A HISTORY OF THE HOLOCAUST

A HISTORY OF THE HOLOCAUST

REVISED EDITION

Yehuda Bauer

Institute of Contemporary Jewry
Hebrew University of Jerusalem

With the assistance of Nili Keren

FRANKLIN WATTS
A Division of Scholastic Inc.
New York ▪ Toronto ▪ London ▪ Auckland
Sydney ▪ Mexico City ▪ New Delhi ▪ Hong Kong
Danbury, Connecticut

Interior Design by Molly Heron
Maps by Bob Italiano
Cover photograph copyright © United States Holocaust Memorial Museum/State Archives of the Russian Federation

Photographs ©: Archive Photos: 163 bottom (Imperial War Museum), 163 top, 166 top, 166 bottom (Popperfoto), 167 top left, 167 bottom, 168 top (Anthony Potter Collection), 161 bottom left, 164 top, 165 bottom, 167 top right, 297 top left, 297 top right, 300 bottom, 301 top left, 301 bottom left, 303 bottom, 304 top; Corbis-Bettmann: 162 top, 302 bottom, 302 top (UPI), 161 top, 165 top, 297 bottom, 299 top, 304 bottom; Library of Congress: 161 bottom right (LC-USZC4-2290); National Archives at College Park: 162 bottom; United States Holocaust Memorial Museum: 164 bottom (Institute of Contemporary History and Wiener Library Limited), 301 right, 303 top (National Archives), 168 bottom (Institute of National Memory/Instytut Pamieci Narodowej), cover (State Archives of the Russian Federation), 298 bottom (Rose Stein-Broseliten), 298 top (Thomas Veres), 299 bottom, 300 top (Yad Veshem Photo Archives).

Library of Congress Cataloging-in-Publication Data

Bauer, Yehuda
A history of the Holocaust/Yehuda Bauer with the assistance of Nili Keren.—Rev. ed.
    p. cm.
Includes bibliographical references (p.) and index.
ISBN 0-531-11884-3 (lib. bdg.)   0-531-15576-5 (pbk.)
1.   Holocaust, Jewish (193901945)—Juvenile literature. 2. Jews—History—1789–1945—Juvenile literature. [1. Holocaust, Jewish (1939–1945)] I. Keren, Nili, II. Title.

D804.34. B38 2001
940.53`18—dc21   00-033033

FRANKLIN WATTS
   A Division of Scholastic Inc.
   90 Sherman Turnpike
   Danbury, CT 06816

8 9 10 11 R 09 08 07

CONTENTS

LIST OF MAPS

LIST OF TABLES AND CHARTS

PREFACE

THE PREFACE to the first edition of this book was written in 1981, while the present one is being written in mid-1999. Obviously, a great deal has happened in the meantime, and the book that is now presented to the reader has undergone some major revisions. But the statement, eighteen years ago, that the Holocaust must be considered a watershed event in modern history not only stands, but is the basic reason that hundreds of university and college courses in the United States and Canada, as well as in other countries, are devoted to this subject. One of the additions to the original volume which I thought was important is a discussion on why the burning interest in a series of events that happened about sixty years ago, on another continent, to people who were not citizens of the countries of the Western Hemisphere, should be maintained by young people who have absolutely no personal connection to those events. That discussion has been added to the historical chapters. A number of errors have been corrected, and new findings incorporated in the story told in this book. Historical research is continuing, and new insights will undoubtedly have to be added in the future.

Again, some of what I said eighteen years ago still stands. I then argued that by *watershed event* is meant a historical occurrence that is in some sense radically new, an occurrence that changes human perspective. I said then, and hold now, that as a historical event, the Holocaust can be understood from various disciplinary points of view. However, in order to approach the Holocaust from literary, philosophical, or theological vantage points, it first must be understood historically—one must know what actually happened. From the facts, some possible conclusions might be formulated as to the "why" question. Many people think that we already have all the facts. How wrong they are! The opening of archives, not only in Eastern Europe, but also in the West (including the United States), has enabled us to answer some questions, and has opened up new ones. Many historians, philosophers, and others, have addressed the "why" questions, and some of their thoughts are included in the discussions presented in this new edition.

However, we have to start with the history, and the history has to be placed in the proper context. Therefore, we must first look backward to the history of the Jewish people and their relationship to the non-Jewish world and to antisemitism in ancient, medieval, and modern times. The period of the Holocaust itself is understood in this book to be essentially the period of 1933 to 1945. However, because the immediate after-effects of the Holocaust—the events of 1945 to 1948 and the establishment of the State of Israel—are equally pertinent; the immediate political, demographic, and sociological consequences are also included and, in this edition, broadened. A revised, selected bibliography is included and more detailed bibliographies can be found in most works cited.

I am deeply grateful to Dr. Nili Keren, who originally participated in the writing of this book, for her help and her patience. I am equally indebted, but in a different way, to Elana, my wife, who picks me up when I fall down.

Yehuda Bauer
Jerusalem, Israel

one
WHO ARE THE JEWS?

TO THE JEWS, the Bible is the Tanakh, an acronym for the Law (Torah), the Prophets (Nevi'im), and the Writings (Ktuvim); to the Christians, the Tanakh is the Old Testament, and the Bible includes the New Testament as well. Many believe the Tanakh is divinely inspired; many others view it as a tremendously important collective product of a people's religious, historical, and literary imagination spanning perhaps a thousand years or more. From the many and conflicting theories about the emergence of the Jewish people, one can perhaps arrive at a story that will be accepted by most, though not all. The Hebrews, a nomadic, tribal bedouin people, or a group of them, were enslaved by the powerful Egyptian empire at some time in the second half of the second millennium B.C.E.[1] Under the charismatic leadership of Moshe (Moses), they escaped from that bondage, to wander for a long period of time in the Sinai desert. During this period, a religious, moral, social, and legal tradition emerged, both similar and dissimilar to those of ancient empires. The similarities are understandable; they were the result of the influence, on the Hebrews, of the cultures amidst which they developed. The dissimilarities were obviously the result of an internal development. A newer theory, which is accepted by some, argues that the Hebrews were the result of a mix between the groups that came up from Egypt, and others who had developed a similar culture in the Land of Canaan. The importance of the stories about the Exodus from Egypt and the Law Giving at Mount Sinai, whose factual details are lost in antiquity, lies in the twin traditions they initiated. Integral today to the self-understanding not only of the Jews themselves but of the entire Christian and the Moslem world, these traditions, centrally important to the Jewish people, are a basic common precept of Western civilization.

The Exodus was taken and understood as a symbol of emergence from slavery to freedom, as a symbol of hope, and in religious thought as proof of the possibility of grace—the beneficial intervention of God in human history. These interpretations are common to Jews and to many groups in Western societies (e.g., African-Americans in the United States), who share in the Jewish tradition and who, for reasons of their own, are in need of symbols to express their own strivings for freedom and salvation.

The story of the Law Giving at Mount Sinai is equally important. The concepts contained in the traditions handed down from the time of Moses not only have shaped the Jewish people but have influenced, in time, others as well. Although the idea of a strict and uncompromising monotheism took root slowly, it became basic to the Jews' understanding of themselves and the world. God, without shape or form, rules a universe created by Him absolutely. In later interpretations, the many biblical passages where He speaks are explained as symbolical, because God, of course, does not actually speak. There can be no minor deities in Judaism as it developed over time, no adoration of pictures or statues. In the ancient world, as well as later, the concept of one God meant that all humans were His children—that all humans are equal, a revolutionary idea indeed.

The laws that bear the imprint of the Mosaic tradition include the provision of liberating slaves after seven years (Ex. 21:2), of freeing all slaves who are maltreated (Ex. 21:26–27), of equality before the law (Ex. 21:20,

23–25), of the prohibition of murder and theft, and of the absolute sanctity of human life—all ideas or concepts logically connected to the idea of monotheism. There were compromises, too, but in the context of ancient empires, the Jews were a strange and, indeed, dangerous phenomenon. Other peoples could trade one god for another, one image or name for that of another. The Jews could not. The ancient civilizations of Egypt, Babylon, Greece, and Rome were built on slavery and strictly hierarchical. One might even argue that ideas running counter to the accepted hierarchical structure were reactionary, in the sense that without slavery and hierarchies the advances (or were they advances?) in civilization of those empires could not have been achieved. One may perhaps conclude that although the Jews were not better or worse than anyone else, they certainly were radically different.

Why the Jews? That is a problem that has not been explained satisfactorily by historians, although one can report some of the explanations that have been given. The radical difference may stem from the Jews' feeling of being chosen—chosen to be different. To the Jews, this sense of being chosen was a burden forced on their ancestors—described to be like a mountain in the form of a water tub turned upside down and put over their heads (har ke-gigit); although, in a parallel tradition, when asked whether they accepted the Law, they agreed. They felt, perhaps, that their choice was negligible. Their task, as they later came to understand it, was to observe the 613 commandments of the slowly evolving and crystallizing Jewish tradition, which would bring nearer the redemption of the world. With the coming of the Messiah, the special Jewish function in the world would cease. Until then, they were to be alone in the strict observance of the commandments, with no special rewards. In Jewish tradition, every non-Jew who observed the "seven laws of Noah"—no idolatry, no incest, no murder, no vivisection of animals, no cursing of God, no theft, and justice toward fellow human beings—was as righteous in the eyes of God as any observant Jew. The Jews felt a certain pride and a deep sense of obligation throughout the ages to observe the commandments with no reward—that is, no reward beyond the satisfaction derived in obeying God's command.

The Hebrew tribes conquered the territory of Cana'an (Palestine, the land of the Philistines, who actually occupied only a narrow coastal strip), which has remained for the Jews the Land of Israel (Eretz Israel). In time, the tribes united under three great kings, Saul, David, and Solomon (about 1000–900 B.C.E.), and then split into the kingdoms of Israel in the north and Judah (Yehudah, Judea) in the south. Solomon's temple in Jerusalem became the center of religious and social life. Jewish monotheism (belief in one God) developed slowly, and for long periods Jews (Hebrews) worshipped both their own God and also gods of the surrounding cultures, despite the fact that the prophets preached against these customs. Only gradually did the teachings of the prophets and the priests penetrate into the minds of the whole Jewish population.

The two kingdoms, actually only small principalities in an area of instability between the warring empires of Egypt and Assyria (Babylonia), fell victim to the vagaries of international power politics. Israel was destroyed in 721 B.C.E., and Judah was conquered in 586 B.C.E. The Israelites (the 'Ten Tribes'), whose link with the ancestral religious, social, and ethnic traditions had weakened under ruling cliques who became "assimilated" to the prevalent pagan concepts, were dispersed and exiled, no longer a recognizable group. The Judeans, more closely attached to what was emerging as Judaism, maintained their distinctiveness in their Babylonian exile, despite the destruction of their temple, aristocracy, priesthood, and other cultural elements. Under Cyrus, the Persian conqueror of Babylon, the Jews were permitted to return to Jerusalem in 538 B.C.E.; although few in number (most of them remained in Babylon), those who returned rebuilt the temple, persuaded the descendants of those who had stayed in the country while the aristocracy had gone into exile to return to Judaism, and began what became known as the Second Commonwealth. Under Persian and later Hellenic rule, Judea became an autonomous province, and in Babylon, Egypt, and elsewhere a Jewish Diaspora maintained and developed Jewish civilization. During the Hasmonean dynasty when Hellenistic efforts to create a universalistic pagan Greek culture clashed with the monotheistic and 'parochial' Jewish tradition, an independent Jewish kingdom (the Hasmonean dynasty) was established (second century B.C.E.). Under the Hasmoneans, Jewish religious and ethnic identity expanded by conversion and adaptation, and when the Romans conquered Jerusalem in 64 B.C.E. the Jews were a large majority of the population. Numbering 3 or 4 million throughout the land of Israel, they were mainly farmers, while most of the large cities along the coast and in the plains were Hellenized.

The opposition to the Romans was, as in the case of the fight against the Hellenizers, ethnoreligious: The Romans tried to merge the Jews in the Greco-Roman pagan civilization; the Jews insisted on being different. The differences, at first cultural and religious, were accompanied by intense inter-Jewish quarrels between the Pharisees, loyal and popular adherents to the Jewish traditions, and the upper-class Sadducees, who favored a compromise with Greco-Roman civilization. In the end, discontent, anger, and bitterness against Roman rule, exacerbated by often unintended Roman provocations directed against sacred Jewish traditions, combined with Messianic dreams of a near redemption to provoke an ill-conceived, disunited and badly led rebellion in 67–70 C.E. The Second Commonwealth and the temple were destroyed. Jerusalem was destroyed. Although some Jews were exiled, most remained in the Land of Israel.

In 132–135 C.E., a second, and in a sense more important, rebellion took place after the Romans had erected a temple to Jupiter on the site of the Jewish temple in Jerusalem, which they renamed Aelia Capitolina. Led by Shimon Bar-Kochba (Bar-Koziva), who saw himself as the Messiah, and sanctioned by one of the greatest Jewish sages of all time, Rabbi Akiva, it ended in a terrible catastrophe. Judea was almost completely depopulated. The Jews there were mass murdered or sold as slaves. Elsewhere, however, and especially in the Galilee, a large Jewish majority continued to exist until the seventh century, when Palestine was conquered by the Arabs.

CHRISTIANITY AND THE DEVELOPING JEWISH CIVILIZATION

Jesus of Nazareth, his birth, his teachings, his ministry, and his death by crucifixion are central to the history of Western civilization. An observant Jew and at the same time a rebel—very much in the Jewish tradition—he tried to adapt old and contemporary Jewish ideas to a new mold or form. According to passages in the Gospels, his death at Roman hands was demanded by the Judean supporters of the High Priest because he was seen as presenting himself as king of the Jews, or Messiah—a false Messiah, in Jewish eyes. This complicated story, told a fairly long time after the event in a number of different versions, was later interpreted by Christian antisemites as "proof" that " the Jews" had killed the Christ. The false myth of the Jews' supposed responsibility, one of the most destructive and murderous legends in human history, has whipped up passion and aggressions against a whole people and their civilization for many centuries. In fact, however, according to the Gospels, a random Judean mob had demanded that the Romans kill a Galilean Jew (there were bitter dissensions between Judeans and Galileans at the time), a Jew who in their eyes was a false Messiah. In recent times (1965), the Roman Catholic Church has declared that "the Jews" of Jesus' time could not be held responsible for the crucifixion.[2] Nor could the descendants of all Jews who lived at the time of the crucifixion be held responsible. The false myth persists, however.

After the death of Jesus, his ideas of love and understanding between humans were spread by both Jews within the Jewish fold and those who went among the Gentiles to propagate his ideas. A new religion emerged, a religion that saw in Jesus the Christ-Messiah who had come to redeem the world. In the decadence of the Roman Empire, Christianity, Judaism, and Mithraite (Persian) influences competed with each other until the early part of the fourth century when Christianity became the official religion of the Roman empire.

In its struggle to legitimate itself as a new religion, Christianity turned against the mother religion from which it had sprung, Judaism. Fortified by the power it had won as the officially enforced state religion, it developed the supersession myth, namely, the idea that with its rise it had become a New Israel; it was the subject of God's covenant, rather than the old Israel, which stood rejected from divine grace because it had refused to accept Jesus as the Messiah. This denial of the legitimacy of Judaism as a religion that in its own way seeks religious truth could be interpreted as a first signal for the denial of the existence of the Jews. If Jews could not exist as a separate entity, the next step may be seen as the denial of their existence altogether.

Many of the church fathers and some of the great figures of Christianity in the early and later Middle Ages held extreme anti-Jewish views. Ignatius of Antioch, for example, enunciated most clearly the supersession myth, and St. Cyprian (third century C.E.) taught: "Now the peoplehood of the Jews has been cancelled; the destruction of Jerusalem was a judgment upon them; the gentiles rather than the Jews will inherit the Kingdom."[3] And St. John Chrysostom said:

> The Jews sacrifice their children to Satan . . . They are worse than wild beasts. . . . The synagogue is a brothel, a den of scoundrels, the temple of demons devoted to idolatrous cults, a criminal assembly of Jews, a place of meeting for the assassins of Christ, a house of ill fame, a dwelling of iniquity, a gulf and abyss of perdition. . . .The synagogue is a curse. Obstinate in her error, she refuses to see or hear; she has deliberately perverted her judgment; she has extinguished within herself the light of the Holy Spirit. . . .[the Jews] had fallen into a condition lower than the vilest animals. Debauchery and drunkenness had brought them to the level of the lusty goat and the pig. They know only one thing: to satisfy their stomachs, to get drunk, to kill and beat each other up like stage villains and coachmen. . . . I hate the Jews, because they violate the Law. I hate the Synagogue because it has the Law and the Prophets. It is the duty of all Christians to hate the Jews.[4]

In a special sermon to the Jews, the "Tractatus Adversus Iudaeos,"[5] St. Augustine, bishop of Hippo (354–430 C.E.), an important Father of the Christian church, said:

> You then belong to that nation to which "the Lord hath spoken, and called the earth from the rising of the sun unto the going down thereof" (Ps. 50:1).
> Have you not been led out of Egypt to the Land of Canaan? But you were not called there from sunrise to sunset, but dispersed from there, towards sunrise and sunset. Do you not rather belong to the enemies of him who says in the psalm: "Slay them not, lest my people forget: scatter them by thy power; and bring them down, O Lord our shield" (Ps. 59:11).
> Therefore you do not forget the law of God, but carry it everywhere, a witness to the nations, a shame for you, and without understanding it you give it to the people that has been called upon from sunrise to sunset.[6]

In other words, Jews should not be killed but humiliated and persecuted, because they are supposedly condemned by God to be dispersed and in their dispersion are to prove the glory of God. The same idea is repeated by St. Augustine in "De Civitas Dei" (18.46).[7] The Jews should not be annihilated, he said, but kept in misery, in fulfillment of prophecy. St. Thomas Aquinas (1225–74) wrote:

> It would be licit, according to custom, to hold Jews, because of their crime, in perpetual servitude, and therefore the princes may regard the possessions of Jews as belonging to the state; however, they must use them with a certain moderation and not deprive Jews of things necessary to life.[8]

The church in the Middle Ages adopted a double, and in a sense contradictory, attitude toward Jews. Jews were humans with souls and could therefore be "saved," but only if they gave up their birthright and converted. The official church insisted, at least theoretically, that conversion had to be voluntary. The obvious conclusion was that Jews must not be murdered. On the other hand, they should be humiliated and set apart as the vanquished religion; debased, they were proof of the victory of the church over the synagogue. A satanic influence in the world, Jews nevertheless had souls. Yet caricatures of the late Middle Ages depict Jews as satanic, demonic figures, clearly not humans. Church propaganda had great effect; the official church sometimes had to defend the lives of Jews against the logical results of its own preachings. Yet it has to be emphasized that no branch of Christianity ever developed a genocidal plan to murder all Jews—that was left to the secularized European world in our own times.

One of the most pernicious legends spread in Christendom, apparently motivated by the characterization of the Jew as the devil, was that of the blood libel. The murder of Christian children for religious purposes was attributed to the Jews, a people who had not only elevated the sanctity of life to a near absolute but had been the first to condemn vivisection and the use of any kind of blood from any creature. Paganism here invaded Christianity and the blood-libel accusation (starting in 1144 C.E. in Norwich, England) against the Jews constitutes one of the darkest pages in human relationships throughout history. The last known blood libel was leveled against the Jews as late as 1946 in Kielce, Poland.

During the Middle Ages the Jews wandered from place to place in Christendom in search of a haven. From all, with the exception of Poland, they were brutally expelled. As will be detailed below, major massacres occurred in Germany during the Crusades, especially in 1196, in England in 1290, throughout Europe during the Black Death epidemic in 1347–50, and in 1648–49 in Poland, when a rebellion of Ukrainian peasants under Bogdan Chmielnicki against their Polish overlords provoked mass murders of Jews all over eastern and central Poland.

In Western, Central, and Southern Europe Jews were marked (usually by a yellow sign), had to wear distinctive clothing, were segregated in certain town areas (later, in Italy, called ghettoes), and were forced to engage in certain occupations, often moneylending, to the exclusion of others. Charged with developing trade and money transactions, they were periodically deprived of their property by taxation or outright confiscation and then expelled (e.g., England 1290, France 1306).

JEWISH REACTIONS UNTIL MODERN TIMES

Throughout the centuries, Jews developed ways and means of survival. As early as the second and first centuries B.C.E. an interpretative process adapted Jewish tradition to changing circumstances. In terse and simple Hebrew language, the Mishna, completed in the second century C.E. by Rabbi Yehuda Hanassi (the Prince), reinterpreted biblical traditions. At that time, Hebrew, the original language of the Jewish people, coexisted with its sister language Aramaic, the lingua franca of much of the Middle East. When the Romans destroyed the temple in 70 C.E., Judaism experienced a spiritual revolution. Religious observance, until then centered in the sanctuary itself, now acquired a new home in the Houses of Assembly (*Batei Knesset)*, or synagogues in Greek; prayer replaced sacrifices, and concentration on study, on learning the laws and traditions and developing the richness of the interpretative moral story (sing., *midrash;* pl., *midrashim),* increasingly surpassed concern with political life. This major switch, the beginnings of which go back to early mishnaic times prior to the destruction of the temple, was dramatically reinforced by the foundation of an academy at Yavneh (today in Israel's coastal plain) by Yohanan ben Zakkai at the time of the conquest of Jerusalem by the Romans. Until today, Yavneh continues to serve as the prototype of orthodox academies for learning the Law (*yeshivot*).

This turning inward, aimed at enriching the spiritual and social life of the community, was probably the salvation of the Jews—their rich social and intellectual inner world allowed them to face hostile external reality. The process of reinterpreting biblical sources reached a peak about 500 C.E. with the final editing of the Babylonian Talmud by Rabbis Yossi of Pombadita and Rabina of Sura (both centers of Jewish learning in what today is Iraq). The Talmud, a vast compilation based essentially on a reinterpretation and elaboration of the Mishna, attempts to regulate the life of the individual and the community in accordance with the religious customs, laws, and social mores handed down from biblical times. The Talmud also includes literary pieces, midrashim, aphorisms, and legends (Hebrew sing., *aggadah)*. A parallel compilation of the Talmud was made in the Land of Israel (the Jerusalem Talmud, ca. 400 C.E.), but not all of it survived. The Talmud, written mostly in Aramaic, developed a system of logical thinking and of internal community legislation that became the basis of Jewish life and learning until modern times. As a result, tremendous stress was laid on study. The purpose of life in Judaism was often defined as consisting of devotion to study of the Torah (Law), that is, the Bible, the Mishna, the Talmud, and a vast later literature that reexamines and reinterprets the Talmud. Strict rules governing individual and social moral conduct were laid down, based on the authority of scholars whose moral superiority was recognized by the community.

Throughout the period 500 C.E.–1800 C.E., the writings and teachings of these scholars influenced the daily life of the Jewish community. In what is now Iraq, Sa'adia Ga'on was the undisputed spiritual head of the Jewish people in the tenth century. Maimonides (Rabbi Moshe ben Maimon; Hebrew acronym: Rambam; 1135–1204), probably the most influential medieval Jewish thinker, developed a rationalistic approach to religion and life in general and to Judaism in particular.

The Jews served as intermediaries between the Moslem and the Christian civilizations in the Middle Ages, both in developing commerce and in the exchange of ideas. Through their works, they transmitted Arab science and Greek traditions preserved in the Moslem world to Christendom.

Jews in Moslem and Christian countries fared somewhat differently, but arguably it was a matter of degree only. Both Jews and Christians were considered to be "People of the Book" by the Moslem conquerors of vast areas of the seventh-century world and thus were a notch higher than pagans, against whom a war of destruction and forced conversion to Islam was waged. As in Christendom, however, Jews in the Moslem world proved to be an obstinate and hard nut to crack. Refusing to disavow their religious and ethnic identity, they were relegated to second-class citizenship, in which toleration alternated with persecutions and massacres.

Thus, under Moslem rule, Jews were massacred in Cordoba, Spain, in 1010, 1013, and 1066. In the southern Arabian state of Yemen, where for a short time there was even a Jewish royal dynasty, Jews were subjected to discrimination and mass killings (e.g., 1627–29) and held in a state of abject humiliation until their mass exodus to Israel in 1949. Blood-libel accusations occurred under Shi'ite rule in Iran in Tabriz in 1826 and under Turkish rule in Damascus in 1840.

JEWISH MYSTICISM AND MESSIANISM

In Judaism, a mystical interpretative view coexisted with the basically rationalistic view previously described. Apparently motivated by the tragedies and problems that were the lot of the Jewish people, some thinkers turned to mysticism to seek direct communion with the Deity. Mysticism was connected to the immediacy of an expectation of the Messiah's coming—in Jewish belief, the Messiah would come to lead the Jews back to their ancestral home in Israel and thus end their troubles and wanderings. Although the belief in the coming of the Messiah was one of the principles of Judaism laid down by the Rambam (Maimonides), traditional orthodox Judaism deprecated attempts at calculating the date of his arrival. A suspicion of such mystical undertakings was justified, as in the course of Jewish history not a few false messiahs brought catastrophe on their followers and usually on themselves as well.

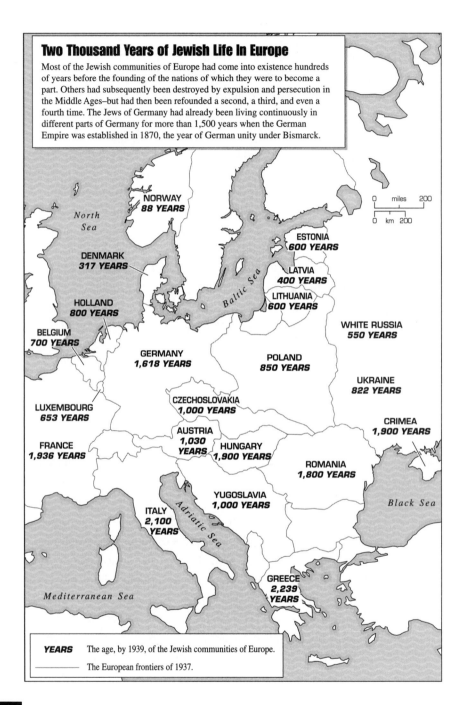

Two Thousand Years of Jewish Life In Europe

Most of the Jewish communities of Europe had come into existence hundreds of years before the founding of the nations of which they were to become a part. Others had subsequently been destroyed by expulsion and persecution in the Middle Ages—but had then been refounded a second, a third, and even a fourth time. The Jews of Germany had already been living continuously in different parts of Germany for more than 1,500 years when the German Empire was established in 1870, the year of German unity under Bismarck.

North Sea

Baltic Sea

Adriatic Sea

Black Sea

Mediterranean Sea

NORWAY
88 YEARS

ESTONIA
600 YEARS

DENMARK
317 YEARS

LATVIA
400 YEARS

LITHUANIA
600 YEARS

HOLLAND
800 YEARS

WHITE RUSSIA
550 YEARS

BELGIUM
700 YEARS

GERMANY
1,618 YEARS

POLAND
850 YEARS

UKRAINE
822 YEARS

LUXEMBOURG
653 YEARS

CZECHOSLOVAKIA
1,000 YEARS

CRIMEA
1,900 YEARS

AUSTRIA
1,030 YEARS

HUNGARY
1,900 YEARS

FRANCE
1,936 YEARS

ROMANIA
1,800 YEARS

YUGOSLAVIA
1,000 YEARS

ITALY
2,100 YEARS

GREECE
2,239 YEARS

0   miles   200
0   km   200

YEARS   The age, by 1939, of the Jewish communities of Europe.

————   The European frontiers of 1937.

Some Early Records of Jewish Town Life in Europe Before 1600

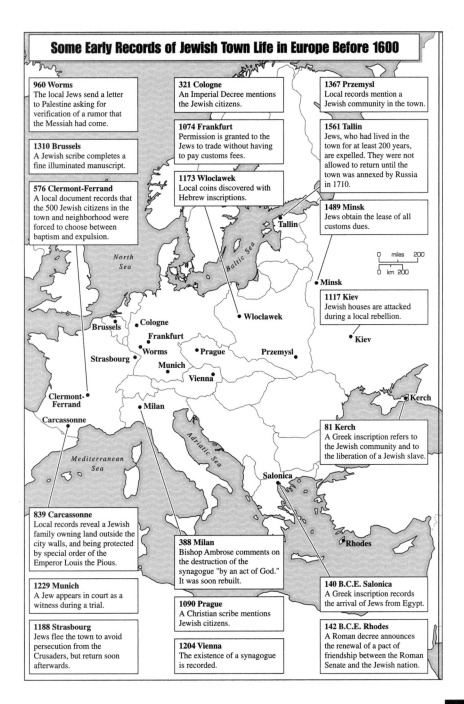

960 Worms
The local Jews send a letter to Palestine asking for verification of a rumor that the Messiah had come.

1310 Brussels
A Jewish scribe completes a fine illuminated manuscript.

576 Clermont-Ferrand
A local document records that the 500 Jewish citizens in the town and neighborhood were forced to choose between baptism and expulsion.

321 Cologne
An Imperial Decree mentions the Jewish citizens.

1074 Frankfurt
Permission is granted to the Jews to trade without having to pay customs fees.

1173 Wloclawek
Local coins discovered with Hebrew inscriptions.

1367 Przemysl
Local records mention a Jewish community in the town.

1561 Tallin
Jews, who had lived in the town for at least 200 years, are expelled. They were not allowed to return until the town was annexed by Russia in 1710.

1489 Minsk
Jews obtain the lease of all customs dues.

1117 Kiev
Jewish houses are attacked during a local rebellion.

81 Kerch
A Greek inscription refers to the Jewish community and to the liberation of a Jewish slave.

839 Carcassonne
Local records reveal a Jewish family owning land outside the city walls, and being protected by special order of the Emperor Louis the Pious.

1229 Munich
A Jew appears in court as a witness during a trial.

1188 Strasbourg
Jews flee the town to avoid persecution from the Crusaders, but return soon afterwards.

388 Milan
Bishop Ambrose comments on the destruction of the synagogue "by an act of God." It was soon rebuilt.

1090 Prague
A Christian scribe mentions Jewish citizens.

1204 Vienna
The existence of a synagogue is recorded.

140 B.C.E. Salonica
A Greek inscription records the arrival of Jews from Egypt.

142 B.C.E. Rhodes
A Roman decree announces the renewal of a pact of friendship between the Roman Senate and the Jewish nation.

North Sea

Baltic Sea

Tallin

Minsk

0 miles 200
0 km 200

Wloclawek

Brussels
Cologne
Frankfurt
Worms
Strasbourg
Munich
Prague
Vienna
Przemysl

Kiev

Clermont-Ferrand
Carcassonne

Milan

Kerch

Adriatic Sea

Mediterranean Sea

Salonica

Rhodes

Jewish mysticism was in many ways parallel to the Christian variety developed in Germany and France in the twelfth and thirteenth centuries during and after the Crusades, which were accompanied by massacres of the Jewish populations in many German and Central European centers. A major turning point was the publication of the Zohar, the basic text of Jewish mysticism, in Spain in the thirteenth century, apparently written by Rabbi Moshe de Leon of Guadalajara. From the Zohar a tradition of mysticism (Hebrew, *kabbala*) developed, which found expression in the School of Safed (in the Land of Israel), where a number of important *kabbala* scholars taught in the sixteenth century.

Messianism, or the appearance of false messiahs, was connected with both the tribulations of the Jews and their hopes of an early redemption. Among the false messiahs who promised a return to Israel were Abu Issa (Yitzhak ben Ya'akov) in Persia in the eighth century, David Alroi in the twelfth century in Kurdistan, and David Hareuveni, who appeared in 1524 in Italy and negotiated with Pope Clemens VII for a combined Christian-Jewish crusade against the Turks, aiming at a reconquest of the Holy Land.

In the mid-seventeenth century another false messiah, Shabtai Tsvi, caused a tremendous upheaval in the Jewish world. In 1665–66 many Jews, believing the messiah had actually come, sold their property and started walking toward Palestine. When the false messiah apostatized and converted to Islam in 1666, the resulting disillusionment provoked a severe moral crisis in Judaism. Until the end of the eighteenth century, the Jewish spiritual leadership waged a bitter struggle against the remnants of the Shabtai Tsvi movement, which continued to exist underground and refused to give up the messianic hope. Some of the early forerunners of a Jewish national revival, as well as secularist millenarian trends among the Jews, seem to have been influenced by the Shabbatean movement.

JEWISH SOCIAL AND ECONOMIC LIFE IN THE DIASPORA

As already noted, Jews were an important element in whatever remained of international commerce in the early Middle Ages. At the same time, the Jewish settlements in Mesopotamia (Iraq) and elsewhere were farming communities, as were Jewish villages in the Galilee. Urban Jewish settlements spread to India and China. Jewish tribes for a time controlled the Yemen, and the rulers of an important Mongol tribe, the Khazars, adopted Judaism, probably in the early part of the eighth century. The Khazars maintained a multi-religious kingdom in the general area of the southern Ukraine and the northern Caucasus. Weakened in the ninth century, the Khazar kingdom was destroyed in the tenth and eleventh centuries. Although most of the inhabitants apparently became Moslems, some small Jewish groups may have emigrated north to Russia, Poland, and Lithuania.

In Western and Southern Europe, where Jews were prevented from owning land or becoming part of the Christian and, later, Moslem communities, they became traders and artisans. Wherever local middle classes emerged, competition with the Jews ensued and provoked some of the persecutions and expulsions previously mentioned.

For certain periods of time in the later Middle Ages (e.g., twelfth-century Germany) only Jews could engage in loaning money for interest, because the church, in theory, at least, did not permit Christians to engage in usury. In effect, the Jews became middlemen between the aristocracy and the peasantry, causing enmity to develop toward them from both sides. Coupled with religious animosity, this hatred was a powerful incentive for attacks and local massacres, especially in Germany and France.

Mass attacks by mobs occurred during the Crusades in Germany and elsewhere, especially in the mass murders of 1196 in the towns of western Germany. Prior to these persecutions, German and French Jewish sages had developed new advances in Jewish culture. Although polygamy among Jews had ceased much earlier, Rabbi Gershom (called 'Light of the Diaspora', 960–1028) made the prohibition official. Rashi (1040–1105), a brilliant interpreter of the Talmud, who lived in Troyes, France, had studied in Germany. After the Crusades, when the Jews migrated from the affected communities, mainly eastward, German Jews experienced a decline. In 1347–50, when the plague, or Black Death, decimated European countries, the Jews were held responsible. A major catastrophe like the Black Death could only be explained in mystical or demonic terms, and the Jews, after all, had been

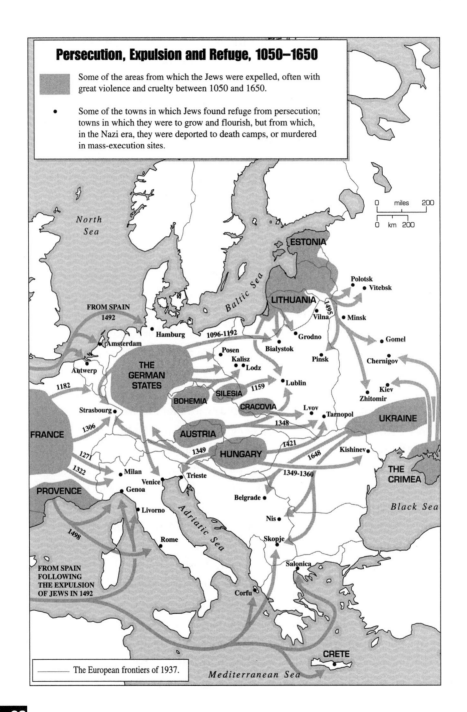

Persecution, Expulsion and Refuge, 1050–1650

Some of the areas from which the Jews were expelled, often with great violence and cruelty between 1050 and 1650.

• Some of the towns in which Jews found refuge from persecution; towns in which they were to grow and flourish, but from which, in the Nazi era, they were deported to death camps, or murdered in mass-execution sites.

0 miles 200
0 km 200

North Sea

Baltic Sea

ESTONIA

LITHUANIA

Polotsk
• Vitebsk

FROM SPAIN
1492

Hamburg   1096-1192

Vilna   • Minsk

• Grodno

• Gomel

1495

• Amsterdam

Posen   Bialystok   Pinsk

Chernigov

Antwerp   Kalisz
•Lodz

THE
GERMAN
STATES   1159   •Lublin   Kiev

1182   BOHEMIA   SILESIA   Zhitomir

Strasbourg •   CRACOVIA   Lvov   Tarnopol   UKRAINE

FRANCE   1306   1348   AUSTRIA   1421   Kishinev •

1271   1349   HUNGARY   1648   THE
CRIMEA

1322   • Milan   1349-1360

PROVENCE   Venice   Trieste   Belgrade •   Black Sea

• Genoa

• Livorno   Nis •

Adriatic Sea

1498   • Rome   Skopje •

FROM SPAIN
FOLLOWING
THE EXPULSION
OF JEWS IN 1492   Salonica

Corfu •

CRETE

The European frontiers of 1937.   Mediterranean Sea

30

viewed as the satanic element in history. Wholesale murder of Jews throughout Europe ensued.

Throughout the Middle Ages Christianity continued to seek the conversion of the Jews. Let us reemphasize that there never existed any Christian intention, much less a program, that we would today call 'genocide'. Christian opposition to the murder of the Jewish people as a whole, despite all the persecutions, clearly marks it off against what happened under the National Socialists (Nazis) in Germany.

During the Middle Ages, the Jewish defense mechanism reserved martyrdom for extreme situations only. When threatened with attacks on his/her religion and his social structure, the Jew was prepared temporarily to yield, to evade. However, when faced with the demand to murder, to commit incest, or to convert, s/he was prepared for martyrdom, or Sanctification of the Lord's Name (Kiddush Ha'shem). Thousands of Jews died in the name of Kiddush Ha'shem, a concept that was to be revived, in a different form, during the Holocaust.

In Christian as well as Moslem Spain, Jewish commerce, trade, and intellectual influence were considerable from the eleventh to fourteenth century. Despite occasional violent persecutions and mass murders (e.g., 1066 in Moslem Granada, 1147 in all of Spain by the Almohades, in the late eleventh century in Christian Toledo, in 1348 in Catalonia, in 1391 in Seville), Jews were to look back on those centuries in Spain as the Golden Age. Jewish philosophers influenced contemporary Christian and Moslem thinking, sages developed Jewish learning, some of the greatest poets in the Hebrew language flourished (Shlomo [Solomon] Ibn Gabirol in the eleventh century, Moshe [Moses] Ibn Ezra and Yehuda Halevi in the early twelfth), and Jewish statesmen and military leaders emerged (e.g., Shmuel Hanaggid, 993–1056).

The rise of a middle class in Christian Spain and the religious and ethnic fanaticism engendered by the reconquest of Spain from the vestiges of Moslem power brought about the expulsion of the Jews (and Moslems) from Spain in 1492. Strong pressure caused voluntary and forced conversion in the decades prior to 1492, and during the year of expulsion many more converted. Many who converted and attempted secretly to adhere to their Jewish beliefs were exposed. These "new Christians," called Marranos (Pigs) by their opponents, were persecuted by the Catholic Inquisition from 1478 to 1765. Between these dates, several thousands of Jews were tortured or burned at the stake for their religious beliefs, sanctioned by the earlier edict of the Fourth Lateran Council (1215), which called upon secular powers to "exterminate" all heretics. The persecution of the Marranos had a distinctly modern tinge, as the idea spread that Jews were poisoning Christian Spain by their "blood." Consequently, the Marranos, or "new Christians," were kept apart from "old Christians" in something like the racist segregation of a later age. According to Spanish law between the sixteenth and the eighteenth centuries, individuals who aspired to high positions in the civil and religious societies had to prove their 'purity of blood' (*limpieza de sangre*), i.e., attest that they were not descended from Jews or 'Moors' (Arabs).

Spanish Jews fled to the Middle East (to Turkey and Palestine, where they settled in Tiberias and Safed, and to Bulgaria, Greece, and Egypt), Western Europe (Holland, Germany, England, and southern France), and the Western Hemisphere (especially the Caribbean islands and the British colonies in North America). They became the source of Sephardi (Spanish) or Sephardic Jewry, speaking a Spanish-Jewish language called Ladino (written in Hebrew letters). Local Jewish populations in the Middle East and North Africa tended to accept Sephardi leadership, though among themselves they spoke an Arab-Jewish dialect. In Europe, in the meantime, ever since the period of the Crusades, another Jewish language developed from Middle High German, with the addition of Hebrew and, later, Slavonic words, namely, Yiddish. Yiddish, written in Hebrew letters and spoken in a number of dialects, became a language of poetry and literature, as well as of daily life, for Ashkenazi (German) or Ashkenazic Jewry in Central and Eastern Europe. Hebrew, the literary language of Spanish Jewry as late as the Golden Age, became the vehicle for liturgy and correspondence; religious commentaries were written in Hebrew or Aramaic. Rabbis and sages all over the Jewish world corresponded with each other in Hebrew until modern times.

In the early modern period, Jewish traders and craftsmen played an important role in the economic and social developments that set the stage for the birth of capitalism. Though they were not found among the great early captains of industry and banking in Western Europe, they were instrumental in the development of commerce. The split in Christendom that came in the sixteenth century and the later developments in Protestantism and the Catholic Church did not aid the Jews. Lutheran Protestanism, in particular, disappointed by the refusal of the Jews to accept their new religion, was rabidly hostile. In his booklet *Of the Jews and Their Lies,* Martin Luther (1483–1546) proposed:

> First, their synagogues or churches should be set on fire, and whatever does not burn up should be covered or spread over with dirt so that no one may ever be able to see a cinder or stone of it. . . .Secondly, their homes should likewise be broken down and destroyed. . . .They ought to be put under one roof or in a stable, like gypsies. . . .Thirdly, they should be deprived of their prayerbooks and Talmuds. . . .Fourthly, their rabbis must be forbidden under threat of death to teach any more. . . .If, however, we are afraid that they might harm us personally, then let us apply the same cleverness [expulsion] as the other nations, such as France, Spain, Bohemia, etc., and settle with them for that which they have extorted usuriously from us, and after having divided it up fairly let us drive them out of the country for all time.[9]

In Eastern Europe, Poland had welcomed Jewish immigration in the thirteenth and fourteenth centuries. A charter by the Polish king in 1364 expressly insured the physical safety of Jews. In the following centuries, despite occasional attempts by some members of the Catholic priesthood to make life difficult, the Jews played an important role in urban settlement and developed crafts and commerce throughout Poland and Lithuania. A kind of judicial and economic autonomy was granted to them, and a Jewish institution called the Council of the Four Regions of Poland and Lithuania was responsible for much of the administration of Jewish communities from the sixteenth until well into the eighteenth century.

However, with the great upheavals in the seventeenth and eighteenth centuries in Eastern Europe came the decline, economically and socially, of Polish Jewry. As mentioned earlier, the Chmielnicki riots provoked an exodus of many Jews to Germany, Austria, and Holland. The wars ruined Poland and caused suffering and dislocation to everyone, including Jewish trade and industry. In 1707, 1734, 1740, and particularly in 1768, Ukrainian peasant hostility toward Poles and Jews caused widespread massacres (the so-called Haidamak riots). Throughout the eighteenth century dozens of blood libels were initiated to divert peasants' attention from their own suffering—to an imagined crime. In 1753, for instance, eleven Jews were killed at the instigation of the local bishop in the town of Zhitomir. Yet at the same time, throughout Poland, the Jewish population increased, poverty and increasing hostility notwithstanding. In 1755, there were 750,000 Jews in Poland, out of 1,250,000 Jews in all of Europe.

In the wake of an increasingly difficult situation, and more than one hundred years after the Shabbatean movement, a new faction arose within Judaism, namely Hassidism. Founded by the half-legendary Israel Ba'al Shem Tov (Rabbi Israel, the Holder of God's True Name or Master of the Good Name) around the middle of the eighteenth century, Hassidism was a mystical movement aimed at reconstituting the Jewish believer's communion with God directly and through nature by joyful worship. At that time about one-quarter of the Jewish population—the poorest—lived in villages; and the others lived in small townships and engaged in hard physical labor. The Ba'al Shem Tov (acronym, the Besht) taught simplicity, modesty, love, without openly negating the traditional function of learning in Judaism. The leader of the Hassidic group was the tsaddik (pl., *tsaddikim),* the holy man, who alone knew how to reach God with prayer and whose intercession was vital for the life of the individual and the community. In time, "courts" of *tsaddikim* developed, with some friction between them; on the whole, however, the initial appearance of the Hassidic movement infused new life and new hope. Oriented toward a return to the Holy Land, Hassidic groups— along with Moroccan and other Oriental Jews— played an important role in attempts to resettle in Israel from 1777 (with the immigration to Israel of Rabbi Menahem Mendel of Vitebsk). Hassidism was opposed by the Mitnagdim (Opponents), traditional orthodox Jews led by Rabbi Eliyahu (the Sage of Vilna) who argued, not without some basis in fact, that the Hassidim were actually continuing the mystical traditions of the Shabbatean movement. Modern secular Zionism owes a debt to Hassidism.

On the eve of the French Revolution, then, the Jews were spread, thinly, over all the Mideast and Europe, with the exception of Scandinavia, Switzerland and Spain,—and in England and the New World. By origin, they were (and are) mixed: white, brown, and black, certainly not "Caucasian." Numbering about 2.5 million, they functioned as middlemen in Gentile society, being neither very poor nor very rich but very visible. Their religious and cultural patterns, crystallized by the interpretative tradition of the Talmud and the later reinterpretations, set them apart in communities governed by civic leaders who observed the traditional moral and religious precepts. The stress on study and learning persisted.

Although relationships with the Christian world in Europe were difficult and contradictory, between the periods of persecution long years of relative peace ensued, with socioeconomic ties developing between the Jews and their neighbors. Intermarriage did not occur, but there were social contacts and much fruitful interchange. In the sixteenth century and especially the seventeenth, some Christian scholars attempted to understand Judaism. Among them, friends of Jews emerged, especially in Britain among dissenting Protestants. Jews were viewed, in some intellectual circles, not as ossified remnants from a past that had somehow survived to the present but as men and women with strong traditions who had much to contribute to society. A different Christian approach to Jews seemed possible, one that would slay the pernicious legends of Jewish responsibility for the crucifixion and the even more dangerous ritual-murder accusation. It would view the Jews not as demons but as humans, as representatives of one of the most ancient civilizations on earth, as a people who had the right to be different. Yet at the same time, these deistic philosophers, attacking Christianity, saw the root cause of the evils in Christian theology in Judaism. This liberal brand of anti-Jewishness was repeated in pre-1789 France with the liberal philosophers called the 'encyclopedists.' Their main spokesman, Francois-Marie de Voltaire, expressed views that did not differ materially from the extreme anti-Jewishness of St. John Chrysostom.

two
LIBERALISM, EMANCIPATION, AND ANTISEMITISM

IN THE NINETEENTH CENTURY the Jews achieved civic equality in many Christian European states. The French Revolution set the tone. On December 22, 1789, Count Stanislas de Clermont-Tonnerre declared that "Jews should be denied everything as a nation, but granted everything as individuals," an attitude that differed in principle from that developing in the fledgling United States, where both individual and group religious equality were accepted from the start. Between the Congress of Vienna in 1815 and the Congress of Berlin in 1878, Jewish equality advanced in most countries, with the exception of Russia, where the majority of Europe's Jews lived (after Poland had been dismembered at the end of the 18th century), and Turkey. Despite the defeat of the liberals and democrats in the 1848 revolutions, the legal equality of all citizens became an accepted principle of political life in the decades that followed. The principle of Jewish emancipation, that is, their legal and civic equality with all other citizens, became accepted not only by revolutionaries and radicals but by liberals as well. Britain accorded emancipation in 1826 and practical equality with the election of a Jewish member to Parliament in 1858. In Germany equal citizenship was first proclaimed in 1808 by the French conquerors of western Germany. With the defeat of Napoleon, however, emancipation was abolished, and a second attempt that followed in 1848 did not last. In northern Germany, emancipation finally came in 1869 and was confirmed in 1871 with the establishment of the Second Empire under Bismarck and Wilhelm I. Other European states preceded or followed these examples.

At the Congress of Berlin (1878) it was determined, mainly at British insistence, that the principle of equality would be initiated in the Balkans. Russia declared that its time would come in Eastern Europe, but that the time was not now; Rumania accepted the principle for local Jews but not for that majority who were, in Rumanian eyes, recent immigrants. Although both countries were strongly antisemitic, it was impossible to avow such views openly. Public opinion in the West saw anti-Jewish acts as reasons or pretenses to attack reactionary eastern governments, and Britain and the United States occasionally intervened to protect Jews there.

When liberals opposed the autocratic powers of the throne and the altar in the name of equality, Jewish emancipation followed. Jews could not be excluded although some liberal philosophers, following Voltaire, despised and hated the Jews. In the wake of the French Revolution, the rapid industrialization and social transformation of Europe brought to the fore moderate liberal and radical democratic tendencies, on the one hand, and an awakening of national or nationalistic trends, on the other, although for a time it seemed all factions might march to the same drummer.

Jews and non-Jews had, however, some rather different perceptions of the meaning of emancipation. For many non-Jews, the abolition of legal constrictions would give the Jews an opportunity to become members of the new nation (French or German or Italian, etc.) or state; in so doing, they would shed their "reprehensible" habits, that is, their religious traditions, and in time disappear as a distinguishable group through the process of assimilation. Most Jews outside Russia agreed regarding acculturation, but not at the expense of their religion and customs.

In the earlier part of the century, many among the social, economic, and intellectual Jewish elite in the West tended to convert to Christianity—the "passport" to European culture, as Heinrich Heine, the German-Jewish poet, put it. Moses Mendelsohn, who became intellectually, socially, and politically a participant in German public life, was the founder of Jewish enlightenment, a movement to make Jews more aware of the world around them, to break down traditional obstacles to a better informed society that would stand up to the challenge of the times. Although Mendelsohn retained his Jewish religion and customs, his grandchildren and later descendants, including the composer Felix Mendelsohn, were Christians. The same was true of the Jewish religious judge in Trier at the end of the eighteenth century, whose grandson, Karl Marx, was converted as a child. Heine in Germany, Benjamin Disraeli in England, and others were converts or descendants of converts.

In the second half of the century, Western or westernized Jews tried to find a middle road between their Jewish heritage and the Western culture to which they aspired. The rise of national consciousness and the exclusive claims of what has been called "integral" or "organic" nationalism, however, complicated the problem.

SOCIAL AND POLITICAL DEVELOPMENTS IN EASTERN EUROPE

The rapid industrialization of Eastern Europe impoverished Jewish traders and craftsmen and gave rise to both a working class and a pauperized population of no fixed occupation. The surrounding society did not, as it turned out, take kindly to this development. The demographic and economic changes in Jewish society in Europe can best be observed by considering the following maps and charts.

The Jewish population exploded in the nineteenth century (Table 2.1). In Russia, Austria, and Germany—the main Jewish centers—the explosion was accompanied by a movement from countryside to towns that deepened the class cleavage among the Jewish people. As growing numbers of Western or westernized Jews entered the middle classes and the professions, they were assimilated into the surrounding society and able to reach the pinnacles

TABLE 2.1.
JEWISH POPULATION *(ESTIMATED)*

Year	Jews in Europe	Total Jews, worldwide
1650	700,000	1,750,000
1700	1,000,000	2,000,000
1750	1,250,000	2,250,000
1800	1,500,000	2,500,000
1825	2,730,000	3,281,000
1840	3,600,000	4,500,000
1850	4,127,500	4,764,500
1860	5,200,000	6,000,000

SOURCE: Arthur Ruppin, *Soziologie der Juden* (Berlin, 1931), pp. 81, 89.

of economic success or cultural and intellectual prominence. Those in Eastern Europe, however, were poverty-stricken inhabitants of towns, townlets and villages. In Tsarist Russia, they lived in an area called the Pale of Settlement, which was created in 1791 after the first partition of Poland and added to when Russia conquered additional areas from Turkey and finally annexed the Polish kingdom in 1815. Jews were not permitted to leave the area. Their middleman function was constantly interfered with by government regulations and edicts. As early as 1804 they were forbidden to live in villages—an unenforceable decree that nevertheless caused a great deal of suffering. Considered a politically unreliable element, they were later forbidden to live along the borders. Victims of contradictory policies, they were encouraged to work the land, however, and by the end of the nineteenth century 160,000 Jews were farmers, half of them in some three hundred Jewish colonies.

Early in the century, under Tsar Nicholas I (1825–55), Jewish communities were required to supply quotas of recruits between the ages of 12 and 25 years to the Tsar's army to serve for twenty-five years. In many cases children younger than twelve were forcibly taken from their homes

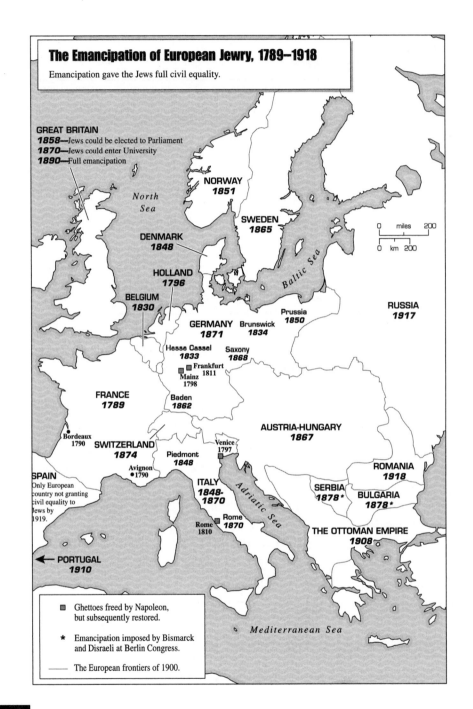

The Emancipation of European Jewry, 1789–1918

Emancipation gave the Jews full civil equality.

GREAT BRITAIN
1858—Jews could be elected to Parliament
1870—Jews could enter University
1890—Full emancipation

North Sea

NORWAY
1851

SWEDEN
1865

Baltic Sea

DENMARK
1848

HOLLAND
1796

BELGIUM
1830

Prussia
1850

RUSSIA
1917

GERMANY Brunswick
1871 **1834**

Hesse Cassel Saxony
1833 **1868**

Frankfurt
1811

Mainz
1798

FRANCE
1789

Baden
1862

•Bordeaux
1790

SWITZERLAND
1874

Venice
1797

Piedmont
1848

Avignon
•1790

AUSTRIA-HUNGARY
1867

ROMANIA
1918

SPAIN
Only European
country not granting
civil equality to
Jews by
1919.

ITALY
1848-
1870

SERBIA
1878*

BULGARIA
1878*

Adriatic Sea

Rome
1810

Rome
1870

THE OTTOMAN EMPIRE
1908

PORTUGAL
1910

Mediterranean Sea

0 miles 200
0 km 200

Ghettoes freed by Napoleon,
but subsequently restored.

★ Emancipation imposed by Bismarck
and Disraeli at Berlin Congress.

—— The European frontiers of 1900.

and sent to strict schools, where most of those who survived—many did not—were forced to abandon their Jewishness. Special "trustees" in the communities were responsible for the recruitment. As desperate parents tried to escape the net, corruption became rampant—the poor and defenseless were deprived of their children, the few who were rich paid for freedom. The recruitment of the cantonists (the kidnapped children) caused untold suffering and left a deep scar on the collective memory of Russian Jewry.

With the ascension of Tsar Alexander II (1855–81), a relative easing of governmental restrictions was accompanied by the beginnings of industrialization. Jews began to flock to towns to work in small industrial enterprises. Working conditions were very harsh, the exploitation of labor was rampant, and a Jewish proletariat began to emerge. Better hygienic conditions allowed the Russian Jewish population to increase from 2,350,000 in 1850 to 5,190,000 in 1897; a parallel increase in employment possibilities did not occur, however. As Russian culture spread among the Jews, cleavages between the traditionally minded majority and a new acculturating intelligentsia deepened. Here and there a few Jews became involved in Russian cultural life and a few became captains of industry (railways, the wood industry, sugar, tobacco, etc.), although Russian industry generally was developed by either foreign capital or aristocratic entrepreneurs and their allies after the economic reforms of Alexander II began to take effect. The rising Russian middle class and intelligentsia—among them the great writers Fyodor M. Dostoyevsky and Ivan S. Aksakov—saw the Jews as competitors to be ousted, however, and masses of peasants and impoverished urban dwellers were easily aroused against the Jewish scapegoat.

In 1881, with the assassination of Alexander II, the government of his successor, Alexander III (1881–94), welcomed the diversion of popular discontent provided by the persecution of the Jewish minority. Massive pogroms shook the foundations of Jewish life in 1881–83 and provoked the first big waves of emigration to the West, chiefly to the United States. In 1882 Jews were again forbidden to dwell in villages, and their numbers in high schools were limited to certain percentages (Lat., *numerus clausus,* "closed number"). Constantine Pobiedonostsev, adviser to the tsar, defined

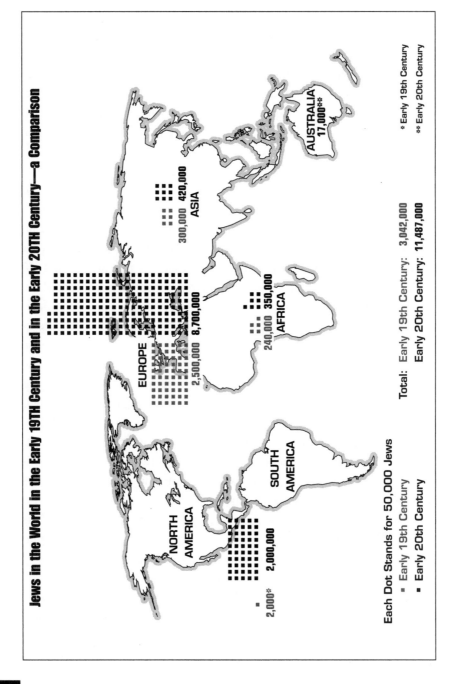

Jews in the World in the Early 19TH Century and in the Early 20TH Century—a Comparison

NORTH AMERICA

2,000* 2,000,000

SOUTH AMERICA

EUROPE

2,500,000 8,700,000

ASIA
300,000 420,000

AFRICA
240,000 350,000

AUSTRALIA
17,000**

Each Dot Stands for 50,000 Jews

■ Early 19th Century

■ Early 20th Century

Total: Early 19th Century: 3,042,000
Early 20th Century: 11,487,000

* Early 19th Century
** Early 20th Century

the Russian policy on Jews: one-third would convert, one-third would die, and one-third would emigrate. Economic and social measures against Jews multiplied, and in 1891 Jews were expelled from Moscow. With the active help of the Tsarist police, pogroms flared again in 1903, especially in the southern town of Kishinev, where forty-five persons were killed and many more wounded, raped, or robbed. Under Nicholas II (1894–1917), the pogroms became, to all intents and purposes, official policy, especially during the first Russian Revolution of 1905–06, again used to divert the population from discontent and revolutionary propaganda.

During the nineteenth century, the Jewish social structure in Eastern Europe changed radically. Although many Jews who had lived in small townships (Yiddish, sing. *shtetl;* pl., *shtetlach)* had moved to larger urban centers, in 1897, 33 percent still lived in *shtetlach* and 18 percent in villages. In the *shtetl* and the village the Jews continued to fulfill their traditional roles as middlemen between the peasants and the town, supplying the villages with manufactured goods, and as craftsmen and artisans. The deeply religious and traditionally minded population, who were converts to Hassidism, lived a way of life immortalized by such writers as Sholom Aleichem (Solomon Rabinowitz, 1859–1911), Yehuda L. Peretz (1852–1915), and more recently by a chiefly American nostalgic literature (as in the musical *Fiddler on the Roof*). However, at the turn of the century, the orientation in the *shtetl* began to move toward a secular, Jewish nationalism (Zionism), and anti-religious socialism, which was to coexist with remnants of the traditionalist approach until the Holocaust.

The growing Jewish population in the Tsarist empire and Austria-Hungary became increasingly poverty-stricken and suffered intensifying political persecution. Insecure among the Gentiles, whose rising nationalisms identified the Jews as a foreign element, the Jews sought safety in flight westward, some to Western Europe, but most to the western hemisphere, chiefly to the United States. Of 885,000 emigrants in 1889–99, 88 percent (780,000) went to the United States; in 1900–24, of 2,119,000 Jewish emigrants from Europe, 85 percent (1,810,752) went to the United States. Thus, most of the close to six million Jews in the United States today are descendants of people who fled from an unbearable situation in Eastern Europe.

THE IDEOLOGICAL AND ORGANIZATIONAL STRUCTURE OF NINETEENTH-CENTURY JEWISH SOCIETY

During the first half of the nineteenth century, attempts to accommodate Jewish life to the revolutionary changes that were occurring, especially in Western and Central Europe, denied the unity of the Jewish people and Jewish ethnicity generally. As Jewish enlightenment—a movement to bring the intellectual achievements of general civilization into Jewish life—spread into Eastern Europe, it distanced itself from the Jewish masses and their organizations, though it did not deny Jewish peoplehood. In Russia, the enlightenment served the interests of the Tsarist regime, which tried to dismantle Jewish communal self-government by introducing new ideas and norms and thereby created a new cleavage in Jewish life. Although the supporters of enlightenment, or *maskilim* (Hebrew, "enlightened people"), sometimes forced secular education on unwilling communities, they often did so in Hebrew, which had been for many centuries the language of prayer and correspondence between literate Jews.

Traditionally minded orthodox Jewry reacted defensively. Along with excommunications, harangues, and sermons, the orthodox also, in some cases (i.e., Hungary in 1868–69), employed liberal principles politically to establish a separate, closed, orthodox community that would preserve traditional values. Among the religiously orthodox, the disputes between the Hassidim and the Mitnagdim gradually diminished as the entire orthodox community faced the upheavals of the time, although some enmity persisted into the twentieth century. The great Hassidic dynasties (Lubavitch, Belz, Ger, Karlin, Vyzhnitz, Satmar, and others) vied with the mitnagdic rabbis of the Lithuanian *yeshivot* for control over the faithful. In Lithuania, the rise of the Mussar (Hebrew, "ethics" or " morals") movement, founded by Rabbi Israel Salanter (Lipkin) at the end of the century, attempted to return to the pristine morality of Jewish tradition, to escape from the Hassidic-Mitnagdic controversy, and to offer an ethical solution to religious problems that would fit the modern world.

In the second half of the century, attempts at reunification and an emphasis on the uniqueness of the Jewish tradition became more marked as extreme adherents of enlightenment in Germany adapted Jewish religious

TABLE 2.2
CHANGES IN JEWISH OCCUPATIONAL STUCTURE IN EUROPE

Agriculture

Western Europe	1%	[early 19th century]
Eastern Europe	4%	[early 19th century]

Trade and Finance

Western Europe	70%	[early 20th century]
	55%	[early 19th century]
Eastern Europe	42%	[early 20th century]
	38%	[early 19th century]

Industry and Craft

Western Europe	7%	[early 20th century]
	23%	[early 19th century]
Eastern Europe	33%	[early 20th century]
	36%	[early 19th century]

Free Professions

Western Europe	10%	[early 20th century]
	14%	[early 19th century]
Eastern Europe	10%	[early 20th century]
	11%	[early 19th century]

Other

Western Europe	13%	[early 20th century]
	7%	[early 19th century]
Eastern Europe	15%	[early 20th century]
	11%	[early 19th century]

traditions to German Protestant forms and saw themselves as another German tribe. A neo-messianic ideology prevailed: Jewish religion, it was claimed, was purely monotheistic and not Trinitarian, or postmessianic, as Christianity was. This pure monotheism with its equally pure Old Testament ethical message had to convince the world of its beauty. Reform Judaism saw itself as unique, as the bearer of messianic ethics to the world. The more it divorced itself from Jewish tradition, the clearer and more universal it thought its message would become. To Reform Jews, as well as their opponents at the other end of the Jewish spectrum, the Hassidim, Judaism was not a marginal note to civilization but a centrally important factor in the development of humanity to a higher plane.

Within Jewish society, there was a combination of a yearning for unity on the one hand, and dissensions and social conflict on the other hand. There was no equality of the sexes. Jewish religious traditions, like those of most other civilizations, are basically anti-feminist and, arguably, even mysogenic (women-hating). Women were not permitted to be witnesses at trials, and could not participate in public life; there were very few exceptions. Family traditions were strictly patriarchal, and while in many orthodox families women were the main providers—men were often engaged in the study of Torah—their position within the family was definitely secondary.

In the early part of the century Western and Central European Jewry frowned on any attempts at the national of international organization of Jews. Emancipation had removed the community as a quasi-governmental agency, empowered by non-Jewish rulers to enforce its rule over individual members. Whereas before emancipation the Jewish community had levied taxes, policed its area, and sanctioned the use of force to ensure conformity, this no longer was the case in Western and Central Europe after emancipation. In some countries, to be sure (e.g., Germany) as long as a Jew had not left Judaism he continued to belong to a Jewish community. But apart from a limited power of taxation, the granting of the rites of birth, entry into the community at the coming of age (the bar-mitzva ceremony at the age of 13 for boys—there was no parallel ceremony for girls), marriage, and death, an individual's participation in Jewish community life was purely voluntary. The renewed attacks on Jews later in the century, the growing uneasiness and insecurity of the Jews, and the realization that the fate of their brethren ("co-religionists" as they were called) elsewhere might well affect their own lives caused the rise of Jewish organizations on denominational and later national and international lines. Contacts between such organizations tended to increase Jewish solidarity as they consolidated to fight anti-Jewish policies at home and abroad. The Alliance Israelite Universelle, for example, founded in France in 1860, was a reaction to two events: In Damascus in 1840 Jews were accused of murdering a Catholic monk and his Arab servant for ritual purposes, an allegation supported by French diplomatic representatives; eventually Jewish innocence was proved. In 1858 a Jewish child, Edgar Mortara, was kidnapped in Italy and forcibly converted to Catholicism. The Alliance worked to protect Jews from such outrages and set up a Francophone school system for Jewish children in the Middle East and North Africa. The Central-Verein (Central Organization of German Citizens of the Jewish Faith), founded in 1893, fought antisemitism in Germany. The German Hilfsverein (Aid Society), founded in 1902, and the Israelitische Allianz zu Wien in Austria-Hungary helped Jewish emigrants from the East to reach havens overseas.

THE RESULTS OF EMANCIPATION

With the attainment of equal legal rights in Western and Central Europe, Jews in those countries thought, in general, that the "Jewish problem" had been solved. In the past, Jewish security had been guaranteed by a charter or various kinds of permits granted by potentates. Now, constitutions and popularly approved laws performed that task. It soon became clear, however, that legal status did not convey equality in the non-Jewish social world. Hidden and open discrimination persisted—Jews were not accepted in certain types of British social organizations or in certain schools, and in Germany, Jews could not become military officers, judges, professors, diplomats. The Jewish "problem" became a social problem.

In a sense, the Jews did not fulfill the expectations of either the general society or their friends. They did not disappear; they did not conform to the officially Christian majority. What centuries of pressure by persecuting churches had not achieved was not reversed by the appeal of toleration.

Jews saw themselves as equal citizens, German or French nationals, for example, and their religion as their own private affair. Many German Jews considered themselves to be another German tribe, like the Bavarians or the Saxons, albeit of a different religion. In their majority, they had no intention of giving up their religious separateness. In addition, Jewish communities had concentrated in the past in such areas as Alsace, Hesse, and Polish Galicia. Toward the end of the century, however, urbanization brought large numbers of Jews to Paris, Berlin, and Vienna where they worked in middle-class positions and the professions. This new concentration of Jews hampered their smooth absorption, or perhaps merger, into non-Jewish society. Despite assimilation and acculturation and the abandonment of traditional ways, in the intellectual world of many Jews the long-range impact of the Jewish moral and intellectual heritage can be discerned: the yearning for a world of justice and purity, the intense feeling of insecurity and the search for a way out of it. The rising nationalism provoked two general Jewish intellectual reactions: A minority of Jewish intellectuals tried to compromise, or even identify, with Europe's exclusive nationalisms; a majority identified with various universalist and internationalist ideas, because security would be achieved only with the defeat of narrow nationalism. Thus, a disproportionately large number of Jews tried to find security—a false security, unfortunately—in a universal all-embracing liberalism, international socialism, modern art, modern philosophy, Esperanto (an artificial universal language), Freemasonry, and so on. The number of Jewish radicals and revolutionaries was (and is) considerable. Revolutions eat their children, and whenever revolutions succeeded, the Jews were no exception to that rule.

MODERN ANTISEMITISM

Traditional antisemitism was based on Christian anti-Judaism—the deicide accusation, the supersession myth, the myth of the supposed moral turpitude and deserved punishment resulting from the rejection of Jesus Christ as the Messiah, as well as economic misbehavior and, in more extreme cases, the myth of the Jews' "desire to control the world." "Ritual" murder accusations persisted (Damascus, 1840; Tisza-Eszlar [in Hungary], 1882; the Beilis affair in Kiev, 1911–13, etc.). Resentment and hatred were focused on the stereotype of the Jew—it had little to do with the people who lived in actual Jewish communities. As only a people possessed by the Devil could have killed God, Jews and Judaism were often seen as the work or the symbol of Satan.

Modern antisemitism has several components. The romantic movement in the first half of the century excluded the Jews. Exalting folkways and emphasizing the purity of the national tradition, it evoked the image of a bygone mythical golden age whose supposed superiority must again be reached. In Germany, for instance, such emphasis produced a yearning for the pre-Christian pagan era and an idealization of the Middle Ages, with legends of knights, chivalry, and endless strife and wars. The romantic trend contributed to an increasingly exclusive, or integral, nationalism, and thus excluded from its purview all those who could claim no part in this idealized past. Unable to claim title to French, Germanic, or British pagan origins or the lores of Christian knights, the Jews were strangers who lived as not-quite-equal citizens in the countries of Europe.

The class antagonism that derived from modern capitalism is another element of modern antisemitism. Such socialist and anarchist thinkers as Charles Fourier, Pierre Proudhon, Michael Bakunin, and Karl Marx took an extreme anti-Jewish stand, accusing Jews of initiating capitalism and thus exaggerating out of all proportion the important, though limited, contribution of Jewish traders and industrialists to the growth of industry and commerce. The Rothschild bankers family served as a stereotype to attack all Jews. Marx equated Judaism with the ideology and practice of capitalism and the Jewish spirit with the spirit of capitalism. With the defeat of capitalism, Judaism and Jews would vanish. In different hands, such theories would later light genocidal fires. In the last decades of the century, however, when antisemitism became part of the stock-in-trade of right-wing movements, socialist parties turned against antisemitism and became its staunch opponents.

Social Darwinism was another contributing factor to modern antisemitism. In England in 1850 Herbert Spencer propounded the theory of constant struggle between humans, in which the strongest would win. In 1859 Charles Darwin proposed (in his *Origins of the Species*) that the various types of life had developed and survived insofar as they managed to adapt themselves to the changing environment. Spencer's ideology—survival not of the fittest but of the strongest—a distortion of ideas later developed by Darwin, has been termed Social Darwinism. Spencer and his disciples concluded that the protection of the weak and the poor by society ran afoul of natural laws. Among nations, too, the strongest was the fittest, therefore the best, and consequently had an inherent right to rule.

The progression of antisemitism to racism was accomplished with linguistic research. Christian Lassen, a German linguist (1800–1876), argued as early as the 1840s that "Semites," who spoke a variety of tongues, were egotistical and exclusive, whereas Indo-Europeans, whose languages stemmed from a common origin, were tolerant and altruistic. The linguists did not, however, insist on common physical characteristics in the same linguistic groups. Count Arthur Joseph de Gobineau (author of the *Inequality of Human Races,* 1854) saw in what he called the "Aryan" race—blond, tall, blue-eyed—a superior, culture-bearing people in line with Social Darwinist thought. Gobineau did not single out the Jews as inferior; this was left for later racists. In the 1880s, French anthropologist Vacher-de-Lafouge argued that the long-faced, blonde Aryans were richer, paid more taxes, were largely urban, tended to migrate, were more intelligent, and preferred to ride bicycles. He added: "I am convinced that in the course of the next century millions of people will kill each other because of a one-degree difference in their skull-index.[1]

The German composer Richard Wagner (and later his family), a radical, but perhaps not a racist, antisemite, fueled the racial difference theory. Wagner expressed a German nationalistic terminology called *völkisch* (people-integral nationalistic). He too talked about emancipation—but emancipation from Judaism and Christianity, which he considered a Judaized religion. Hence his artistic attempts to glorify a Germanic religion based on pagan elements. Eugen Duehring, a Social Darwinist, and Paul de Lagarde, a 'volkist' antisemite, developed the anti-Judaic and anti-Christian element still further. If the decisive element in a person's makeup was race, which was hereditary, then no amount of baptismal water could change a Jew. They and others, especially writers of popular novels, developed the symbol of "blood"—blood carried the characteristics of race and was both the symbol and the content of purity or lack of it. The biologization of antisemitism found its expression also in the idea that the Jew was not human. The racist German oriental scholar Paul de Lagarde (1827–1891) wrote, for example:

One ought "to despise those who—out of humanity!—defend these Jews or who are too cowardly to trample this usurious vermin to death. With trichinae and bacilli one does not negotiate, nor are trichinae and bacilli to be educated: they are exterminated as quickly and thoroughly as possible." [2] To the imagery of the Jew as Satan, derived from earlier Christian antisemitism, was added the biologically oriented imagery of the parasite. Both images, that of the Devil and that of the parasite, dehumanized the Jews and made theorizing about their physical destruction possible.

Wagner's son-in-law, Houston Stewart Chamberlain (1855–1927), in his book *Foundations of the Nineteenth Century,* disregarded the physical indications of race and emphasized the "spirit" of race. Everything Jewish was black and demonic, destructive and corrupting. Its opposite was the pure Germanic spirit. These simplistic Manichean (black and white) definitions indicate that antisemitism converted racism into a tool to propagate antisemitic doctrine. Or it might be said that antisemitism was not a specific development of racist ideas but that racism was a cover and a rationale for antisemitic doctrine. Its Manichean element allowed it to be absorbed and accepted. Thus mass antisemitism could become a valuable propaganda weapon.

The term antisemitism was apparently first used by a racist ideologist in Germany, Wilhelm Marr, in 1878 or 1879. Prior to that the term Judenhass was current in German, Jew-hatred in English, and Judeophobia in intellectual circles, terms essentially inherited from the Christian period. But in an increasingly secularized society in which there was no belief in Jesus, the question of who was responsible for his death seemed irrelevant. Marr, Duehring, de Lagarde, and the other racists, violently anti-Christian, saw Christianity—quite rightly, of course—as derived from Judaism and therefore utterly condemnable. They needed a "modern," "scientific" term, hygienic, neutral, one that would not include the word *Jew.* Antisemitism was such a term—but in the Central European context everyone knew who was meant when the word Semite was used. Sixty-odd years later, in 1941, when the Nazis had to deal with Hajj Amin el-Husseini, Mufti of Jerusalem, the leader of Palestinian Arabs, who had fled to Berlin to join Hitler's forces, the question was solved simply: The Arabs were declared "honorary

Aryans." The term antisemitic did not apply to them. There were no "Semites" against whom a movement arose—the movement was anti-Jewish; the new term was a semantic cover, and so it has remained (and should be spelled as one word, not as 'anti-Semitism', because there is no 'Semitism' one can be 'anti' to).

The supposed Jewish desire to control the world was actually an old concept derived from the Satanic image. Just as Satan is out to control the world, so the Jew, possessed by the Devil, must be. Psychologically, this is easily explicable. Fears and aggressions were projected onto a weak and totally powerless minority, identified with an all-powerful "Satan" that was, in fact, a weak people easily attacked and "destroyed." One can find the idea of the supposed Jewish craving for world power expressed not only in literature but also in caricatures.

In 1806 Napoleon convened a group of Jewish notables to arrange for the integration of Jews into his Empire—he called it the Sanhedrin, in a grandiose, Napoleonesque gesture, borrowing the term *Sanhedrin* from the Jewish High Court in the period of the Second Temple (538 B.C.E.–70 C.E.). From the viewpoint of orthodox anti-Jewish Christian circles throughout Europe, Napoleon, the modern Anti-Christ, had thus given legitimation to the mythical secret Jewish government that had existed throughout the ages. In 1806, a French captain addressed a letter to Abbe Augustin Barruel, a prolific and influential author and an inveterate anti-democrat and Jew-hater, in which he claimed that the "Jewish sect" was a "most formidable power. . . .What they promise themselves is that within less than one century they would become masters of the world, abolish all the other religions in order to rule alone, and turn Christian churches into synagogues."[3]

In a manner characteristic of later Nazism, these figments of panic-stricken imaginations appeared on the Left as well. Such left-wing democrats as the Prussian Friedrich Buchholz accused the Jews in 1807 of plotting with the aristocracy to rule society.[4] In 1816 the world-conspiracy theme was repeated by Johann Ehrmann, a German anti-Napoleonic nationalist. The same idea was propagated in *Le Juif, le Judaism et la Judaisation des Peoples Chretiens* (1869) by Roger G. de Mousseaux. Later, Freemasonry, an organization of God-fearing liberals of all religious faiths, whose purpose is to advance religious equality, social justice, and the brotherhood of man, was attacked by the same groups that in the nineteenth century had developed the false myth of the Jewish desire to control the world.

The famous forgery called "The Protocols of the Elders of Zion" (published in two slightly different versions in 1903 and 1905) purported to be the record of a meeting of the "real" rulers of the West, the Jewish elders at the first Zionist Congress at Basle in 1897. In actual fact, the "Protocols" were concocted in Paris between 1897 and 1899 by agents of the chief of the Russian secret police, General Rachkowski, who based their forgeries on a French satirical essay by Maurice July, "Dialogue in Hell between Macchiavelli and Montesquieu" (1865), which attacked Napoleon III. In the paranoiac imagination of the forgers, the Jewish elders met regularly in the Middle Ages in the old Jewish graveyard in Prague to plot the control of the world, a concoction "borrowed" from the German writer Gedsche who wrote under the pseudonym of Sir John Radcliffe in the 1860s and 1870s. According to the "Protocols" the elders met at the Zionist Congress to plot the subversion of all civilization and the imposition of Jewish rule. The "Protocols" were published in Germany in 1919, in France and the United States in 1920, and in Britain in 1920–21, although an investigation by the *London Times* soon revealed the forgery. Exposed again as a forgery in a trial for libel in Switzerland in 1934, the "Protocols" nevertheless are being spread all over the contemporary world; their influence continues to be considerable in the countries of the former Soviet Union and the so-called Third World. The identification of Zionism with Judaism presages the use in the post-Holocaust world of the term anti-Zionism, which has largely replaced the older term antisemitism as a code word for Jew-hatred and which uses the idea of a Jewish world conspiracy as an integral part of its propaganda. The "Protocols" undoubtedly answered a deep-seated need for a simplistic explanation of the evils and failures of the modern world. As in times past, the satanic element in history—the Jews, defined as such by Christian antisemitism—could be held responsible by imputing to the Jews a world conspiracy. In time, the "Protocols" would become an essential weapon in the arsenal of Nazism.

The historian George L. Mosse traced the complex relations between Germans and Jews to ideas and ideologies that prevailed in Germany prior to the nineteenth century:

> German antisemitism is a part of German intellectual history. It does not stand outside it. Above all, it became involved with the peculiar turn which German thought took after the first decade of the 19th century. German thought became at once provincial, in its search for roots, and idealistic, in its rejection of mere outward progress, in its belief in the irrationality of culture. Here the Jew was the outsider, and if he could at times gatecrash by assimilation in the 19th century, that did not fundamentally alter the emerging image of the Jew. Culture was closed to him for he lacked the necessary foundations.[5]

In dealing with the image of the Jew in popular German literature, Mosse wrote:

> The stereotype Jew that emerges from this segment of popular culture provided one of the most important roots of German anti-Semitism. It was an ominous image, the more so as it was in all instances associated not only with contempt but with actual cruelty. It became a reality in the early days of National Socialism with the pictures of the captured Eastern Jews sweeping the streets or having their beards pulled amid the hilarity of the mob. . . .The image of the Jew was outside the range of serious political and social analysis, and that was its strength. In this way it provided the emotional basis for a totalitarian solution of these problems. There must have been many who, like Hitler, when faced with real problems, first awakened to the stereotype of the "Jew" and then built their ideology around it. . . .Only in this way will we be able to understand fully the continued influence of anti-Semitism, which distressingly, seems to predate and to outlast its immediate political or social relevance.[6]

In other words, the Jew was the stranger, the outsider, and in the self-understanding of many Europeans, including Germans, he could simply never be considered a member of what in Germany was known as the *Volk*.

Popular literature solicited this perception by presenting the Jew as the eternal "other," the symbol of foreignness, of dark and evil forces, forever polluting the purity of the German people. In this, the Jews and the Roma ('Gypsies') had much in common in the popular perception. Stereotypes of these peoples developed, with definite and extreme negative slants; that they were stereotypes and not representative of the peoples themselves mattered not at all.

Mosse illustrated his point with two books: Felix Kahn's *Flight from Rome* (1869), which was one of the most popular novels of the century, and Gustav Freytag's *Debit and Credit* (1855), which was written under the influence of the Italian Risorgimento as a "contribution to the movement for German unification."[7] The Jewish hero of Kahn's book, Jocham, bears all the characteristics of the Jewish stereotype. Jocham, a traitor, speaks a foreign language and performs the destructive acts of the novel. The real hero is, of course, the Germanic people.

In appealing to the middle classes in his novel, Freytag writes about the merchant house of Schröter, old, honest, pure, the German ideal of the middle classes. The Jewish merchant Veitel Itzig is described as "puny, pale, has red curly hair, is poor and slovenly in dress." Whereas Schröter's establishment is old, solid, clean, and comfortable, Itzig's store is dirty, small, and cramped. The German family is described as full of love, the Jewish family as full of hate.

POLITICAL ANTISEMITISM

Politically, antisemitism became a force in Germany when the famous historian Heinrich von Treitschke published a series of antisemitic articles in the prestigious *Preussische Jahrbücher* in 1879.[8] He ended the series with: "The Jews are our misfortune." A year later an antisemitic petition that demanded the exclusion of Jews from government positions and teaching posts obtained almost a quarter of a million signatures. Intended to wean away support from the Social-Democrats and led by the court preacher, Adolf Stöcker, the conservative, government-supported Christian Social

Workers' party espoused antisemitism in 1879. The other antisemitic parties and groups that were formed in 1880 and the following years began flourishing after 1887, when the first antisemite was elected to the Reichstag (Parliament). A virulent antisemite, Hermann Ahlwardt, who had written a book in which he claimed that the Jews were ruling Germany, was elected in 1892.

The 1890s were a time of economic and social unrest in Germany, particularly the latter years of the decade. The lower middle class was especially hard hit and nationalism and antisemitism were an obvious answer to many. The Pan-German League (Alldeutscher Verband), founded in 1893, became a supporter of German imperialism. Under Heinrich Class (from 1908), it became a major transmitter of racist antisemitism. In 1912, Class published (under a pseudonym) *If I Were Kaiser (Wenn Ich der Kaiser wär)*, in which his notions of German aggrandizement and hatred of Jews and foreigners are clearly expressed.

Although the ideologists (e.g., Houston Stewart Chamberlain) continued their propaganda, antisemitism seemed to decline politically after 1907. The antisemitic parties lost seats, and social democracy, rather than the extreme right, seemed to be the force that expressed social discontent; social democracy, opposed to antisemitism, turned against the monarchy and the capitalist system rather than against real or imagined foreign enemies.

It is important to note that while antisemitism, including its radical and potentially lethal manifestations, became influential among the German intellectual and power elites, it was far from endemic in German society. In 1912, the Social Democrats gained a plurality in the general elections, and together with the liberals they probably represented a majority of the German people. It is therefore mistaken to argue for some kind of almost genetic German inclination toward Jew-hatred from the Middle Ages on, as some observers (e.g., Daniel J. Goldhagen) have done. Among the elites, too, different forms of antisemitism were spreading—less radical and more radical ones, and the latter did not necessarily predominate until much later. The development of German society towards identification with the Nazi project of killing the Jews was not pre-ordained or pre-determined.

JEWISH REACTIONS

Zionism and Palestine

Zionism is the national movement of the Jews that postulates the unity of the Jewish people on the basis of their past history, their common fate, their common culture, and the centrality of their political and social regeneration in Palestine-Israel, their ancient homeland.

The rise of Zionism in Europe, before and after the first Zionist Congress at Basle in 1897, was associated with the rise of European and national movements, of which the Jewish national revival is really a part, and of modern antisemitism, to which Zionism reacted. Zionism sought an answer for the Jewish masses in Eastern Europe who were seeking to escape impoverishment and persecution, especially after the 1881–82 pogroms in Russia.

As early as the mid-nineteenth century, Moses Hess, one of the first European socialists, had advanced the idea of a Jewish return to Palestine. Later in the century groups of young Jews sought to return to find a haven for both the Jewish people and the Jewish civilization. The first pioneers, such as the "Bilu" group, which founded the first modern Jewish settlements in Palestine in the early 1880s, were building on solid religious and traditional foundations. Jewish tradition was quite firmly bound to the Land of Israel, and repeated attempts, messianic and others, had been made to settle there. In Jerusalem, the majority of the population was Jewish throughout the nineteenth century, whereas in Palestine generally there was a large Arab majority. Religious dreamers and Oriental Jewish merchants and craftsmen were now shaken by a modern national revival. Lovers of the Zion (Hebrew, *Hovevei Zion)* groups sprang up, especially in Eastern Europe, to advance settlement in Palestine. When the early settlers ran into trouble, Baron Edmond de Rothschild of Paris intervened to provide help. The revival movement was urged along largely, but not solely, by the suffering of the Jewish masses in Eastern Europe.

Theodor Herzl, a Viennese journalist, was moved not by the East European persecutions but by the resurgence of antisemitism in Western Europe.

57

He reported the trial of Alfred Dreyfus, a French Jewish officer who was framed by a group of antisemitic French officers and wrongly accused of betraying French military secrets to Germany (1894). The affair, which lasted until Dreyfus was finally acquitted and reinstated in 1906, was the occasion for an outbreak of militant antisemitism in France, and Herzl, moved by anti-Jewish propaganda generally and not specifically by the Dreyfus affair, organized the Jewish national movement that became known as Zionism at Basle in 1897. The political aim of Zionism was to establish an internationally recognized Jewish political entity. Under the influence of Russian Jews, Herzl, who was an assimilated Jew with weak roots in the Jewish past, agreed to identify Jewish national endeavors with Palestine, though he had supported a proposal to settle Jews temporarily in Uganda in 1903. His idea was to convince the Great Powers to support this movement, as Italian nationalism had sought the support of France against Austria, and Greek nationalism had sought the support of Britain against Turkey. He failed in obtaining a charter for Jewish settlement in Palestine, but the movement he founded survived his death in 1904 to place the Jewish national problem on the map of world politics. Britain became interested in Zionism, partly because of mistaken notions regarding a supposedly considerable world Jewish influence, which would be useful to have on Britain's side.

Among traditionally minded East European Jews, Zionism as a sentiment was widely accepted. Jews had for thousands of years repeated daily prayers for a return to the Land of Israel, had observed customs and laws that made sense only in the homeland, and had connected their whole existence with it. However, as a political force, Zionism grew slowly; it became a major influence only during and after World War I. It was even slower to develop in Western Europe and America. Everywhere it remained a minority group among Jews, until after World War II. Zionism faced opposition from the religiously orthodox and the universalist-assimilationist Jews. Whereas Jewish orthodoxy saw in Zionism a secular movement blasphemously preempting the Messiah's task in returning the Jews to their homeland, the liberals, the assimilated Jews, and the socialists saw in Zionism an obstacle to their integration in the Gentile society.

The Bund

In Russia, revolutionary sentiments spread among the downtrodden urban population, including the Jews. A Jewish socialist party was founded in 1897, the year of the Basle Zionist Congress. It was called the General Jewish Workers' Alliance, or in Yiddish, Allgemener Yiddisher Arbeter-Bund, or Bund (not to be confused with a pro-Nazi organization of German Americans of the same name, in the thirties). The Bund saw the future of the Jewish masses in terms of a socialist Russian society, built on equality and justice, in which Jews would maintain a cultural (non-religious) autonomy based on the Yiddish language and literature, as equals with other nationalities. The Russian Social Democrats did not accept this idea, and Lenin's Bolsheviks expressly rejected it (1903), demanding a full integration of Jews in the all-Russian movement. In effect, Russian socialists repeated to the Jews what the French Revolution had proclaimed: to the Jews as individuals, everything, to the Jews as a group, nothing. To become equals, the Jews would have to deny their ethnic and/or religious identity. Most Jews were not prepared to do that.

The Bund rejoined the Russian Social Democratic party (the Mensheviks) in 1906 and took part in the social and political upheavals of the Tsarist Empire until its downfall in 1917. The Bund's determined opposition to the rising Bolshevik party resulted in its dissolution and suppression when the Bolsheviks took power in late 1917.

Anti-Zionist and Other Reactions

Orthodox, anti-Zionist Jewry, faced with organized ideological movements in the Jewish world, also sought ways of establishing itself as a political force. In 1912 Agudat Israel (Agudas Yisroel in Yiddish), the political wing of Jewish orthodoxy, was founded. Led by rabbis from Eastern Europe and Germany, it fought to preserve strict adherence to ancient religious norms and withdrew from the political struggles of the Gentile world. If left to its own devices internally, orthodoxy promised unswerving loyalty to whatever regime happened to be in power in any given country. Zionism, assimilation, socialism, Western democratic values—all were rejected in favor of strict observances of customary law.

Other solutions appeared at the turn of the century. Large numbers of Jews, especially in America and Eastern Europe, sought security in acculturation and assimilation to the surrounding society. Others (e.g., the great Jewish historian Simon Dubnow in Latvia) demanded cultural autonomy for Jews in a democratic world. But on the eve of World War I, insecurity was marked. Antisemitism was a fact of life. Jews in the West were outwardly equal, but their equality was far from genuine. Social and political restrictions were applied to Jews at every turn. In Eastern Europe, autocratic regimes hostile to Jews even revived the blood-libel accusation (the Beilis case in Russia, 1911–13).

The Jews, probably the most ancient people with an uninterrupted cultural tradition, emerged on the eve of World War I as a group that, surprisingly, had begun a national revival. Their religion and culture, adamantly adhered to and developed over millennia, had worn well. They were not a fossilized remnant from the past but a live community throbbing with excitement and cultural achievements. Confronted by hostility and discrimination, they nevertheless had contributed very much more than their share of scientists, artists, poets, writers, actors, and musicians to Western culture. Would that civilization overcome its prejudices and grant the Jews the right to be different but equal?

three
WORLD WAR I
AND ITS AFTERMATH

THE BACKGROUND: 1914–1918

THE OUTBREAK OF WORLD WAR I signaled not only the end of an era; it marked a crucial landmark in Jewish history as well. The war released aggressions and revealed potentials for mutual mass annihilation that had been undreamed of in previous generations. The mass carnage of the 1914–18 war, the murder of 8.5 million men on the battlefield, put an end to the positivist European dreams of uninterrupted progress. The way was now paved for victory of the so-called cultural pessimists, who had rejected the Western democratic tradition and were looking to a revived autocratic society to impose s rigid rule of one kind or another.[1]

Most European Jews lived in the Russian Pale of Settlement in Eastern Poland, the western parts of Belorussia (now Belarus) and the Ukraine, in the Austro-Russian border region of Polish Galicia, and in Lithuania, where warring armies had struggled almost constantly. In 1915 the Tsarist

Massacre, Pogrom, and Emigration 1600–1920

By 1914, more than eight million Jews lived between the Baltic Sea and the Black Sea. Another two million had sought a new life, and greater security, in the United States. In addition, by 1914, three hundred thousand went to Britain and sixty thousand to Palestine.

- - - - - - Russia's western border, 1815–1917.

———— Poland's frontiers, 1920–1939, bringing nearly three million Jews under the sovereignty of the new Polish Republic by 1921.

Area of anti-Jewish massacres, 1648–1651. Over 100,000 Jews were killed. Many more were tortured or ill-treated. Others fled to Germany and the Balkans.

⊙ Some of the towns, then in Tsarist Russia, in which the mob attacked the Jews between 1881 and 1907, killing many hundreds, looting shops, and burning homes.

Area where, in 1919, more than 60,000 Jews were murdered by Ukrainian nationalists. As a result, tens of thousands of Jews fled to other parts of Europe, to the United States, and to Palestine.

command, blaming the Jews for its defeat, expelled them from certain border areas. The Pale itself was abolished, and hundreds of thousands of Jews were forced to move inland, to Russia itself. Starvation and disease, which took many lives, were alleviated somewhat by help from more affluent Russian and, particularly, American Jews.

German, Austro-Hungarian, French, British, and American Jews participated in the war in numbers that were generally higher than their percentage in the population would warrant. Of 600,000 German Jews, fully 100,000 served in the German army, and 12,000 fell on the battlefields. A similar picture emerges elsewhere. Jewish enlistment appears to have been prompted by a basic feeling of insecurity in the Gentile environment and a consequent desire to prove a loyalty equal to, or beyond, that shown by others. But their patriotism availed them not. Stereotyped as unmilitary, German Jews suffered humiliating inquiry into their collective behavior and were frequently the victims of pent-up aggressions.

The overall political situation of the Jews during the war was, however, favorable in at least one sense: Germany was fighting against tsarist Russia, the home of the "Protocols," the pogroms, destitution, and persecution. In conquering Poland and western Russia, German armies brought succor and rescue from persecution.[2] (When Nazi troops occupied East European Jewish centers in World War II, people expected them to behave as their fathers had. "Der Daitch" [Yiddish, "the German"] was pictured in 1914–18 terms; people could not comprehend the new reality.) On the other hand, Western democracy had proved to be the climate best suited for the well-being of the Jewish population. Despite the alliance of Britain and France, and even more so the United States, with the Tsar, many Jews saw the Western democracies as bastions against the overweening dreams of conquest of Kaiser Wilhelm II.

The center of the weak Zionist organization was in Berlin and the old German Zionist leadership was loyal to Germany. At the outbreak of war, a liaison office was set up in neutral Denmark. In Palestine itself, the young Zionist settlers sought at first to identify with the Ottoman regime, but hostile Turkish attitudes persuaded them otherwise.

Chaim Weizmann, a young Russian Jewish scientist, had settled in Manchester, England, prior to the war. He established close relations with a number of influential British statesmen and sought British support for a Jewish Palestine under British tutelage after the defeat of Turkey. With the assistance of another Russian Jewish intellectual, Vladimir (Zeev) Jabotinsky, Weizmann initiated the Jewish volunteer movement for the British army. Fleeing from Turkish persecutions in Palestine, Jewish exiles in Egypt joined the Zion Mule Corps under the legendary one-armed Joseph Trumpeldor. Those who survived the unsuccessful British Gallipoli invasion of the Turkish heartland in 1915 made up the backbone of a Jewish battalion that was formed in England and fought in Palestine from June 1918 to the end of the war. Members of another Zionist battalion, formed in the United States, saw action in Palestine in the last period of the war. By the time a third battalion composed of Palestinian Jews was formed in 1918, the war was over.

British policy on Palestine vacillated during the war. Prime Minister Herbert Asquith, who was hostile to Zionist aspirations, resigned in December 1916; the succeeding government, headed by David Lloyd George, was influenced by the strategic thinking of Sir Mark Sykes of the British Foreign Office. Sykes sought to base British influence on a coalition with the Jewish, Arab, and Armenian national movements. In late 1917, with revolution raging in Russia, Britain was moved also by the idea that if Palestine was promised to the Jews, Jewish influence in Russia might prolong Russia's participation in the war as well as intensify American participation. Information regarding Germany's impending promise of Palestine to the Zionist movement also influenced the British. It appears that Britain's support of Zionism was connected, in a sense, with the antisemitic legend of decisive Jewish world influence. If, the British thought, the Jewish power was so great, it would be useful to have them firmly on the allied side. With the Balfour Declaration of November 2, 1917, the British promised to establish a Jewish National Home in Palestine. The fact that there was an Arab majority (of some 90%) in the country in 1918 was known, but British supporters of Zionism as well as the liberal leadership of the Zionist movement believed that a compromise could be struck between an Arab national movement aspiring to a large, united Arab political entity in the Middle East, and the Jewish national movement asking for that very small part of it called Palestine.

The outcome of the war made a large-scale effort to establish an autonomous Jewish settlement in Palestine extremely difficult. The Bolshevik revolution in Russia (November 1917) triggered a bloody civil war that was to last until 1921. The rightist (White) armies fighting the Bolsheviks vented their rage on Jewish populations, especially in the Ukraine. The nationalist Ukrainian government under Semyon Petliura (after November 1918) failed to prevent outrages against Jews, and General Anton Denikin's White armies committed even worse carnage. By 1921, from 70,000 to 100,000 Jews in the Ukraine had been murdered, 500 communities were destroyed, and hundreds of thousands were wounded. More than 100,000 Jewish emigrants entered the United States in 1920-21; many others were prevented from emigrating by the victorious Bolshevik government, which had closed all exits. The massacres and pogroms executed by antisemitic soldiers in the Ukraine and Poland after World War I were among the worst experiences of the Jewish people since the seventeenth century.

Many Jews responded by identifying with Zionism or, especially in Russia, with socialist or communist universalist doctrines that were to create a world without discrimination. The tragedy of Zionism was its lack of sufficient time to establish a political base for the Jewish people, a base that might serve both as a haven and as a political influence to counteract antisemitism.

Genocide of the Armenians

The massacre of the Armenian people in Turkish Anatolia in some ways parallels the Holocaust. Starting in 1894 with the murder of at least 20,000 Armenians at Sassun, Turkey, the systematic and planned campaign of murder under the Young Turk regime (Talaat Bey and Enver Bey were primarily responsible) continued at Adana in 1909. In 1915 and 1916 a concentrated effort was made, under the leadership of the Young Turkish leadership, to eliminate the Armenian population in Turkish ethnic areas.

At least one million Armenians were murdered. Turkish regular troops killed Armenian recruits in the Turkish army; other regulars evicted Armenians from their homes and forced them to undertake long marches into the desert, during which large numbers were barbarously killed by Turks, or

Kurdish or Circassian auxiliaries. Those who reached the desert died of thirst and starvation in very large numbers. The military planned the massacre, which was facilitated by the use of the modern telegraph for the transmission of messages, and the railway for the transportation of troops.

The motivation of the genocide was clearly nationalistic. Armenians were seen as a local menace to Turkish nationalism, not as a worldwide satanic threat to human culture. To the Turkish leaders, the Armenians were an obstacle to their dream of establishing a pan-Turanian (Turkic) empire that would include Turkic-speaking peoples from European Turkey to Russian Central Asia. The motivation was thus ideological, though the threat by Armenian nationalism to Ottoman rule was largely imaginary: Armenian nationalists demanded autonomy (though some aspired to independence), and, in fact, had supported the Young Turk revolution of 1908. Some Armenian political groups allied themselves with Russian imperialism, as a result of the enmity of the Turks toward them. This fact served as a justification for massive murders by the Turkish authorities. However, there was no pseudo-religious, eschatological element involved in the Turkish opposition to the Armenians, though there certainly was a long tradition of enmity to them. Although Turkish politicians referred to the Armenians as a "race," the racial element per se was absent. Nor was racist purity an issue, for Armenians who converted to Islam, Armenian women who were recruited for Turkish harems, and Armenian children who were kidnapped and reared as Turks, survived. Although there were important parallels with the Holocaust, the differences were marked. Mainly, the motivation differed.[13]

THE BACKGROUND: 1918–1933

World War I was evidence of the massive brutalization of the twentieth century; it was a major new departure in the history of mankind. For the first time in history had mass killing on such scale taken place between civilized societies. The killing, mutilation, and gas poisoning of millions of soldiers on both sides had broken taboos and decisively blunted moral sensitivities. Auschwitz cannot be explained without reference to World War I.

The destruction of tsarist Russia, and imperial Austria-Hungary and

Germany, brought about the establishment of new states (Poland, Czecho-slovakia, and Yugoslavia) and changes in the frontiers of existing ones. The rise of new nationalities was to find its expression in these new entities. However, the fact that all these nationalities were entwined and intermin-gled, increased national enmities, as each nation or ethnic group clamored for separateness. The defeated nations—Germany, Austria, Hungary, Russia —were deeply dissatisfied. Economic structures established in the larger empires in the pre-war period were thrown into severe crises by the tariff walls erected by each small new state. The textile industry of Lódtz in Poland, for example, founded and developed by Jews when the city was under Russian rule and the vast Russian empire could be expected to serve as a market, suffered losses after 1918 when limited to the small Polish home market.

Following the Bolshevik revolution, the national communist parties in Europe became, in fact, local agencies of the foreign policy of the Soviet Union. The political fights fed by economic crises, which culminated in the Great Depression that began in October 1929, increased the influence of the extreme left and the extreme right at the expense of the center, especially of liberals and socialists or social-democrats.

The legal status of the Jews in Britain, France, Holland, and Scandinavia remained the same. Tens of thousands of East European Jews immigrated to Belgium, and approximately 100,000 settled in France—Jews unable to make a living at home, those who wanted to better their situation, those of leftwing views who had run afoul of the authorities, and refugees from the communist take-over in Russia.

In the new East European states the Jewish minorities were unable to identify with their "homeland." In Austria-Hungary, where Jews had been guaranteed equality of opportunity and had enjoyed the vision and culture of a large European state, they had been, on the whole, ardent supporters of the Emperor. In attempting to identify with nationalities who were fighting each other for control, Jews felt like outsiders; the foreignness of the Jew was emphasized—s/he was not a Pole, nor a German, a Czech, or a Slovak. However, the need for protection quickly produced whole sectors in Jewish society eager to identify as members of these nationalities, albeit of a different religion. In dealing with the problems generated by their minorities—Germans, Ukrainians, Belorussians, and Lithuanians in Poland; Germans and Hungarians in Czechoslovakia—none of the new nations saw the Jews as belonging to themselves.

A Jewish delegation at the Paris peace negotiation in 1919, which was composed of representatives of the American Jewish Congress, the Board of Deputies of British Jews, and other organizations (including the Zionist leader, Chaim Weizmann), obtained the inclusion of paragraphs protecting the rights of minorities, explicitly including Jews, in the various treaties establishing or acknowledging the existence of the new East European states. Considered in most cases as interference by the Big Powers in the internal affairs of such countries as Poland or Rumania, the "protection" was, at best, with the exception of democratic and liberal Czechoslovakia, temporary; in fact, it has been argued that they only increased already prevalent antisemitic tendencies. Nevertheless, in Eastern Europe the minority treaties did enable the Jews to develop networks of social and economic organizations and political parties.

Of the approximately 9.4 million Jews in Europe in 1933, more than 78 percent lived in Poland, the USSR, Rumania, and Hungary. The greatest concentration of Jews—3.1 million—lived in Poland, about 2.5 million in the USSR, about 750,000 in Rumania, and 444,000 in Hungary.

The position of Jews in West and Central Europe (the latter including Germany, Czechoslovakia, Austria, and Hungary) was quite different from that of those in Eastern Europe. In the developed countries of the industrialized West, the Jews were, by and large, an economically well-integrated group of merchants, industrialists, craftsmen, and professionals. In the East, with its relatively backward economic structure, there were no large-scale industries to absorb the Jewish working class or to support a commerce that would provide employment to Jewish traders. The peasants, the majority of the population, panicked by the economic crises, turned against the Jewish traders who sold their produce and provided them with industrial products. In addition, as urbanization increased, peasants settled in towns to compete with Jews in crafts and trade. Fired by economic competition and nationalistic slogans, the middle classes once again viewed the Jews as foreign competitors who had to be suppressed by the government.

And the governments in Poland and Rumania complied. About 10 percent of the population in Poland, the Jews paid 40 percent of the taxes. Although they were 27.3 percent of the Polish urban population, their share in municipal administration in 1931 was 3.4 percent. Among Warsaw's 20,000 city employees, 50 were Jews. In state administration and the courts the number of Jews came to 2 percent; in the police, customs, and prisons, to 0.18 percent.[4] Because they failed tests in Polish history, geography, and language, thousands of Jewish shoemakers and tailors were deprived of their licenses in 1927. When Poland nationalized the railways in the late twenties, 6,000 Jews were dismissed. Of the 3,000 Jews in the tobacco industry, only 440 retained their jobs. All the Jews—25,000—in the wood industry were fired. By 1931, 48.86 percent of Polish Jews had an income of less than $10 a week. Against a background of economic crisis which hit everyone, not only the Jews, one-third of Polish Jewry in the thirties was on the verge of starvation or beyond it. The drought in employment opportunities was not peculiar to Poland, of course. In Hungary, for example, the number of Jews among all traders declined from 41 percent in 1920 to 35.8 percent in 1930.

Traditional Christian antisemitism served as an anvil for the hammer of economic measures. In 1936 the Polish Catholic Press Agency, accusing the Jews of communist leanings and of fighting against Christianity, declared its belief in "the cultural separation of Poles and Jews." Catholic writers considered the Jews "ulcers in the Polish body," and stated that the hatred between Poles and Jews—a hatred "highly beneficial to our Polish trade and to our country"[5]—cannot be stopped.

The Polish and Rumanian governments supported an economic boycott of the Jews. Expressing his opposition to physical attacks on Jews in 1935, Polish Premier Felicjan Skladkowski said "of course" *(owszem)* he favored an economic boycott.

A visitor to Warsaw in the thirties wrote:

You look at the Jews of Warsaw and it looks to you that except for a minority they have been hungry from birth, and that they grew up under the pressure of hatred and persecution, so much so that they are unable anymore to stand up straight. They have lost all hope for a decent human existence, and they carry on doggedly out of inertia—a typical characteristic of their race; they would be better off dead. It is indeed a most unhappy scene; not even in this extremity could the Jews find a solution to their desperate plight.[6]

Despite all this, and quite inexplicably, there was a tremendously active, productive social and cultural life in Jewish Eastern Europe, especially in Poland. Religious and secular organizations and political parties, schools, theatres, orchestras, and learned institutions, as well as a plethora of newspapers and books, served as evidence of intense cultural activity—an escape, perhaps, from grim economic realities into matters of the spirit, for there was little hope of physical escape. The Polish and Rumanian governments were not successful in persuading the Western countries to permit Jewish immigration. The yearly Polish immigration quota to the United States, for example, was limited in the twenties to less than 700. Palestine, a small, struggling Jewish community, could not provide a haven for the masses. There was nowhere to go.

This prelude to the Holocaust may serve to explain, in part at least, why the mass destruction that followed succeeded and, on the other hand, what the basis for Jewish resistance was.

SOVIET JEWRY

The fate of Soviet Jews between the wars differed radically from that of their brethren elsewhere. As early as 1903 Lenin had formulated the official communist ideology on Jews: The Jews, he said, were not a nation because they did not have a territory. Assimilation was the solution to the Jewish problem, a solution, he thought, that would be in the interest of the Jewish working class. Stalin's theory regarding nationalities, as set down in his *Marxism and the National Question* (1913—actually, it may have been written, and was certainly inspired, by Lenin), derived from his opposition to Zionism. A nation had to have territory, a common language, a common economic market, and a common psychological and cultural character; the Jews, therefore, were not a nation, nor could they become one. They would soon disappear. But the large Jewish working class in pre-revolutionary Russia was well organized, had a language of its own (Yiddish), and fought not only for its economic interests but also demanded certain national rights. The Jews posed a problem for the communist movement.

After the revolution, in their confrontation with the middle classes, the Soviet regime destroyed the economic foundation of most Jewish families. "Capitalists"—anyone who employed one apprentice or worker or more—were deprived of their civil rights and labeled *lishentsy* (non-citizen). They could not occupy administrative positions, they were excluded from all social and medical services, and their children could not attend state schools. Of the 2.7 million Jews in Russia in the early twenties, about 830,000 were *lishentsy.*[7]

The Jewish population had two choices, if they wanted to become involved in the Soviet system: They could become peasants or industrial workers. In 1926, 5.9 percent of the Jews were farmers and 14.7 percent were factory workers. With the help of the American Jewish Joint Distribution Committee (JDC), large numbers of Jews were settled in the Crimea and the southern Ukraine. By the mid-thirties, about 160,000 Jews were settled on land, 40,000 to 60,000 of them by the JDC. Interested in "productivizing" the *lishentsy,* the Soviet government gave full support to the resettlement efforts of American Jews.

In addition to the Crimea, the Soviet government tried to establish a Jewish autonomous region in Birobidzhan, an area on the Soviet-Manchurian border, to provide a defense against the Japanese, who controlled Manchuria, and at the same time solve the Jewish problem, a kind of Soviet Zionism. In stark contradiction to the theories of Lenin and Stalin, the establishment of a Jewish autonomous region recognized, or so it seemed, the validity of the claims of Jewish nationhood. Although the project was first proposed in 1928, serious attempts at settlement were not made until May 1934. Under harsh local conditions, the fairly large numbers of Jews who chose this solution found the "autonomy" severely limited. By the time of the 1936-38 purges in the Soviet Union by the Stalin dictatorship, only about 30,000 Jews remained. The sole Yiddish newspaper printed only 1,500 copies.

By 1938, both Birobidzhan and the Crimea had a much reduced Jewish population. Jewish nationhood could not develop in such areas—there was no historical, moral, or religious motivation; Birobidzhan was not Jerusalem and the Black Sea was not the Lake of Gennasaret. In addition, the rise of Soviet industry had increased the demand for an intelligent working class. The Jews left the old Pale of Settlement, Crimea, and Birobidzhan, in large numbers, to go to work in factories and plants.

The industrial revolution in the Soviet Union was accomplished by the implementation of Stalin's Five-Year plans (1929–33, 1934–38). During the first Five-Year plan, 350,000 Jews, *lishentsy* and others, became factory workers. With their families, and with those Jews who had been factory workers before, this accounted for about one-half, or more, of the Jewish population. The *lishentsy* problem, in effect, was solved, along with the basic economic problem of Soviet Jewry. Now on a par with their non-Jewish fellow citizens, their quality of life had improved and they did not suffer overt discrimination. In time, Jews became prominent in all walks of life, particularly the professions, in a considerably higher proportion than their share in population.

However, the Soviet policies that allowed Jews to overcome their economic problems at the same time gradually deprived them of all self-expression as Jews. Although a law against antisemitism was enforced until the late thirties, all independent Jewish political and social activities were eradicated. Zionist groups were particularly persecuted. In their struggle to ban religions, the communists took drastic action in the Jewish case. By 1941, only a handful of active rabbis remained, work on the Sabbath was enforced, and education was strictly anti-religious. Although other nationalities were allowed to retain their languages, the use of Hebrew was forbidden, and Yiddish was rewritten to eliminate Hebrew spelling or linguistic influence. Yiddish-speaking schools were at first supported, as was Yiddish literature, which in the twenties experienced a renaissance, but in the thirties the trend was reversed. Slowly, Yiddish schools were emptied of any specifically Jewish content, although Soviet propaganda was taught in the Yiddish language.

As Yiddish education increasingly became a dead end, parents began to prefer Russian schools and the number of Yiddish schools declined. Required to conform to the paean of Stalinist adulation, Yiddish literature began to wither. Slowly and thoroughly, Jewish national and cultural existence was being eliminated.

BRITISH AND FRENCH JEWRY

At the end of World War I extreme rightist groups, basing their position on the "Protocols of the Learned Elders of Zion," blamed the Jews for the social disruption, political instability, and economic crises that ensued. In France the extreme right-wing Action Francaise under Charles Maurras fought against the supposed Judeo-Masonic conspiracy. In Britain, the Bolshevik revolution had rocked the foundation of middle- and upper-class British society—there was a connection, it was said, between Bolshevism and "International Jewry." The publication of the "Protocols" in English in 1920–21 caused a sensation. Although The London *Times* exposed the forgery in 1921, the spread of the "Protocols" continued.

ANTISEMITISM IN BRITAIN AND FRANCE

Although the small British Union of Fascists, led by renegade Labor party leader Sir Oswald Mosley, never attracted much public support in Britain, it nevertheless had connections to those circles in the Conservative party who had accepted the "Protocols" and became admirers of the Hitler regime after 1933. Popular and social antisemitism existed, but British Jewry was fairly well integrated into British society and had itself become a traditional element in it.

The situation was not quite the same in France, where the Popular Front government of socialists, communists, and radicals was led, between 1936 and 1938, by the Jewish socialist leader Leon Blum. Because many Jews were among the volunteers in the International Brigades that fought in Spain to support the republican government against General Franco's fascist rebellion, anti-Jewish feelings were exacerbated in both Britain and France.

In France, the Right, opposing the anti-Nazi policies of the Popular Front, favored antisemitism. It was a very French antisemitism that recognized the rights of "old" French Jews, especially those who had fought in the 1914–18 war; it was directed, rather, against foreign Jews and belittled the plight of Jews under Hitler. Aid to Jewish refugees in France was hampered by the opposition of rightists who combined French jingoism with an admiration of Hitler, including his antisemitic policies.

AMERICAN JEWRY

The spread of the "Protocols" to the United States provoked extensive antisemitic agitation, under the aegis of automobile magnate Henry Ford. Basing his arguments on the "Protocols," he published a series of rabidly antisemitic articles against "International Jewry" in his weekly newspaper *The Dearborn Independent,* as a separate publication. In 1927, he was forced to publish a retraction and recognize the "Protocols" as a forgery.

At Harvard a proposal was made in 1922 to introduce a *numerus clausus* (a fixed number, or percentage) for Jewish students. Antisemitism, however, did not become an officially sanctioned policy in either the United States or Britain, although American Jews particularly were threatened by its constant shadow.

In 1920–21, 119,000 East European Jews entered the United States.[8] Anxious to prevent a recurrence of such magnitude, the restrictionists passed a quota law in 1924 that limited immigration to 2 percent of the members of any national group that lived in the United States in 1890. Between 1881 and 1924, some 2.25 million Jews had arrived in the United States from Eastern Europe. Of 4.5 million Jews in the United States in 1928, 3 million had East European origins.[9] But by the end of the twenties, total yearly Jewish immigration was down to 11,000.

Although the economic and social situation in the twenties militated against immigration to the West generally, the efforts to limit Jewish immigration in particular leave little doubt that anti-Jewish prejudices were significant.

The Great Depression generated a radicalization of antisemitism in

America, which was later aggravated by the deliberate antisemitic agitation perpetrated abroad by the Nazis. Fascist and Nazi sympathizers, such as the German-American Bund[10] led by Fritz Kuhn, spread racist Nazi propaganda laced with obscurantist Christian traditions. On Washington's Birthday in 1939, for example, a Bund speaker in Madison Square Garden explained that white Christians adhered to the Golden Rule because of their superior racial heritage. The Bund had some 25,000 members, including 8,000 Storm Troopers.[11]

Another antisemitic organization, the Silver Shirts, was led by William D. Pelley, a New Englander with spiritualist leanings. Based on the "Protocols," his propaganda reported that 7 million Jewish communists had overrun the country. Although the Silver Shirts numbered several tens of thousands, the most influential antisemite of all was Father Charles E. Coughlin of Royal Oak, Michigan, whose attacks were propagated by an organization called the Christian Front. His weekly magazine, *Social Justice,* had a circulation of up to 350,000; his Sunday radio broadcasts were listened to by 3.5 million people on a regular basis and another 15 million occasionally; 51 percent of the latter approved of the priest's opinions. In 1938 Coughlin blamed the workers' economic plight on the American financial system, which was controlled, he said, by Jewish communists. In the summer of that year Coughlin published large segments of the "Protocols."[12]

Polls conducted between 1938 and 1942 reported that 10 to 15 percent of Americans were willing to support government antisemitism actively; another 20 percent were sympathetic to such a policy; one-third were opposed, and the others polled were undecided.[13] Antisemitic agitation was directed against the New Deal ("Jew Deal") and against the Roosevelt administration, which had to consider the spread of antisemitic feeling among its own supporters. In the thirties, social discrimination ("Christians only"—unofficial bans on Jewish students and faculty at universities; refusal to hire Jews and to admit them to hotels, etc.) and much economic discrimination went hand in hand. Although there were regional and social differences, antisemitism had much in common with anti-Black and -anti-Catholic discrimination. Antisemitism was opposed, however, by

America's liberal and democratic tradition. In the late thirties, a Christian opposition to antisemitism could be discerned, especially in those Christian communities that advocated the Old Testament traditions, where antisemitism was never very popular. As time went on, antisemitism was identified more and more with opposition to American involvement in World War II. After the Holocaust, when American soldiers had seen the end result of antisemitism with their own eyes in liberated concentration camps, antisemitism diminished considerably and became, from the fifties on, a relatively marginal phenomenon.

THE NEW JEWISH CENTER IN THE UNITED STATES

Of the 17 million Jews in the world in the early twenties, 4.5 million, or 27 percent, lived in the United States, about 2.5 percent of the American population. Although more than 1.5 million Jews lived in New York City, other traditional Jewish centers existed in Philadelphia and Chicago, and a new major Jewish center was growing on the West Coast.

The East European Jews who had entered the States after 1881 had been craftsmen and petty traders in a backward, largely preindustrial economy. As members of the working class, they were employed in the manufacture of clothing, including gloves and furs, and furniture. The growth of the American trade-union movement is due in large measure to the leadership of its many Jewish members. A marked dichotomy existed, however, between the post-1881 East European immigrants and the minority (200,000) of "uptown" Central European Jews who had arrived beginning in 1848, mainly from Germany, In the early twenties the Central European Jews were being swiftly assimilated, and had there been no East European immigration, they may well have disappeared completely in American society. By the twenties, they provided a moneyed, status-conscious leadership. They identified for the most part with the Reform movement, whereas the East European Jewish community was split between Orthodox Jews, who were trying to re-create the small, intimate Hassidic or Mitnagdic congregation, and anti-religious socialists, who were rebelling against Jewish tradition. Both groups were quite out of sympathy with the upper-middle-class American-ized values of the German Jews.

The German Jewish leadership was strongly committed to philanthropic work, which derived from their sense of moral responsibility for their "less fortunate co-religionists" as they called them. They organized the American Jewish Committee, a "defense" organization—as the German Jews had done before them—to fight antisemitism, as early as 1906. Led by a prominent lawyer, Louis Marshall, the oligarchic AJC was wedded to the idea of quiet diplomacy; it tried to influence the government and public-opinion makers to take action against antisemitism at home and to intervene to protect human rights abroad, although it was opposed to a Jewish ethnicity or nationality and viewed Jewry as a religious community only.

In 1914 the American Jewish Joint Distribution Committee (JDC) was organized by Reform, Orthodox, and labor elements. Led essentially by the same German Jews who directed the AJC, the new group's purpose was to distribute social aid to Jews abroad. The JDC aided Palestine Jewry during World War I and East European and German Jewry between the wars and during and after the Holocaust. The JDC supported the Jew-ish national endeavor in Palestine economically, but opposed Zionist dreams for an independent Jewish entity there. It was led by circum-stances to support Jewish ethnic institutions in Europe. Both organiza-tions (AJC and JDC) are still very active at present. In 1918 East European immigrants joined up with Marshall to establish the American Jewish Congress, which represented American Jewry at the Paris Peace Conference and was instrumental in securing national minority rights for Jews in Eastern Europe.

Early in the twentieth century, Americanization led to a slow decline in Yiddish culture among the new immigrants. In the twenties and thirties, as East European immigrants or their sons and daughters began moving out of their original neighborhoods, such as New York's Lower East Side, into "better" areas, they moved as well into the middle classes and the profes-sions, and their numbers were growing. In 1933, 30.6 percent of New York Jews were employed in working-class occupations and the crafts; 35 percent were engaged in trade; 21.6 percent were in clerical occupations; and 7.4

percent were in the professions. "De-proletarization" continued in the forties and after, although a Jewish working class continued to exist and some Jews were still active in trade-union leadership. At the same time, although the outmarriage rate remained low, growing numbers of Jews were drifting away from Jewish identification.

As Jews entered American society, they became prominent in cultural life—literature, music, painting, sculpture, journalism, the film, and, later, the television industry. They entered the new technological industries as experts and technicians. Jews were prominent in the middle ranges of commercial life, especially retail trade and the new supermarkets. But they were almost non-existent in major industrial production, in agriculture and mining, and, with a few exceptions, in the oil industry. They became a largely middle-class community; they no longer belonged to the disadvantaged poor, as on their arrival in America, but neither did they control the American economy. Their economic clout, and consequently their political influence, was limited. They voted for the New Deal administration, because it was opposed to antisemitism and sympathetic to the plight of Jews in Germany. Relatively few Jews voted Republican, and because the Democrats thought of the Jewish vote as a "safe" vote, Jews wielded no political clout. A number of Jews were among Roosevelt's advisers—Bernard Baruch, Judge Samuel Rosenman, Judge Felix Frankfurter, and Judge Louis D. Brandeis, a famous liberal and the erstwhile leader of American Zionism. But these men had practically no influence on major political and international decisions. They did not act in concert and did not represent a constituency. Mainly, they desisted from arguing any policies that concerned Jews. The Jewish group in the United States in the thirties was visible, relatively prosperous, and politically powerless.

Internally, the influence of the old German-Jewish social aristocracy was diminishing. Opposition to Jewish ethnicity also weakened. The Zionist movement in the United States claimed 807,000 members in its various suborganizations in 1935.[14] Socialist groups were also influential during the Great Depression. In their religious affiliations, American Jewry was composed of three main groups: Reform, Conservative, and Orthodox. Reform congregations advocated the Americanized version of the original liberal

German Reform movement in which the flight from Jewish ethnicity was still predominant (though some Reform rabbis were among the leaders of the Zionist movement). Conservative Judaism, introduced into America by Solomon Schechter, attempted to reconcile Jewish orthodoxy with the modern world without diminishing either. It became the major force in American Jewry, and its Jewish Theological Seminary, under the spiritual guidance of Abraham J. Heschel and, later, Louis Finkelstein, trained a large number of rabbis for its congregations. Conservative Judaism was ethnic and generally supportive of Zionism. Orthodoxy was, in the thirties, still largely in a chaotic stage. Divided between strictly traditional anti-Zionists and religious nationalists, it was the weakest group, although beginning in the forties its importance would increase.

JEWISH REACTIONS

After the achievement contained in the Balfour Declaration of November 2, 1917, and after the end of the war in 1918, the Zionist movement reorganized to achieve its goal of national self-determination. It was, and is, based on two postulates: that the Jewish people are an ethnic or national group with a common history, tradition, and future; and that this scattered people desire to reestablish a political and cultural center for themselves in their ancient homeland.

The Zionists, led after 1918 by Chaim Weizmann, supported the occupation of Palestine by Britain, which had expressed its support of Zionism in the Balfour Declaration. Weizmann also sought the support of the developing Arab national movement. In June 1918 and again in Paris at the Peace Conference in 1919, a tentative agreement was reached between Weizmann and Feisal, the leader of the Arab revolt against the Turks and the son of the king of Hejaz, who controlled the Islamic holy city of Mecca. (Feisal would later become king of Iraq and, later still, his great-nephew, Hussein, would be the king of Jordan, who died in 1999.) In return for Jewish support for Arab national aspirations in the rest of the Middle East, Feisal promised that the Arab national movement would support the return of the Jews to Palestine. However, because Feisal was evicted by the French in 1920 and consequently never consolidated his rule over Syria, the agreement was aborted.

In 1922 Britain formally received from the League of Nations the right to rule Palestine as a Mandated Territory, in trust, until the country was ready for independence. The Zionist movement attempted to encourage immigration to Palestine by investing funds and buying land. Although progress was made, against increasing opposition from Arab nationalism, by 1931 there were only 175,000 Jews in Palestine, in a population of just over 1 million, and the economic base was not sufficient to absorb any mass influx from abroad. Therefore, although Zionism as a national movement was gaining membership among Jews in Europe and America, its expansion was slow; it could not offer early solutions to the mass plight of Jews outside Palestine.

Nor could other Jewish political movements offer better alternatives. The Allgemeiner Yiddisher Arbeter-Bund, destroyed by the Bolshevik regime in Russia, became a mass party in Poland between the wars, commanding the allegiance of about one-third of Polish Jewry. But government and popular antisemitism precluded any integration with the workers and peasants of Poland; the Bund's love affair with Polish socialists, it seemed, was rather one-sided. In America, the non-Zionist liberals and assimilationists fought antisemitism by proclaiming absolute loyalty to the majority's value system. Various marginal Jewish groups advocating Jewish settlement in out-of-the-way areas such as West Australia, the so-called territorialists, did not gain mass support among Jews or non-Jews

By the early thirties, Jewish powerlessness was compounded by the effects of the Great Depression: Jews had little or no economic clout and less political influence. Their center in Palestine was growing too slowly to provide the necessary power, and British politicians soon saw that their reliance on a supposedly influential Jewish factor in America and Russia had been a mistake. In 1933 Jews were finally seen by Western governments as what they were: an unpopular minority, whose moral claims on the conscience of the West—a conscience formed to no small degree by Jewish values—stood in inverse proportion to their real influence.

four

THE WEIMAR REPUBLIC

- Weimar was not genuine; more to please Western world
- 20 govnts btwn. 1919-1933
- Economic problems: Free market
- Hitler took over DAP, turned to National Socialist party
- Many high seats unchanged, Germany still unfair to lower-class
- 1930, Nazis took over

THE REVOLUTIONARY ERA

THE NAZI MOVEMENT BEGAN, in effect, with the first German experiment in republican democracy. After the flight of Emperor Wilhelm II to Holland, a new regime constituted itself at Weimar, the birthplace of the humanist writer and poet Johann Wolfgang Goethe. Buchenwald, the Nazi concentration camp, is nearby. The new regime was reluctantly proclaimed a republic on November 9, 1918. Although the emperor's abdication had been demanded by members of the parliamentary Left, the republic came into being because the General Staff believed that a Germany remade in the spirit of the West would receive better terms from the Allies. In effect, therefore, the reins of government were given to Friedrich Ebert and Philipp Scheidemann, the socialist members of the last imperial government under Prince Max of Baden, by the German General Staff. Through their lukewarm support, the new government of

- Republic was ingenuine

Extremes on both sides

the moderate Left was able to maintain itself against attacks from the extreme Left and extreme Right.

The new republic had not resulted from a popular rebellion. Neither did it institute thoroughgoing reforms, in politics or in the realms of society or the economy. Nor did it change the bureaucratic apparatus inherited from the empire. Key positions in the judiciary, the military, and the financial community remained in the same hands. Members of the aristocracy and captains of industry, who supported the army, retained their privileges. The ultimate fate of the Weimar Republic was in no small degree foreordained by this policy. ← *Many high Sects remained unchanged*

Although the majority of Social Democrats and a number of radical independent Socialists supported parliamentary democracy, the Soviet system was advocated by the Spartacists, an extreme leftist group, but they failed to gain majorities in the Soviets—councils of workers, soldiers, and peasants—that sprang up all over Germany. Led by Rosa Luxemburg and Karl Liebknecht, the Spartacists established the German Communist party. However, a Congress of Soviets in December 1918 decided to hold parliamentary elections. Right-wing elements in the endangered government goaded the Spartacists into an ill-prepared and premature uprising, which was easily squashed. A similar fate befell the short-lived communist republic of Bavaria in April-May 1919. Luxemburg and Liebknecht were murdered by right-wingers in January 1919.

1. Social Dem.
2.

The Social Democrats (Sozialdemokratische Partei Deutschlands, SPD) gathered some 40 percent of the vote in the January 1919 election. Along with the Catholic Center (Zentrum) party and the small Democratic party, the SPD formed the Weimar coalition to attempt to make the new republic work.

The peace treaty presented to the Germans by the Allies in May 1919 in the form of an ultimatum included the statement that Germany alone had been responsible for the outbreak of the war and the following stipulations: the army would be limited to 100,000 men, the navy to 15,000; unification with Austria would not be allowed; reparations would be necessary in an as yet unknown amount; and Germany would lose its overseas colonies as well as areas in the East (such as today's Poznan, and parts of Upper Silesia) and the West (Alsace-Lorraine). The treaty was signed in June 1919.

Because the armistice was signed—at the desperate urging of the German generals—while the German army was still deep in Belgium, northern France, and Russia, after a four-year-old struggle in which the Germans had won many great victories, many Germans failed to understand why Germany had lost the war. In November 1919, when the former quartermaster-general of the German General Staff, General Erich von Ludendorff, and the chief of the General Staff, General Paul von Hindenburg, appeared before a parliamentary inquiry committee, Ludendorff offered an answer to that question. After the signing of the armistice a British general had said to him that the German army had been defeated not by the external enemy but by an internal enemy who had stabbed it in the back. Ludendorff, a rabid and violent antisemite who would soon become an ally of the young Nazi party, identified the back stabbers as those who in the last stages of the war expressed the German people's yearning for peace—the Democrats, the Catholic Center party, the Socialists, and, of course, he said, the Jews. The legend of the stab in the back *(Dolchstosslegende)* was to become a favorite theme of Nazi propaganda. → WWI failed because of internal problems

To German nationalists, all Socialists, Communists, Liberals, Democrats, sundry revolutionaries, and Jews were birds of a feather. They refused to observe that the Jewish intellectuals prominent in contemporary revolutionary movements—Lev Trotsky in Russia, Rosa Luxemburg and Kurt Eisner in Germany, Bela Kun in Hungary—had reached their positions by explicitly renouncing their contacts with Jewish life. The voting pattern of Jews in both Russia and Germany, whenever free elections were held (in Russia, between March and November 1917), was consistently middle-of-the-road and moderately Left, that is, Liberal, Democratic, and Social Democratic. But no rational arguments about the voting patterns of the half million German Jews (in a population of some 62 million) could prevail against a nationalist agitation with deep, and less than rational, historical and psychological roots. The few Jewish names prominent in politics symbolized the "Jewification" of the new democratic republic. That the Weimar Republic's constitution was written largely by Hugo Preuss, a Jewish Democrat, served to intensify the opposition of authoritarians against the "Jewish republic." Faced by such hostility, the number of Jews actively involved in

German political life had dwindled considerably by 1919. The majority of the Jewish population, however, viewed the republic as the guarantee of their civil and social rights. After long years of struggles and expectations, it seemed that full emancipation had been achieved at last.

SOCIAL AND ECONOMIC PROBLEMS

The old bureaucracy continued to serve the new regime reluctantly, evincing little sympathy with the democratic principles of the German republic. The judiciary, especially, was unsympathetic. When assassination attempts and other rebellious strikes against the republic were brought before them, the German judges handed down severe sentences only to members of the far Left. Right-wing rebels or assassins were viewed by the judiciary as patriots and treated with demonstrative leniency.

Many upper-class, aristocratic former army officers, who had enjoyed special social status and privileges under the empire, were especially opposed to the republic. Only a few of them found employment in the new truncated army, the Reichswehr, and many turned to the new *völkisch* armed movements that became the scourge of the new Germany and the hotbed of later Nazism. These armed groups, Freikorps (free corps), roamed the border regions and sometimes the inner provinces of Germany, murdering, looting, seeking out enemies—those they identified as being responsible for the demise of the old social structure that had given them security and status. Ernst von Salomon, a free corpsman who was to be involved in the assassination of the Jewish statesman Walter Rathenau, described the corps:

> We were a band of fighters drunk with all the passions of the world; full of lust, exultant in action. What we wanted we did not know. And what we knew we did not want! War and adventure, excitement and destruction. An indefinable, surging force welled up from every part of our being and flayed us onward. . . . Anyone who judges the Freikorps fighters by the standards of the civilization it was their task to help to destroy is utilizing the standards of the enemy.[1]

These paramilitary units, such as the Stahlhelm (Steel Helmet), Captain Ehrhardt's Naval Brigade, the Bavarian Home Guard, and many others, were to provide the recruits for the Nazi SA (Sturmabteilung, Storm Troops) and SS (Schutzstaffel, Defense Corps). Their defiance of democracy and its dreams of equality and justice was expressed in such formulations as:

> I hate
> The crowd
> The little men
> The mean men
> Who bow their heads
> And eat, sleep and beget children
> I hate
> The crowd
> The impotent crowd
> The pliable crowd
> Which believes in me today
> And tomorrow will tear my heart out.[2]

Neither was the new regime assured of the loyalty of the Reichswehr itself. When an attempt was made in 1920 by rightist forces under Dr. Wolfgang Kapp to overthrow the republic and restore a monarchist regime, the Reichswehr refused to protect the legitimate government, which was saved by a general strike against the military.

Hostility toward the republic was expressed in violent ways, including the murder of politicians of the Left and the Center. Matthias Erzberger, a leader of the Catholic Zentrum, was perhaps the man most hated by the Right in Germany. He had been an adamant protagonist of peace during the final stages of the war, had led the German delegation that signed the peace treaty, and had publicly attacked the German wartime leadership in the Reichstag (Parliament). A staunch Republican and representative of Weimar democracy, Erzberger was murdered on August 26, 1921.

Walter Rathenau, the scion of a wealthy Jewish family, a thinker and writer, had been very successful during the war in organizing the supply of scarce raw materials and thus contributed significantly to Germany's war effort. An ardent German patriot, he demanded a popular *levee* (mass mobilization) to save the fatherland in 1918 when the war seemed lost. He could hardly be accused of defeatism by the Right, nor of Bolshevik leanings. However, in the great debate that was raging in Germany in the early twenties regarding whether or not to implement the Allies' demands, especially in the area of reparations, Rathenau opposed an anti-Allies nationalistic stand. He hoped that the Allies would desist when they realized that the reparations demanded ($33 billion in 1921) could not be paid. However, the main provocation of his murder on June 24, 1922, was that, as foreign minister, he, a Jew, had advanced democratic Germany's European position by a treaty with the Soviets. In his murder, the right-wing extremists identified Jews with both bolshevism and democracy.

In the second elections to the Reichstag in July 1920, the vote of the Weimar coalition parties was reduced from 76 to 42 percent. Right- and left-wing opposition to the regime gained adherents, and the democratic parties were never to regain a true and effective majority (Table 4.1) (Between 1919 and 1933, twenty governments, some ruling by presidential fiat without a parliamentary majority, followed one after another, thus creating a political climate that severely jeopardized the survival of the Weimar Republic.)

20 govs.

A massive inflation (induced by the government to avoid the payment of reparations, according to some historians) struck the country in 1923. In January the dollar was worth 1,800 marks; later in the year it was worth 4.2 billion marks. Extreme leftists and extreme rightists tried to bring down the government by armed uprisings. On November 9, 1923, the National Socialists tried to seize power in Munich, Bavaria, in alliance with the former general Erich von Ludendorff, but the half-baked attempt was put down with ease. Inflation was brought under control, however, by a moderate Center-Right coalition led by Gustav Stresemann, and between 1924 and 1929 Germany enjoyed relative stability and prosperity.

ADOLF HITLER AND THE NAZI PARTY

In early 1918, the Thule Society was founded by a political adventurer who gloried in the name of Rudolf von Sebottendorf, the adopted son of an Austrian nobleman. Supported by disgruntled members of the right-wing nobility and middle class, the Thule Society was anti-Christian, racist, and, of course, violently antisemitic. It chose the swastika for its symbol. In its newspaper, the *Münchener Beobachter,* Jews were denounced as the "mortal foe of the German people."[3] To gain support among the masses, the society founded, with the help of Anton Drexler, a railway machinist, the German Workers' Party (DAP, Deutsche Arbeiterpartei) in January 1919. In September 1919 the group was investigated by a propaganda agent of the Army. The investigator decided to join the group. He became board member Number 7. His name was Adolf Hitler.

Hitler was born in 1889 in Braunau, a small Austrian town not far from the Bavarian border, to a family of peasant, probably Czech, background. His father, Alois, was the illegitimate son of a maid-servant, Maria Anna Schicklgruber, who later married a journeyman, Georg Hiedler (variously spelled Hüttler, Hütler, Hitler). Alois, a customs official, died in 1903, leaving his third wife, Klara, in comfortable circumstances, with her two children, Adolf and Paula. A bright, but indolent, pupil, Hitler was forced to leave high school in the town of Linz because of total academic failure. With his mother's financial support, he went to Vienna in October 1907 to gain admittance to the Viennese Academy of Fine Arts. But he failed; his drawings were judged unsatisfactory. He returned to Linz where his mother died of cancer in December 1907. (She had been the patient of a devoted Jewish doctor, Dr. Eduard Bloch, who later testified to Hitler's love for his mother and the deep respect he had shown to him.)[4] Relying on his orphan's pension, Hitler went to Vienna to stay in early 1908. In October, he failed again to be admitted to the Academy of Fine Arts.

In 1909 he lived in a night asylum, or flophouse. Impoverished and destitute, he was apparently unaware of a small pension still available to him, which he then reclaimed. Between 1910 and 1912 Hitler lived in a home for men who could afford to pay a certain basic minimum for a cubicle with a bed; the men could not stay in the cubicle during the day, however, for they were expected to be looking for work. During that time, Hitler painted postcards and sold them to Jewish dealers who pitied him. He began again to draw his pension and thus maintained himself, more or less. In 1913, after receiving the inheritance from his father as a result of reaching his 24th birthday, he moved to Munich, in order to avoid being drafted to the Austrian army.[5] There he lived as a boarder and painted postcards. When the Austrian military authorities finally caught up with him, he avoided punishment by claiming that he had not received the summons in time. He was discharged by the Austrian military authorities in early 1914, after a medical examination showed him unfit for service. It does not appear, however, that Hitler was a coward. Although he tried to avoid serving in the Austrian army, he hoped for a war in which he could serve as a German soldier.

Hitler was a voracious, if unsystematic, reader of history, architecture, and possibly other disciplines as well. His hatred in the early years was directed toward the world in which he had grown up, a world that had failed to recognize his genius, not against Jews specifically, quite the contrary. His mother's doctor and Josef Neumann, who had helped to support him by buying his postcards and giving him presents, were his closest known Jewish contacts. Yet it is possible that during his Vienna period, his hatred slowly began to focus on the Jews, as the key to understanding why the world was bad.

Hitler was influenced by the German nationalist and racist wave that swept Austria at the end of the nineteenth century and early in the twentieth. From Karl Lueger, the charismatic, populist leader of the rabidly anti-semitic Christian-Social party, who was mayor of Vienna when Hitler came there, he learned the value of mass support and the apparent ease with which it could be attained. From Georg von Schönerer, leader of the German Nationalists in the Austrian Parliament, he took his German nationalism. Schönerer advocated the unity of German Austria with Germany and the exercise of German supremacy over the mixture of nationalities—Czechs, Poles, Slovaks, Serbs, Croats, and others—that made up the Austro-Hungarian monarchy. The racist component was strikingly expressed in *Ostara,* a series of pamphlets published by a defrocked monk who had assumed the name of Jörg Lanz von Liebenfels. Lanz tried to establish an order of blond male masters who would propagate genetically pure Aryan offspring; those less pure were to be sterilized or eliminated. Through the fantasies of Lanz and others, Hitler became aware of the theories of the nineteenth-century racists.

Hitler rebelled against all ideas of leveling, of equality, of democracy, such as that represented by the Social Democrats. Having never been a worker, contrary to his later claims, he was representative of that group of itinerant, uprooted intellectuals who scoffed at all ideas of equality and supported elites of which they saw themselves a part. But he appreciated the methods used by socialists to organize large bodies of people, as well as the way in which the Catholic Church, in which he had grown up, used liturgy, pomp, and physical and emotional effects to fortify the loyalty of its believers. Christianity itself, however, was abandoned. He turned, instead, to a kind of pantheistic philosophy with a nebulous supreme being, who could be representative of pagan traditions as well as of racist principles.

Upon the outbreak of World War I, in August 1914, Adolf Hitler volunteered to serve in the so-called List infantry regiment of the Bavarian army. He served at the front as a dispatch runner for more than four years, was wounded in 1916, and received a number of decorations, including the Iron Cross, First Class, for which he was proposed by his Jewish commander, Lieutenant Hugo Gutmann. In proving his physical courage, he remained aloof, strange, and fanatic. He was almost blinded and severely wounded in a gas attack in October 1918, and by the time he had recovered, the German empire had collapsed. Like other disillusioned ex-soldiers, whose only profession had been to fight and kill, Hitler joined in the search for the lost security of a hierarchical, authoritarian system that had collapsed.

In 1919 Hitler seemed to be back at the beginning, a young man without an occupation, without any training, alone and bitter. Employed by the army to observe radical political groups, he stumbled on Drexler's DAP. Quickly gaining control of the tiny group, he began to speak for it in October 1919 in the beer cellars of Munich, where his talent as a public speaker came to the fore.

The name of the party was changed to National Socialist German Workers' Party (Nationalsozialistische Deutsche Arbeiterpartei, NSDAP), and early in 1920 Drexler and Hitler wrote a twenty-five-point party program. In primitive political language, it gave a first utterance to what later became

Nazi ideology. The program demanded the abrogation of the Versailles treaties and the restoration of the German colonies. It vaguely formulated demands for the supremacy of the state and the subjection of individualism to a nebulous common good. It opposed "unearned income," that is, interest, and large retail stores, as well as working-class (Marxist) movements. Foreigners and foreign influence—the Jews—were considered the major source of Germany's problems, although Jews were mentioned only occasionally and in some cases obliquely. Jews could not be German citizens, the program said, but only alien guests of Germany. All recent Jewish immigrants were to be returned to the countries they had come from.

Between 1920 and 1923, Nazism grew as a party and an ideological movement, but it was still largely confined to Bavaria. Hitler became the leader, though his leadership was not undisputed. Like Hitler, the NSDAP's leadership was of middle- or lower-middle-class origin—with some notable aristocratic exceptions—and included embittered ex-soldiers, rejected intellectuals, and condottieri. They included: Major Ernst Röhm, a typical Freikorps condottiere who became the leader of the brown-clad Storm Troops (Sturmabteilung, SA); Herman Göring, a much-decorated intellectual fighter-pilot who could not accept Germany's defeat and had spent the early postwar years in Sweden in an attempt to restore his mental and physical health; Dr. Josef Goebbels, a gifted journalist, who hated a world that did not appreciate his talents; and Heinrich Himmler, an agronomist and dilettante farmer, who rebelled against the strict Catholic upbringing of his middle-class home.

By 1921 the NSDAP claimed a membership of 4,500 and the growing support of extreme right-wing circles, especially in Bavaria. Hitler founded the SA as a paramilitary formation to "protect" party gatherings, that is, physically to confront opponents in and out of party assemblies. Men in search of violent adventures flocked to the SA, which numbered about 400 members in 1922. During the economic collapse in 1923, as the Nazis gained status in Bavaria, as well as the support of Ludendorff, Hitler decided to overthrow the conservative local government in Munich and then march on Berlin, imitating somewhat the recent surge to power of Mussolini and his Fascists in Italy. However, in August 1923 Gustav Stresemann's conservative government began to restore confidence in the economy and the government. Communist attempts at rebellion were thwarted. Had Hitler succeeded in taking over Bavaria, he would have had to face a Reichswehr deeply contemptuous of the upstart extremists of the NSDAP as well as the reaction of the trade unions, whose general strike had overcome Wolfgang Kapp's putsch in 1920.

On November 8, 1923, Hitler, Goering and about sixty SA men threatened a crowd of 3,000 in a large beer cellar in Munich and arrested three Bavarian administrators, including Otto von Lossow, the general in command of the local army garrison. They were half persuaded, half forced—by Hitler and Ludendorff, who had joined the rebels—to sign a declaration handing over the government to Hitler. Lossow repudiated his signature the next morning, however, and his men and the police fired into a troop of Nazis as they marched through Munich to occupy government buildings. Eighteen Nazis were killed; Hitler fled from the scene; Ludendorff walked through the hail of bullets erect, unscathed.

At first, Hitler considered the Munich putsch a disaster; hysterically, he contemplated suicide. He soon recovered, however, and used the ensuing trial (February-March 1924) as a vehicle for a propaganda attack on the hated democratic regime. Three mediocre, cowed, and basically sympathetic judges sentenced him to five years in prison, but he was released by Christmas 1924. During his short imprisonment, he dictated *Mein Kampf* (My Struggle) to admiring secretaries in his well-furnished Landsberg prison cell.

Mein Kampf, the holy writ of the Nazi movement, had a tremendous influence. In his biography of Hitler, Robert Payne wrote:

> It is a great book in the sense that Machiavelli's *The Prince* is a great book, casting a long shadow. The Renaissance word *terribilita* implies superb daring, immense disdain, an absolute lack of scruples, and a terrifying determination to ride roughshod over all obstacles, and the book possesses all these qualities. The author says: "This is the kind of man I am, and this is what I shall do," and he conceals nothing, as though too disdainful of his enemies to wear a disguise. The armed bohemian describes in minute detail how he will stalk his prey. . . .

There is no evidence that Baldwin, Chamberlain, Churchill, Roosevelt, Stalin, or any of the political leaders most directly affected did anything more than glance at it. If they had read it with the attention it deserves, they would have seen that it was a blueprint for the total destruction of bourgeois society and the conquest of the world. . . . Just as Hitler's speeches lack any sense of progression, for he is continually circling round a small, hard core of primitive ideas announced with complete conviction, so in *Mein Kampf* he disdains any reasoned argument but repeats his ideas ad nauseam, loudly, firmly, unhesitatingly, until the reader becomes deafened. . . . The ideas he expresses—hatred for the Jews, the insignificance of men, the necessity of a Fuehrer [leader] figure possessing supreme authority, the purity of the German race so immeasurably superior to all other races, the need for living space in the East, his absolute detestation of Bolshevism—all these are announced with manic force.[6]

Hitler's analysis of the receptivity of large masses of people to the blandishments of propaganda is a classic. The masses, Hitler says, are essentially "feminine," that is, in his view, feelings and emotions are far more important than logical, reasoned thought. Successful propaganda must concentrate on a few points only and hammer at those points incessantly. His purpose, Hitler said, was to concentrate on one enemy only and through him attack all others. That one enemy was "the Jew".

In *Mein Kampf* the primitive idea of a "Fuehrer-State" is hinted at: It should be neither capitalist nor socialist but a society of racial brothers manipulating the state machinery under the guidance of a charismatic leader. But the years that followed were not conducive to Nazi blandishments. Germany was recovering economically, enjoying a newfound prosperity. The cosmopolitan culture of Berlin seemed far removed from the crude ravings of the Nazis. Some Nazi intellectuals attempted to develop approaches that differed from those of Hitler. A kind of left-wing Nazism, developed by the brothers Gregor and Otto Strasser, ranted against the middle classes and the aristocracy and demanded a populist-nationalist dictatorship. For a time, Dr. Josef Goebbels belonged to the Strasser group. Walther Darre, later the Nazi minister of agriculture, and Alfred Rosenberg, a Baltic German intellectual, emphasized a confused racist ideology. Through a series of crises, Hitler maneuvered cleverly to maintain and strengthen his position. His opponents were either denied party membership (some, like Gregor Strasser, were later murdered) or, in most cases, persuaded to accept his authority. In 1928 the Nazi party received only 12 of 491 Reichstag seats and a popular vote of 2.6 percent. They were a marginal, almost invisible factor in German life. Yet five years later they came to power.

Underneath a veneer of prosperity and liberalism, Germany harbored disappointment and discontent. Defeat in the war had not been accepted by the nationalistic upper and middle classes. The republic was seen as an artificial import forced on Germany by the Allies. Still largely monarchistic, the bureaucracy despised the new democratic rulers, as did the army officers in the Reichswehr and those former officers who were now unemployed. Disaffected and bitter members of the working class supported the communist party. Old hatreds persisted.

In 1929 the New York Stock Exchange collapsed. As the economic crisis spread worldwide, unemployed millions struggled bitterly for a piece of bread, a sack of coal. The German people yearned for strong leadership that would end the misery and degradation rampant in the land. Between 1929 and 1933 political crises followed one upon another, expressing the reality of a deeply divided people. Beginning in the elections of September 1930, no possible coalition of parties received a parliamentary majority (Table 4.1). Of 547 seats in 1930, the National Socialists (Nazis) won 107 seats, the Nationalists 41 and the Communists 47—35.6 percent of the Reichstag representatives were committed to the overthrow of the republic. The Social Democrats, the Catholic Centrists, and the Democrats, who were committed to maintaining it, had 250 seats, or 40 percent, not enough for a majority. The rest represented a wavering middle element. In the subsequent elections of July and November 1932, the situation did not improve. With 7 million unemployed, the validity of the free-enterprise system and of democracy itself seemed denied.

Yet the fact of the matter is that the economic crisis hit the United States and Britain no less than it did Germany. In both these countries, democracy emerged victorious. Yet in January 1933, the Nazis came to power in Germany.

TABLE 4.1
REICHSTAG REPRESENTATION, 1919–1932

	1919	1920	May 1924	December 1924	1928	1930	July 1932	November 1932
Total seats	421	459	478	493	491	547	599	572
Left								
Communists	—	4	62	45	54	47	89	100
Independent Socialists	22	84	—	—	—	—	—	—
Social Democrats	165	102	100	131	153	143	133	121
Total	187	190	162	176	207	190	222	221
No. of seats lost or gained	—	+3	−28	+14	+31	−17	+32	−1
Center and Right								
Catholic Center party	91	85	81	88	78	87	97	90
National party	19	65	45	51	45	30	7	11
Economic party		10	17	23	23	2		
Nationalist party	44	71	95	103	78	41	37	52
Miscellaneous	5	9	25	12	23	49	—	—
Total	159	230	256	271	247	230	143	153
No. of seats lost or gained	—	+71	+26	+15	−24	−17	−87	+10
Democrats	75	39	28	32	25	20	4	2
No. of seats lost or gained	—	−36	−11	+4	−7	−5	−16	−2
National Socialists	32	14	12	107	230	196	230	153
No. of seats lost or gained	—	—	—	−18	−2	+95	+123	−34

SOURCE: Documents on the Holocaust, p. 31.

The 1930–32 governments tried to stem the tide of economic crisis by budgetary cuts and other stringent measures that only deepened the misery of the masses. The president of the republic, the old hero—real or supposed—of the late war, Marshal Paul von Hindenburg, was enamored of neither the republic nor the democratic idea. Using a suitable paragraph in the constitution, he enabled three chancellors—the Catholic leader Heinrich Brüning (1930–32), the Catholic aristocrat Franz von Papen (1932), and the former army general Kurt von Schleicher (1932–33)—to rule by decree in his name. Parliamentary democracy, in effect, was thus rendered impotent more than two years before Hitler's accession.

The Nazi party grew stronger, feeding on the discontent of the middle and lower-middle classes. The working class did not abandon the mutually warring factions of the Social Democrats and the Communists. Nor did the Catholic voters join the Nazis; even the right-wing Nationalists held their own, more or less, against the Nazi onslaught, But the moderate right and the Democratic party collapsed. Millions of new voters—many of them middle-class and unemployed Germans who had not bothered previously to vote and people voting for the first time—cast their ballots for the Nazis.

[handwritten margin note: Weimar became economically unstable]

The Nazis were still a minority, however, when Hitler came to power. Of the 585 seats contested in the Reichstag elections of November 1932, the Nazis won 196 (33.1 percent of the vote, or 33.5 percent of the seats). They had actually lost 2 million votes, 34 seats, and more than 4 percent of the popular vote, as compared to the previous elections, whereas the Communists and the right-wing Nationalists registered important gains. They had less seats than the left-wing parties (221 seats). Why, then, did Hitler come to power in January, 1933? A theory has been put forward, by Daniel J. Goldhagen, that extreme murderous antisemitism has been a social norm in German society since the Middle Ages, and that Germans supported Hitler's party, in part at least, one has to suppose, because they had been socialized to accept the extreme message of the Nazis to start with. However, it is clear that the majority of Germans did not accept the Nazi ideas until a few weeks before they came to power—including the Nazis' anti-semitism, presumably[2].

In the early months of 1932 the economic crisis in Germany had reached its nadir. During the summer months industrial production was stabilized, and later in the year production was on the rise (Table 4.2). Although economic recovery did not begin as early in other countries, neither did it have as far to go (Table 4.3).

TABLE 4.2.
INDUSTRIAL PRODUCTION IN GERMANY, 1932 (1928 = 100)

	1st quarter	2nd quarter	Aug.	Sept.	Oct.	Nov.
Index	55.0	57.7	52.3	56.3	59.9	62.9

SOURCE: Karl D. Bracher, *Die Auflösung der Weimarer Republik* (Villingen, 1960), p. 226.

TABLE 4.3.
INDUSTRIAL PRODUCTION IN DEVELOPED COUNTRIES, 1932 (1929 =100)

	Germany	United States	Great Britain	France
1st quarter	54.2	58.8	85.1	72.3
2nd quarter	56.9	51.4	84.3	67.3
October	59.1	55.1	78.1	68.0
November	62.0	–	–	–

SOURCE: Karl D. Bracher, *Die Auflösung der Weimarer Republik* (Villingen, 1960), p. 227.

Hitler came to power as the strength of the Nazi party was beginning to wane and Germany was beginning to emerge from the depth of the economic crisis. The right-wing politicians surrounding Hindenburg no longer trusted the Catholic Center party; nor would they ally themselves with social democracy; their experiment with a relatively 'progressive' army general (Schleicher) had failed. Hitler, it seemed, could provide a mass following as well as a deterrent to the growing Communist movement. As a front for the right-wing nationalists, he could be controlled—after all, he had been weakened in the November elections. After much wavering, Hindenburg accepted the idea. A government with only three Nazis (Hitler; Wilhelm Frick, minister of the interior; and Hermann Göring, minister for Prussia) among a conservative majority would be a safe solution. Hitler became chancellor in January 1933.

NAZI ANTISEMITISM

Nazi propaganda of 1929–33 stressed unemployment, social security, tariffs on agricultural products, war reparations to foreign nations, Germany's status among nations, and the territories it lost in World War I. Antisemitism itself was not the main focus, though it was never absent from Nazi pamphlets or speeches.

The Nazis did not add any new elements to antisemitism—except for their determination to implement it—but the full-blown antisemitic ideology that eventually developed, combined elements of both traditional Christian and pseudoscientific nineteenth-century antisemitism. The Protocols of the Learned Elders of Zion, containing the Jewish world-conspiracy theory, were adopted as an article of faith. The concept of the satanic Jew was taken over from Christianity, as only a people possessed by Satan could have killed the Messiah. But whereas traditional Christian antisemitism viewed the Jew as a human being possessed by the Devil, Nazi ideology viewed the Jew as the Devil himself. The Medieval Church had hoped to save Jewish souls through baptism, and had never developed a genocidal plan to murder all Jews, though popular Christian antisemitism had not been limited to the deprivation of all civil and most economic rights, as the many murderous outbreaks show. Nevertheless, it remained for the National Socialists to turn the symbol of the Devil, the Jew, into content: the Jew *was* the Devil, in Nazi eyes.

An "International World Jewry," a kind of Jewish world government, actually existed, according to the Nazis, and they attempted throughout the Holocaust period to discover its location and the identity of its members and leaders. In support of their "world Jewish domination psychosis," the Nazis cited an imaginary Jewish "control" of the Western "plutocracies" and Russian bolshevism. In the Nazi mind, the illogical concept of Jewish "control" of *both* bolshevik Russia and the capitalist West was rationalized by the attribution of demonism to the Jew.

Hitler classified countries as enemy or friend by the measure of supposed Jewish control in their administrations. France, for example, was considered under Jewish control and therefore an enemy. England, however, struggling against "Jewish domination," was a friend, a potential German ally. (Hitler refused to believe until the last moment that "Aryan" England would enter the war against Germany.)[7]

To establish a historical basis for his analysis of the Jewish "plot" to rule the world, Hitler contended that the Jews had introduced into civilization unnatural concepts—humanism, Christianity, equality, liberalism, compassion, conscience—to weaken the resistance of other peoples to their rule. Did not Christianity, introduced into the all-powerful Roman empire by the Jews, weaken and ultimately destroy Rome? The survival of the human race depended not on humanitarian, egalitarian Judaic concepts but on natural, pagan, hierarchical strength and force.

Nineteenth-century racism, that is, the idea of a superiority of one race over another, was appropriately congruent with Nazi ideology. The Germanic peoples were a superior part of the "Aryan" race and were, therefore, along with other nations of similar "blood," the rightful rulers of the world. Indeed, they were the only true humans. Because of the Germanic "blood" in their veins, certain nations (e.g., the Scandinavians and the British) might become Germany's allies. Other Europeans (e.g., Latins and Slavs), although they were "Aryans," too, would be ruled by Germany because of their lack of Germanic blood. Due to past contacts between Germans and Slavs, the latter had absorbed some Germanic "blood," which was to be "rescued" by kidnapping blue-eyed, blond-haired Slav children, and by permitting Poles with German names or German ancestry (real or supposed) to be considered Germans. Some of the other Slavs were often termed "subhuman,"[8] and though there never was any plan to annihilate completely any of the Slav nations, their leadership was to be eliminated along with their religious and educational institutions. With their culture reduced to a primitive level, the Czechs, Poles, Russians, and others were to become, essentially, slaves, and serve the aims of the superior Teutons.[9] Other Slavs, however, the Slovaks, Bulgarians and Croats, became allies of Nazi Germany, and were treated with relative respect.

Whereas some Slavs were subhuman, the Jews were non-human. Hitler saw the Jews as a kind of anti-race, a nomadic mongrel group. Because contact with Jews would corrupt German blood and culture, Jews would be segregated,[10] a segregation that led to the possibility of annihilation. In segregating the Jews, the Nazis followed the traditional Christian policy that viewed the Jew, the "Other," as essentially different and somehow inherently dangerous. In elaborating their concept of the Jews as non-human, the Nazis described them as parasites, viruses, or loathsome creatures from the animal and insect world (rats, cockroaches). As a parasitic force, the Jews corroded, and would ultimately destroy, the cultures of their host nations.

To the Nazis, the "Jewish problem" was a problem of cosmic importance. Human survival itself depended on the fate of the 17 million Jews inhabiting the globe. Should the Jews be successful in their quest for world domination, the Nazis said, they would deny existence to all others. Human survival depended, therefore, on the victory of the forces of light (Aryans) over the forces of darkness (Jews). In the Nazi *Weltanschauung* (ideology, world view), the Germanic Aryans, not the Jews, had been commissioned by Providence to rule the world.[11] This Manichean juxtaposition of Jews and Germanics might indicate that their contradictory racist ideology really served as a rationalization for that central pillar in their world view: antisemitism. In addition, it must be emphasized that the Nazis, that is in effect the German intellectual elite supporting them, actually believed in this nonsense.

In a memorandum on the Four-Year Plan in 1936, Hitler wrote:

Since the beginning of the French Revolution the world has been drifting with increasing speed towards a new conflict, whose most extreme solution is named Bolshevism, but whose content and aim is only the removal of those strata which provided the leadership to humanity up to the present, and their replacement by international Jewry. . . . Germany has a duty to make its own existence secure by all means in face of this catastrophe and to protect itself against it; a number of conclusions follow from this necessity, and these involve the most important tasks that our nation has ever faced. For a victory of Bolshevism over Germany would not lead to a Versailles Treaty but to the final destruction, even the extermination, of the German people.[12]

The Nazis, then, accused the Jews of wanting to do what they, the Nazis, were out to do themselves: control the world and annihilate their enemies. In this inverted picture of themselves, they described the Jews as the demonic force of evil that Nazism itself was. In doing this, they dehumanized themselves first, and that enabled them to strip the Jews, in their own minds, of any human quality. This was a necessary ideological prelude to a gradual political development that turned ideology into murderous reality. The very fact that the process, as we shall see, was gradual, indicates that it might have been stopped somewhere on the way. Once, however, the victim became completely devoid of humanity in the perpetrator's eye, he or she could be killed. Annihilation followed.

five
THE EVOLUTION OF NAZI JEWISH POLICY, 1933–1938

RANK AND FILE GERMANS who voted for the Nazi party in 1932 were voting for a regeneration of the German people, for new and decisive leadership, and for an economic revival to be initiated by a new national sense of purpose. They did not necessarily vote for the extremist positions of the party. As with all political parties on the assumption of office, it was expected that the power and responsibility of governing would in this case too dampen Nazi extremism and produce rational compromises with reality. This did not happen, however.

On February 27, 1933, the Reichstag (German parliament) burned down. Marinus van der Lubbe, a Dutch anarchist, was accused by the Nazis of executing a Communist plot to set the fire. It appears, however, that van der Lubbe did it on his own. Regardless of the fire's origin, however, the burning of the Reichstag served the Nazis well. Using it as a pretext, they arrested Communist leaders and Communist Reichstag deputies.

On February 28, they persuaded President von Hindenburg to issue a decree, "for the protection of the People and the State" (supposedly from the Communist menace), suspending the constitutional guarantees of personal liberty, the right of free expression of opinion—including freedom of the press—and the rights of assembly and association. The privacy of postal, telegraphic, and telephonic communication was no longer guaranteed, and warrants for house searches and orders for confiscations of, as well as restrictions on, property were also permissible beyond the legal limits otherwise prescribed.[1]

To eliminate both their Communist, Socialist, and Catholic opposition, and their right-wing bedfellows, the Nazis called for new elections on March 5, 1933. Again using the burning of the Reichstag as a pretext, the Nazis denied the Communist party inclusion on the ballot. Despite the of official elimination of the Communists (many of whom nevertheless voted for the illegal Communist party) and a widespread reign of terror on election day, the Nazi party was unable to achieve a parliamentary majority. Of 647 seats, the Nazis gained 288. With the support of right wingers, however, Hitler pushed through the "Law for Removing the Distress of People and Reich," the so-called Enabling Act, on March 23, which removed the power of legislation from the Reichstag and gave it to the Nazi-controlled government. By the time the Law expired in 1937, the Nazi dictatorship was complete. Authorized by the Enabling Act, the dictatorship ruled Germany until its defeat in 1945.

During the spring of 1933, the other political parties were forced out of existence by a combination of threats, force, and cajoling. On July 14, a law was enacted declaring the Nazi party (NSDAP) the only legal party in Germany. On December 1, 1933, the "unity of Party and the State" was officially decreed. In effect, the government as such ceased to function. All authority emanated from the Führer (Leader), Adolf Hitler, and the various ministers became his executive officers.

After Hindenburg's death on August 3, 1934, Hitler combined the presidency and the office of the Chancellor (Reichskanzler), and assumed the title of Führer and Reichskanzler. In June 1934 the leadership of the SA (Storm Troops) was purged. SA leader Ernst Röhm had demanded that the SA become a part of the Reichswehr, the official German army, hoping to become its main force. Röhm and the SA, who supported an anti-aristocratic, populist version of Nazi doctrine, stood in stark contradiction to Hitler's careful wooing of the propertied classes and the aristocratic caste of the mainly Prussian military. Röhm might become a dangerous rival. The rebuilding of the army as an instrument of Nazi policy demanded, at that stage at least, an alliance with the military rather than a surrender to social demagogy. On June 30, 1934, after much wavering, Hitler agreed to the murder of his loyal SA commanders, including Röhm. The opportunity was also used to rid the regime of other opponents, particularly right-wing opposition leaders such as Schleicher, Hitler's predecessor.

Following the June 30 assassinations, the SS (Schutzstaffel, the Defense Corps), a special elite corps under SA stewardship, became independent. Control of the concentration camps was also in SS hands. Heinrich Himmler, the leader of the SS since 1929, gained complete control of the police by 1936 and became Reich Leader (Reichsführer) of both the SS and the Police. The SD (Sicherheitsdienst, the Intelligence branch of the SS) was established in 1931 with Reinhard Heydrich at its head.

By late 1932 and particularly early 1933 the German economy, as previously noted, had passed its lowest point and was experiencing the beginnings of an upturn. The effort of the new government's economic policies, which included a lowering of wages, the commencement of great public works (the autobahns [freeways], for example), rearmament, and the gradual elimination of unemployment, meshed with the economic upturn already in progress.

With the abolition of free trade unions and the establishment of a government-organized Labor Front (May 1933), wages were no longer negotiated but determined by the state. Under the slogan "Joy through Work," workers were treated to state-organized pastimes to take their minds off "dangerous" thoughts.

Similarly, the spiritual and artistic life of Germany was regimented. Reich Propaganda Minister Josef Goebbels directed the press, literature, arts, and science in accordance with Nazi thought. Books written by Jews and those deemed dangerous to Nazi ideology were removed from public libraries. In May 1933 such books were publicly burned in Berlin and elsewhere. Artists and scientists who refused to adhere to the Nazi line either emigrated or were silenced. However, large numbers—it is safe to say a great majority—of creative people accepted the Nazi line, sometimes hesitatingly at first, and allowed themselves to be used in Nazi propaganda both at home and abroad.

Special emphasis was placed on the 'education' of youth. Dissident teachers were gradually removed. New textbooks were written in the spirit of Nazism—for example national-socialist physics, national-socialist chemistry, and soon young people were forced, by social pressure, to join Nazi youth movements—the Hitler Youth (Hitlerjugend, HJ) for boys and the League of German Girls (Bund deutscher Mädel, BdM)—where blind obedience and loyalty to Hitler and the regime were propagated.

GERMAN FOREIGN POLICY

Because the weakness of the German army in 1933 delayed Hitler's demand for *Lebensraum* (living space) for supposedly overpopulated Germany in the East (i.e., in the Soviet Union), he appeared at first as the apostle of peace in Europe, whose sole aim was to recoup losses unjustly suffered by Germany at Versailles. Gradually, however, the underlying principles of Nazi foreign policy unfolded. The Nazis took the first offensive step in October 1933 when they withdrew from the League of Nations. With the signing of a treaty of neutrality with Poland in February 1934, the eastern flank was protected and the Franco-Polish treaty, which was directed toward the encirclement of Germany, was negated. In accordance with the provisions of the Versailles treaty, a plebiscite in the Saar region in 1935 determined by an overwhelming majority to return the region to Germany. A region of great mineral wealth and of industry, the Saar served as a site for the rearmament of Germany. In a parallel development, the 1935 Naval Agreement with Great Britain allowed Germany to build up a fleet equal to 35 percent of the British fleet's tonnage—a vast building program that soon turned Germany into a major naval power.

In March 1936, with the rearmament program successfully underway, Hitler started bluffing his way through Europe. The Rhine province, a demilitarized zone according to the Versailles treaty, was occupied by the as yet unprepared German army. At the slightest sign of French opposition, the troops were to withdraw. But the French did not react, and the occupation, in defiance of the Versailles provisions, stood.

In his quest for allies, Hitler achieved a binding agreement with Italy, which had become isolated following its aggression and conquest of Ethiopia in 1936. The weaknesses of the Italian fascist dictatorship were not apparent, and in 1936 the Berlin-Rome Axis appeared to be a strong combination in the European power game. In defiance of the St. Germain treaty between the Allies and Austria, the Nazis forced the *Anschluss* (annexation) of Austria by a combination of threats and propaganda in March 1938. To Britain, Nazi Germany was a bulwark against European communism and a countervailing force to French power on the Continent. The blindness of British politicians was matched by the weakness of the French state. Finally, using the grievances of the German minority in the Sudeten borderlands of Bohemia and Moravia against the Czech majority of the democratic Czechoslovak republic, Hitler demanded and, after difficult negotiations with British Prime Minister Neville Chamberlain, obtained the annexation of the Sudetenland to Germany, in an agreement signed in late September 1938 at Munich by Germany, Britain, France, and Italy. The hapless Czechs surrendered without fighting. The conquest of the Sudetenland eliminated the powerful Czech army, whose main fortifications lay in the Sudeten region, and effectively dismantled the Czechoslovak republic, thereby giving the Nazis a predominant position in Central Europe. Hungary and Poland used the dismemberment of Czechoslovakia to obtain portions of Czech territory as well and in the process became Germany's allies. Chamberlain returned to London from Munich in the belief that he had secured "peace in our time." On March 15, 1939, Hitler repudiated the Munich agreement by occupying the Czech lands of Bohemia and Moravia. Declaring them a German Protectorate, he forced the Slovak fascists to declare the independence of the Slovak state.

During these maneuvers, appearances to the contrary, the German Army was still unprepared for war. Tanks and armored vehicles became mired in the spring mud as they entered Austria. During the Sudeten negotiations, German generals offered to rebel against Hitler if the British would not sign the agreement. But the British were not interested; they preferred to rely on Hitler's promises.

On November 5, 1937, Hitler informed his chief generals and confidants that Germany was to be prepared for war within the next few years, that Czechoslovakia and Poland would be eliminated, and that Germany would expand into Russian territory (as recorded by officer Friedrich Hossbach). In the course of such a policy, Hitler was prepared to face the Western Powers as well. During 1938 and 1939, consequently, preparation for war intensified. After the repudiation of the Munich agreement in March 1939, Britain understood that appeasement was not possible. Faced with British and French guarantees to Poland, Hitler decided to isolate the struggle against Poland as far as possible and to avoid a two-front struggle by reaching an understanding with the Soviets. The Soviets, who had followed a straight anti-Nazi line since 1933, were concerned by British prevarications. In their eyes, Britain and France seemed to want a war between Germany and the Soviet Union, in which the Western Powers would watch while Germans and Soviets killed each other. Stalin therefore agreed to turn the tables on the West and on August 23, 1939, signed a neutrality pact (the Molotov-Ribbentrop pact) with the Germans. The agreement guaranteed the Germans the import of essential raw materials from the Soviet Union and effectively neutralized the USSR in the coming struggle against Poland. In addition, in a secret protocol attached to the pact, the Germans agreed to another partition of Poland, in which Eastern Poland would be annexed by the Soviets, and Latvia and Estonia (and by a later addition Lithuania as well) would come under their so-called 'sphere of influence'. These previously independent states were subsequently annexed by the Russians in 1940. At this time, the Germans and the Russians were also seeking to postpone a war between themselves; both countries knew that war would one day come, but that neither were yet ready for it.

NAZI ANTISEMITIC POLICY

Affected by the development of both domestic and foreign Nazi policies, the realization of their antisemitic intentions evolved gradually, and was marked by considerable vacillations.

Upon the Nazi accession to power, the SA and the SS began their campaign of terrorism, against political opponents in the main, and mostly did not target Jews as such. However, there were many exceptions; apartments, offices, and stores were invaded in order to arrest Jews, in particular lawyers, doctors, and other professional people. They were later released, after being tortured, and upon signing a statement that they had been treated well. Nazi brutality turned especially against leftists generally, Jewish leftists in particular. Detailed reports of maltreatment published in the Western press were quickly defined by the Nazis as "Jewish atrocity stories." In retaliation for such "anti-Nazi propaganda," the Nazis announced an economic boycott of the Jews to start on April 1, 1933. The extremists were Goebbels, Julius Streicher, the Franconian area leader (Gauleiter) and publisher of the pornographic antisemitic weekly "Der Stürmer," and others. These viewed the boycott as an opportunity to rid the German economy of the Jews altogether. Along with the devastation of German Jewry, a permanent boycott would have shattered, perhaps, the illusions indulged in by large numbers of Jews as to the transitory nature of their troubles. But this was not to be.

To protest the Nazi persecution of the Jews, a mass rally was organized for March 27 at Madison Square Garden in New York City by Rabbi Stephen S. Wise, leader of the American Jewish Congress and American Zionism. Threatened by Göring with reprisals if the rally was not stopped, German Jewish liberals and Zionists appealed to their American brethren and even to the American Embassy in Berlin to cancel the rally, but to no avail. The rally raised the consciousness of Americans and thoroughly frightened conservative Reich cabinet ministers, who cited the adverse results a war of "international Jewry" would have on the German economy. They pleaded with the Nazi hierarchy to stop the boycott. On March 31 Goebbels announced a one-day boycott for Saturday, April 1, a day on which many Jewish shops and offices were closed in any case. Both the Nazis and their right-wing allies thus fell victim to their own ideology. In the Madison Square Garden rally they saw the expression of that mysterious international Jew they had invented, their all-consuming fear. In calling off the permanent boycott in fear of the counter-reaction of the Jews, the Nazis yielded, in effect, to the figment of their own imagination.

Nevertheless, the April 1 boycott was implemented with much brutality by party members. The attitude of the population in general left much to be desired from a Nazi point of view, which indicated the need the Nazis felt to intensify their antisemitic propaganda. On the other hand, there was no outright opposition to the boycott, and many Germans agreed with this kind of measure.

On April 7, 1933, the Law for the Re-establishment of the Professional Civil Service, which provided for the dismissal of "non-Aryans," was promulgated. The few exceptions—those who had been serving in the German army since August 14, 1914, or prior to that date, those who had fought at the front for Germany (or one of its allies), and those whose fathers or sons had died in the German cause—a concession to Hindenburg, were quietly and gradually abolished after his death. The importance of the law lies in its definition of "non-Aryan" : In practice the term non-Aryan applied only to Jews. By a subsequent definition of April 11, a person who had one Jewish parent or one Jewish grandparent was identified as "of non-Aryan descent." One can see how confused Nazi racism was when Jewish grandparents were defined by religion rather than so-called racial criteria.

Although detailed anti-Jewish legislation had not been prepared prior to the Nazi accession to power, the general proposals contained in Heinrich Class's book *Wenn Ich der Kaiser wäre* (If I Were the Kaiser, Berlin 1913), were to be translated into action: elimination of Jews from public life, from the armed forces, from state education, from influence on the press, from the management of corporate banks, and from the ownership of rural property. Jews who had acquired German citizenship were to be denaturalized and Jewish names that had been translated into German were to be nullified.[32] Internal memoranda show that the decision to implement such proposals was clear before 1933.

A series of laws and administrative orders promulgated or issued between April and October 1933 translated these laws and orders into reality. Jews were excluded from such occupations as assessors, jurors, and commercial judges (April 7); a *numerus clausus* law limiting Jewish students in institutions of higher learning to 1.5 percent of new admissions was promulgated on April 25. In the professional sphere, the establishment of a

Reich Chamber of Culture (September 29, 1933) provided a means for excluding Jews from entertainment enterprises (art, literature, theatre, movies); the National Press Law (October 4, 1933) excluded Jews from the press. Jewish ritual slaughter was forbidden; Jews could no longer farm land; and on July 14, 1934 the Law on the Revocation of Naturalization and Annulment of German Citizenship deprived relatively recent Jewish imigrants, especially those of East European background, of German citizenship.

Pressure from the party rank and file and from the SA especially to go beyond these legal restrictions was resisted on several grounds. First, the conservatives were opposed, especially those like Hjalmar Schacht, the minister responsible for the restoration of the German economy. To them, any such action was likely to disrupt economic recovery. Schacht and others like him, although no friends of the Jews, opposed drastic anti-Jewish actions because Jews were considered an important middle-class element in Germany and a powerful force abroad. Second, what the next step should be was not clear. The Nazis wanted the Jews to leave Germany, but they were not quite sure how to achieve their goal (see the quotations at the end of this chapter). Third, in 1934 the Nazi party was facing serious internal problems (e.g., the purge of SA leadership and other opponents), and the "Jewish problem" had a lower priority.

The relative quiet of 1934 acted as a dangerous sedative on the Jewish community, lulling many into a false sense of security. Insofar as Jews were not members of opposition groups, they were not arrested. But an unofficial boycott and public humiliation continued, and life for Jews, in many small places especially, was becoming unbearable. Although about 20 percent of German Jews had lost their livelihood, according to JDC estimates, the mood prevalent among German Jews was that Hitler's rule could not last, that the country of Goethe and Schiller, Beethoven and Schubert would soon shake off the barbarians who had temporarily gained control.

In 1935 ominous signs appeared. The increasingly violent hate articles appearing in Julius Streicher's *Der Stürmer* (The Attacker) were echoed in Goebbels' *Der Angriff* (The Attack), another party magazine in Berlin, *Der Judenkenner* (The Jew-Expert), and elsewhere. The exclusion of Jews from

German life altogether was demanded. On May 21, 1935, Jews were, excluded from the armed forces. Goebbels and the party apparently linked their attacks on the Jews with their desire to eliminate centers of conservative power. On July 16, 1935, shops were destroyed and Jewish passers-by were beaten up on Berlin's main thoroughfare, the Kurfürstendamm. The next day, *Der Angriff* carried the headline: "Berlin is being cleansed of Communism, Reaction and the Jews." The beatings and destruction of property continued for about a week.

But there were other views in the party as well. Frick and Bormann intervened against the disorder, and the conservatives, led by Schacht, warned the party leadership energetically against excesses. Schacht spoke in this vein publicly on August 18 and convened a conference of experts on August 20, although a unanimous stand was not achieved. On June 18, 1935, the German-British Naval Agreement was signed, and economic negotiations were begun on June 17 with France. There was no point in proving at that point that disorder and insecurity were reigning in Germany.

Hitler, apparently, had kept aloof from these developments. However, after the signing of the Anglo-German and French-German accords he intervened, because he saw that the situation was ripe for a legal disenfranchisement of the Jews. Disenfranchisement would gratify party activists, especially if accompanied by dramatic acts of humiliation; and the conservatives would see it as an end to insecurity, a legal definition of the rights of second-class citizens.

Various laws designed to disenfranchise the Jews had been prepared earlier, but what became known as the Nuremberg laws resulted from a direct order by Hitler on September 13. The two laws promulgated at the Reichstag in Nuremberg on September 15, 1935, and the first decree to the Reich citizenship law of November 14 are usually included in what is known as the Nuremberg laws.

The Reich citizenship law of September 15 says in part:

1. (1) A subject is anyone who enjoys the protection of the German Reich and for this reason is specifically obligated to it.

(2) Nationality is acquired according to the provisions of the Reich and state nationality law.

2. (1) A Reich citizen is only that subject of German or kindred blood who proves by his conduct that he is willing and suited loyally to serve the German people and the Reich.

(2) Reich citizenship is acquired through the conferment of a certificate of Reich citizenship.

(3) The Reich citizen is the sole bearer of full political rights as provided by the laws.[3]

The Law for the Protection of German Blood and German Honor, passed on the same day, says in part:

Imbued with the insight that the purity of German blood is a prerequisite for the continued existence of the German people and inspired by the inflexible will to ensure the existence of the German nation for all times, the Reichstag has unanimously adopted the following law, which is hereby promulgated:

1. (1) Marriages between Jews and subjects of German or kindred blood are forbidden. Marriages nevertheless concluded are invalid, even if concluded abroad to circumvent this law.

(2) Only the State Attorney may initiate the annulment suit.

2. Extramarital intercourse between Jews and subjects of German or kindred blood is forbidden.

3. Jews must not employ in their households female subjects of German or kindred blood who are under 45 years old.

4. (1) Jews are forbidden to fly the Reich or national flag and to display the Reich colors.

(2) They are, on the other hand, allowed to display the Jewish colors. The exercise of this right enjoys the protection of the state.[4]

The decree of November 14, which defined so-called *Mischlinge,* or persons of "mixed blood," is perhaps more indicative of Nazi ideology than the others. It reads, in part:

2. (2) A Jewish "Mischling" is anyone who is descended from one or two grandparents who are fully Jewish as regards race, unless he is deemed a Jew under 5, Paragraph 2. A grandparent is deemed fully Jewish without further ado, if he has belonged to the Jewish religious community.

3. Only a Reich citizen, as bearer of full political rights, can exercise the right to vote on political matters, or hold public office. The Reich Minister of the Interior or an agency designated by him may, in the transition period, permit exceptions with regard to admission to public office. The affairs of religious associations are not affected . . .

5. (1) A Jew is anyone descended from at least three grandparents who are fully Jewish as regards race. Paragraph 2, Sentence 2 applies.

(2) Also deemed a Jew is a Jewish Mischling subject who is descended from two fully Jewish grandparents and who belonged to the Jewish religious community when the law was issued or has subsequently been admitted to it; . . .

b. who was married to a Jew when the law was issued or has subsequently married one;

c. who is the offspring of a marriage concluded by a Jew, within the meaning of Paragraph 1, after the Law for the Protection of German Blood and German Honor of September 15, 1935 took effect;

d. who is the offspring of extramarital intercourse with a Jew, within the meaning of Paragraph 1, and will have been born out of wedlock after July 31, 1936.[5]

Believing that the laws would allow the establishment of a bearable relationship with the Germans, the Jews accepted their status as second-class citizens.

To create a good impression on visitors to the Olympic Games in 1936, the Nazis splashed a coat of whitewash on Berlin. Anti-Jewish signs disappeared from shops, theaters, and the town gates. Jewish sportsmen and sportswomen were invited to participate in the games. The international community sent athletes from the world around, ignoring not only the Nuremberg laws and the other anti-Jewish measures but also the military occupation of the Rhineland by Nazi forces in March 1936, three months before the games. The effect of the Nuremberg laws did not appear until the games were over, when the Jewish situation began to deteriorate. As in 1934, the 1936 Olympic Games episode tended to delude the Jews into a false sense of relative stability, if not security.

The fate of the Jews was linked to Hitler's preparation for war. As early as the end of 1935 at a meeting of Gauleiters, Hitler reported that war would be launched in four years when preparations were complete.[6] As we have seen already, Hitler prepared a memorandum outlining his program for Hermann Göring, who assumed responsibility for the Nazi Four-Year Plan in September 1936.

The war was to insure the dominance of Europe by the Aryan race and through it the dominance of the world as well. To accomplish this goal, Germany would have to eliminate the Jews within the four-year period of preparation, for if Germany did not eliminate the Jews under their control, the Jewish Satan, still residing in Germany, would, according to Hitler, eliminate the German people. Clearly, therefore, as war approached, Nazi policies toward the Jews became more extreme.

These developments took place at a time when Jews were not leaving Germany fast enough. On October 14, 1937, the SS journal *Das Schwarze Korps* stated that Jewish businesses should "disappear," that is, be confiscated. In February 1938, Economic Affairs Minister Hjalmar Schacht, who had objected to anti-Jewish measures out of economic considerations, was replaced by Walther Funk. One of Funk's priorities was to remove the Jews from the German economy. An SD internal report of January 1938 demanded the removal of all the poor Jews. A similar line was taken by *Das Schwarze Korps* in February, although more radical laws proposed by extreme Nazis in various ministeries and supported by Hitler were temporarily shelved.[7]

The annexation of Austria on March 13, 1938, increased the Jewish population by approximately 200,000.[8] The Jewish communities of Germany and Austria were quite different. Jews in Austria were, for the most part, a relatively new group, most of them having arrived over the past one hundred years from Polish Galicia, Bukovina, and the Czech lands. In Vienna, where the overwhelming majority of Austrian Jews lived, they engaged in trade—mostly small businesses—and the professions. In 1937, the Jewish proportion of various industries were: advertising, 90 percent; furniture manufacturing, 85 percent; newspapers and shoe manufacturing, 80 percent. Of the doctors and dentists, 51.6 percent were Jewish, as were 62 percent of the lawyers. In the slums of Vienna, 30 percent of the Jews lived in great poverty, many dependent on charity, and 35.5 percent of the Jewish working population were unemployed.[9]

As we have seen, early in the twentieth century Vienna had been the hotbed of a populist, Christian-Socialist antisemitism, personified by Mayor Karl Lueger. After the dissolution of the Habsburg monarchy, dislike of the stranger—in the Jewish case both visible and vulnerable—increased rather than decreased. At the same time, social democracy was a powerful factor and the Social-Democrats opposed antisemitism. Socialism—the universalist ideas of a working-class movement that promised security and brotherhood to the outsiders—quite naturally appealed to the Jews. Leaders such as Otto Bauer, Viktor Adler, and Friedrich Adler were Jews who had cut their relationships to the Jewish community. In early 1934, however, with the defeat of a socialist uprising against the dictatorship of Christian-Socialist Engelbert Dollfuss, the Socialist party was suppressed.

The Jewish community—the Israelitische Kultusgemeinde (IKG)—was organized on party lines: the Unionists, who were the Austrian equivalent of the liberal, assimilationist Central-Verein in Germany, and the Zionists, who were in the majority.

When the Nazis marched into Austria in 1938, the Austrian population, especially the Viennese, rallied to them with great enthusiasm. The arrest of political opponents was accompanied by massive action against the Jews. The process of degradation, terror, and expropriation that had taken five years in Germany was completed—indeed surpassed—in a few months in Austria. Men and women were forced to scrub streets on their knees, while crowds of Viennese stood by and cheered; shops were invaded, robbed, and their owners beaten; arbitrary arrests deprived families of fathers who were never seen again.

In Germany, the legal campaign against the Jews continued. On April 22, 1938, a law against "hiding" the identity of Jewish businesses was enacted. On April 26 an order was issued requiring the registration of all Jewish businesses worth more than 5,000 marks. Such businesses were officially identified on June 14. Until then, although deprived of governmental or public posts, Jews could operate private businesses and pursue legal and medical professions, albeit under increasingly difficult conditions that included unofficial boycott. Jewish artisans and laborers could still work if they could find someone willing to employ them. In the spring of 1938, however, the laws took on a new character.

On March 28, 1938, the German Jewish communities were deprived of the right to act as legal personalities (i.e., own property, etc.). As of September 30, Jewish doctors could no longer treat Aryans, although they were allowed to function as medical orderlies for their Jewish patients; Jewish lawyers were forbidden to practice law as of November 30. On August 17 a law was issued requiring that all male Jews assume the name Israel and all females the name Sarah by January 1, 1939. On October 5, a law was issued requiring all Jewish passports to be marked with the letter "J" (for "Jude," Jew)— which originated with the head of the Swiss Alien police, Dr. Heinrich Rothmund, who wanted to limit the entry of Jews into Switzerland.[10]

On June 9, 1938, the synagogue in Munich was set on fire. On June 15 some 1,500 Jews who had police records (including traffic violations) were put into concentration camps. Until then, Jews had not been systematically incarcerated in such camps, whose overall population in mid-1935 was 3,500, in 1936 4,761, in November 1938, before the so-called Kristallnacht pogrom, over 24,000 (a year after that, before the outbreak of World War II, when most of the arrested Jews had been either released or had died, it was about 21,000).

On August 10, Julius Streicher caused the destruction of the Nuremberg synagogue. Meanwhile in Austria, anti-Jewish attacks tended to be more extreme than in Germany itself. By September 1938, 4,000 Austrian Jews had been sent to concentration camps. Suicides multiplied. In some small communities (Horn in Lower Austria and the Burgenland) expulsions took place in September and early October. Berlin cancelled a plan to expel all the Jews from three Viennese districts on October 5, Yom Kippur, the Day of Atonement, the holiest of Jewish holidays, a day of repentance and fasting.[11]

To prevent Polish Jews who were living in Vienna from fleeing to Poland after the annexation of Austria on March 13, a Polish law was promulgated on March 25 decreeing that Polish citizens who had not visited Poland for five consecutive years would be deprived of their citizenship. In June it was reported that Polish Jews affected by this regulation who nevertheless returned to Poland would be put into a concentration camp for political prisoners (at Bereza Kartuska).

Of the 98,747 non-German Jews in Germany in 1933, 56,480 were Polish nationals. On October 6, 1938, the Polish government declared that citizenship would be denied to those whose passports were not renewed by October 29. On October 26 the German Foreign Office requested the Gestapo to deport as many Polish Jews as possible. The Gestapo was eager to comply. On the night of October 27–28, some 18,000 Jews were put on special trains and sent to the Polish border. Denied entrance into Poland, many were nevertheless forced across the border illegally by the Nazis; others, some 5,000 were forced to camp in a tiny Polish frontier village, Zbazsyn. When Herschel Grynszpan, a 17-year-old student living in Paris, received a letter from his family telling him what had happened to them in Zbazsyn, he went to the German Embassy in Paris on November 7 to kill the ambassador. Instead, he shot a third secretary of the embassy, Ernst vom Rath, who was not a Nazi, and who died on November 9. Grynszpan's action triggered the Kristallnacht (Night of the Broken Glass) pogrom (the term is a Nazi term; a more correct term would be 'the November pogrom').

Vom Rath's death was a convenience for the Nazis, allowing them to justify mass action against the Jews as revenge for the German diplomat's death, but mass arrests had actually been planned long before the shooting in Paris—barracks to accommodate tens of thousands of Jews had been built in concentration camps before November.

Hitler and Goebbels discussed their strategy in Munich on the night of November 9 as Nazi leaders assembled to celebrate the anniversary of Hitler's 1923 putsch. In an attempt to seize control of the Jewish question from his Nazi competitors, Göring and Himmler, Goebbels activated the SA and tens of thousands of loyal party members to burn all the synagogues in Germany, destroy and loot Jewish shops, and physically abuse large numbers of Jews. Ninety-one Jews were reported dead. But the German population at large did not respond enthusiastically to the pogrom. Although little help was extended to the victims, neither was there a joyous participation in the orgy of destruction. Many Germans were shocked or disinterested. Himmler and Heydrich quickly regained control and emphasized their own anti-Jewish hallmark: supposedly cold, "scientific," unemotional brutality. SS units were ordered to capture Jewish archives, to insure the confiscation, not the looting, of individual and community property. In a major action, they arrested and sent to concentration camps some 26,000 Jewish men at least.

Three major points emerge from the documentation: (1) the details of a new Jewish policy were worked out *after* the Kristallnacht, not before, so that the pogrom itself can hardly be considered a way-station to the Holocaust in terms of a planned policy; (2) the Jews had to pay the Nazis a so-called indemnity (for the death of vom Rath) of 1 billion reichsmarks, as well as insurance benefits for their destroyed property, which came to another 250 million reichsmarks; and (3) following the Kristallnacht, the Jews were finally and totally evicted from German economic life. By January 1, 1939, a Jew could be employed only by a Jewish organization. As businesses were taken over by "Aryan" Germans ("aryanized"), employees were fired. The ultimate goal, the eviction of all Jews from Germany, was within reach. Those in concentration camps were released, provided frantic relatives arranged for emigration. A mass panic and mass exodus ensued to anywhere, at any price. Of the approximately 500,000 Jews in Germany and 200,000 Jews in Austria, about one-half had emigrated by the outbreak of war (Table 5.1).

The evolution of the Nazi Jewish policy in the thirties can be best illustrated perhaps by a few excerpts from Nazi statements:

> In this matter of the struggle against the Jews, a certain arrangement has been reached . . . and the life and security of the Jews in Germany will not be endangered. [Hans Frank, chief Nazi lawyer, in a speech at a party congress on October 4, 1933.][12]

TABLE 5.1

JEWISH EMIGRATION FROM GERMANY, 1933–1939, AND AUSTRIA, 1938–1939*

	Germany	Austria	
1933	37,000		
1934	23,000		
1935	21,000		
1936	25,000		
1937	23,000		
1938	35,369	62,958	
1939	68,000	54,451	
Total	232,000	117,409	=350,000

SOURCE: Bauer, Yehuda. *American Jewry and the Holocaust* (Detroit, 1981), pp. 26, 66.

*Round figures are given because emigration figures for Germany—except for 1938—are estimates only.

It emerged from the discussion that the participants supported the Party program on the Jewish problem in principle, but criticism was leveled against the methods used. The limitless expansion of antisemitic activity on the part of irresponsible organizations or individuals, which is penetrating many and varied areas of public life, should be curbed by legal means. At the same time, special aspects of Jewish life, especially the economic aspects, should be regulated by special legislation. Apart from that their liberty should be guaranteed in principle.

From the discussion there did not emerge a broad and unanimous aim for German policy towards the Jews. [From a discussion among German ministers on the economic effects of the anti-Jewish policy, August 20, 1935][13]

The government of the German Reich is guided by the thought that it may be possible, by a unique secular solution, to achieve a basic situation which may enable the German people to arrive at a tolerable relationship toward the Jews. Should this hope not be realized, and Jewish incitement continue in Germany and in the international arena, the situation will be evaluated anew. [Hitler's speech in the Reichstag on the Nuremberg laws, September 15, 1935][14]

The Führer pointed to the fact that the National-Socialist legislation opens up the only possibility of arriving at tolerable relations with the Jews living in Germany. The Führer emphasized especially that in accordance with these laws an autonomous national life in all spheres will be made possible for the Jews of Germany, such as is not the case in any other country. Accordingly, the Führer renewed the order to the Party to refrain, as hitherto, from sporadic actions against the Jews. [A summary ofHitler's speech to party leaders September 15, 1935][15]

Gentlemen, today's meeting is of decisive importance. I received a letter written to me by Bormann,[16] the head of the office of the Deputy Führer,[17] on the Führer's instructions.

According to this letter we must arrive at a unified and overall approach to the Jewish question and to bring it to a solution one way or the other. In a telephone conversation yesterday the Führer instructed me yet again to concentrate the main steps centrally. . . . At the first meeting on this question we decided on the Aryanization of the German economy. Kick out the Jews from the economy and turn them into debtors and recipients of welfare allowances. [Hermann Göring, November 12, 1938, in the wake of Kristallnacht][18]

With all the extrusion of the Jews from the economy, in the end we are always left with the basic problem, that the Jew should leave Germany. May I make a few suggestions on this matter? In Vienna we established, on instructions from the Reichskommissar,[19]a Central Jew-Emigration office [Judenauswanderungszentrale] with whose help we managed after all to get rid of 50,000 Austrian Jews; at the same time, no more than 19,000 Jews were extruded from the Old Reich. . . . [20] May I therefore suggest that we should establish in the Reich area a similar central authority, with the participation of the responsible Reich departments, and that we should achieve in the whole Reich area a solution that would base itself on our experience [in Austria]. . . . The second thing is that in order to get rid of the Jews an emigration action for all Reich Jews should be instituted that will take eight to ten years. . . . As to isolation I would like briefly to suggest a number of proposals from a purely police standpoint, which would also have a psychological effect on public opinion, such as: a personal identification sign for each Jew that would indicate that every Jew

as defined in the Nuremberg laws should wear a certain outward marking. . . .
The ghetto, in the form of parts of a town totally set apart for Jews, is in my opinion impossible from a police point of view. [Reinhard Heydrich, November 12, 1938, in the wake of Kristallnacht][21]

Jews, What Now?

We shall now bring the Jewish problem to its complete solution, because it is essential, because we will no longer listen to the outcry in the world, and because actually there is no longer any force in the world that can prevent us from doing so. The plan is clear: total removal, total separation!

What does this mean?

This means not only the removal of the Jews from the economy of the German people, which they damage by their murderous attacks and their incitement to war and to murder.

It means more than that!

No German should be asked to live under the same roof with Jews, who are a race marked as murderers and criminals, and who are the mortal enemies of the German people. Therefore, we must expel the Jews from our houses and our living areas and house them in separate blocks or streets, where they will live among themselves with as little contact with Germans as possible. They should be marked by a special outward mark, and they should be forbidden to own houses or land, or be partners in any such ownership in Germany. Because it is out of the question to demand of any German that he should be under the authority of a Jewish landowner and that he should keep him by his work. . . .

To criminality.

But let nobody imagine that we can view such a development with equanimity. The German people have no wish to suffer in their midst hundreds of thousands of criminals, who not only maintain themselves by their crime but will also want to take revenge. . . . We would be faced with the hard necessity of exterminating the Jewish underworld in the way we generally exterminate crime in our well-ordered state: with fire and sword. The result would be the actual and final end of Jewry in Germany, its complete destruction. [*Das Schwarze Korps,* SS journal, November 24, 1938][22]

six
GERMAN JEWRY IN THE PREWAR ERA, 1933–1938

OF THE 522,000 JEWS living in Germany in 1933, 20 percent were recent immigrants from Eastern Europe and 80 percent were German citizens, the descendants of Jews who had settled there during the past two thousand years. They participated in German economic, cultural, and political life as members of the German community. They were loyal to Germany and most of them remained loyal even after the Nazis came to power. German Jews, and particularly German Jewish organizations, although aware of Nazi propaganda during the last years of the Weimar Republic, did not truly understand the extent of Nazi antisemitism. Except for the hardships of the postwar period, which they shared with the total German population, their lives went on undisturbed.

The attitude of the majority of Jews did not appreciably change during the first two or three years of Nazi rule. Well-established German Jews did not jump to any extreme conclusions at the sight of the terror exercised by

SA and SS on the streets of German towns. However, a sizable minority thinking otherwise emigrated in a wave of panic in 1933. The boycott of April 1, 1933, and the discriminatory laws that followed shook the self-awareness of some.

On April 4, the German Zionist leader Robert Weltsch published an article in the Zionist weekly *Jüdische Rundschau* (No. 27), which said:

> The first of April, 1933, will remain an important date in the history of German Jewry—indeed, in the history of the entire Jewish people. The events of that day have aspects that are not only political and economic, but moral and spiritual as well . . . To speak of the moral aspect, that is our task. For however much the Jewish question is now debated, nobody except ourselves can express what is to be said of these events from the Jewish point of view, what is happening in the soul of the German Jew. Today the Jews cannot speak except as Jews. Anything else is utterly senseless. . . . Gone is the fatal misapprehension of many Jews that Jewish interests can be pressed under some cover. On April 1 [the day of the anti-Jewish boycott] the German Jews learned a lesson which penetrates far more deeply than even their embittered and now triumphant opponents could assume. . . .
>
> April 1, 1933, can become the day of Jewish awakening and Jewish rebirth. If the Jews will it. If the Jews are mature and have greatness in them.
>
> They accuse us today of treason against the German people: The Nationalist-Socialist Press calls us the "enemy of the Nation," and leaves us defenseless.
>
> It is not true that the Jews betrayed Germany. If they betrayed anyone, it was themselves, the Jews.
>
> Because the Jew did not display his Judaism with pride, because he tried to avoid the Jewish issue, he must bear part of the blame for the degradation of the Jews.
>
> Despite all the bitterness that we must feel in full measure when we read the National-Socialist boycott proclamations and unjust accusations, there is one point for which we may be grateful to the Boycott Committee. Para. 3 of the Directives reads: "The reference is . . . of course to businesses owned by members of the Jewish race. Religion plays no part here. Businessmen who were baptized Catholic or Protestant, or Jews who left their Community remain Jews

for the purpose of this Order." This is a (painful) reminder for all those who betrayed their Judaism. Those who steal away from the Community in order to benefit their personal position should not collect the wages of their betrayal. In taking up this position against the renegades there is the beginning of a clarification. The Jew who denies his Judaism is no better a citizen than his fellow who avows it openly. It is shameful to be a renegade, but as long as the world around us rewarded it, it appeared an advantage. Now even that is no longer an advantage. The Jew is marked as a Jew. He gets the yellow badge.

A powerful symbol is to be found in the fact that the boycott leadership gave orders that a sign "with a yellow badge on a black background" was to be pasted on the boycotted shops. This regulation is intended as a brand, a sign of contempt. We will take it up and make of it a badge of honor.

Many Jews suffered a crushing experience on Saturday. Suddenly they were revealed as Jews, not as a matter of inner avowal, not in loyalty to their own community, not in pride in a great past and great achievements, but by the impress of a red placard with a yellow patch. The patrols moved from house to house, stuck their placards on shops and signboards, daubed the windows, and for 24 hours the German Jews were exhibited in the stocks, so to speak. In addition to other signs and inscriptions one often saw windows bearing a large Magen David, the Shield of David the King. It was intended as dishonor. Jews, take it up, the Shield of David, and wear it with pride!

And in the *C.V. Zeitung*, the paper of the liberal, anti-Zionist Jews, of April 27, 1933, the following proclamation appeared:

. . . There is great distress in German Jewry. We German Jews bore our share in the general distress in Germany. We contributed our contingent to the great army of people who were without work and without income, and seemed to be excluded from meaningful life. New distress has overtaken us. Jewish people are torn away from their work; the sense and basis of their lives has been destroyed.

The purpose of a community reveals itself in times of trouble. When the individual can no longer see any sense in his existence, when he is alone, the community can direct him to a purpose and an aim; when he alone can no longer do anything, then the community must show its strength. In times of distress the community must grow anew, gain life and existence. It is from the community that the individual must draw the strength to live and be active. . .

We are faced with new tasks of unknown magnitude. It is not enough to give bread to those who do not know how they are to survive the next few days. Of course it is our first task to make sure that none of our people goes hungry or lacks a roof over his head. Of course we must make sure that the institutions remain that we have built for our children, for our old and our sick, as we . . . German Jews, show that you are able to rise to the magnitude of your task! Do not imagine that the problems of German Jewry can be solved without the greatest of sacrifices, by means of undirected emigration. There is no honor in leaving Germany in order to live untroubled on your income abroad, free of the fate of your brothers in Germany. It will not help anybody to go abroad aimlessly, with no prospect of making a living, but only increase the numbers there who are without work and means. Every prospect will be examined, every possibility exploited to help those who no longer have a prospect of earning a living in their German Fatherland to find some means of settling abroad! But don't leave Germany senselessly! Do your duty *here!* Don't push people off blindly to an uncertain fate.

Let nobody fail in his duty in this hour of trial! Let everybody contribute according to his ability, and in his own place, to the task of helping others! The hour of German Jewry has arrived, the hour of responsibility, the hour of trial. Let German Jewry prove itself capable of facing this hour.

The central organization of liberal Jews in Germany, the Central-Verein, stated, in the C.V. *Zeitung* (No. 22) of June 1, 1933, that

. . . the great majority of German Jews remains firmly rooted in the soil of its German homeland, despite everything. There may be some who have been shaken in their feeling for the German Fatherland by the weight of recent events. They will overcome the shock, and if they do not overcome it then the roots which bound them to the German mother earth were never sufficiently strong. But according to the ruling of the laws and regulations directed against us only the "Aryans" now belong to the German people. What are we, then? Before the Law we are non-Germans without equal rights; to ourselves we are

Germans with full rights. We reject it, to be a folk or national minority, perhaps like the Germans in Poland or the Poles in Germany, because we cannot deceive our own innermost (feelings). We wish to be subjects as Germans, with equal rights, to the new Government and not to some other creation, whether it is called League of Nations or anything else . . .

Thus we are suspended between heaven and earth. We will have to fight with courage and strength in order to get back to earth, in the eyes of State and Law too. . . .

On the other hand, the orthodox community leaders wrote to Hitler, in October 1933, as follows:[1]

. . .The position of German Jewry today, as it has been shaped by the German People, is wholly intolerable, both as regards their legal position and their economic existence, and also as regards their public standing and their freedom of religious action . . .

. . . even where no law applies, economic activity has been made extraordinarily difficult. Even if Jewish activity in the economic field has not been limited directly by the law, there is in practice in all of Germany an anti-Jewish boycott. National, local and public enterprises have been forbidden to buy from Jews, while the Nazi Party has made a similar ruling for all members of the NSDAP. In many cases even low-level Jewish employees have been removed from economic enterprises, to say nothing of Jewish members of their management . . .

This means, then, that the German Jew has been sentenced to a slow but certain death by starvation.

Added to this is the defamation of the Jews, whose good name is sullied, which prejudices the people even more sharply against the Jews and robs them of the air they need to breathe.

. . . Thus the position of German Jewry must be perceived as altogether desperate by the most objective of observers the world over, and one must understand that the German National Government might all too easily be suspected of aiming deliberately at the destruction of German Jewry. This false concept must be disproved with concrete arguments if an information campaign is to have any effect.

Orthodox Jewry is unwilling to abandon the conviction that it is not the aim of the German Government to destroy the German Jews. Even if some individuals harbor such an intention, we do not believe that it has the approval of the Führer and the Government of Germany.

But if we should be mistaken, if you, Mr. Reich Chancellor, and the National Government which you head, if the responsible members of the National Administration of the NSDAP have indeed set themselves the ultimate aim of the elimination of German Jewry from the German People, then we do not wish to cling to illusions any longer, and would prefer to know the bitter truth.

It is in your interest, and in that of the whole German People, to tell us the truth openly. We would then prefer to consider your intention as fact and make our arrangements accordingly.

We confess that this would be an unspeakable tragedy for us. We have learned to love the German soil. It contains the graves of our ancestors, of many great and holy Jewish men and women. Our link with this soil goes back through history for 2,000 years; we have learned to love the German sun; all through the centuries it has let our children grow and mature and has added special and good elements to their Jewish characteristics. And we have learned to love the German people. At times it hurt us, particularly in the Middle Ages. But we were also present at its rise. We feel closely linked to its culture. It has become a part of our intellectual being and has given us German Jews a stamp of our own.

And yet we would and could muster up the courage to bear our tragic fate and to leave its reversal confidently to the God of History . . .

We do aspire to living space within the living space of the German people, to the possibility of practicing our religion and carrying out our occupations without threats and without abuse. In accordance with our religious duties we will always remain loyal to the Government of the State. Within the framework of the German people the German Jew will gladly take part in the task of reconstruction of the German Nation and do what is within his power to win friends beyond the German borders.

As the Jews experienced disorientation and internal turmoil, there rose a real, tragic tension between genuine feelings of patriotism and loyalty to

Germany and the need to evaluate realistically their position as aliens in their own land. The great achievement of Jewish enlightenment, namely, Jewish equality within German society, had been shattered. Assimilated Jews found adjustment to their new status difficult. The Zionist-oriented minority had consistently argued that Jews were not Germans, although they could be citizens of Germany and as such entitled to equality; they now demanded that Jews stop playing at being Germans and instead turn inward to discover their own great traditions.

Although young or wealthy Zionists, who could help develop Jewish Palestine were encouraged to emigrate, the Zionists generally did not favor a mass exodus immediately. Palestine had to be prepared to absorb German Jews, and German Jews had to prepare themselves, to become worthy, proud Jews, and conscious of their national character. During the interim, they were determined to keep the Jewish community alive and to adjust to the new situation. Generally, the German Jewish community was determined to stay put, to defend their rights, to work and live and create in the land of their forebears. They intended to prove to the world that the Nazi antisemitic policy was a result of misunderstanding.

To meet the external threat, the Jewish community, traditionally disunited and split into factions, had to give up differences and unite. Although first attempts in 1932 and in April 1933 to establish a united Jewish organization had failed, a social agency was set up, the Central Committee for Help and Reconstruction (Zentralausschuss für Hilfe und Aufbau, ZA), headed by the Berlin rabbi Dr. Leo Baeck and the leader of the Jewish community in the province of Württemberg, Dr. Otto Hirsch. In September 1933 a further attempt at establishing an overall political body succeeded. The Central Representation of German Jews (Reichsvertretung der deutschen Juden, RV) resulted from a compromise between the liberal and the Zionist wings, and despite occasional disagreements, the RV and the ZA represented German Jews throughout the period. Some groups, such as the orthodox, did not, initially, participate.

From 1933 to 1935, the RV tried to remain loyal to the new German regime. The Berlin Jewish community, for example, wrote to the British chief rabbi protesting anti-Nazi propaganda outside Germany. They demanded that "acts of propaganda and boycott be stopped. . . . Spreading false news. . . will create difficulties and tarnish the reputation of our homeland."[2]

The new RV itself published the following proclamation in the *Jüdische Rundschau* No. 78 of September 29, 1933:

At a time that is as hard and difficult as any in Jewish history, but also significant as few times have been, we are entrusted with the leadership and representation of the German Jews by a joint decision of the State Association of the Jewish Communities (Landesverbände), the major Jewish organizations and the large Jewish communities of Germany . . .

In the new State the position of individual groups has changed, even of those which are far more numerous and stronger than we are. Legislation and economic policy have taken their own authorized road, including [some] and excluding [others]. We must understand this and not deceive ourselves. Only then will we be able to discover every honorable opportunity, and to struggle for every right, for every place, for every opportunity to continue to exist. The German Jews will be able to make their way in the new State as a working community that accepts work and gives work.

There is only one area in which we are permitted to carry out our own ideas, our own aims, but it is a decisive area, that of our Jewish life and Jewish future. This is where the most clearly defined tasks exist.

There are new duties in Jewish education, new areas of Jewish schooling must be created, and existing ones must be nurtured and protected, in order that the rising generation may find spiritual strength, inner resistance, and physical competence. There must be thoughtful selection in order to develop and re-direct our youth towards professions which offer them a place in life and prospects of a future . . .

Much of our former economic security has been taken from us German Jews, or at least reduced . . .There will be not a few who will be refused a place of work or the exercise of their profession on German soil. We are faced by the fact which can no longer be questioned or opposed, of a clear, historic necessity to give our youth new (living) space. It has become a great task to discover places and open roads, as on the sacred soil of Palestine, for which Providence has decreed a new era, as there the character, industry and ability of the German

Jews can prove themselves, robbing none of their bread, but creating a livelihood for others.

For all this and all else we hope for the understanding assistance of the Authorities, and the respect of our gentile fellow citizens, whom we join in love and loyalty to Germany.

We place our faith in the active sense of community and of responsibility of the German Jews, as also in the willingness to sacrifice of our brethren everywhere.

We will stand united and, in confidence in our God, labor for the honor of the Jewish Name. May the nature of the German Jews arise anew from the tribulations of this time!

To the RV leaders, the Nuremberg laws were a welcome sign of stabilization. They anticipated that the preceding insecurity, particularly in light of Hitler's speech to the Reichstag on September 15, 1935, and other similar statements by Nazi leaders, would no longer prevail and that Jewish life in Germany would be assured, albeit on the basis of discrimination and second-class citizenship. In a civilized country such as Germany, they reasoned, this regime of terror could not possibly last. Using the words "tolerable relations" from Hitler's speech to the Reichstag, the RV published a statement on September 24, 1935:

The laws passed in the Reichstag at Nuremberg hit the Jews of Germany very hard, but they are designed to create a basis that will enable tolerable relations to develop between the German nation and the Jewish nation. The RV is willing to contribute whatever it can to the achievement of that goal. A precondition for "tolerable relations" is the hope that the cessation of destruction and boycott may make moral and economic existence possible for Jews and their communities in Germany. The organization of Jewish life in Germany should oblige the state to recognize Jewish autonomous leadership. The RV is the proper body for that.[3]

For the first time the RV spoke of the Jewish nation; until then, most Jews had thought of themselves as Germans of the Jewish religious faith.

However, the Nazis never recognized the RV as the representative of a Jewish nation in Germany, and the guiding RV principle even as late as 1935 remained the desire to insure a continuation of Jewish life in Germany. At the same time, some voices within the RV urged a different approach; in private conversations the top RV leaders spoke of the death of German Jewry and of the need to emigrate as quickly as possible. This was the message German Jewish leaders sent to American Jews; the message that prompted the suggestion in 1935 by banker Max M. Warburg, an important German Jewish leader, to James G. McDonald, the League of Nations High Commissioner for Refugees, to arrange for the emigration of 150,000 German Jews over a five-year period. Young people would emigrate first, and their families would follow. Time was necessary to locate countries that would accept immigrants. To buy that time, the RV attempted to create a tolerable existence for those on the waiting list, especially older people, who were a growing part in a community that had been aging and declining even before Hitler.

A veritable cultural revolution occurred by means of the educational and cultural networks that were established in order to fortify Jewish morale. Jewish elementary and secondary schools were supported by Jewish funds from abroad. Humanism, Jewish tradition, and skills that might be useful in emigration were stressed by teachers who had been dismissed from their previous positions as a result of the new Nazi policy. Many countries of immigration would not accept persons whose occupations were not needed or which might threaten the livelihood of their own citizens. Vocational centers were therefore organized to retrain Jewish merchants, professional men, and artisans, who formed the vast majority of German Jews. Adults joined the Kulturbund (Cultural Association), which reintroduced Jewish tradition in a modern form to a Jewish community searching for values and meanings. Under the leadership of people like the philosopher Martin Buber, who had translated the Bible into German, the Kulturbund and similar groups fostered humanism in an increasingly brutalized environment. Through the efforts of many, in those few years of decline the German Jewish culture flourished as it had not done for generations.

JEWISH EMIGRATION

Of the 53,000 Jews (10 percent of the Jewish population) who fled in the panic exodus of 1933, 16,000 returned rather than suffer the humiliation, deprivation, and even starvation (especially in Paris) that greeted them in the countries of destination. In the following years, emigration became better organized, both within and without, and about 5 percent of the 1933 Jewish population emigrated annually, despite considerable difficulties.

Although publicly Nazi policies were calculated to encourage emigration, the reality of the Nazi position was somewhat different. Influenced, perhaps, by their belief in the mythical world power of the Jews, Nazi economists thought an immediate major exodus would endanger the fragile German economy that was just then emerging from the Great Depression. With the exception of a few Jewish industrialists and major retailers, however, the Jewish significance to the German economy was minimal.

Well-off Jews would in any case find havens of refuge, but then the poor would be left behind and would become a burden for the Nazis. On quite another level, the Nazis wanted poor Jews to emigrate because, according to their theory, they would generate antisemitism wherever they fled. In so doing, they would effectively counteract international protests over Germany's treatment of the Jews and increase sympathy for Germany's position. The emigration of poor, not rich, Jews would further the Nazi purpose of turning the Jews into a world problem.

A policy of property confiscation was the practical solution to their dilemma. The Flight Tax (Reichsfluchtsteuer), which had been introduced in 1932 before the Nazis came to power, could in effect rob the richer elements of much of their property. To emigrate, a person had to pay a flight tax of 25 percent of his property. The larger the property, the greater the loss, of course, and, consequently, wealthy people were not inclined to leave. They deluded themselves into thinking that their position was still relatively strong, that the Nazi regime would not last long enough to cause their ruin. Those who did leave provided considerable sums to the Nazi coffers. (See Table 6.1)

TABLE 6.1.
INCOME FROM FLIGHT TAX

Year	Reichsmarks (RM) in thousands (RM 2.50 = $1)
1932–33	1,000
1933–34	50,000
1936–37	70,000
1937–38	81,000
1938–39	342,000

Leo Baeck, *institute Yearbook* 1980 (Vol.25), p. 343; in Jewish Emigration from Germany—
Nazi Policies and Jewish Responses (1). by Herbert A. Strauss, pp. 313–361

Delay often compounded the emigration problem, for entry permits to countries of immigration were usually issued only to those who could prove that they had sufficient capital to sustain themselves. Consequently, those who delayed too long frequently found entry permits difficult to obtain, for after paying their taxes and buying their tickets, there was little left. Emigration was further hampered by the stipulation that only small amounts of foreign currency at exorbitant exchange rates could be purchased with the prospective emigrant's Reichsmarks (German currency).

To rescue German Jewry (not from murder, at that stage, but from persecution), two essentials were necessary: countries willing to receive the immigrants and funds not only to cover the cost of emigration and settlement but also to meet the needs of the increasingly impoverished German Jewish community (52,000 Jews were on welfare in 1935; in 1938, with a Jewish population of 380,000, 100,000 were receiving relief). The American Jewish Joint Distribution Committee (JDC) extended aid to German Jews. Funds were also provided by the Central British Fund for German Jewry, established in 1933 by a merger of British Jewry's Zionist and non-Zionist groups and the

Jewish Colonization Association (JCA), which had been founded in 1891 to settle Jews on land, mainly in Argentina.

To help German Jews without sending American dollars to Nazi Germany, the JDC supported the youngsters of wealthy families who were sent abroad, mainly to Britain; the parents of the children, in turn, paid the equivalent in marks to the ZA. Similarly, after 1935 prospective emigrants paid their marks to the ZA, and their tickets and expenses outside Germany were paid by the JDC (Table 6.2). Thus, the ZA was financed without aiding the Nazi economy by introducing dollars into Germany.

However, the chief obstacle to emigration was the unwillingness of countries to accept German Jews, an unwillingness motivated largely by the fear of swamping labor markets with new immigrants at a time of world economic crisis. Those who were accepted were usually farmers or miners; middle-class and professional persons were not. And, of course, many countries were reluctant to open their doors because of traditional antisemitism.

The High Commission for Refugees (Jewish and Others) Coming from Germany, headed by James G. McDonald, former chairman of the Foreign Policy Association in the United States, was a voluntary intergovernmental body, not technically associated with, but a part of, the League of Nations. From October 1933 until December 1935, McDonald tried unsuccessfully to convince the governments of countries of immigration (including his own) to

TABLE 6.2

COMPARISON OF ZA AND JDC FUNDS, 1934–1937 (in RM)

Year	Total ZA budget	Total raised in Germany	JDC expenditure	Others
1934	2,418,146	?	855,427	?
1935	2,863,000	1,225,364	933,000	704,636
1936	4,123,125	1,690,481	1,188,884	1,243,760
1937	4,400,000	1,575,000	1,610,000	1,215,000

SOURCE: Bauer, *My Brother's Keeper* (Philadelphia, 1974), p. 122.

liberalize admittance procedures. In his letter of resignation in December 1935, which was published in the Western press, he demanded a drastic change in the free world's attitude to Nazi Germany and declared that the Nazi treatment of the Jews was a matter not of internal German affairs but a world concern. The persecutions in Nazi Germany were not a temporary affair, he said; the "plague" threatened to become pandemic and demanded coordinated action. His practical proposal, which did not require a change in U.S. quotas, was submitted to President Roosevelt; in line with the Jewish initiative mentioned above, it suggested that 150,000 young Jews emigrate within a five-year period, with their relatives to follow later, and was dependent on locating countries of destination. He emphasized that the Jewish problem in Germany was relatively small—only half a million persons were involved, and civilized humanity surely could find a solution for them. McDonald's successor, a retired British Army general, Sir Neil Malcolm, took a different position: "I have no policy, but the policy of the League is to deal with the political and legal status of the refugees. It has nothing to do with the domestic policy of Germany. That's not the affair of the League. We deal with persons when they become refugees and not before."[4]

Immigration to the United States had been limited since the early thirties by an administrative regulation of September 8, 1930, in which President Herbert Hoover announced, in a press release, that if "the consular officer believes that the applicant may probably be a public charge at any time, even during a considerable period subsequent to his arrival, he must refuse the visa."[5] This rebirth of the so-called LPC (Liable-to-become-a-public-charge) clause was used frequently by consuls to restrict immigration for ethnic or religious reasons. In general they sympathized with the then prevalent restrictionist tendencies in American life. Of the annual quota from Germany of about 26,000, 4,392 came in 1933–34, 5,201 in 1934–35, and 6,346 in 1935–36, of whom some 80 to 85 percent were Jews. In October 1935, McDonald asked the leaders of the Jewish community in the United States to seek a review of the administration's policy. On November 1, Herbert H. Lehman, former governor of New York, wrote to Roosevelt to ask him to ease the regulations, within the quota system. The people who wanted to come, he said, were like "my father, Carl Schurz, and other Germans who came over here in the days of 1848."[6] The refugees were presented as "Germans," not "Jews," which was the anti-ethnic approach espoused by Jewish leaders. Roosevelt replied on November 13: The State Department had issued instructions, "now in effect," that refugees should receive "the most considerate attention and the most generous and favorable treatment possible under the laws of this country."[7] Although Roosevelt's statement was a vast exaggeration and although restrictive practices persisted, total immigration from Germany increased to 10,895 in 1936–37, 17,199 in 1937–38, and in 1938–39, 32,753 people were admitted—again, about 80 to 85 percent were Jews (roughly 38,000 to 40,000 between July 1936 and December 1938). About 380,000 Jews were still in Germany in 1938. Had the 1938–39 flow persisted, a sizable proportion of German Jewry might have been saved.

The number of immigrants to be admitted to Palestine was based on an estimate of the economic absorptive capacity of the country as determined by the British administration in Palestine, which issued a labor schedule every six months listing the need for various kinds of workers. The Jewish Agency for Palestine (JA), which had been organized in 1929 by Zionist and non-Zionist Jews to develop the Jewish National Home in Palestine, selected those to receive immigration permits on the basis of the labor schedule and the needs of the countries of origin. Because the economic situation in Poland was desperate and because Polish Jews were the least acceptable in other countries, the JA gave priority to East European immigrants. People with £1,000 or more, called capitalists, entered the country more or less without limitations, although few German and Polish Jews could marshal such sums. Of the 199,676 persons who immigrated to Palestine between 1933 and 1938, 44,537 (22.3%) were from Germany and Austria (Table 6.3).

In 1931, there were 175,000 Jews in Palestine. There was practically no industry and the development of agriculture was just beginning. There was no economic basis for mass immigration. The Great Depression was raging and Jewish contributions to Zionist funds had dwindled to a trickle. That 140,267 persons immigrated in 1933–35 (22,747, or 16.2%, from Germany) is evidence of both the positive attitude of the British administration at that time, and the diligence of the Jewish Agency. The situation was to change, however, in the following years.

TABLE 6.3.
IMMIGRATION TO PALESTINE OF JEWS FROM GERMANY AND AUSTRIA

	From Germany		From Austria	Total	Total immigration to Palestine (legal)
1933	6,803		328	7,131	31,977
1934	8,497	22,747	928	9,425	44,143
1935	7,447		1,376	8,823	64,147
1936	7,896		581	8,477	31,671
1937	3,280	15,399	214	3,494	12,475
1938	4,223		2,964	7,187	12,263
Total	38,146		6,391	44,537	199,676

SOURCE: Bauer, *My Brother's Keeper* (Philadelphia, 1974), p. 163.

In 1935–36 Italy was at war with Ethiopia, and Britain's position in the Mediterranean and the Middle East was endangered. Viewing the strengthening of the Jewish National Home with increasing alarm, the Palestinian Arabs, under Haj Amin el-Hussaini, the Mufti (Moslem cleric) of Jerusalem, decided to oppose the Jews and Britain, obtaining moral (and some, but very little, material) support from Mussolini's Italy and Hitler's Germany (Arab Rebellion, 1936–39). To avoid a quarrel with the Arab world, Britain began to withdraw its support of the Zionist movement in late 1935; immigration, consequently, dropped sharply in 1936–38.

Immigration to Palestine was aided by the transfer (Heb., *ha'avara*) agreement signed in 1933 by the Nazi Ministry of Economic Affairs and representatives of the Jewish Agency. Designed to transfer capital from Germany to Palestine, the agreement stipulated that a prospective Jewish emigrant was permitted to buy machinery or finished products in Germany with his German Reichsmarks and ship the goods to Palestine, where they would be sold to local constructors or industrialists; on his arrival in Palestine, he would receive most of the sterling equivalent that had been realized for his property. Although no foreign currency accrued to Germany, the German economy was bolstered by the sale of exports. For Jewish Palestine, the absorption of German and other immigration was thus aided by an inflow of Jewish capital from Germany at a time when capital imports from America and elsewhere had dwindled. However, the Jewish boycott on German goods to protest the Nazi persecutions in Germany was, in effect, subverted by the transfer agreement. Although the efficiency of the boycott was minimal, bitter controversy nevertheless arose between supporters of the ha'avara and its opponents, who accused them of treason in the Jewish struggle against Nazism. In the end, the £8 million ($36 million—at the end of the century this would be $360 million approximately) of capital imports that reached Jewish Palestine in 1933–39 made possible the absorption of many thousands of Jewish immigrants.

The year 1938 marked the turning-point for German and European Jewry. As Nazi Germany began provoking armed conflict, radicalization of the Nazi Jewish policy followed. The Western powers scarcely reacted. To solve the problem of the refugees from Germany, however, President Roosevelt, under pressure from his liberal supporters to do something for the Jews, invited thirty-three nations to participate in an international conference in March 1938. The purpose was to have the burden of the refugees to be shared by many countries, and thus not alienate conservative and isolationist sentiment.

Twenty-nine countries attended the conference at Evian, France, between July 6 and 15, 1938. Britain declared Palestine was not to be discussed, the United States demanded that U.S. quotas were not to be discussed, and the other countries, with the exception of the Dominican Republic, limited themselves largely to stating what they could *not* do. The Dominican Republic declared its willingness to accept up to 100,000 Jewish refugees—however, this was no more than a diplomatic ploy arranged with the State Department, to encourage more serious offers by other countries to follow—but no one did. The Dominicans accepted a small number of refugees in the years that followed. The Inter-Governmental Committee on Refugees (IGCR) was established, however, to negotiate with the Nazis to allow emigrants to retain some of their property and thus facilitate entry into the countries of immigration.

In the panic that followed the Kristallnacht pogrom, thousands of Jews emigrated—to Palestine, to Britain, to North and South America, and to Shanghai. Further, to press reluctant Jews to emigrate, the Nazis established a Central Office for Jewish Emigration (Zentralstelle für jüdische Auswanderung) in Vienna in 1938. Headed by Adolf Eichmann, the emigration office fostered a reign of institutionalized terror.

Between early 1938 and September 1939, forty derelict ships transported some 16,000 illegal immigrants—from Poland before Kristallnacht, from Germany and Eastern Europe after Kristallnacht—to Palestine, despite violent British opposition. The illegal immigration was organized by the Mossad le'Aliyah Beth (Institute for "B" immigration), an agency of the Haganah, the underground military organization of the JA; the Irgun Tsvai Leumi (National Military Organization), the rightist split-off from the Haganah; and private entrepreneurs. Illegal immigration to Palestine—and to Latin American and Shanghai as well—was supported by the Gestapo, and many people on shipboard had been released from concentration camps on the condition that they leave Germany more or less immediately.

By January 1939, 13,500 Jewish and non-Jewish German refugees had found asylum in Britain. Following Kristallnacht, British public opinion urged that "something" be done. Although a JA request to permit 10,000 children to enter Palestine was rejected, the British government offered to accept not only the children but also female domestic servants and others. There were also a few illegal entries aided by British sailors, who were not deported on the recommendation of British judges. Between January and September 1939, some 50,000 refugees from Germany, Austria, and the Czech lands entered Britain, including 9,354 unaccompanied children.

Latin America was another destination. In September 1938 the S.S. *Iberia* docked in Mexico with 43 Jews; the S.S. *Orinoco* with 300 passengers arrived in October. By March 1939, 1,740 passengers, sailing on twenty-three ships, had found havens in Cuba, Venezuela, Colombia, Chile, Costa Rica, and landlocked Bolivia. At least two ships, the S.S. *General Martin* and the S.S. *Caparcona,* had to return their distraught passengers to Europe. The 907 passengers of the S.S. *St. Louis,* who were refused entry to Cuba, although they had Cuban visas, were refused entry to the United States as well, which sent out Coast Guard ships to prevent them from landing.[8] They, along with passengers of similar ships, finally found refuge in West European countries, upon payment of large sums by the JDC to the governments concerned. However, those who were taken in by the Netherlands, Belgium, and France were later caught by the Nazi occupation of these countries and most of them were murdered.

Another haven for desperate, visa-less German and Austrian Jews was provided by Shanghai. In 1937 Shanghai was actually three cities: the International Settlement, directed by the consuls of foreign powers, the French Settlement, and the Chinese city that recently had been conquered by the Japanese. In the summer of 1938 the Jewish community of Vienna (Israelitische Kultusgemeinde—IKG) learned that no visas were required for entry into the International Settlement; by June 1939, some 10,000 German and Austrian Jews had entered Shanghai. After spending their German marks for passage on the Soviet Trans-Siberian railroad, refugees arrived in Shanghai literally penniless. Although the JDC and other charities sent aid, the refugees suffered near starvation in a completely foreign civilization that was constantly threatened by revolutionary upheavals. Many refugees often asked themselves whether starvation in Vienna and Berlin was not to be preferred to starvation in China. They survived, however. Those who stayed behind, did not.

A more centralized Jewish organization became necessary after the Jewish communities in Germany were denied legal rights in March 1938 and particularly after Kristallnacht, when many RV leaders, along with other men, were arrested. Because such an organization was also needed by the Nazis to facilitate their dealings with the Jews, appropriate orders were issued by the Nazis, and the Gestapo finally approved the reorganization in July 1939. Called the Reichsvereinigung der Juden in Deutschland (National Union of the Jews in Germany, RVE), the group was led by the former leaders of the RV: Rabbi Baeck, Dr. Hirsch, and others. To label them, as some have done, as slaves of Nazi terror is to deny the truth. They worked courageously to aid Jews in their escape from Germany, and represented those that remained with dignity.

The IGCR set up at Evian managed to contact the Nazis at the end of

1938 to facilitate emigration. IGCR director George Rublee, an American corporation lawyer and an ardent supporter of the Roosevelt administration, established contact with Hjalmar Schacht, then the head of Germany's State Bank (Reichsbank). After an intensive exchange of proposals, they agreed upon a complicated arrangement, whereby 150,000 Jews of working age would emigrate, to be followed by 250,000 dependents. The remainder, an estimated but much exaggerated figure of 200,000, who were considered "non-emigrable"—the old, the sick, and those without families—were to stay in Germany, with the assurance that they would not be molested. One-fourth of the Jewish property in Germany would be used to buy German goods to be taken out by the emigrants, and an equivalent sum would be raised by a nebulous "world Jewry" abroad to facilitate settlement. Schacht got Hitler's approval for this arrangement on January 2, 1939. Although he himself resigned from the Reichsbank on January 21, for reasons unconnected with these negotiations, Göring assured Rublee on January 23 that the agreement stood.

Jewish organizations had many misgivings about this project. It would, in effect, legitimize the confiscation of German Jewish property by the Nazis, bolster Nazi Germany's exports, and create a "world Jewish" institution in the Nazi image to deal with the Nazis. At a time of economic crisis, 1938–39, moreover, there was no hope of reaching the sum of $2.4 billion required by the project. However, with the U.S. administration eager to show results for its efforts to satisfy American liberal opinion, pressure was exerted on the Jews to accept the proposal. After much soul-searching, a group of Jewish leaders in America set up the Coordinating Foundation on June 6, 1939, with a total capital of only $1 million, to start implementation.

In the meantime, the European situation had critically worsened on March 15 with the German annexation of the Czech lands (Bohemia and Moravia), home to 117,000 Jews. On March 14, Slovakia declared its "independence," completing the break-up of the liberal Czechoslovak republic. On January 24, 1939, Heydrich, acting on Göring's instructions, had set up a Central Office for Jewish Emigration on the Viennese model in Berlin. Heydrich stated that two parallel policies would be pursued: Jews would emigrate via the Schacht-Rublee agreement or be forced out via terror. A similar office was set up in Prague after it was occupied in March.

The Zionist leader Chaim Weizmann said, in a bitter comment on this situation, that the countries of the world were divided into two camps: those that wanted to get rid of the Jews, and those that refused to take them in. On May 17, 1939, the British government published its White Paper on Palestine: within ten years, a Palestinian state with a permanent Arab majority was to be set up; establishment of a Jewish National Home was terminated; 75,000 additional immigrants would be permitted to enter; any Jewish immigration after that would be dependent on Arab consent—in other words, would not take place. To allay the expected outcry of liberal public opinion against such an anti-humanitarian policy, the British Colonial Secretary, Malcolm McDonald, announced on the same day that British Guiana would be investigated for possible Jewish immigration. Nothing came of it.

In this atmosphere of despair, the Coordinating Foundation was unable to find havens for fleeing Jews. On July 19 the British government offered to support settlement projects financially (apparently, their Guiana project) if other governments would also cooperate. But other governments did not respond. There were no havens, there was no money—but mainly, there was no time. On September 1, 1939, the Nazis attacked Poland. Night descended on the world; the Jews of Europe were destined to die.

After the failure of the economic boycott in April 1933, the totality of the Nazi anti-Jewish policy unfolded one step at a time. The barring of Jews from government and other public employment in the spring and summer of 1933 affected some 20 percent of the Jewish population. Although the Nuremberg laws denied the Jews citizenship in 1935, they were at the same time promised existence at least as a minority. A Jewry that had considered itself German first and foremost and Jewish only secondarily, now turned inward to develop a new-found Jewish identity. They maintained their dignity despite rejection by what they thought was their fatherland. From time to time a semblance of stability tended to delude them into thinking that their situation might improve. The pressure was insidious, but never drastic enough to jolt the victims into radical reaction. Emigration continued, however, and at any given time there were considerably more visa seekers than there were opportunities of exit.

Beginning in 1935, the leaders of German Jewry tried to inform the non-Jewish world outside of their predicament. When there was little response, they realized that to survive, both physically and spiritually, in an immoral society, they would largely have to depend on themselves.

CHRISTIANITY AND THE NAZIS

Nazism was an anti-Christian movement. By denying the brotherhood of man, racism denied the Fatherhood of God and was therefore anti-Christian. The Nazi ideology promoted a *volk* community that would be free of the influence of churches. The Führer was not only the secular authority but the messenger of God, the interpreter of the scriptures. Christ had been an Aryan, the Nazis said, misinterpreted by Christianity. The "maintenance of racial purity [was] a commandment of God and Christianity."[9]

Cuius regio, eius religio (whoever rules determines the religion) was a strong tradition in mainstream German Protestantism. Unless it subverted scriptural commandments, secular Christian authority was to be obeyed.

In 1930 a so-called German Christian Church, led largely by ex-Freikorps men and other extreme nationalists, was founded as the representatives in the Protestant Church of the Hitler-led forces of "national revival." The fight against pacifism, socialism, Freemasonry, and the Jews was their fight.

A rather simple military pastor of the German Christians (Deutsche Christen), Ludwig Müller, was nominated by Hitler to be his "Delegate and Plenipotentiary" for all problems concerning Protestant churches. A Reich Church was to be established, led by a national bishop. When Müller was defeated by a traditionalist candidate, the Nazis cancelled the elections, and in July 1933, after tremendous pressure had been exerted, Müller was "elected." In Prussia, the new church authorities denied church membership to those of Jewish descent and those married to Jews. Opponents were cowed, youth groups were dissolved, and by February 1934 some seventy pastors had been sent to concentration camps.[10]

The traditionalist opponents of the new dispensation were led by Martin

Niemöller, pastor of the church at Dahlem, a suburb of Berlin. Niemöller, a German nationalist, commander of a submarine in World War I, and a national hero, had welcomed the Nazi regime and as late as 1934 used the Nazi salute. But he refused to recognize the right of secular authorities to determine matters of conscience for the individual and denied the state's claims of supremacy over Christians—only God and God's word had that right.

In August 1933 Niemöller helped establish the Pastors' Emergency League, which soon claimed the allegiance of one third of Germany's Protestant pastors. Through public prayers, the movement became increasingly influential and even gained the release of arrested clergymen. Niemöller was eventually sent to the Dachau concentration center himself.

In May 1934 a traditionalist synod was held at Barmen to establish the Confessing Church (Bekennende Kirche, BK). In a statement largely written by Karl Barth, the Protestant theologian at Basle, the BK acknowledged that "the inviolable foundation of the German Evangelical Church is the Gospel of Jesus Christ, as it is witnessed to by the Holy Scriptures and as it comes to light anew in the Confessions of the Reformation." It rejected "the false doctrine that the Church is able or at liberty apart from this ministry to take to itself or to accept special 'Leaders' [Führer] equipped with power to rule." It rejected equally "the false doctrine that the State can become the single and total order of human life, thus fulfilling also the Church vocation."[11] Although the Barmen declaration did not go beyond purely church affairs, its denial of the absolute supremacy of the state demanded tremendous courage in the Germany of 1934.

The BK in some cases refused to remove converted Jews or descendants of Jews from its congregations or its ministry and was clearly anti-racialist, although few dared to protest the persecutions of the Jews. Niemöller himself was arrested in July 1937 and spent the war years in Nazi camps. Bishop Theophil Wurm of Württemberg spoke out against so-called "mercy killings" (euthanasia) and the persecution of the Jews. Ludwig Steil defended the Jews and died in a Nazi camp; Pastor Heinrich Grüber of Berlin, who helped both converted and non-converted Jews, was sent to a concentration camp. He survived to testify at the trial of Adolf Eichmann in Jerusalem in 1961. Eichmann, Dr. Grüber said, had told him:

"No one will thank you for your doings, for your activities for the benefit of
the Jews. There will be no thanks coming from them." I answered him . . . "Do
you know the road leading from Jerusalem to Jericho?" and he nodded. I said,
"On this road there was once a Jew brought down by robbers, and he who had
helped that Jew was a man who was not a Jew. The God whom I worship, He
told me, 'Go and do as he did.'[12]

Of the thousands of pastors and church leaders imprisoned, about 500
died.[13]

During the war, Dietrich Bonhoeffer, a member of the BK, concluded
that a Christian should not stop at Church affairs when opposing a state evil.
Although he considered the separation of Jews from German society legitimate and the deicide and supersession myths valid, he nevertheless determined, from a Christian viewpoint, that the Jewish question was at the center
of the controversy with Nazi paganism and that "only he who cries out for
the Jews may sing Gregorian chant."[14] He was murdered in a Nazi prison as
an anti-Nazi resister.

A community of interest between the Catholic Church and Nazi Germany has been noted.[15] The Nazi opposition to bolshevism and socialism
was shared by the church. Because preservation of the Catholic Church was a
supreme command from God, church leaders were inclined to preach moder-
ation and submission rather than endanger its existence.

In July 1933 Nazi Germany signed a concordat with the Vatican, under
Pope Pius XI, that guaranteed the freedom of Catholicism. In return, the
Catholics, in effect, abandoned political activity in Germany and dissolved
their political organizations. To the Nazis, however, the Concordat was no
more than a truce in the fight against the Catholic Church. Between 1933 and
1938 Catholic youth organizations were dissolved, confessional schools
abolished, priests arrested, and priests, the priesthood, and the church were
vilified, and the Vatican submitted. However, the sermons of Cardinal
Michael Faulhaber of Munich condemned Nazi racist and secularist teachings; German bishops meeting in 1934 at Fulda condemned Alfred Rosenberg's *Myth of the Twentieth Century,* a Nazi ideological tract based on
racism, blood, soil, and other Nazi pagan symbols; and Bishop Clemens A.

von Galen of Münster defended the church against the totalitarian pretensions of Nazism and, especially, euthanasia. As in the case of the Protestants, the Catholic leaders opposed the Nazi position only as it pertained to church matters and interests. Yet they were loyal Germans and supported the regime as well as being faithful Catholics; for example, Bishop von Galen considered it his duty to advocate the defense of Germany against the Western Allies, and conducted a mass for Hitler, after the latter's suicide, three days before the war ended.

In 1937 Pope Pius XI had issued an encyclical, "Mit Brennender Sorge" (With Burning Concern), which condemned the racial myth, but while the church tried to protect Jewish converts to Catholicism, it did not oppose Nazi antisemitic policy. A proposal for a papal encyclical against racial antisemitism, which however repeated Christian antisemitic stereotypes, was rejected by Pius XII. Provost Bernhard Lichtenberg of Berlin was an exception. After the Kristallnacht pogrom, he prayed for the persecuted Jews as well as for the so-called non-Aryan Christians (the converts): "What took place yesterday, we know; what will be tomorrow, we do not know; but what happens today that we have witnessed; outside [this church] the synagogue is burning, and that also is a house of God."[16]

Christianity, born of Judaism, and anti-humanist Nazism could not coexist. During the Nazi rule of terror, 4,000 priests from all over Europe were murdered. At Dachau alone there were 2,771 priests. For defending their beliefs against Hitler, 129 German Catholic priests and 2 Protestant pastors were sentenced to death.[17]

There were 30 million Catholics in Germany. Although Jews were helped clandestinely, the church never publicly recognized that the defense of the Jews was a Christian duty.

Franklin H. Littell, a Methodist minister and professor of religion at Temple University, wrote:

> The cheap and easy view of the Church struggle is that it was like the persecutions of old in which martyrs and confessors stood to the death against heathenism. And now the purveyors of cheap grace are beginning to use the faithfulness of a few Christians like Dietrich Bonhoeffer to boast of the Church's

record of courage in the face of this spiritual enemy! The truth is that the Church Struggle was fought out within the institutions themselves, not between "insiders" and "outsiders," that most Church constituents apostatized and only a small percentage remained faithful, and that most of the theological and ecclesiastical vises which surfaced during this time of trial are yet unresolved. . . . In the triumph of anti-Christian ideologies, parties, and systems in the twentieth century, supported enthusiastically by the vast majority of apostate baptized, the Jewish people has supplied by far the largest number of martyrs and witnesses to the God of Abraham, Isaac and Jacob. He is also the Christians' God, when they remember who they are.[18]

As a prisoner in Dachau, Martin Niemöller is reported as having said that first the Nazis went after the Jews, but he was not a Jew so he did not react. Then they went after the socialists, but he was not a socialist. Then they went after the trade unions, but he was not a worker, so he did not stand up. Then they went after him, and by then it was too late for anybody to stand up. The so-called Church struggle, one must conclude, was the work of the few; as regards the Jews, the opponents of Nazism among the clergy were much fewer even than that. On the whole, to use Littell's terminology, the vast majority of German Christians apostatized.

seven
POLAND—
THE SIEGE BEGINS

THE GERMAN INVASION

ON SEPTEMBER 1, 1939, Germany invaded Poland without a declaration of war, a further act in Hitler's scenario of world conquest.

On September 3 France and Britain declared war on Germany to fulfill their treaty obligations with Poland. But they did not extend military aid to their ally; no bombing raids on Germany took place from the West, and the huge French army on the denuded German western front moved slowly. Poland, ill-equipped and badly led, was dying, despite tremendous heroism on the battlefield. On September 6 Warsaw radio announced the removal of the government to the east and asked able-bodied citizens to join the armed forces there. A panic exodus from the city followed.

On September 17, in accordance with the Molotov-Ribbentrop treaty, the Soviet army invaded Poland from the east. The Polish government fled into Romania and in effect dissolved. General Wladyslaw Sikorski, an opponent

The German Partition of Poland 1939/41–1945

————	Boundary of Poland up to September 1, 1939
- - - - -	German-Russian border, September 1939–June 1941
░░	General Government of Poland after July 1941 (under German administration)
▓▓	Incorporated into the German Reich
✠	Death camps

LATVIA

LITHUANIA

Baltic Sea

Kovno
(Kaunas)

Vilna
(Vilnius)

Danzig

EAST PRUSSIA
(GERMANY)

Grodna

Incorporated into
Reichskommissariat
Ostland

• Minsk

Generalkommissariat
(quasi-incorporated with East Prussia)

USSR

Wartheland

Bialystok

Baranowicze

• Poznan

Treblinka ✠

Chelmno ✠

Brest Litovsk

Pinsk

• Warsaw

Lódz •

GERMANY

Radom •

Sobibór ✠

Incorporated into
Reichskommmissariat
Ukraine

• Breslau

Lublin (Majdanek)
Majdanek ✠

• Czestgochowa

Belzec ✠

Dubno •

Oswiecim
(Auschwitz) Cracow

General Government

PROTECTORATE
OF BOHEMIA
AND MORAVIA

✠ Auschwitz

Przemysl

• Lwów

Ukraine

Tarnopol •

(added to General Government
in July 1941)

SLOVAKIA

HUNGARY

Sniatyn •

ROMANIA

0	miles	100
0	km	100

of the previous regime, established a government in exile, first in France and later in London. Although remnants of the Polish army continued to fight, they could do little for a Warsaw surrounded and besieged by German forces. On September 27, confronted by a lack of military equipment and the prospect of death by starvation, the Poles surrendered. During the bombing and artillery shelling, the Jewish sections of the capital were specifically targeted for particularly savage destruction.

On September 28 the USSR and Nazi Germany redivided Poland. The Soviets withdrew from the mainly Polish ethnic areas promised to them under the Molotov-Ribbentrop agreement and in return obtained control of Lithuania. Western and central Poland, with a population of some 22 million, came under German rule. On October 8 Hitler decreed the "return" to the Reich of the Polish areas that until 1918 had been part of the German Empire, as well as other areas that had never been German at all—areas adjacent to eastern Prussia, Danzig (Gdansk) and Pomerania, the so-called Warthegau with the Polish industrial city of Lodz (with the second largest Jewish population in Poland), and eastern Silesia, including the cities of Katowice and Bedzin, among others. The rest of the country was organized as a protectorate, called General Government *(Generalgouvernement),* and the Nazi minister of justice, Hans Frank, was appointed General Governor. Poland, partitioned by its territory-grabbing neighbors at the end of the eighteenth century, had been repartitioned after a short twenty-one years of independence.

Terrorism raged. In the *A-B Aktion* (A-B Action), the code name for the mass destruction of the Polish intellectual elite, about ten thousand Polish priests, teachers, technicians, and political leaders were murdered. Although the major annihilation occurred during the first months of occupation, it continued intermittently until the spring of 1940 and occasionally was renewed after that. Thousands of men were sent to concentration camps, and the Nazis began a mass expulsion of Poles from the newly annexed western Polish territories to the General Government. A rigid separation was maintained in Poland between the German master race and the Poles. Only Germans were allowed to frequent certain restaurants, cafes, cinemas, and shops. When food rationing was introduced, Germans received much higher rations than Poles.

To sustain life, many Polish working-class families sought supplies on the black market that developed in a general atmosphere of near starvation. Some Poles, or their children, who evinced what Himmler called "good" racial characteristics, were permitted to register as Germans. In some cases, children were kidnapped and taken to Germany to be reared as Germans. Suffering from financial loss, many Poles signed up for labor in Germany, which was voluntary at first. Later, people were rounded up, often simply taken by force from the city streets, and forced to labor in Germany. Polish industry was either dismantled and transported to Germany or controlled by Germans. Basic to the German policy was the Nazi concept of the superiority of the Germanic race, endowed with the right to enslave others. The Poles, considered Aryans of a lesser breed and often termed "subhumans," were to be the slaves who would build a Nazi culture of the future. According to the UN Genocide Convention of 1948, German policy towards the Polish people was clearly a case of genocide.

THE JEWS IN PREWAR POLAND

In 1939 there were about 3.3 million Jews in Poland. Since its independence in 1918, the country had suffered economic crisis. The middle class, in particular, had been hurt, and bitter competition for employment had drastically increased antisemitic acts, including boycotts and pogroms. During the autocratic reign of Marshal Jozef Pilsudski (1926–35), the government did not succumb to the blandishments of antisemitism. After his death in 1935, however, his weak successor, Marshal Edward Smigly-Rydz, permitted the government to drift to the Right and compete with the antisemitic policies of the Endek (National Democratic) party, the major middle-class opposition. In fact, the government party founded in 1937, known as OZN, exhibited fascist tendencies no less virulent than those practiced by the ONR, an extreme faction that split off from the Endeks to found what was, in effect, a fascist group. Although the left-wing opposition—a faction of the Peasant party under Stanislaw Mikolajczyk and especially the Polish Socialist party (PPS) opposed the antisemitic policy of the others, antisemitic tendencies of a milder sort were occasionally evident here too.

Antisemitic acts mounted in the mid-thirties. Jewish students, separated from others at Polish universities, were subjected to harassment and attacks by fellow students (1935–37). Boycotts against Jews, with open government approval, spread from early 1935 on. Between 1935 and 1937, 118 Jews were killed and 1,350 were wounded in sixteen pogroms (for example, in Przytyk, March 9, 1936, and in Czestochowa and Brest Litovsk in 1937). A total of 348 separate mass assaults on Jews took place. Nor did the situation improve in 1937–38. There were five severe pogroms in Central Poland in August 1937, followed by anti-Jewish demonstrations in Warsaw. Riots occurred several times in early 1938 in Warsaw. In early 1939 Jews were forced to leave certain frontier towns because they were considered unreliable elements.

Pogroms were motivated by hatred of the stranger, and the economic crisis. A hungry and bitter people struck out against the stranger, who was equally poor. Antisemites wanted to effect "the revision of citizenship and the elimination of Jews from the economic and cultural life of Poland."[1]

In 1931, 1,123,025 Jews were gainfully employed. Of these, 277,555 were laborers, about 200,000 were artisans, 428,965 were traders (with their families, 1,140,532). By 1935, 400,000 traders and their families were living in poverty. Of the laborers and employees, 60 percent were unemployed or working only part time. Of the 120,000 intellectuals and their families, 60,000 had no steady income. According to JDC estimates, 1 million Jews, or about one-third of the total, were unemployed or working part time. On January 8, 1937, the *London Jewish Chronicle* described the Jews of Poland as "a helpless minority sunk in squalid poverty and misery such as can surely be paralleled nowhere on the face of the earth." In October 1936 the New York-based Jewish writer Sholem Asch said the Polish Jews seemed to be "buried alive. Every second person was undernourished, skeletons of skin and bones, crippled, candidates for the grave."

The most serious results of this general situation were evident among Jewish children. A detailed investigation in the town of Ostrog showed that, out of a sample of 386 Jewish children in four out of fifteen "Jewish" streets, 262 were of school age but only 109 attended school. Of the other 153, 12 were ill, 3 were retarded, 6 had no documents for registration, 9 had not enrolled in time, 6 were not accounted for, and 117 could not go to school because they had insufficient clothes or shoes. Of the total of 386, only 67 were healthy; 196 were weak or anemic, 61 were scrofulous. A total of 71% of the children were in various stages of undernourishment down to and including starvation. This was the situation three years before the establishment of ghettoes in Poland.[2]

Despite a hopeless and deepening poverty, however, intellectual, artistic, and political activities continued to be pursued. In 1938, 17,720 pupils were studying in vocational schools. At the end of 1935, of 523,852 Jewish children of school age in Poland, 180,181 attended Jewish schools that received only token or no government assistance. *Yeshivot* abounded, as did secularist Hebrew and Yiddish schools. Newspapers and books were published in large numbers. Theaters were well attended. Orchestras performed.

Politically, Polish Jewry was divided into three main, mutually hostile camps: the religious fundamentalists, the Agudat Israel party; the secularist, anti-Zionist Bund; and the Zionists, who themselves were split into many factions (the right-wing Revisionists, the middle-of-the-road General Zionists, and the Socialist factions of Right Poalei Zion and Left Poalei Zion, and many others). Each main group claimed the allegiance of about a third of the Jewish population. In addition, a very small, but important, group of Jews were trying to become assimilated into the society of the Polish intelligentsia.

The Agudat Israel party tried to trade their support at the polls for a government guarantee of Agudist supremacy in internal matters concerning the Jewish community. The Bund hoped for a free, secular, socialistic Poland where Jews would receive a certain amount of cultural autonomy. The Zionists campaigned for Jewish political and economic rights until emigration to Palestine was possible. None of these programs was realistic. The Jews in Poland had no recourse to any governmental consideration. Nor could they emigrate, for the gates of the world were closed—Palestine by the British, America by the quota system, and so on. Polish Jewry was sick unto death before the first German soldier crossed the frontiers.

The Zionist youth groups, which claimed between 70,000 and 100,000 members in 1939 attracted disillusioned youth who sought a regeneration in

Palestine. The largest groups were the Dror (Freedom) and Hashomer Hatzair (Young Guardian). Dror, affiliated with the Right Poalei Zion party, was oriented to a collective settlement movement *(kibbutz;* pl., *kibbutzim)* in Palestine called Kibbutz Meuchad (United Kibbutz) and led by Yitzhak Zuckermann and his wife, Zivia Lubetkin. Hashomer Hatzair, a radical socialist group, unaffiliated with a political party, was oriented toward Kibbutz Artzi (National Kibbutz Federation) in Palestine and led by Joseph Kaplan, Tossia Altman, and 20-year-old Mordechai Anielewicz, who was to become the commander of the Warsaw ghetto uprising in 1943. Smaller groups included Gordonia, moderate Social Democrats affiliated with another *kibbutz* federation in Palestine, and Akiva, a liberal Zionist youth group. These four groups formed the Hehalutz (Pioneer) Federation, which was the central moving force in later ghetto rebellions. In addition, there was a centrist group, the small Noar Zioni (Zionist Youth), and on the Right the large, right-wing Betar, whose leader, Menahem Begin, was to leave Poland when the war broke out and reach Palestine in 1942 after spending time in a Soviet concentration camp.

THE JEWS IN OCCUPIED POLAND

A woman who left Poland on June 7, 1940, reported:

> A few days after their entry in Wloclawek, on the eve of the Day of Atonement [Yom Kippur], the Germans forced their way into a private house, where Jews were praying, and ordered those present to go out and run; then they ordered "halt," but several Jews did not hear and carried on running; they then opened fire and killed five or six of them. On Yom Kippur itself the Germans burned down the two large synagogues. The fire spread to some private houses. The Jews threw their possessions out of the window and were thereupon robbed by a mob of non-Jews. The arsonists were mainly S.S. men. The Jews tried to save the burning buildings. The Germans then took out all the Jewish men from one of the houses, twenty-six of them, and forced them to sign a declaration that they had laid fire to the house. After receiving the declaration the Germans then told those arrested that they will be punished for the arson unless they pay 250,000 zloty [about

$5,000 prewar] to ransom their lives. The Jewish population of Wloclawek col-
lected the money and the arrested men were released. Then hunting expeditions
on Jewish houses took place. They caught 350 Jews and put some of them into
military barracks and others into Muhsam's factory. From there they were taken
out daily for work, but received no food—only their families were allowed to bring
them something to eat. . . The Judenrat [Jewish Council], which was nominated
instead of the former community council, and whose activity was designed merely
to fulfill the Germans' orders, produced daily a certain number of Jewish workers
in accordance with German demands. Those who were taken, or caught in the
street, were beaten up and humiliated endlessly. The way they treated the Jews
during work can be seen from the fact that one of these Jews, Jacob Heimann, 52
years old and too weak for physical labor, was beaten, and stabbed with a dagger
during work, and died a few days after being brought home.

In October the Germans decreed that the Jews should attach on the back of
their clothes a yellow star, and that they should not walk on the side-walks but in
the middle of the road. After levying the fine on account of the imaginary arson-
ists of 250,000 zloty, they fined the Jewish population another 500,000 zloty for
supposedly not observing the order forbidding them to use the side-walks. The
schools were closed.

A few days after their entry into the town, the Germans closed and confiscated the Jewish factories and shops. Jews were required to register all their
property, and no Jew was permitted to keep more than 200 zloty in his house
[2,000 zloty in Warsaw]. Cases of beating and abuse of Jews were frequent.
These occurred not only during forced labor, and not only under some pretext,
but also for no reason at all: simply, they used to walk up to Jewish passersby
and, shouting "Jude," beat him up.[3]

Of the total Jewish population in prewar Poland (approximately 3.3 million), somewhat less than 2 million remained under German rule (600,000 or
slightly more in the western territories annexed by Germany and probably
about 1.3 million in the General Government). During the fighting and immediately afterward an estimated 120,000 Jews were killed—as soldiers in the
Polish army, in aerial bombardments, or as victims of special SS murder
squads, the five *Einsatzgruppen*, whose main targets were Polish intellectuals.

About 350,000 Jews fled to the east and found themselves under Soviet rule. As the new borders stabilized, however, some Polish Jews wandered back to the German-controlled areas to be with families they had left behind. As the German terror was directed at first primarily against the Poles, and as the situation in the east was far from being satisfactory, many Jews saw little difference between the two locations. Approximately 250,000 Jews remained in the east; the others had returned by the beginning of 1940.

THE GERMAN PLAN FOR JEWISH CONTAINMENT

On September 21, 1939, before the fall of Warsaw, Reinhard Heydrich, chief of the Security Police (Sicherheitspolizei, SIPO), sent a *Schnellbrief* (express letter) to the *Einsatzgruppen* leaders which read in part:

SECRET

To: Chiefs of all Einsatzgruppen of the Security Police Subject: Jewish question in the occupied territory

I refer to the conference held in Berlin today and once more point out that the planned *overall measures* (i.e., the final aim) are to be kept *strictly secret.* Distinction must be made between:

(1) The final aim (which will require an extended period of time), and

(2) The stages leading to the fulfillment of this final aim (which will be carried out in the short term).

The planned measures demand the most thorough preparation in their technical as well as economic aspects.

It is obvious that the tasks that lie ahead cannot be laid down in full detail from here. The instructions and guidelines below will at the same time serve the purpose of urging the chiefs of the Einsatzgruppen to give the matter their practical thought.

I

For the time being, the first prerequisite for the final aim is the concentration of the Jews from the countryside into the larger cities. This is to be carried out with all speed.

In doing so, distinction must be made:

(1) between the areas of Danzig and West Prussia, Posen, Eastern Upper Silesia, and

(2) the rest of the occupied territories.[4]

As far as possible, the area mentioned (in item 1) is to be cleared of Jews; at least the aim should be to establish only a few cities of concentration.

In the areas mentioned in item 2, as few concentration points as possible are to be set up, so as to facilitate subsequent measures. In this connection, it is to be borne in mind that only cities which are rail junctions, or at least are located along railroad lines, are to be designated as concentration points.

On principle, Jewish communities of fewer than 500 persons are to be dissolved and to be transferred to the nearest city of concentration.

This decree does not apply to the area of Einsatzgruppe, which is situated east of Cracow and is bounded roughly by Polanica, Jaroslaw, the new line of demarcation, and the former Slovak-Polish border. Within this area, only an improvised census of Jews is to be carried out. Furthermore, Councils of Jewish Elders, as discussed below, are to be set up.

II

Councils of Jewish Elders (Jüdische Ältestenräte)

(1) In each Jewish community, a Council of Jewish Elders is to be set up, to be composed, as far as possible, of the remaining influential personalities and rabbis. The council is to comprise up to 24 male Jews (depending upon the size of the Jewish community).

The council is to be made *fully responsible,* in the literal sense of the word, for the exact and punctual execution of all directives issued or yet to be issued.

(2) In case of sabotage of such instructions, the councils are to be warned of the severest measures.

(3) The Jewish councils are to take an improvised census of the Jews in their

local areas—broken down if possible by sex (age groups): a) up to 16 years of age, b) from 16 to 20 years of age, and c) over, as well as by principal occupational groups—and are to report the results in the shortest possible time.

(4) The Councils of Elders are to be informed of the dates and deadlines for departure, departure facilities, and finally departure routes. They are then to be made personally responsible for the departure of the Jews from the countryside.

The reason to be given for the concentration of the Jews into the cities is that Jews have most influentially participated in guerilla attacks and plundering actions.

(5) The Councils of Elders in the cities of concentration are to be made responsible for appropriately housing the Jews moving in from the countryside.

For general reasons of security, the concentration of Jews in the cities will probably necessitate orders altogether barring Jews from certain sections of cities, or, for example, forbidding them to leave the ghetto or go out after a designated evening hour, etc. However, economic necessities are always to be considered in this connection.

(6) The Councils of Elders are also to be made responsible for appropriate provisioning of the Jews during the transport to the cities. No objections are to be voiced in the event that migrating Jews take their movable possessions with them, to the extent that this is technically possible.

(7) Jews who do not comply with the order to move into the cities are to be allowed a short additional period of grace where circumstances warrant. They are to be warned of strictest punishment if they should fail to comply with this latter deadline. . . . .

IV

The chiefs of the Einsatzgruppen will report to me continuously on the following matters:

(1) Numerical survey of the Jews present in their territories (broken down as indicated above, if possible). The numbers of Jews who are being evacuated

from the countryside and those who are already in the cities are to reported separately.

(2) Names of cities which have been designated as concentration points.

(3) Deadlines set for the Jews to migrate to the cities.

(4) Survey of all Jewish-owned essential or war industries and enterprises, as well as those important for the Four Year Plan, within their areas.

If possible, the following should be specified:

a. Kind of enterprise (also statement on possible conversion into enterprises that are truly essential or war-related, or important for the Four Year Plan).

b. Which of these enterprises need to be Aryanized most promptly (in order to forestall any kind of loss)? What kind of Aryanization is suggested? Germans or Poles? (This decision depends on the importance of the enterprise.)

c. How large is the number of Jews working in these enterprises (including leading positions)?

Can the enterprise simply be kept up after the removal of the Jews, or will such continued operation require assignment of German or Polish workers? On what scale? Insofar as Polish workers have to be introduced, care should be taken that they are mainly brought in from the former German provinces, so as to begin the weeding out of the Polish element there. These questions can be solved only through involvement and participation of the German labor offices which have been set up."[6]

It is clear that considerable deliberation preceded Heydrich's order. The Jews were to be concentrated in larger towns with rail connections in preparation for the "final aim" (not "solution"). Although the "final aim" is not spelled out, ghettoes seem to be a foregone conclusion and the Councils of Elders are discussed in detail. Exemption of the Einsatzgruppen 1 area (Polanica, Jaroslaw, and the Slovak border, section 1, last paragraph) from these preparations appears puzzling at first sight.

Some historians have argued that Heydrich's order is proof that the total murder of the Jews—the "final solution"—was being planned by September 1939. In support of the "final solution" theory, some historians have pointed out that Hitler earlier (on January 20, 1939) had threatened the Jews with annihilation in the event of another war. Although Heydrich's orders seem to be part of a detailed Nazi plan, the only documentation to support such a thesis is the order itself, which however seems to point to a different answer regarding the ultimate destination of the Jews. Immediately after the release of *Schnellbrief,* mass expulsion of Jews from west Polish territories and elsewhere commenced. But many were sent to precisely the area exempted by the *Schnellbrief* which is around Nisko near Lublin, later called by the Nazis the "reservation" area (borrowing the term used in the United States for land allocated to American Indians). Consequently, Heydrich's "final aim" was expulsion, and the concentration of Jews near railways was a logical location for future deportation to such a "reservation." The "Final Solution" was not envisaged at that stage.

On October 17, 1939, 1,000 Jewish men were sent to the Nisko area from the Czech lands. They were left in open fields or sometimes quartered in poor Jewish villages and told to build new settlements. Thousands of others soon followed. The winter of 1939–40 was particularly severe, with temperatures of -20°C and under. The Jews dug wells, built huts and fences, and drained marshy areas. Many Jews were allowed to escape from the Nisko area into nearby Soviet-held territory, which is what the Nazis eventually intended, that is, expulsion beyond the German frontier. By March about 95,000 had been expelled to Nisko. Governor Hans Frank objected—the General Government was not the proper place into which to dump Jews he thought, nor was it economically feasible. Heeding his protests, the Nazis abandoned the plan to expel Jews into the Nisko area in April 1940.

It is important to add that Heydrich's *Schnellbrief* was sent out after a meeting of top Nazi police officials had taken place the same day (9/21/39). In the minutes of the meeting a Hitler directive is mentioned that all the Jews under German rule should ultimately be sent into Soviet territory. The directive makes clear Heydrich's order: Jews should be concentrated in the Lublin area, or near rail hubs, in order to facilitate their ultimate expulsion into the Soviet sphere. Obviously, the plan was unrealistic, and beyond the suffering of tens of thousands of Jews, nothing came of it.

In early March 1940, 12,000 Jews were expelled from Stettin, then a north German harbor (today Sczeczin in Poland), and arrived near Lublin, Poland. Their numbers were reduced by 72 deaths on the fourteen-hour march in a snowstorm to their village destination. By March 12, 230 had died.

THE GHETTOES

By the fifth of March, 1940, all Jews had to leave the town. Every day one could see them in snow-covered streets. Caravans of people carrying on their backs pieces of furniture, bags and suitcases, sledges piled high with possessions and small hand-carts pushed along by frightened children. . . .

Grandma's apartment consisted of a large room and a kitchen. It was not easy to accommodate sixteen persons in it. But there were people who did not even have that option and many huddled together outside with no roof over their heads. . . . It was in the middle of winter, there was no heating material. We froze in the rooms. In most of the ghetto houses there were no water pipes and people lined up at a well. When the water of the well froze, they carried water from streets farther away, because there there were wells that had not frozen.[7]

In accordance with Heydrich's order to abolish Jewish communities with fewer than five hundred inhabitants, thousands of Jews were concentrated in ghettoes of larger communities. Set apart from the rest of the town, ghettoes were in most cases surrounded by a fence or a wall and were usually the poorest and least developed areas of the community. The non-Jewish inhabitants were ordered to move out of the designated areas, and thousands of Jews, both those who lived in other parts of the community and those from outlying villages, moved in. Housing accommodations were limited and the consequent overcrowding was a major cause of epidemics. In January 1941, a top German official in Warsaw, Waldemar Schön, reported:

"The Jewish quarter extends over about 1,016 acres. . . . Occupancy therefore works out at 15.1 persons per apartment and six to seven persons per room . . . ."[8]

Part of the Nazi propaganda effort was to persuade non-Jews that the ghettoes were necessary in order to protect them from the Jews. Jews were

This engraving shows a riot against Jews that occurred in August 1614 in Frankfurt, Germany. When economic depressions hit Europe, disorder often resulted, usually with Jews becoming the targets of brutal attacks.

This photo shows Adolf Hitler giving the Nazi salute during a parade in the 1940s.

Propaganda posters such as this one encouraged German young people to devote their lives to the Nazi party. The poster says, "Serve the Fuhrer." The Nazi party youth organization was called the Hitler Youth.

German children, carrying Nazi flags, are receiving the Nazi salute as they participate in a Berlin march in 1934.

By 1933, German Jews faced Nazi persecution on several levels. Here, a Nazi storm trooper guards a store in Berlin. A Jewish star has been painted on a display window of the store with a sign that warns Germans not to buy at this business owned by Jews. Storm troopers harassed or beat people who dared to shop in Jewish stores.

German students are helping Nazi soldiers unload boxes of books for the bonfire in front of the Berlin Opera House in 1933. The books, mostly poetry and fiction, are by Jewish or foreign authors whom the Nazis consider unacceptable. The sign in front says, "German students march against the un-German spirit."

Here, a crowd watches as books are burned.

These men are buying tickets at a public bath with a posted sign that says, "No admittance to Jews."

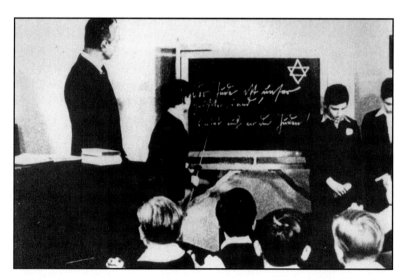

German students were encouraged to humiliate their Jewish classmates. Here, the Jewish boys must stand next to a chalkboard on which an anti-Semitic slogan has been written. The student with the pointer reads the slogan, "The Jew is our greatest enemy." German officials believed that the primary function of education was to create Nazis.

Nazi humiliation existed in the streets of every village. Here, Nazi soldiers force a Jewish son to cut his father's beard. In the background, the soldiers jeer.

The mayor of Vinkeveen, Holland, demonstrates that he is a loyal Nazi supporter by erecting a sign that states, "Jews not wanted here."

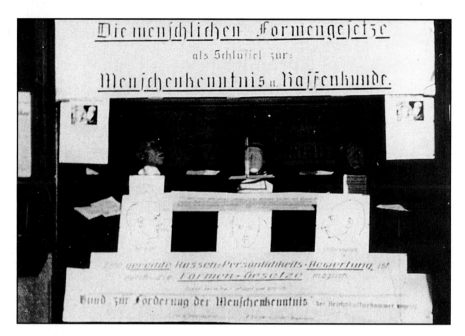

Phrenology is a pseudo-science that supports the idea that the bumps on a person's head can be "read" by feeling them and that they determine a person's character. This photo shows the sign in a Berlin shop where a phrenologist displays the difference between the head of a Nazi Aryan German and a Jew. The idea of the sign is to show how much more superior the head of the Aryan is compared to the head of the Jew.

Soon after the Nazis took power, the government ordered a boycott of Jewish businesses. Here, a crowd of Germans reads a notice announcing the boycott.

This photo shows the Fasanenstrasse Synagogue, Berlin's largest house of Jewish worship, before Kristallnacht.

This is a scene of the Fasanenstrasse Synagogue burned in anti-Semitic riots during Kristallnacht.

November 9, 1938 is known as Kristallnacht (Night of Broken Glass). Nazi mobs shattered the glass in Jewish homes and stores. Synagogues became the most common targets. Nazis burned more than 200 synagogues. This photo shows smoke billowing from the Great Synagogue of Berlin after it was set on fire.

These women stand on a street in front of a Jewish shop with its windows broken after Kristallnacht in Berlin. Nazis destroyed more than 7,000 Jewish-owned shops and businesses.

On April 19, 1943, about 2,000 Nazi soldiers marched into Warsaw to put down the resistance. Jewish fighters held out for four weeks. This photo shows Jewish women and children that the Nazis have captured as the resistance ends.

said to be carriers of epidemic illnesses while non-Jews were immune to them. In many instances, the Jews were also accused of cooperating with Germany's enemies and that supposedly was another reason why they had to be shut up in ghettoes. The Nazis told the Jews the ghettoes would help protect them from the attacks of Polish thugs, which were becoming more and more common. In actual fact the reason behind the establishment of the ghettoes was ideological—the removal of the Jews; as far as epidemics were concerned, the ghettoes created them and the numbers of Jewish victims were tremendous. The very use of the term "ghetto" was misleading, because Jewish ghettoes first arose in early modern times in Italy and served largely as a means of self-defense against possible persecutions. The original ghettoes were not isolated from their non-Jewish environments, nor did they necessarily serve as tools for persecution.

The first ghetto in Poland was established on October 28, 1939, in Piotrkow Tribunalski; the second was set up in the industrial center of Lódz. In Lódz, an ordinance published on February 8, 1940, detailed the area limits, times of entry and exit, and other restrictions. The ghetto was established in the "Baloty" quarter, known for its poverty and its underworld characters. There were 31,962 apartments there, of which about 60 percent were one-room flats, and 30 percent two-room flats. The houses were old, mostly built of wood, and usually had no toilets or running water or sewage of any sort. By March 5 all Jews were to be concentrated in the ghetto, and the following night German police killed a number of Jews found outside the ghetto area. After that date, those who were still outside hurried into the enclosure for fear of their lives.

The Lódz ghetto was viewed by the Germans at first as a temporary expedient, for they intended to deport all Jews from the newly annexed Polish territories. But in both Lódz and the area of Sosnowice-Bedzin (eastern Upper Silesia, or Zaglebie in Polish), where a regional Judenrat was established, deportation did not occur. The Lódz ghetto gradually became a large slave labor camp of workshops and factories. Hunger, overcrowding, and a lack of sanitation caused epidemics, mainly typhus. Mortality soared.

The ghettoes established by the Nazis differed in many ways, including the degree of isolation. Lódz was the most completely isolated ghetto—there was literally no possibility of any contact with the outside world. The ghetto was fenced with barbed wire and exits were guarded by police who had standing orders to shoot to kill. Entry by non-Jews was also well-nigh impossible. Food was therefore limited to that supplied by the supervisors of the ghetto, whereas in other ghettoes smuggling and economic exchange eased the situation to a smaller or greater degree. The poverty was such, however, that the starved population could not buy even the meager supplies provided. In August 1940, 47 percent of the food supplied to the Lódz ghetto was not purchased. The number of deaths escalated, the number of births declined; the total population declined from 160,423 in June 1940 to 148,547 in May 1941. To the Nazis, however, the Lódz experiment was a "success."

The SD decided as early as November 1939 to establish a ghetto in Warsaw, but the head of the Judenrat, Adam Czerniakow, obtained a postponement from the military governor. In October 1940, the ghetto was finally established, however, and on November 15 the gates of the ghetto were closed. Non-Jews were forced to leave the area chosen, a Jewish neighborhood in the center of the city, and 183,000 Jews who lived in other parts of Warsaw moved in. On November 16 the Jews still outside the ghetto, at least 10,000, were moved into it by force. Emmanuel Ringelblum, the chief chronicler of the Warsaw ghetto, wrote:

> The Saturday the Ghetto was introduced was terrible. People in the street didn't know it was to be a closed Ghetto, so it came like a thunderbolt. Details of German, Polish and Jewish guards stood at every street corner searching passersby to decide whether or not they had the right to pass.[9]

In most cases, the Jews could transport only a few essentials, and most of their property—houses, apartments, stores, furniture, clothing—was seized. The boundaries of the ghetto remained vague, and houses on the periphery were frequently confiscated for use by "Aryans." Overcrowding in the ghetto, compounded by the inclusion of large numbers of refugees from other parts of Poland, increased misery and internal problems.

Ghettoes were established in Poland, though not everywhere. They were later also set up in some territories occupied in the Soviet Union, and in

Romanian-held territories (in Bessarabia, Bukovina, and Transnistria). With the exception of Terezin (Theresienstadt) in Bohemia, which was a ghetto-like concentration camp rather than a ghetto on the Polish model, no ghettoes were established on Czechoslovak, Austrian, German, or Western territories or in the Balkans (with the exception of short-lived ghettoes in Greece and Hungary in 1943–44). The first ghetto in Poland was established in 1939, the last, in 1943.

The evidence seems to suggest that the ghettoes were initially to be used during a transition period that would lead to the expulsion of Jews from the German Reich or Europe; the decision to murder the Jews came later. Whether the Nazi dehumanization of the Jews was consciously planned cannot be determined because only fragments of the SS and Gestapo archives have survived and there appears to have been, in any event, a consensus that orders and discussion concerning Jews were to be verbal, not written (according to a later order by Martin Bormann, Hitler's secretary and leader of the Nazi party in 1943).[10]

THE JEWISH COUNCILS—THE JUDENRÄTE

The Nazis sought to achieve their aims within the Jewish community via the Judenrat (Jewish Council; pl., Judenräte), or Ältestenrat (Council of Elders), led by Judenälteste (Jewish elders); other names were used in different places. Heydrich's *Schnellbrief* decreed the establishment of Councils of Jewish Elders composed of twenty-four "of the remaining influential personalities and rabbis."[11] The councils were responsible for the immediate and accurate execution of all Nazi orders. Their tasks included registration of all Jews, by age and profession, and an accurate survey of all Jewish property, as well as the internal administration of the ghetto (e.g., housing, health, police, etc.).

Practically all Judenrat leaders believed that the Germans would lose the war.[12] They based their policy, therefore, on the assumption that temporary cooperation would lead to survival and eventual liberation. The Judenräte were not unique; similar administrative bodies performed similar functions in all German-occupied territory. There is no evidence that non-Jewish local leaders—Czech, French, and Dutch mayors, for example—behaved differently (see bibliography). But there was of course a basic difference: German policy towards the Jews ended in total murder; this was not the case for any other population under German rule. In the hope of satisfying the Nazis, the Judenräte cooperated in providing labor and facilitating the confiscation of property. They attempted to "normalize" ghetto life, for stability in both ghetto conditions and the Nazi attitude toward the Jews might promise survival—*Mir vellen sei iberlebn* (Yid., "We will outlive them").

Some historians view the Judenrat as not only an obedient tool of the Nazis but an essential element in the Nazi destruction of the Jews (e.g., Raul Hilberg). According to this viewpoint, even "good" Judenrat leaders, that is, those who tried by various subterfuges to protect the Jews, were, in fact, aiding in the process of destruction because they simply kept more Jews alive to supply temporary labor for the Nazis. That is, in keeping the Jews under control, the Judenräte were an instrument of the German bureaucracy. Other historians (e.g., Yisrael Gutman and myself) consider not only the end results (the murder of the Jewish communities) but the intentions of the Judenrat members as well. But even when only the actions of Judenräte are considered, they range from complete submission to rebellion, with many variations in between. The Judenräte were victims of the Nazi onslaught—more victims, perhaps, than others, faced, as they were, with life and death decisions in circumstances that no leaders of communities in recent times had been faced with. However one views the Judenräte, the ultimate responsibility lies, of course, with the Nazis, not with those who were, at worst, but tools.

The major leaders of Polish Jewry fled during the September 1939 war or shortly thereafter. The first-term Judenräte were composed of former local community workers and their local leaders. Second- and third-term Judenräte leaders—that is, those nominated by the Nazis after the removal (usually by murder) of the first—were sometimes chosen from among refugees, individuals without roots in the community who were often weak as well, individuals easily manipulated by the Nazis. The histories of most ghettoes can be divided, therefore, into two periods: before and after the first mass murders.

Historian Aharon Weiss has isolated four major behavioral patterns of Judenrat leaders, based on an analysis of the behavior of 146 first-term and

100 later-term leaders, as reported by the testimony of survivors.[13] The four patterns are: (1) complete non-cooperation with the Nazis, (2) cooperation on questions of property but non-cooperation in regard to delivering people for deportation, (3) sacrifice of the lives of some people in the hope of saving others, and (4) full cooperation with Nazis in the hope of saving their own lives. Although Weiss's figures should be taken as a general indication rather than as scientific findings, his analysis nevertheless tends to emphasize the complex nature of the ghetto environment.

FOUR JEWISH COUNCILS

The Lódz Judenrat

On October 13, 1939, Mordechai Hayim Rumkowski, member of the prewar Lódz Jewish community board (its chairman fled before the Germans entered the city), was nominated Judenälteste. Instructed to choose a Beirat (consultative committee), he sent letters of invitation to thirty-one well-known members of the community on the same day: "In accordance with the order of the Stadtkommissar [city governor] you are nominated to be a member of the Council of Elders of the Jewish religious community in Lódz. The acceptance of the mandate is obligatory."[14]

On November 7 the Beirat members, including Rumkowski, were ordered to appear at the Gestapo offices. With the exception of Rumkowski and two others, they were arrested and sent to a punitive camp near Lódz, where most of them died. Three months later, on February 5, 1940, the nomination of a new Beirat of twenty-one members was announced by Rumkowski. Rumkowski became, in effect, the sole arbiter of the Lódz ghetto. Rumkowski, a megalomaniac, printed ghetto currency with his likeness on it. Already an older man (aged 62), gifted and ambitious, he was known among the Jews as "the king." His credo throughout the ghetto period was "calm and work." By calm he meant obedience to the Germans. By work he meant making the ghetto indispensable to the German war machine. Obedience and work would keep the Jews alive until the end of the war.

Rumkowski's rule can be divided into two periods. In the early part of

TABLE 7.1.
COMPARISON OF FIRST AND LAST-TERM JUDENRAT LEADERS

	First term		Last term	
	N	%	N	%
Assisted the community, refused to carry out financial directives, warned of approaching actions– unanimous positive evaluation	45			
Resigned, unwilling to acquiesce to Nazi policy	11			
Removed by Nazis for disobeying orders	26			
Murdered, refused to supply people for deportation	18			
Total–Positive evaluation	100	68.6	30	29.6
Had connections with underground	2			
Committed suicide	5			
Died soon after taking office	4			
Removed by Jewish community	1			
Evaluation controversial	13			
Total–In between evaluation	25	17.1	10	10.0
Total–Negative evaluation	21	14.3	61	60.4
N	146	100	101	100

SOURCE: Aharon Weiss, "Jewish Leadership in Occupied Poland," in Yad Vashem Studies, Vol. 12 (Jerusalem, 1977) p. 356.

the war he acted forcefully, efficiently, and speedily to establish a well-run ghetto empire—workshops, police, courts of justice, jails, and schools. To visit the various departments, he traveled in a horse-drawn carriage given to him by the Germans. He surprised workers in the public kitchens as they doled out soup to the starving population and checked on the food shops. He spoke ironically about the Warsaw Judenrat with whom he had visited. In Warsaw, he said, chaos reigned, children were dying in the streets while food was plentiful in elegant cafes and restaurants. In actual fact, starvation in Lódz was even worse than in Warsaw. Nevertheless, he seems to have viewed himself as the savior who would rescue the Jews of Lódz.

Some ghetto inhabitants, including members of Rumkowski's administration, agreed with his strategy of remaining inconspicuous, obeying orders promptly, and refraining from anti-Nazi activity. Others, however, frequently rebelled. When a "work slow" movement began in the workshops, Rumkowski spread rumors among the workers to either calm them down or threaten them with reprisals, as occasion demanded. Order was maintained by all and every means. To silence his opponents, he used unemployment, starvation, and finally deportation. Anyone who raised a doubt regarding the wisdom of Rumkowski's decisions laid himself open to the old man's revenge.

The situation changed, however, in mid-1942. Rumors regarding the fate of Jews in other parts of Poland began reaching him. By mid-1942 at the latest, he knew that Jews were being murdered. To rescue the remaining 60,000 to 70,000 Jews in the ghetto he continued to obey Nazi orders and help deport Jews. To save some, as he hoped, he decided to sacrifice others. And he determined who should die and who should live.

Rumkowski's strategy was almost successful. The Lódz ghetto was the last one in existence in Poland. It had survived because, as Rumkowski had intended, it was producing clothes and other articles that the German war economy needed. But in July 1944 the Soviet army, advancing rapidly through Poland, stopped sixty miles from Lódz. In August, the Nazis sent Rumkowski and most of the ghetto inhabitants to Auschwitz. When the Soviets overran the German army and covered the distance to Lódz in three days in January 1945, they found 870 survivors. Had the Soviets continued their July 1944 offensive for another 60 miles, they might have liberated at least some of the 69,000 Jews then still in Lódz. Would Rumkowski have been vindicated at a postwar trial for saving their lives, or would he have been condemned as the murderer of tens of thousands of others?

The Vilna (Vilnius) Judenrat

On June 22, 1941, the Germans invaded the Soviet Union, and on the 26th they occupied Vilna. A few thousand Jews managed to flee with the retreating Soviet army. Two ghettoes were established: a so-called small ghetto, which housed "unproductive" elements, and a large ghetto for the workers and their families. The small ghetto was liquidated in October. By December 23, of the 57,000 Jews living in the city on June 22, 33,500 had been murdered. The large ghetto housed about 20,000 persons in early 1942.

In September the Nazis set up a Judenrat and a Jewish police force. Jacob Gens was appointed chief of police. Born in Kovno, the prewar capital of Lithuania, Gens was a member of the right-wing Zionist Revisionist party. At the end of World War I, Gens was an officer in the Lithuanian army, fighting against the Bolsheviks. His wife was Lithuanian and his contacts with nationalist Lithuanian politicians resulted in their recommendation of him for the post of police chief. His wife and daughter were living as Lithuanians in the "Aryan" part of the city; he chose not to seek a similar solution.

As the Nazis undertook to murder the Jews of Vilna, the job of the Jewish police was to rope in and guard the victims to prevent them from running away. In his first letter to his wife from the ghetto, Gens wrote: "For the first time in my life I have taken upon myself to fulfill such tasks. My heart bleeds, but I shall always do whatever is necessary for the ghetto Jews."

When the mass murders ceased in December 1941, the remaining Jews, crowded into the ghetto, deluded themselves into thinking that the Nazi thirst for Jewish blood had been quenched. In the main, the young and strong, those who were "productive," remained to work for Germany. Like Rumkowski, Gens believed that those who were necessary to the German economy would survive:

> We must show the Germans that we are extremely useful to them. Work, and especially work for the army, is the order of the day. . . . We now have 14,000 workers in the ghetto and we must do everything to increase the usefulness of our labor. . . . Jewish workers must give up easy and comfortable workplaces for more difficult ones, so as to be more useful. . . . That is necessary for the general welfare of the ghetto.[15]

The Vilna Judenrat was officially dissolved in July 1942 when Gens's power became supreme. Known as "the commander," and "Jacob the First," he issued a call to the ghetto inhabitants in which he reiterated his credo: "The basis for the existence of the ghetto is: labor, law and order. Every ghetto inhabitant who is capable of labor must do so, for that is the cornerstone of our lives."[16]

During 1942 ghetto inhabitants attended theaters and lectures on scientific topics; they organized festivities, literary clubs, a music school, an orchestra, choirs, elementary schools, and sports activities; teachers, writers, and technicians organized lectures in Yiddish and Hebrew. Gens actively supported all the cultural activities. In a speech to children he said: "My brothers, be good friends to each other, protect your parents, love your people, work for the ghetto and be proud and courageous Jewish children."[17]

Among other small concessions, Gens obtained from the Germans permission to cut wood in a nearby forest for the ghetto. Those who went out to cut the wood not only enjoyed being outside the ghetto but also contacted local people to obtain more food and even managed to get in touch with Soviet partisans. Gens himself had partisan contacts.

Because of his success in organizing the Vilna ghetto, the Germans made Gens responsible for a number of small ghettoes in the vicinity. He sent his police to the other ghettoes, to eradicate petty larceny and other criminal acts resulting from overcrowding and starvation, and he obtained permission to arrest unauthorized Germans when they entered the ghetto to terrorize its inhabitants without Gestapo approval.

There was much opposition and even demonstrations against Gens. In October 1942 Gens sent Salek Dessler, his deputy and the new chief of the police, to the nearby ghetto of Oszmiana (population: 4,000) to select 400 elderly people to be murdered. In a speech on October 27 Gens reported that the Gestapo had ordered the murder of all women and children, and that by negotiation he had managed to save them: "And so the police saved all those that had to remain alive. Those who did not have much time to live anyway went. With all due respect, the old Jews have to excuse us. They were sacrificed on the altar of our future."[18] In another speech Gens said:

Many of you see in me a traitor, and many wonder what I am doing here among you, at a literary gathering in the ghetto. I, Gens, lead you to death. I, Gens, want to save you from death. I, Gens, ordered the uncovering of hiding places [Gens' police delivered Jews in hiding to the German police]; I, Gens, am trying to find work permits, more working places [people who were necessary were not killed] and am trying to help the ghetto. I care for Jewish blood, and not for Jewish honor. When the Germans come and ask for 1,000 people I provide them for them, for if we Jews do not give of our own free will, they will come and fetch them by force, but they will not take one thousand, but thousands—and the whole ghetto will be in danger. You are the people of the intellect and the pen, you do not come into contact with the filth of the ghetto. You will emerge from the ghetto and your hands will be clean, and if you survive you will be able to say: we emerged and our conscience is clean. But I, Jacob Gens, if I survive, I will come out and my hands will be dirty and dripping with blood. Nevertheless, I will stand before a Jewish court and I will say: I did everything in my power to save Jews, to bring them to the gates of deliverance; and in order to ensure that there should be a remnant left, I myself had to lead Jews to their deaths. And in order to ensure that people come out with clean hands, I had to be infected with all the filth, to behave like a person without a conscience.[19]

When the Gestapo discovered that Gens had partisan contacts, he was ordered to report to the Gestapo office on September 9, 1943. To a friend who suggested that he hide, Gens answered: "If I, the head of the ghetto, run away, thousands of Jews will pay for it with their lives." He assembled the ghetto police, told them about his impending visit to the Gestapo, and nominated a successor. He went to the Gestapo the next day and did not come back. A Gestapo officer named Keitel told the Jewish Police that Gens had been shot for insubordination. The Jewish police organized a commemorative assembly for him in the ghetto, and two girls stole out of the ghetto to lay a wreath on his grave. A few days later, the ghetto was liquidated.

The Warsaw Judenrat

Adam Czerniakow, the leader of the Warsaw Judenrat, had been a member of the prewar Jewish community council. Nominated by the Polish regime during the last days of the siege, he was confirmed by the Germans and told to nominate a Judenrat council. An engineer by profession, who had headed an organization of Jewish artisans and craftsmen before the war, Czerniakow was torn between identification with the Jewish lower middle class and his love of things Polish.

The Warsaw ghetto was established by the Nazis in mid-November 1940. In May 1941 Czerniakow was authorized to act as mayor of a separate municipality by Heinz Auerswald, the Nazi ghetto commissar. An *Ordnungs-dienst* (lit., Order Service, the Jewish ghetto police) was organized, which numbered about 2,000 and was recruited by Jozef Szerynski, a professional policeman and a convert to Christianity. When the Nazis drew this force into their orbit, corruption in the Jewish administration became rampant

From his and other diaries and documents, Czerniakow emerges as a man who tried to do his utmost to alleviate the suffering of ghetto inhabitants, but failed. Although his attempts to cajole the Nazis into concessions testify to his personal courage, he presided over a largely corrupt and inefficient administration. He described the situation in his diary:

October 5, 1941—During the meeting Dr. Schipper [a historian] again behaved foolishly. Since he contrasted those present with the "true mentors of the people" I asked him where those "mentors" [20] were? Should we not look for them among those who have fled or among those who tried to leave but did not succeed? (He himself had a passport in his pocket.) He replied that those people would be punished. His own actions were entirely honorable.

November 1, 1941—Auerswald [the German administrator of the ghetto] maintains that a worker should labor at extracting bricks from the ruins all day for a bowl of soup. I remarked that he could also have a wife and children. Auer-swald retorted that 2 bowls of soup might be made available. And how is he going to have his shoes repaired? As for myself, although I could afford it, I pur-chased only one pair of late. I then permitted myself to observe that as a recently married man Auerswald could not understand what it means to have a family. I added that, although in his mind I am just a Spiessbürger [bourgeois], I neverthe-less have a strong conviction that people should be paid for work.

I mentioned for the "nth" time that the Order Service receives no pay. I also commented that when it came to the worst I could explain to the Order Service functionary that Dr Fribolin [German paymaster] has not given us any money. He [the functionary] will understand, but a [cart] horse which is not given any fodder will not.

All this toil, as I see it, bears no fruit. My head spins and my thinking is getting muddled. Not one single positive achievement. The food rations were to be increased. The mountain gave birth to a mouse. The population will reportedly receive, per person, 10 1/2 ounces of sugar per month, 3 1/2 ounces of marmalade a month, 1 egg per month, 220 pounds of potatoes per year. The bread ration is to remain as before: not a chance of increasing it.

May 5, 1942—Disturbing rumors about deportations persist in the city.

July 8, 1942—Many people hold a grudge against me for organizing play activity for the children, for arranging festive openings of playgrounds, for the music, etc. I am reminded of a film: a ship is sinking and the captain, to raise the spirits of the passengers, orders the orchestra to play a jazz piece. I had made up my mind to emulate the captain.

July 18, 1942—in the morning with Leikin to Brandt and Mende [Gestapo officials]. A day full of foreboding. Rumors that the deportations will start on Monday evening (All?!). I asked the Kommissar whether he knew anything about it. He replied that he did not and that he did not believe the rumors.

July 22,1940 [sic]—in the morning at 7:30 at the Community. The borders of the Small Ghetto surrounded by a special unit in addition to the regular one.

Sturmbannführer Höfle and associates came at 10 o'clock. We disconnected the telephone. Children were moved from the playground opposite the Community building.

We were told that all the Jews irrespective of sex and age, with certain exceptions, will be deported to the East. By 4 p.m. today a contingent of 6,000 people must be provided. And this (at the minimum) will be the daily quota.[21]

The next day, July 23, was the second day of the mass deportation of

Warsaw Jews (300,000) to their deaths in Treblinka. An eyewitness testimony reports:

> On July 23, they took away the car from Czerniakow—the last symbol of his authority. On that same day, at 7 o'clock in the evening, a small car pulled up in front of the Judenrat building, and from it emerged two hitherto unknown Gestapo officers. They demanded that the Judenrat head be brought to them immediately. Two [Jewish] policemen hastened to Czerniakow's home. Upon receiving the message, Czerniakow took a rickshaw (man-drawn vehicle on two wheels) for the first and last time in his life—and arrived at the Judenrat building. The conversation with the two Gestapo men was very short this time—it took no more than a few minutes. The Germans drove away. After they had gone, Czerniakow rang, and his aide came to his study. He asked her to bring him a glass of water. His wish was immediately fulfilled. His secretary later said that Czerniakow was white as a sheet and as he took the glass of water from her with trembling hands he made a weak attempt to smile. "Thanks," he said. That was the last thing he said. Ten minutes later, the Judenrat cashier who was in the building heard a telephone ringing. The sound came from Czerniakow's office. Surprised that Czerniakow did not answer, the man cautiously opened the door of the study and saw Czerniakow dead in his chair. On the table stood a tiny bottle with cyanide, half a glass of water and two brief letters. One of them was a parting letter to his wife, in which he asked her to forgive him for leaving her. He explained that he could not do otherwise. The other note said: "They are demanding ten thousand for to-morrow, after that seven thousand," and then two illegible words. His sudden death left a deep impression on everyone and was a telling demonstration of the hopeless situation.[22]

The Minsk Judenrat

Minsk, the capital of Soviet Belorussia (today Belarus), was conquered on June 30, 1941, by the German armies. Jews from the surrounding areas were concentrated in the ghetto, which was established in late July and numbered between 80,000 and 100,000 inmates.

Ilya Mishkin, who had been born in Minsk and was a middle-grade local government official before the war, was appointed leader of the Judenrat. Two underground movements were organized, one in the ghetto, under Hersh Smolar and one in the city of Minsk, under Isai (Isaiah) Kasinetz, a Jewish engineer. Mishkin, and other Judenrat members, including Zyama Serebriansky, the Jewish police chief, coordinated the two groups and established a communication with the first partisan detachments that began to organize in the forests nearby. At the end of 1941, the first group of armed ghetto Jews left for the forests. Their exit and the later exit of thousands of others, resulted from the cooperation of the Judenrat and the underground. Wounded partisans were occasionally treated in the ghetto hospital, which became a center of underground resistance.

On November 7 and November 20, 1941, 20,000 Jews were murdered. The Germans, not the Judenrat, ordered the Jews to concentrate in the central square. When a third "action" was ordered on March 2, 1942, the Jewish police were forewarned and in turn warned ghetto inhabitants.

Mishkin was arrested in February 1942 for hiding an anti-Nazi German officer, who then betrayed him. He was executed in March. His successor, Moshe Yaffe, continued his policies. When the Nazis identified Hersh Smolar (they only knew his false identity) as the leader of the resistance group, they demanded his surrender. Because it was generally believed that Smolar's surrender would protect the ghetto, even some members of the resistance group advised him to give himself up. Yaffe, however, did not share this viewpoint. He saved Smolar by showing the Germans a bloodsmeared identity card, purportedly Smolar's, as proof that he had been killed.

On July 28, 1942, 25,000 Jews were assembled in the ghetto square. Yaffe was ordered to calm them down. Instead, he told them to run for their lives. He was shot immediately and they, too, were soon dead.

eight

LIFE IN THE GHETTOES

GHETTOES IN POLAND

THE GHETTOES PROVIDED slave labor for the Nazi war machine. From the first days of German occupation, in addition to slave labor camps, the ghettoes supplied labor for German offices, installations, and workshops. In other instances, Jewish slave labor had no recognizable purpose other than dehumanization. In some locations, wages were not paid; in others a minimal sum of 0.50–0.80 Reichsmarks ($1 = 2.50 RM) per day was paid. Although the wage rate in Lódz was higher, the workers actually received only 35 percent of their wages, for the Germans retained 65 percent in a special "Jewish Fund."

Generally isolated, the ghettoes were cut off from provisions that might have been supplied by the neighboring population. The food provided by the Nazis was minimal. In Lódz the cost of the daily ration did not exceed 0.30

RM, which was less than that provided for convicts. In Warsaw the daily bread ration was less than 100 grams (3.5 ounces). The total daily caloric value of food supplied in Warsaw was 220, or about 15 percent of the normal daily requirement. Food was smuggled in on a large scale in some ghettoes, for example, Warsaw, where children, among others, were able to use their agility to circumvent Nazi guards. Such opportunities were not available in Lódz. Dependent on official rations, the Lódz population suffered chronic starvation, which led, in turn, to disease, to epidemics, and to the eventual demoralization of the ghetto population.

In the Warsaw ghetto a new aristocracy arose, an aristocracy of smugglers who frequented expensive cafes and restaurants to obtain food. Ruthless and lacking in social consciousness, the smugglers nevertheless risked their lives to bring in food and other essential products. Without them, the ghetto would have died out quickly. Formerly wealthy people, in contrast, frequently lost their will to live and joined those begging for food on the streets.

Forty percent of the social aid program in Warsaw was supported by indirect taxes, which even the poorest were required to pay—2 zloty ($1 equaled about 40 to 50 zloty on the black market) for each bread ration, for example. The tax policy was clearly discriminatory, for the Judenrat lacked the power to tax the wealth of the smugglers.

In the Warsaw ghetto, the most serious problem was the tremendous influx of refugees. Following the Heydrich *Schnellbrief,* some 100,000 additional Jews arrived. In September 1940, 50,000 additional Jews were evicted from the area around Warsaw and sent to the Warsaw ghetto. Of a population of close to 450,000 early in 1941, 150,000 were refugees. Elsewhere in occupied Poland, 470,000 other refugees were crammed into the ghettoes, 230,000 of whom were evicted between April and August 1940 from western and southern Poland.

Driven out of their homes with only small bundles on their backs and thrust into a strange environment, the refugees became dependent on social welfare. The meager resources of the Judenrat, especially in Warsaw, were incapable of feeding this multitude, and the refugees, consequently, were the first victims of starvation and epidemics. In Warsaw, they lived in cellars, synagogues, former schools and cinemas, often without heat and with many broken windows; sanitary facilities were inadequate or nonexistent. They became candidates for death. When efforts to help themselves failed, thousands of adults and children resorted to the streets to beg for food from Warsaw Jews who were themselves underfed and starving. The typhoid epidemic, which began in late 1940, claimed 43,239 lives in 1941 (out of a population of 420,116 in August 1941) and 22,760 in January-May 1942. These deaths reflect the spread of typhoid and other starvation-induced illnesses. Because not all deaths were reported, the actual figures are probably even higher. The 1941–42 deathrate of 10 percent of the ghetto population began to decline in the spring of 1942, as the typhoid epidemic receded. The weakest had died. As time went on, through the efforts of the illicit workshops selling their produce to Poles and also of the smugglers, the situation at least stabilized. A major proportion of the inhabitants of the ghettoes could have survived had the Nazis not decided otherwise. Did the Jewish will to survive contribute to that decision?

Although the Warsaw ghetto included well over 20 percent of Polish Jewry, the majority lived in ghettoes scattered throughout the country. By

TABLE 8.1
CHILDREN'S MORTALITY IN THE WARSAW GHETTO CHILDREN'S HOMES

1941 month	No. of children first day of month	Added	Left	Died	Mortality (percentage)
January	480	37	5	16	3
February	496	46	4	15	3
March	523	48	4	27	5.1
April	540	81	14	18	3.3
May	589	166	52	78	13.2
June	625	167	30	155	24.8
July	607	121	8	148	24.3
August	572	69	46	115	20.1

SOURCE: Sarah Nishmit, *Ma`avako shel Hagetto* [The struggle of the ghetto] (Tel Aviv, 1965), p. 43.

October 1940, of about 1.6 to 1.9 million Jews in Nazi-occupied Poland, 350,000 were in ghettoes. The major ghettoization occurred between October 1940 and April 1941, although some ghettoes were set up much later, and in some eastern localities later occupied by the Germans there were no ghettoes at all. Because the process of ghettoization was slow, conditions in ghettoes differed markedly. Conditions were desperate in the Lublin and Cracow ghettoes and only slightly better at Radom. In the Czestochowa and Zaglebie (Sosnowice-Bedzin) ghettoes for instance, the Jews never actually starved, although food was scarce. It appears that the Nazi policy regarding the treatment of Jews was not unified. Aside from general brutality, selective murder, extreme humiliation, and minimal sustenance, specific treatment of the Jews seems to have been the prerogative of the Nazi in charge of the ghetto. The inventiveness of the victims was also a contributing factor.

The Will to Survive

Lucy S. Dawidowicz writes:

> Despite the attempts by the Germans to impose a state of barbarism upon them, the Jews persisted in maintaining or in re-creating their organized society and their culture. The milieu in which the Germans confined them was the state of war or condition of insecurity which [Thomas] Hobbes [17th century British philosopher] epitomized: "no arts; no letters, no society; and which is worst of all, continual fear, the danger of violent death; and the life of man, solitary, poor, nasty, brutish and short." Nevertheless, in nearly all the ghettoes, the Jews conspired against the Germans to provide themselves with arts, letters and society—above all, with the protection of the community against man's solitariness and brutishness. Never was human life suspended.[1]

To foil the Nazi goal of breaking their spirit, ghetto inhabitants formed social welfare, religious, educational, cultural, and political (underground) organizations. In some cases, all activities were underground. Membership was usually voluntary. The groups were usually either independent of, or only partially connected with, the Judenrat. Judenräte that refused to cooperate with the Nazis were usually more closely involved in voluntary ghetto organizations.

On September 1, 1939, a municipal Social Service Committee (Polish acronym: SKSS) was set up in Warsaw, and on September 19, before the Germans occupied the city, a Jewish Coordinating Committee (KK) was established by the JDC committee, which was recognized by SKSS as the representative of Jewish social agencies. The leaders of the Warsaw JDC were left-wing Zionists, quite unlike the JDC leaders in New York. In prewar Poland the JDC not only supported but in some cases organized major Jewish welfare organizations—CENTOS, the child-care society; TOZ, the society for the protection of health; ORT, the vocational training society; and TOPOROL, the society for the advancement of agriculture. Although the dissolution of these groups was ordered by the Nazis, they maintained themselves in a semilegal way as part of a JDC network that was in some places (Warsaw, for example) independent of the Judenräte.

As an American organization, the JDC could maintain itself legally until Germany declared war on the US on December 11, 1941. It set up a "front" organization, known as Zetos, which had developed from the KK in September 1939 and was directed by a public committee, to represent unofficially the banned Jewish political parties, from the socialist and anti-Zionist Bund to the right-wing Zionists. Headed by Dr. Emmanuel Ringelblum, the historian of Polish Jewry during the Holocaust who was also a JDC official, Zetos organized public kitchens and supported children's homes, hospitals, and other forms of aid in Warsaw. Working partly through CENTOS and TOZ, they competed with and overshadowed the social welfare department of the Judenräte. The main achievement of Zetos, however, was the development of the "house committees," which had emerged spontaneously during the September war as groups organized to aid all the families in a house, or rather a four-house complex around a central yard, which was the way houses in Warsaw were built. The house committees helped the poor, cared for children, and fostered cultural life. Some committees—poorly organized, given to interminable squabbles, or so poverty-stricken that they were helpless—failed. But most house committees provided at least some solace and contributed to the spiritual survival of ghetto inhabitants. By April 1940 there were 778 house committees; early in 1942 there were 1,108, with 7,500 committee members. Mary Berg had American citizenship and she was able to leave the ghetto. In her diary, she wrote on April 4, 1941, that her "house" cooked a big vat of soup every Friday for the children and the sick and that "spoon actions"—each family contributed a spoonful of flour or sugar to the general pot—were frequent occurrences. The poor helped those who were even poorer; those who had nothing worked for food. Youth groups, especially young Zionists and Bundists, cared for children and organized makeshift kindergartens and schools, sold tickets to cultural activities, and served as scouts to warn of approaching SS or police.

The house committees, however, were powerless against brutality and oppression. The Judenrat had to acquiesce, in 1941, to the Nazi demand for disinfection actions, supposedly instituted against the spread of epidemics. Polish and Nazi doctors, accompanied by Jewish police, entered apartments and took away warm bedding and clothing to be disinfected. If not stolen, these items were returned, often ruined and torn. People were marched off to baths where they had to stand naked in the bitter cold of an unheated building in the Polish winter while their clothes were disinfected. They showered in boiling hot water and then, without benefit of towels, put on their damp and ruined clothes. Many became ill; epidemics and death were spread rather than averted by these practices. Disinfection squads operated throughout 1941; attempts by house committees to bribe them were unsuccessful

For the General Government as a whole, the JDC established the Jewish Social Self-Help (Jüdische Soziale Selbsthilfe, JSS). Dr. Michael Weichert, a JDC worker, was the leader of the JSS, whose headquarters were located at Krakow; as was the German administration for the General Government. The JSS became a member of the only German-recognized Polish organization, NRO (Naczelna Rada Opiekuncza), a welfare agency that also included a Polish ethnic welfare group and a similar Ukrainian group. After protracted negotiations with the Poles, the JSS was allotted 17 percent of all the funds or goods at the NRO's disposal. The JSS was recognized by the Germans until the end of 1941 as an official body because it represented an American organization, the JDC. In establishing welfare committees in the ghettoes of Poland, the JSS tried to maintain its independence from the Judenräte. For a time, the JSS appeared to be developing into an independent organization supported by the Germans, as opposed to the Judenräte. Soon, however, most Judenräte, in effect, gained control over the JSS committees. Financially, the JSS was supported by the JDC and the NRO; its budget, which Weichert estimated at about 1 million zloty per month (about $20,000) in 1940, provided help in a fairly large number of ghettoes. In early 1942, Weichert claimed that 412 committees were functioning in as many ghettoes. Under his aegis, CENTOS operated 26 children's homes and 61 "children's corners" with 12,299 children in late 1941. At the same time, Weichert claimed to be feeding 47,000 children. Although difficult to substantiate, these claims, if correct, would indicate that 15 to 20 percent of the children were helped by the JSS.

Weichert's relations with the Germans were strictly legal, as opposed to the Warsaw JDC's illegal practices. Weichert's close association with German bureaucrats in Krakow made him suspect, at least insofar as the essential illegal activities were concerned, and he was accused of being unreliable and a collaborator. Social aid programs from abroad were, as discussed earlier, financed almost exclusively by the JDC, which appropriated $860,000 for Poland in 1940 (13.8% of its budget) and $972,000 in 1941 (17% of its budget). The appropriations made in New York, however, could not be transmitted to Poland. The official JDC-Warsaw expenditure figures for 1940 were 10.2 million zloty (about $200,000 in real terms, depending on how the money was spent). The official figures do not in all likelihood reflect illegal expenditures, based on the illegal income derived by the JDC from Polish Jews who still had some money left and who were promised postwar repayment in dollars for any zloty they might donate. Although relatively large sums were collected and distributed in this manner, details concerning the transactions are not available.

In Warsaw, refugees were not included in the house committees. The 145 public kitchens and the 46 children's kitchens, which served some 135,000 daily "meals" (soup), could not possibly supply the needs of 150,000 refugees in addition to the local Warsaw Jews. Zetos and the Judenrat competed in social welfare work; although 60 so-called *Landsmannshaftn* (groups of persons originating in the same town), representing the refugees, joined Zetos, there was simply not enough to feed tens of thousands of refugees. The official Warsaw Judenrat welfare budget for May 1941, for instance, was 1,740,000 zloty ($34,800). The direct feeding cost was 991,880 zloty, of which 339,830 zloty (34%) was allocated to refugee areas. In the town of Rzeszow (Krakow district), with 14,000 Jewish inhabitants, the budget for April 1940 was 19,971 zloty, of which 18,584 was spent on food.

In Warsaw Zetos competed with or complemented Judenrat activities in maintaining public kitchens, distributing clothing, and aiding hospitals. It was equally active in supporting clandestine educational and religious activities.

Altogether, Zetos employed some 3,000 people in Warsaw, mostly experienced prewar workers, teachers, and so on. About one-fourth of the ghetto inhabitants (35,000 families or 113,000 individuals) received Zetos help in 1940–41.

Religious Life

The Nazis forbade all public religious practices, despite their claim that their antisemitism was racial, not religious. Jews dressed in traditional garb, especially bearded Jews and others recognizable as believers, were singled out for especially brutal treatment.

Towards the end of 1939 all male Jews of Rawa were forced to assemble in the town square to cut their beards. Among them was Rabbi Rappaport, the rabbi of Rawa, an old man with a white beard. The rabbi had always been on good terms with the local priest, a German, ever since the German occupation during World War 1, and also under Polish rule. The daughter of the rabbi went to the priest and asked him to prevent the cutting off of her father's beard. The priest went to the town square to intervene on the rabbi's behalf. After the officer in charge had heard the priest's request, he upbraided him for intervening in favor of a Jew. But as he did not dare to ignore the priest's request, he declared—either the beard will be cut off, or one hundred lashes will be administered. The rabbi preferred the lashes. After a number of strokes, the rabbi fainted, covered in blood. He was brought to a hospital where he lay for two weeks, but his beard remained intact. . . . When they put fire to the synagogue of Sierpec at the end of

September, 1939, all the Jewish inhabitants were ordered to assemble around the burning synagogue. From among the crowd a young, brilliant student of the Jewish law, Moshe was his name, emerged and ran into the burning house of worship, into the blazing fire, and took out of the ark two scrolls of the Torah, one in each hand. When he came out, he was met with a hail of bullets at the hands of the evil ones. He fell with the Torah scrolls in his hands, and was burned to ashes with them and the synagogue. May the Lord avenge his soul.[2]

Religious life had to go underground. Members of the ultra-orthodox Agudat Israel party participated in Zetos activities in Warsaw and helped organize religious observances.

A fair proportion of East European Jewry observed religious traditions (probably close to half the Jewish population in Poland). Even normally non-religious Jews observed some of the sabbath and dietary laws.[3] Large numbers of synagogues existed, as well as prayer rooms, religious elementary schools *(hadarim),* religious higher academies *(yeshivot),* and religious slaughterhouses (to slaughter meat according to Jewish ritual for the humane slaughtering of animals).

Polish Jews prayed clandestinely. On the 9th day of Ab (the Jewish day of mourning for the destruction of the First and Second Temples in Jerusalem by the Babylonians and Romans in 586 B.C.E. and C.E. 70), August 12, 1940, diarist Chaim Kaplan, a teacher, noted:

Public prayer in these dangerous times is a forbidden act. Anyone caught in this crime is doomed to severe punishment. If you will, it is even sabotage, and anyone engaging in sabotage is subject to execution. But this does not deter us. Jews come to pray in a group in some inside room facing the courtyard, with drawn blinds on the windows. . . [4] Even for the high holy days, there was no permission for communal worship. I don't know whether the Judenrat made any attempt to obtain it, but if it didn't try it was only because everyone knew in advance that the request would be turned down. Even in the darkest days of our exile we were not tested with this trial. Never before was there a government so evil that it would forbid an entire people to pray. Everything is forbidden to us. The wonder is that we are still alive, and that we do everything. And this is true of public prayer too. Secret minyanim[5] by the hundreds throughout Warsaw organize services, and do not skip over even the most difficult hymns in the liturgy. There is not even a shortage of sermons. Everything is in accordance with the ancient customs of Israel. . . . They pick some inside room whose windows look out onto the courtyard, and pour out their supplications before the God of Israel in whispers. This time there are no cantors and choirs, only whispered prayers. But the prayers are heartfelt; it is possible to weep in secret, too, and the gates of tears are not locked.

Although prayer was forbidden in some ghettoes, Ringelblum reported at least 600 *minyanim* in Warsaw alone. In Lódz, public prayer was permitted in 1940. In Riga (Latvia), refugee German Jews were allowed to pray, local Jews were not. In Vilna and Kovno (Lithuania), public prayer was not permitted. In March 1941, Hans Frank, the German governor, permitted religious activity in private homes and in synagogues and prayer houses on the sabbath and holidays. For many people, prayer became more meaningful. Additional liturgy was read, such as prayers for deliverance (e.g., Psalms 22 and 23) and the special prayers written during the Crusades and the persecutions of the Middle Ages when the devout "sanctified the Lord's name" (that is, accepted the martyrdom of death rather than deny the Jewish faith).

Observing the Jewish religious commandments *(mitzvot)* under ghetto conditions was difficult. Keeping the sabbath was impossible because people were forced to labor on that day as well as on festivals and high holy days. Keeping dietary laws *(Kashrut,* the separation of dairy and meat dishes), as well as other commandments, including rules of hygiene, was especially difficult. Starving Jews were prepared to forgo non-kosher meat. In special cases, rabbis permitted the consumption of non-kosher food, because the preservation of life is more important under Jewish law than dietary laws and the sabbath. In Lódz, for instance, rabbis permitted pregnant women to eat non-kosher meat. Jews fasted, especially on the Day of Atonement (Yom Kippur), although their starvation rations forced them to fast on many other days as well.

Education and Cultural Activity

In a memorandum to Hitler in May 1940 Heinrich Himmler wrote:

> For the non-German population of the East there must be no higher school than the four-grade elementary school. The sole goal of this school is to be— Simple arithmetic up to 500 at the most; writing of one's name; the doctrine that it is a divine law to obey Germans and to be honest, industrious, and good. I don't think that reading is necessary [see Appendix].

Himmler was referring to the education of Poles and other non-Jews on Polish territory; the Nazi attitude toward the education of Jews fell short of even that. Following the Nazi entry into Poland, and later the USSR, education was forbidden. Newspapers were not permitted and libraries were closed. Under the auspices of Alfred Rosenberg, the official Nazi ideologue, special Nazi units entered the large ghettoes to liquidate Jewish libraries and rob them and other institutions of Jewish cultural treasures. But some treasures were hidden, especially by youth and children, and ghetto libraries were established. Writers continued to write, and painters to paint, and scientists continued their research. The few archives that survive supply ample evidence of a feverish intellectual activity during the ghetto period. The Jewish reverence for education would not be denied.

Orchestras were active in the Vilna and Warsaw ghettoes and elsewhere as well. In the Kovno ghetto the orchestra was conducted by Misha Hofmekler, formerly conductor of the Lithuanian opera orchestra. The famous choir in Terezin (Theresienstadt, in Bohemia) was immortalized in Josef Bor's "Terezin Requiem." [6] In many ghettoes, kitchens supplied education as well as food, and youngsters also participated in singing and storytelling programs.

Because education was forbidden in Warsaw (in September 1941 the Germans permitted the Judenrat to open some elementary classes) so-called *complets* sprang up, initiated by teachers or parents for groups of 4 to 8 children. No information is available on the number of *complets* in Warsaw or elsewhere or the number of children involved. Teachers usually received a slice of bread in payment. In 1940 and 1941 groups of teachers met to discuss curricula and educational problems, and high school education became more organized. An illegal high school of the Dror Zionist youth movement, which existed between 1940 and the summer of 1942, was supported by Zetos to prepare youngsters for Polish matriculation exams. Beginning with 3 pupils and 7 teachers, by the spring of 1942 there were 120 pupils and 13 teachers. Scientists and educators earned some slices of bread by teaching math, history, biology, philosophy, and literature to half-starved youngsters. Illicit vocational training courses were offered in pharmacology and technical drawing, as well as university-level courses in education, medicine, and technical subjects. The school eventually contained elementary grades 4 to 6, all six high-school grades, and two college-level grades. Most pupils belonged to youth movements and were to participate in the Warsaw ghetto rebellion.

In the Lódz ghetto, education was permitted. During 1940 and 1941, 14,000 students attended 2 kindergartens, 34 secular and 6 religious schools, 2 high schools, 2 college-level schools, and 1 trade school (weaving). In Vilna, 2,700 children, aged 7 to 14, attended school.

Yitzhak Rudashevsky, aged 15, who lived in Vilna, wrote:

> A boring day. My mood is just like the weather outside. I think to myself: what would happen if we did not go to school, to the club, and did not read books? We would die of dejection inside the ghetto walls.[7]

Youth Movements

All political organizations were illegal, and they dwindled in the ghetto; only the core groups of such parties as the Bund, for instance, operated. The ultra-orthodox Agudat Israel party ceased to function. The youth movements, on the other hand, after an initial period of disorganization, resumed their educational work. Illegal, the groups found themselves, most often, in opposition to the Judenräte.

The Hehalutz organization was composed of the Hashomer Hatzair, Dror, Gordonia, and Akiva youth movements, which were secularist Zionist groups preparing their members for life in Palestinian *kibbutzim*. The communal life they lived in the ghetto eased both their material and spiritual life. Grouped around soup kitchens, counselors one or two years older than their charges told stories about the fields and hills of Palestine, creating an ideal world of tomorrow that enabled them to suffer the world of today. Socialist and Zionist ideologies were the subjects of heated arguments. A similar atmosphere prevailed in the non-Zionist movements as well, primarily the Bund youth group, Zukunft (Future), where the vision of Palestine was replaced by the vision of a Polish-Jewish brotherhood standing proud in democratic socialist Poland.

When rumors regarding mass murder penetrated the ghetto, the educational orientation of the youth movements was supplanted by practical political discussion. Underground newspapers had been published from the early days of the Nazi occupation. When the rumors became fact, the youth groups switched from political argumentation to preparing for armed resistance. The following was written by Tossia Altman, a leader of the Hashomer Hatzair. It is dated "Hrubieszow [a town in eastern Poland], 1942" (code words were used, as the letter was sent abroad):

> The illness of Israel [the Jewish people] and of myself—and you know how long we have been fighting it—has now definitely been found to be incurable, so the doctors say. One therefore has to adjust, slowly, to this thought. The terrible thing perhaps is that there is no time for adjustment. I am sure you want to know how the other members of the family are. Praotchik [pogrom, excesses] and Shhita [mass murder] live with Ami [my people] and Israel. There was no choice. It has a fatal influence on Israel's health, and I can see how this will bring the end near. But what can one do—those are the realities. I am doing everything to prevent this, but unfortunately there are factors that hamper even the strongest will. Israel is dying in front of my eyes, and I cannot help.[8]

Historical Documentation

To document Nazi barbarism and to preserve the history of life in the ghettoes, various secret archives were established. The most important, the Oneg

195

Shabbat (cover name: 'the festivity on shabbat eve') of Warsaw, was founded by the leader of Zetos, the young historian Dr. Emmanuel Ringelblum, who persuaded writers, journalists, economists, social scientists, and rabbis to contribute to the documentation.

In addition to a number of permanent workers, the archive commissioned others to investigate specific topics. Journalists reported on life in the ghetto. The leader of the health organization TOZ, Dr. Israel Milejkowski, organized a group of doctors to study the effects of hunger on the human body. Discovered after the war, their study was published in Warsaw in 1946. Others reported on education, on cultural life, on slave labor camps. Writers and poets gave their works to Ringelblum for safe-keeping. The archive's correspondents reported on the situation in other ghettoes. Ringelblum's diary, which he wrote in a kind of personal shorthand and apparently hoped to expand after the war, was published in English in 1958, in a cut and inaccurate version.[9]

The Oneg Shabbat workers were divided into two groups: a scientific group, headed by Ringelblum, which collected materials, and a technical group, whose purpose was to pack and hide the materials. In the summer of 1942, most Oneg Shabbat members were deported to their deaths. Ringelblum managed to hide in the non-Jewish part of Warsaw where he continued to write in his diary. His hideout was discovered in March 1944 and he, his family, and the Polish family with whom they lived were murdered. The archive was buried in the ghetto in three milk pails. Two of these were uncovered after the war; one was never found.

Parts of other archives, collected in Bialystok, by Mordechai Tennenbaum, the commander of the underground, and in Vilna, were discovered after the war. Although many of the diaries written during that period were presumably lost, many others survived, such as those of the Warsaw teachers Chaim A. Kaplan and Abraham Levin (available only in Hebrew), as well as others (see bibliography).

GHETTOES IN THE USSR

Jews in the USSR were living fairly ordinary lives in 1939-41. But their hope that the Germans would not invade Russia or fail to conquer it if they did was shattered with the outbreak of the German-Soviet war on June 22, 1941. On June 24, 1941, Kovno, Lithuania, was captured.

Kovno

A center of Jewish culture and education in the eighteenth and nineteenth centuries, Lithuania was, at the same time, the scene of tsarist persecution. Jews were expelled from various towns, and later, during World War I especially, the tsarist government expelled 120,000 Jews. After World War I, Vilna (Vilnius in Lithuanian), Lithuania's ancient capital, was annexed by Poland, and Kovno (Kaunas) became the capital. The Jewish community numbered 25,104 in 1923 and 38,000 in 1933.

In the early twenties, a democratic Lithuania permitted Jewish cultural autonomy and intensive commercial and industrial activity. An autonomous Jewish National Committee and a number of Jewish political and cultural organizations operated in Kovno. Five Jewish dailies were published in the early thirties. Hebrew and Yiddish schools, kindergartens and teachers' seminaries flourished. Many young people belonged to Zionist youth movements. Later in the thirties, however, the Lithuanian government became authoritarian and effectively abolished Jewish cultural autonomy. Moving to the Right under the influence of pro-Nazi nationalists, Lithuania experienced a rebirth of antisemitism. Jews were effectively debarred from government, and university education became difficult. In June 1940 when Lithuania was occupied by the Soviets, Lithuanian independence was forcibly extinguished, and in the course of Sovietization all Jewish trading and industrial establishments were nationalized. Jewish organizations were closed, as were all Hebrew schools. But the Soviets promised equality, and the gates of higher education and government service were opened to Jews. Therefore, although a part of the Jewish population suffered severely under Soviet rule and all Jewish cultural independence was denied, other Jews, especially the youth, welcomed the Soviet regime and the new opportunities offered. The Lithuanian population as a whole was anti-Soviet and Jewish entry into positions hitherto closed to them was effectively used for anti-Jewish and anti-Soviet propaganda. The fact that some 7,000 Jews were deported by the Soviets from Lithuania to forced labor camps (in the whole area occupied by the Soviets in Eastern Poland, former northern Romania—Bessarabia and Bukovina—and the Baltic Republics, 100,000 Jews were thus deported to the Gulags) was conveniently ignored; in fact, it can be argued that proportionately more Jews than Lithuanians were deported by the Soviet authorities. Yet when the Germans arrived, they were enthusiastically welcomed by a majority of the Lithuanian population.

From the morning of June 23 until the evening of June 24, Kovno was a no-man's-land. Groups of nationalist Lithuanians and armed criminal elements calling themselves partisans and freedom fighters controlled the city. They seized the opportunity to attack Jews, accusing them of handing over Lithuania to the Soviets. They rioted. They robbed and attacked Jews, killing many during the two days of terror. The atrocities initiated when the German army entered Kovno reached a peak on the night of June 25 when whole families in the poverty-stricken district of Slobodka were killed in a house-to-house murder march.

Throughout the first week of occupation Jews were arrested en masse. First taken to jail, they were then removed to the Seventh Fort, one of a series of nineteenth century fortifications surrounding the city. Ten thousand people were kept without food or drink, some of them in the open, others in the cellars of the old fort. Daily, groups of men were taken out and shot not far from the fort. Women were raped and then shot. On July 7 the surviving women were sent back to the town; 6,000 to 7,000 men were buried in large pits that had been dug by Soviet prisoners of war.

Lithuanian extremists, not German Nazis, committed the murders. Here and there some Germans took part, but the authorities described the massacre as a quarrel between Lithuanians and Jews. In actual fact, however, Nazi security police pulled the strings that made the Lithuanians dance. As Dr. Franz Walther Stahlecker, the Einsatzgruppe commander in the Baltic area, reported on October 15, 1941 to Heydrich:

> In order to fulfill the tasks of the security police, it was necessary for us to enter the large cities together with the attacking forces. . . . A small forward group

at whose head I stood myself, entered Kovno on June 25, 1941 The first action was to capture communist activists and communist material. . . . In the first hours after the entry of the forces we also persuaded, not without considerable difficulties, local antisemitic elements to start pogroms against Jews. In accordance with orders, the security police was determined to solve the Jewish question by every means and with determination. But it was preferable that in the first instance at least, the security police should not openly appear in this action, because the methods employed were extraordinarily harsh, and might have caused reactions even in German circles. It was desirable, outwardly, to show that the first steps were made by the local population on its own initiative, as a natural reaction to their subjugation at the hands of the Jews for decades, and to the recent communist terror. . . .

The commander of the partisans, Klimatas, who was specially recruited for this action, succeeded in organizing a pogrom in accordance with instructions he was given by our forward detachment which was activated in Kovno, without it appearing outwardly that instruction or encouragement had been given by the Germans. In the course of the first night of the pogrom, between June 25 and 26, the Lithuanian partisans liquidated 1,500 Jews, many synagogues were burned or were destroyed and a Jewish quarter with about 60 houses was burned. During the following night, 2,300 Jews were killed in a similar way.[10]

On August 7 Lithuanian partisans jailed 1,200 men. About 200 were later released; the others were taken outside the town and killed. Kovno Jews were ordered to move into the ghetto on August 15. On August 8, 534 Jewish intellectuals—teachers, lawyers, doctors—were taken, supposedly to do some special intellectual work in the city archives. They were transported not to the archives but to the Fourth Fort where they were shot.

When the Kovno Jews were ordered to elect a Judenrat leader (in Kovno, the Jewish Council was called the Ältestenrat), they chose Dr. Elhanan Elkes, a popular doctor and a Zionist. Although he refused at first to accept the job, he was persuaded by other community leaders and the intervention of a hassidic Rebbe, Rabbi Yakov Moshe Shmukler.

After the ghetto gates were closed, systematic murder actions began. On September 26, Jewish residents of one ghetto area were assembled in the square, where those fit for work were separated from those less fit. After two days, the "fit" ones were released; the others, about 1,000 men, women, and children, were transported to the Ninth Fort and murdered. On October 4 the whole so-called small ghetto was liquidated. Those who were artisans or members of artisans' families were released into the large ghetto, the others—1,500—were transported to the Ninth Fort. When the hospital in the small ghetto was burned down, its 60 patients and the doctors and nurses were burned alive.

Three weeks later, on October 27, the Judenrat received an order to assemble the inhabitants, without exception, in Democracy Square, for "control." It was clear that a "selection" would be made and that many would die. Some Judenrat members wanted to refuse to convey the German order. But an opinion expressed by the much venerated Rabbi Abraham Duber Shapiro was decisive: "If a Jewish community (may God help it) has been condemned to physical destruction, and there are means of rescuing part of it, the leaders of the community should have courage and assume the responsibility to act and rescue whoever they can."[11]

When the Jews assembled, the square was surrounded by German soldiers and 'partisans' armed with machine guns and rifles; on the hills surrounding the town large numbers of Lithuanians viewed the proceedings. At 9 o'clock in the morning the officials arrived: the security police, the Gestapo official responsible for Jewish affairs, Helmut Raucka, and the city administrator's staff, and Fritz Jordan, who was responsible for Jewish affairs in the civilian administration. The "selection" was made. The survivors were permitted to return to the ghetto; the others, more than 10,000 people, were escorted under heavy guard to the small ghetto to replace those who had been "selected" in the previous murder action. Next morning the death march proceeded through the Slobodka quarter, with Lithuanians and Jews looking on, to the Ninth Fort, where huge pits had been prepared. The Germans and Lithuanians forced the Jews toward the pits in small groups and mowed them down with machine guns. The bodies were covered with lime and earth. This massacre was termed the "big action" by surviving Jews. Mass murder then ceased for two and a half years.

The ghetto became a slave labor camp of nearly 17,000 inhabitants, less than half the original number of Kovno Jews. The labor office of the Judenrat was the most important institution in the ghetto. At first, all men between the ages of 14 and 60 were recruited. Later, women were added. Men worked six or seven days a week; the women worked three days at first, then five. By the spring of 1942, most ghetto inhabitants had been assigned specific jobs. Those without a permanent job were ordered to appear at the gate every morning to be assigned a temporary job. The foremen of the ghetto work-shops were Jewish, which served as a protection of sorts. Outside the ghetto, the foremen were Germans or Lithuanians. Those who worked outside the ghetto were escorted to work by armed Germans or Lithuanian 'partisans'. In return for their work, they received as much food as the Nazis decided to pro-vide, but it was not supplied on a regular basis. Often some rations were sim-ply withheld. The weekly rations per person were: bread, 700 grams (24.6 ounces), or about one small loaf per week; meat, 125 grams (4.4 ounces); flour, 122.5 grams (4.3 ounces); coffee substitute or tea substitute, 75 grams (2.6 ounces); and salt, 50 grams (1.7 ounces). Workers doing heavy work received an additional 700 grams of bread, 125 grams of meat, and 20 grams (0.7 ounces) of fats per week. Water and electricity were provided; taxes and rents were not required. No clothing was supplied.

Typhus and typhoid fever had killed tens of thousands in other ghettoes (e.g., Warsaw) in the period before the mass murder began. But in a ghetto such as Kovno, which was established while mass annihilation was already taking place, it posed a special danger because seriously ill people might be considered useless by the Nazis and killed. Typhus patients were reluctant to go to the ghetto hospital, for discovery by the Germans might result in not only their death but the death of all the patients, and perhaps the death of all ghetto inhabitants as well. Because survival was dependent on smuggled food, the isolation of an epidemic-stricken section of the ghetto would result in starvation. To keep the news of the disease from spreading, the patients themselves were often not told of the diagnosis. When forty ghetto inhabi-tants were stricken by typhoid fever, an underground hospital was estab-lished. Well camouflaged, it was never discovered by the Germans.

Established in the poorest and most backward area in the town, the ghetto had no sewage system. In the overcrowded ghetto, the latrine pits and refuse dumps overflowed. To alleviate the sanitation problem somewhat, the Judenrat set up a public bath, a delousing station, and a public laundry. The hygienic and sanitary situation improved and was actually better than the sanitary conditions in the town.

A grade school was opened, and a second one followed. A few weeks after the mass murder of October 27, 1941, the children presented a special Hannukka[12] program in the school.

At the end of February 1942, Nazis confiscated all books. Schooling continued, however, until August 1942, when any kind of schooling or instruction was forbidden. Although the two schools were closed, education did not cease. Small groups of children continued to study in various homes. Soon the Judenrat obtained permission to organize a vocational school to train young workers for the workshops. In addition to smithery, carpentry, tinnery, sewing, and so on, basic elementary subjects were taught when the Judenrat extended vocational school hours. A choir, a drama circle, and even a ballet group functioned under the auspices of the vocational school.

In the summer of 1942, the well-known musician Misha Hofmekler asked the Judenrat's permission to form an orchestra. Dr. Elkes was doubtful. An orchestra might be interpreted as an expression of joy, which in the ghetto conditions would be an abomination. Explaining that music satisfied an inner emotional need, Hofmekler got his orchestra. The Slobodka Yeshiva (talmudic academy), which for a time had served the Nazis as a place for killing Kovno dogs, became the concert hall. When the chords of the first concert were struck in August 1942, both the performers and the audience cried, tears not only of sorrow but of pride.

Religious observance continued in the Kovno ghetto. Although wearing a beard and sidelocks and showing other outward signs of religious observance were dangerous, many people did so.

A multitude of rabbinical decisions[13] were asked for and given: How should one treat Jews who had been ordered to tear up Torah scrolls and trample on them? Could the clothes of dead Jews be worn? Should those still alive praise God for having been saved?

On August 26, 1941, the Germans closed all prayerhouses. Soon, however, in defiance of the Nazi order, observant Jews reopened illegal prayerhouses to pray and study the Torah. The congregation of one prayerhouse opened in the hospital played hide-and-seek:

> On Yom Kippur, as the Cantor[14] and the congregation were pouring out their feelings in fervent prayers, word spread that two officials of the German town command—one of them a notoriously well-known work foreman—had entered the ghetto and were walking towards the hospital. The hospital was quickly informed, and as during the inquisition period in Spain, the signs of the great "transgression" were quickly removed, the Holy Ark was camouflaged, the candles extinguished, the prayer-shawls and prayer-books were put away, and the congregants were hidden in a special room. The two Germans went around briefly in the hospital and did not find anything suspicious. When they went, everything was returned to its place and the prayers continued to the end.[15]

TEREZIN (THERESIENSTADT)—THE "MODEL" GHETTO

The first deportees from Prague (Bohemia) arrived at Terezin (German: Theresienstadt), an old fortress town in Bohemia, at the end of November 1941; by the end of May 1942, about one-third of the Jews (28,887) of the Bohemia and Moravia Protectorate had arrived. The ghetto was similar to a concentration camp, with one important exception—here entire families remained together. In January 1942, 2,000 Jews were deported to Riga and others soon followed. By July 1942, the original non-Jewish population had been evicted, and conditions improved somewhat. But soon thousands of German and Austrian Jews arrived. In accordance with the Wannsee decisions, most new arrivals were elderly, many had military decorations from World War I, and many others were privileged in some way (see Chapter 9). They had been informed that they would be permitted to buy an apartment at Terezin by signing a legal contract that transferred their property to the Nazis. Shipped to Terezin, they lived in stinking cellar dormitories with wooden bunks, and starved. Their final "apartment": Auschwitz. The Nazis, obviously, had no concern for the words of the prophet Elijah to King Ahab: "Hast thou killed and also taken possession?" (1 Kings 21:10).

By September 1942, 53,004 people were living in an area of 115,004 square meters. During that month an additional 18,639 people arrived; 13,004 were deported to death camps; and 3,941 persons died. By mid-1943 Terezin housed 90 percent of the Protectorate Jews and the remnants of German and Austrian Jewry. Mass deportations to Terezin ceased except for a few small groups of Dutch and Danish Jews who arrived later. Deportations to the death camps continued throughout the period. From October 1942, all major transports went to Auschwitz. At the end of October 1944, only 11,068 inmates remained in Terezin. Of the 86,934 who had been deported from Terezin to Auschwitz, 3,097 returned at the end of the war. In Terezin, 32,497 had died of "natural" causes by October 1944.

Most Terezin inmates were assimilated, Czech and Western Jews. There also were small groups who had converted to Christianity and *Mischlinge,* children of Jewish-"Aryan" marriages. The Zionist-oriented and the assimilated Czech youth leaders developed a lively cultural activity in special lodgings set apart for children and youths. A children's opera (called "Brundibar") was written, composed and performed; wall newspapers were written. The SS controlled the ghetto, of course, and everyday supervision was in the hands of Czech gendarmes. The Judenrat had some leeway in internal administration. The leader of the Council of Elders was a Zionist-socialist, Jacob Edelstein. On November 9, 1943, he was arrested for disobeying the Nazis; he and his family were killed in Auschwitz. The second council leader, Dr. Paul Eppstein, was murdered on October 27, 1944, for unknown reasons. The last council leader, Benjamin Murmelstein, survived. Rabbi Leo Baeck, the former leader of German Jewry, was also an inmate.

The council was responsible for compiling deportation lists, supplying labor, distributing food, arranging accommodations, supervising sanitation and health, dealing with education and the elderly, providing cultural programs, keeping order in the ghetto, and exercising judiciary functions.

Most ghetto children under the age of 16 lived in youth houses where the morale was considerably better than in the adult housing. Despite Nazi orders to the contrary, regular schooling was provided by Zionist and Czech-Jewish assimilationist youth movement instructors as well as by some German Jewish inmates. The children's paintings that survived are ample proof of a spirit of active, non-violent reaction to Nazi oppression.

The many artists, writers, and scientists in residence provided a rich cultural life. Several orchestras and an opera group performed, and a theater provided light entertainment and satirical revues. Lectures and study circles were organized, and a library with 60,000 volumes was opened. Emphasis was placed on Jewish themes, which were something of a novelty for many of the inmates, who today, perhaps would be called marginal Jews. Performances of various kinds were held every week. Although religious life and observance were difficult to pursue, there were no official restrictions.

Designed by Edelstein to maintain morale, this bustling activity was used by the Nazis for their own purposes. At the end of 1943 when information regarding death camps began to spread abroad, an invitation was extended to the International Red Cross to visit Terezin. In preparation for the visit, larger numbers of inmates were shipped to Auschwitz to diminish overcrowding. Phony stores were opened, a phony coffeehouse, a bank, kindergartens, a school and the like. Flower beds were quickly planted. Forced to participate in the deception, inmates were thoroughly trained for their roles by the SS. Most Red Cross members allowed themselves to be fooled when they visited Terezin. Following the visit, the Nazis made a propaganda film about the new life that the Führer was granting the Jews. When the filming was finished, most of the performers—council members as well as ghetto children—were sent to die in Auschwitz.

Illnesses and epidemics took their toll. During 1942 the mortality rate reached 54.4 percent. The establishment of hospitals, with 2,163 beds, and a vaccination campaign, reduced mortality to 29.4 percent in 1942, and 17.2 percent in 1944.

As the end of the war approached, small groups of Jews from Slovakia and *Mischlinge* from the Reich arrived. With the approaching collapse of the Nazis, Himmler agreed to transport 1,200 Jews from the ghetto to Switzerland; they left Terezin on February 5, 1945. On April 15, 413 Danish Jews were shipped to Sweden. The population increased at the end of April, however, when 12,971 prisoners from various camps arrived, of whom 483 died before liberation. Of the 139,654 Jews deported to Terezin before April 1945, 16,832 were freed when the ghetto was liberated after the end of the war, on May 9, 1945. After treatment by a Soviet medical team, the last Jews left on August 17.

THE LIMITS OF UNARMED RESISTANCE

The kind of unarmed Jewish response to German anti-Jewish measures described above did not occur everywhere, of course. Even in Warsaw, for instance, not everyone was a member of a house committee or was helped by one; many children received no education, and many people despaired of religious solace. The same is true for other places. In many ghettoes, apart from the ones that were described here as having developed social, educational, political, and cultural activities, no such actions were possible. Thus, in the areas of Eastern Poland which had been annexed by the Soviet Union in 1939, the German murder groups killed off large numbers of young men and members of the intelligentsia immediately or shortly after they occupied these places. In many places a reign of terror and starvation began which made any kind of action outside of desperate attempts to keep body and soul together illusory. In the town of BrestLitovsk, for instance, which had a Jewish population about the size of those of Vilna or Kovno, very little could be done. The town, which today is on the border between Belarus and Poland, was overrun by the Germans on the day they invaded the Soviet Union, on June 22, 1941, and a few weeks later some 5,000 young Jewish men were arrested, transported out of the town and murdered. Without its young men, the community was crippled. The families did not know for many months what had happened to their sons and husbands. In November 1941, a ghetto was established, with about 17,000 inmates. The daily bread rations were progressively shortened, until in early 1942 they were down to 100 grams—one could not survive on such rations for long. In addition, there was forced labor for men and women for endless hours a day. In such circumstances there was no effort at educating children, no public religious observance, beyond a small circle of older men meeting at the dwelling of an aged rabbi. No youth movements were active, and social welfare was done, with tremendous self-sacrifice, as the survivors (nineteen out of 17,000) unanimously reported, by the Judenrat. As one of the survivors said—when one is hungry to death one does not play Beethoven, even if one has a violin and knows how to play. Surprisingly enough, there was, even under such conditions, a serious attempt to organize an armed rebellion. However, when the Germans finally came to murder the ghetto, in mid-October 1942, someone had betrayed the underground and the weapons and the hide-outs were destroyed; only a very few managed to escape to the forests.

A large number of other places had histories not unlike the one told here, though one must emphasize that each ghetto or locality was slightly different from all the others.

In many places there were Jewish Gestapo agents whose 'work' paralleled that of local non-Jewish collaborators—lost souls who saw their only chance of survival in serving their oppressors, and who were in almost all cases murdered by the Nazis once they had done their despicable job of denouncing others, telling the Germans where the hide-outs were, or serving in Jewish police units that collected Jews for deportation. Apart from the police (called 'Order Service', or 'Ordnungsdienst' in German), these agents may have been few, but they caused tremendous damage. The Jewish police were not made of the same cloth either (in a minority of cases they were actually part of various attempts at opposition or resistance); but in their majority they were the enemies of their people.

In the conditions created by the Germans it is surprising that unarmed opposition or resistance was as wide-spread as it was; but it was not and could not be all-embracing. There is no way of estimating the proportional weight of these activities beyond saying that they took place on a fairly large scale, but that in many places they did not. Even where they took place, they did not manage to do more than try to alleviate the life of the doomed. The main reason for that was undoubtedly the different objective conditions in which the death-throes of Jewish communities took place; but there were undoubtedly also localities or countries where unarmed opposition to the Germans took place without such conditions being present, whereas there were cases where despite there being conditions for unarmed opposition, it did not happen largely because, one assumes, of the personalities of the individuals involved. It is easy to form judgments a long time after these events took place, and one has to ask oneself: what would I have done in such a situation?

nine
THE "FINAL SOLUTION"

THE PLAN TO DEPORT European Jews to Madagascar seems to have been operative as late as October 1940 when 7,500 Jews from western Germany were deported not to the east but to France, an appropriate embarkation point for Madagascar. But deportation was simply not feasible. With the success of their upcoming Soviet campaign, the Nazis thought that they would have to deal with an additional 5 million Jews. Madagascar could not accommodate such numbers, and, in any event, the island was not under German control.

The United States, the only major western power which was still neutral until December, 1941, had not protested the treatment of Jews up to that point; nor had the Vatican. There seemed to be no objection from an international point of view to an intensification of Nazi brutality. However, these pragmatic considerations, while constituting necessary conditions, were not sufficient. What made them sufficient conditions was the desire to murder the Jews inherent in Nazi antisemitism. Up until early 1941, the Nazis—

with the possible exception of Hitler himself—were not conscious of the full implications of this murderous ingredient of their own ideology, perhaps because the practical possibilities of implementing it were not apparent; even if some of them were, they did not explicitly say so. Now, when the invasion of Russia would provide a formidable smokescreen for the mass murder of civilians, the non-human, demonic Jews could be murdered. Annihilation was the practical solution.

In March 1941, in planning for their Soviet offensive, Hitler informed his generals that the coming struggle against the Soviets would be an ideological war in which no mercy would or should be granted to the enemy: the war was to be a race war against the Jewish Bolshevik Soviet Union. In early June, the German Army issued the so-called Commissar directive, which ordered the execution of all Communist Soviet officials, and later another ordering the murder of all "communists" and Jews among the Soviet POWs.[1] In his postwar trial Otto Ohlendorf, the commander of one of the murder squads (no. 'D') established to engage in mass murder (the 'Einsatzgruppen', or Action Groups), testified that the order was delivered to him by SS officer Bruno Streckenbach in Pretzsch, in eastern Germany, where the murder units were being trained, in May 1941. It is clear now that there was no general order at that stage to kill all Jews. A consensus had developed to annihilate, first as many Jews as possible and, later, to kill all Jews that could be found.[2]

In a circular issued by Martin Bormann on July 11, 1943, Hitler said that when "the Jewish question is brought up in public, there must be no discussion of a future overall solution."[3] And Himmler said: "We have never talked about this and never will."[4] From this and other allusions, it would seem, therefore, that no general order to murder Jews was ever committed to paper, although it must be remembered that most of the SS archives were destroyed.

This question of whether there was a general order to kill Soviet and European Jews, whether such an order was given by Hitler, or whether what we call today the Holocaust was the result of a development by stages, and what motivated this development has been the subject of much historical debate. A school of historians developed a thesis known as the 'functionalist' interpretation, which argued that the murder of the Jews generally was the result of development of German society, from before the Nazis' accession to power and throughout the short and stormy history of the Nazi regime; that the Nazi regime, divided as it was into semi-autonomous and mutually antagonistic fiefs of major Nazi figures whose allegiance was to Hitler personally, developed impasses and blind political and economic alleys from which there seemed only one way out: increasing radicalization. Given a general ideological racist and antisemitic background, these impasses led the German authorities into a murder campaign against the Jews. The initiatives for the murder actions came, according to this school of thought, basically from the local chiefs. Hitler was no more than a legitimizing factor, but did not actively intervene in these matters as long as his obsessive radical, racist antisemitism was satisfied by underlings who executed the most radical anti-Jewish measures possible.

Another school of thought, known as 'intentionalists' have argued, on the contrary, that directives came from the Berlin center, from Hitler and Himmler, and from a core of ideological antisemites loyal to Hitler, and developed into a well-organized campaign of mass murder. [5]

In the nineties, both these positions became increasingly outdated. Archival material found in the former Soviet Union became the basis for a reevaluation of other, previously known sources, and has led to what appears now to be at least a partial solution to the question about the decision-making process related to the initiation of the Holocaust. It has become fairly clear that there was no dichotomy between a center headed by Adolf Hitler, and local initiatives. Historians have been able to show that the initiators of murders on a local basis (say, in the area of Eastern Galicia, or Lithuania, or Belarus (were sent to their high posts as SS commanders or civilian administrators precisely *because* they had proved themselves to be convinced Nazis and radical, racist antisemites. They fulfilled the expectations of those who had sent them: they proposed and activated the most radical, murderous measures in the full knowledge that that was what they had been sent to do. On the other hand, the center, in the person, mainly, of Heinrich Himmler, was constantly on the move to visit them in the areas conquered by Germany, encouraging them, listening to their proposals, occasionally giving them orders, and often prodding them to do more. The motivation was very clearly ideological, though of course pragmatic considerations were almost always put forward to justify the unjustifiable. Pragmatic considerations did indeed exist: the Germans decided, for instance, to starve out huge numbers of people in the occupied Soviet territories—a figure of 30 million to be starved to death was mentioned, before the attack on the Soviet Union, as a desired goal. These were to be, largely, inhabitants of Soviet cities; the food thus acquired would prevent shortages in Germany and feed the German Army in the East. Jews were not only, largely, town-dwellers, but for the Nazis the idea that Jews should be fed was absurd, for ideological reasons. Murder would solve the problem in its entirety. The overall starvation plan was not carried out in the end, but the Jews were killed. Another pragmatic issue was that of finding apartments for German bureaucrats, police, and military personnel. In a number of localities the reason given for the murder of Jews was that they had to be killed to make room for these German apartment-seekers. In the area of the Soviet Union, Jews were accused of being behind the menace of pro-Soviet partisans behind German lines (at a time when there were hardly any Soviet partisans at all. In all these cases which in themselves exhibit a total change from pre-Nazi moral values, the question why the Jews and not someone else should have been the target remains unanswered, but of course the only possible answer is that murderous antisemitism had become a matter of a general German consensus, and any practical issue that arose could be 'solved' by 'removing' the Jews. Thus so-called pragmatic, structural, and other such motivations were really secondary appendages to the basic motive: murderous racism and antisemitism.

In this development Hitler's role was crucial. He was indeed the radicalizing and legitimizing factor, and it has now become clear that he met with Himmler every few days (156 times, at least, in the years 1941 and 1942!), and received reports and, presumably (we have no record of the contents of these discussions) expressed views and wishes (Himmler indeed more than once referred to Hitler's 'wishes' and considered them to be orders with the force of law.[6] The Holocaust developed in stages (vague instructions interpreted as meaning that as many Jews as possible should be killed were translated at first, in June and July, 1941, into mass murders of Jewish men in the conquered Soviet areas. From the end of July women and children began to be murdered as well, so that the consensus developed that *all* Soviet Jews should be killed. This was perpetrated, at first, largely by the Einsatzgruppen, and very soon by Order Police battalions, special SS units and a large number of regular German Army units as well. How did this happen?

In the spring of 1941 four Einsatzgruppen were organized and subdivided into smaller units called Einsatzkommandos (Action Commandos) and Sonderkommandos (Special Commandos), a total of 3,000 men. Of the first four Einsatzgruppen commanders, two had Ph.D. degrees: Dr. Dr. Otto Rasch (he had two ph.D. titles to his credit) and Dr. Walther Stahlecker. A third, Otto Ohlendorf, was a well-known economist and lawyer, though he had no academic title. The fourth, Arthur Nebe, was a policeman. A number of lesser officers were also university educated. One was a pastor. An analysis of one of the Einsatzgruppen has shown that only 12.5 percent of the men were Nazi security officials. The rest were ordinary policemen or army soldiers, by no means known sadists. Transfers to other units could be

TABLE 9.1.
COMPOSITION OF EINSATZGRUPPE A*

	Percent
Waffen SS (SS troops)	34.0
Policemen	13.4
Gestapo	9.0
Non-German auxiliaries	8.8
Criminal police force	4.1
SD (SS intelligence)	3.5
Technical personnel and clerks	27.2

*Transfers were available.
SOURCE: Heinz Höhne, *The Order of the Death's Head* (London, 1969), p. 358.

obtained; individual soldiers who expressed a desire not to participate in the killings were transferred elsewhere and were not harmed in any way.

Each unit was to serve in a specific area: Einsatzgruppe A, the Baltic states; D, Bessarabia and the southern Ukraine, in liaison with the Romanian army, and later in the Crimea and the Caucasus; Einsatzgruppen B and C were assigned the areas in between. With the invasion of the USSR on June 22, 1941, the murder machine was ready.

The Soviet areas conquered by the Germans during the first weeks of the war were areas of dense Jewish settlement. Because of the speed of the German advance, only a proportion of the Jews there managed to flee eastward, but the previous deportation of Jews in those areas by the Soviets in 1939–1941 resulted in over 250,000 people from what used to be Poland, and an additional number from the pre-1939 Soviet areas to be saved by flight into the Soviet interior. Local initiatives of Soviet officials or army officers sometimes moved Jews to flee; sometimes obstacles were put in their way, such as orders given to Soviet guards in many places not to permit people from the former Baltic republics and Eastern Poland to enter pre-1939 Soviet territory. In the chaos of defeat in the early weeks of the invasion, no Soviet evacuation plan or policy appears to have been followed. Few non-Jews fled: a large proportion of the population, especially in the Baltic States and the Ukraine, received the Germans as liberators from the Soviet yoke. Had the Germans not treated them brutally, they might well have become active collaborators with Germany. All told, about 2 million Soviet Jews managed to survive, either by fleeing inland, or because they were in any case living in areas not conquered by the Germans. Close to 100,000 others from the territories annexed in 1939–40 "escaped" because they had been exiled by the Soviets to Siberia. As the German advance slowed somewhat after the first few weeks, the Soviets began evacuating factories and offices in places that the German army was threatening to occupy, and as many workers and staff were Jews, they escaped the German advance.

The annihilation procedure was similar in all German-occupied Soviet areas. In many small towns, all the Jews were killed immediately. Local populations were encouraged to murder the Jews—and appropriate their

TABLE 9.2

JEWISH POPULATION OF SOVIET TERRITORIES, 1940

Country	Population [a]
Bessarabia and northern Bukovina [b]	300,000
Estonia	5,000
Latvia	95,000
Lithuania (excluding Vilna)	155,000
Polish territory annexed by USSR	1.5–1.6 million [c]
USSR (pre1939)	3.1 million

[a] Estimated.

[b] Taken by Russia from Romania in June 1940.

[c] Including 200,000 to 300,000 refugees from Nazi-occupied Polish areas.

SOURCE: Jacob Robinson, in: *Encyclopedia Judaica* (Jerusalem, 1971) Vol. 8, pp. 889–890.

properties. Local collaborators were recruited as auxiliaries. In certain areas, particularly large towns, the victims were, at first, young men and the intelligentsia. Later, the opposite happened: the victims were selected from the old and the weak, thus insuring the temporary retention of a supply of those able-bodied people who had not been murdered in the first few weeks. But eventually, the laborers too were killed. In some areas, economic considerations temporarily postponed mass destruction, sometimes for up to a year. At the appointed time, however, the victims were forced out to previously dug pits or trenches where they were shot by machine guns.

The burial pits were dug near the towns or cities. When the Vilna ghetto stabilized at the end of 1941, it sheltered fewer than 20,000 inhabitants; a few miles away, in the woods of Ponary (or Ponar in Yiddish; in Lithuanian: Paneriai or Panierai), 40,000 Jews lay dead. The Minsk ghetto housed some 60,000 people in early 1942; nearby 20,000 were buried. From their ghetto windows, the Kovno Jews could view the Ninth Fort, where most of Kovno's Jews were killed.

Although systematic murder of Jews in the newly conquered Soviet

The Jews of the Western Soviet Union

Following their invasion of Russia in June 1941, the Germans conquered an area in which more than 2,700,000 Jews were living. Probably some hundreds of thousands managed to escape eastwards, into the unoccupied Soviet Union. But of the remaining, all but about 100,000 were murdered, many within a few days of the arrival of German forces. The massacres at Odessa, Nikolaev, and in Transnistria were carried out largely by the Rumanian occupation forces.

Some of the "precise" figures, as for Bobruisk or Mogilev, come from German statistics compiled at the very moment of the executions. Many of these figures, as for Simferopol, are for a single day of killing. The death toll for Minsk is that of three separate days of executions in 1941: one at the end of September, the second on November 6, and the third on November 20. At Smolensk the first to be murdered, in October 1941, were children, old people, and people too sick to do forced labor. Then, in February 1942, all women and all children under 16 were killed. Finally, on May 20, 1942, all the men were shot.

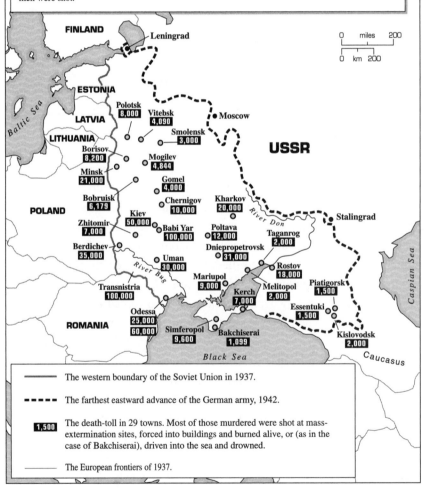

The western boundary of the Soviet Union in 1937.

- - - - The farthest eastward advance of the German army, 1942.

1,500 The death-toll in 29 towns. Most of those murdered were shot at mass-extermination sites, forced into buildings and burned alive, or (as in the case of Bakchiserai), driven into the sea and drowned.

——— The European frontiers of 1937.

territories continued until late 1943, with help of local collaborators, most murder actions had been committed by late 1942. The Soviet government published reports of killings, although Jews were not described as such but hidden under the definition of "Soviet citizens." In a memorandum sent on January 6, 1942, to all countries with which the USSR maintained diplomatic relations, Soviet Foreign Minister Vyacheslav Molotov described the "monstrous villainies, atrocities and outrages committed by the German authorities in the invaded Soviet territories." [7] The memorandum reported the mass murder of Jews in a number of places, chiefly Kiev, which is, perhaps, the best known Holocaust massacre and has been described in poetry and prose as the murder at Babi Yar, the wood on the outskirts of Kiev.

> A frightful slaughter and terror actions were committed by the German invaders in the Ukrainian capital of Kiev. During three days the German robbers shot and killed 52,000 men, women, old people and children,[8] mercilessly killed Ukrainians, Russians and Jews who showed their loyalty to the Soviet government. Soviet citizens who escaped from Kiev give a terrible description of one of these mass murders: in the Jewish cemetery of Kiev a large number of Jews, many of whom were women and children, were brought together; before they were shot they were stripped of their clothes and beaten. The first group destined for death was forced to lie on the bottom of the pit with their faces downward and they were shot with automatic rifles. Afterwards, the Germans covered the corpses with a little earth and put on top a second layer, and killed them as well with automatic rifles. Many murders were committed by the invaders in other Ukrainian towns. The slaughter was directed chiefly against unarmed helpless Jewish toilers. According to incomplete information, no less than 6,000 Jews were shot in Lwow, in Odessa over 8,000, in Kammenets-Podolskyi about 8,500 were shot and hanged, in Dniepropetrovsk over 10,600.[9]

The Jews of Kiev and other Russian cities were murdered not because they were toilers or loyal Soviet citizens but because they were Jews. The 33,000 victims in Kiev were all Jews, but later victims at the same site were Ukrainians and others. And from the Jewish community of Uman in the Ukraine we have this report:

In August 1941, German armies entered Uman. . . . In October an order was published providing for an obligatory registration of all Jews, warning that anyone not registering will be killed. At the same time a local police force was established from among the Ukrainian population. . . In accordance with a special order by the military command they began concentrating the Jews at special points, supposedly in order to send them to Palestine which, as the Germans said, had been conquered by General [Erwin] Rommel. A selection was made at the concentration points: doctors, tailors, cobblers and others were chosen. They were sent to work for the German army. . . . On November 6-8, 1941, "actions" were committed. Groups of Jews were concentrated in synagogues, in the "Red Army House," and in many other houses in the old and new town. The houses were set on fire and the people inside burned alive. Those who tried to jump through the windows were shot with automatic weapons. Notices were put up in the town warning against hiding Jews and encouraging ferreting out of people in hiding and handing them over to the German command. . . . During the "actions" 18,000 people were exterminated. . . . Jews who were caught after the action were mercilessly shot. Slowly the Jewish artisans were also liquidated. . . . The property was stolen by the Germans, and what was left was taken by the Ukrainians.[10]

The British intelligence services during World War II developed the capacity to decipher many German military codes. Between July and September, 1941, they were able to read radio reports from German Order Police units in the occupied Soviet territories. These regularly reported on massacres of civilians, occasionally identified as Jews, sometimes as 'bandits', 'partisans', or other cover names. At least one British analyst concluded that it was clear the Germans were murdering all Jews they could lay their hands on. As historian Richard Breitman has shown,[11] some of these reports landed on the table of Winston Churchill, Britain's Prime Minister. It is, however, doubtful whether the extent of what we today call the Holocaust could be deduced from this. First, because in the summer of 1941 no such overall decision had yet been taken by the Germans; second, because despite the British officer's report, these seemed like horrible local massacres, and not a planned action by a major state. It is even more doubtful whether any-thing could have been done at the time to rescue Jews in those areas: Allied armies were on the run, Western air forces could not at that time reach the Soviet territories, and there was hardly any point of warning the Jews them-selves: they experienced the massive murder actions daily. Any use of these decrypts of German radio message would have exposed the fact that the British were reading them, and would have very seriously hampered the Allied conduct of war.

At the Nuremberg trials of Nazi war criminals after the war, many mass killings were described. Mass killings also occurred in Odessa in the Crimea, at Romanian hands, where 144,000 civilians were murdered, mostly Jews, largely by burning and drowning. In the winter of 1941–2, the German advance was stopped temporarily, and some Soviet territory was reconquered. On reentering Soviet towns and villages, Soviet troops saw the destruction and heard survivors' reports of the mass murders. Reports of the massacres carried in the Western press were often considered either local atrocities or simply anti-Nazi war propaganda. In 1942, when the German army returned to the attack, the Jews in many of the Soviet towns conquered by the Nazis had fled, except where the German advance was very swift and surprised the inhabitants, as for instance in the Northern Caucasus, where the few weeks that the Germans were in the saddle sufficed to murder most of the Jews there. From later testimonies it becomes clear, however, that, locally at least, information regarding the Nazi treatment of Jews was believed.

By the end of 1942, probably over 1.4 million Jews had been murdered in the occupied territories of the USSR. The main ghettoes still in existence were in the western USSR, chiefly in the areas annexed by the Russians in 1940–41: Vilna, Kovno, Siauliai (Yiddish: Shavli), Oszmiana in Lithuania, Riga in Latvia, Minsk in Belarus, Lwow and other large towns in the western Ukraine. About 130 ghettoes existed in small towns until the end of 1942, decimated by selective mass murder at intervals, always on Jewish holy days (the Jewish New Year, Yom Kippur, Purim, etc.).

THE WANNSEE CONFERENCE

It soon became clear that the murder of European Jewry could not be accomplished by the methods employed in the East. In the West especially, the murder of Jews within sight of local populations might provoke opposition. Similar considerations operated against murder on German territory. Moreover, in Western and Central Europe presenting murder as a military necessity would be difficult. The East, under direct Nazi control, with the SS occupying an increasingly important position, was a more appropriate site. It is absolutely clear that the extermination camps were not set up on Polish territory because of Polish antisemitism—the Poles had nothing to do with these camps. Direct control in an area brutally ruled by the Germans where local public opinion had no weight was an important factor, but the main factors were the accessibility of railroads and the fact that most Jews lived in Poland and the adjacent areas. That German industrialists (e.g., I. G. Farben) wanted cheap, expendable slave labor available in areas that were militarily safe undoubtedly contributed to the decision to build the camp at Auschwitz, located in Polish territory annexed to Germany after Poland's defeat. In the East, too, because of direct SS control, secrecy could be maintained more easily than in the West. Everything connected with the "Final Solution," including the term itself, was carefully camouflaged. On July 31, 1941, Göring sent the following order to Heydrich:

> I hereby commission you to carry out all necessary preparations with regard to organizational, substantive and financial viewpoints for a total solution of the Jewish question in the German sphere of influence in Europe.
>
> Insofar as the competencies of other central organizations are hereby affected, these are to be involved.
>
> I further commission you to submit to me promptly an overall plan showing the preliminary organizational, substantive, and financial measures for the execution of the intended final solution of the Jewish question.[12]

Here "final solution" is used for the first time to describe mass murder (the term was used in a different context before that). It is addressed to Hey-

The Fate of the Roma (Gypsies) Under Nazi Rule

By 1939, many German and Austrian Roma had been sent to concentration camps. About 2,500 German Roma were deported to Poland in 1939-40 and 5,000 Austrian Roma to the ghetto of Lodz, from where they were sent to the death camp of Chelmno. On December 16, 1942, Himmler ordered the deportation of German and some other Roma to Auschwitz, where nearly 20,000 were murdered, more than 6,000 of them by gassing.

North Sea

miles 200

km 200

ESTONIA
1,000

LATVIA
5,000

HOLLAND
500

Baltic Sea

LITHUANIA
1,000

BELGIUM
600

WESTERN USSR
?

Bergen-Belsen

GERMANY
29,000

Treblinka

Chelmno

POLAND
?

Düsseldorf

Buchenwald

Gross Rosen

Sobibór

Babi Yar

Valogne

Auschwitz

Majdanek

LUXEMBOURG
200

BOHEMIA
7,000

Belzec

Natzweiler

Dacchau

SLOVAKIA
80,000

Nikolaev

AUSTRIA
11,200

FRANCE
40,000

HUNGARY
100,000

ROMANIA
300,000

Simferopol

ITALY
25,000

Zemun

Black Sea

CROATIA
28,500

SERBIA
115,000

Adriatic Sea

Mediterranean Sea

⊕ Mass murder sites where Roma as well as Jews were slaughtered.

◉ Camps at which Roma were forcibly sterilized.

⊕ Concentration camps in which Roma are known to have been murdered.

10,000 Number of Roma in 1939, country by country (approximation).

——— The European frontiers of 1937.

Plans to Implement the "Final Solution"

One of the macabre features of the numerical list of the Jews submitted to the Wannsee Conference was the fact that no figure was given for the Jews of Estonia, merely a brief note that Estonia was "free of Jews." This was true. The 1,000 Estonian Jews who had come under German rule in October 1941 had all been murdered during the three months before the Wannsee Conference.

The Wannsee Conference also specified the number of Jews in unconquered countries for eventual destruction, including 330,000 from Britain, 18,000 from Switzerland, 6,000 from Spain, and 4,000 from Ireland.

NORWAY 1,300

North Sea

SWEDEN 8,000

ESTONIA "Free of Jews"

DENMARK 5,600

Baltic Sea

LATVIA 3,500

BIALYSTOK DISTRICT 400,000

IRELAND 4,000

HOLLAND 160,800

LITHUANIA 34,000

USSR 5,000,000

BELGIUM 43,000

UNITED KINGDOM 33,000

WHITE RUSSIA 446,484

Berlin

Wannsee ⊗

Chelmno ⊕

GERMANY 131,800

GENERAL GOVERNM'T 2,284,000

EASTERN TERRITORIES 420,000

FRANCE Occupied Zone 165,000

BOHEMIA AND MORAVIA 74,200

UKRAINE 2,994,684

SLOVAKIA 88,000

FRANCE Unoccupied Zone 700,000 (including French North Africa)

SWITZERLAND 18,000

AUSTRIA 43,700

HUNGARY 742,800

ITALY 58,000

CROATIA 40,000

ROMANIA 342,000

SPAIN 6,000

SERBIA 10,000

Adriatic Sea

Black Sea

BULGARIA 48,000

GREECE 69,600

TURKEY 55,500

ALBANIA 200

0 miles 200
0 km 200

Mediterranean Sea

10,000 — The number of Jews mentioned at the Wannsee Conference, country by country and area by area, for eventual deportation, and subsequent death. More than 11 million people were thus marked for death.

⊕ — First Nazi extermination camp.

The Concentration Camps (selected sites)

As many as two million Jews were killed in their own towns and villages, some confined in ghettoes where death by slow starvation was a deliberate Nazi policy, others taken to be shot at mass-murder sites near where they lived.

Among the hundreds of thousands of non-Jews sent to the concentration or death camps were Roma (Gypsies), German, Polish, and other anti-Nazis, Jehovah's Witnesses, and homosexuals. About 100,000, mainly German handicapped people, were murdered in special installations.

In many of the camps shown here, so-called "medical" experiments were carried out, without anaesthetics, solely to satisfy the curiosity and sadism of the doctors. Hundreds of otherwise healthy "patients' were tortured and murdered during these experiments.

drich, who was the head of the Reich Chief Security Office, which included the political police and was also responsible for the Einsatzgruppen. The purpose of the document, as its date indicates, was to legitimize actions that were already in operation, for mass murders commenced after the invasion on June 22, some six weeks before Göring's order. Nazi documents often regularized actions after the fact.

Months passed before the SS acted on Göring's instructions, possibly because the Einsatzgruppen were fully occupied in Soviet territory. The first conference called by the SS in December 1941 to comply with Göring's order was postponed for "technical reasons." On January 20, 1942, the conference finally convened in a Berlin suburb, in a place called *am grossen Wannsee*. The participants included Heydrich, Gestapo chief Heinrich Müller, Adolf Eichmann; secretaries of the ministries of interior, justice, the Four-Year Plan (Göring's ministry), and the General Government of Poland; two top officials of the Ministry for the Occupied Eastern Territories; the undersecretary of the Foreign Office, and top representatives of the Party Chancellery, the Reich Chancellery, and the Race and Resettlement Main Office.

Heydrich reported on the steps taken to "solve" the "Jewish question." He reported on Jewish emigration from the German Reich, which according to his figures had reached 537,000 by October 1941. He then explained:

> In view of the dangers of emigration in time of war and in view of the possibilities in the east, the Reichsführer-SS and Chief of the German Police [Himmler] has forbidden the emigration of Jews. In lieu of emigration, the evacuation of the Jews to the east has emerged, after an appropriate prior authorization by the Führer, as a further solution possibility.[13]

Hitler's order is again invoked, this time by Heydrich, the person responsible, under Himmler, for the murder of the Jews. Heydrich centered his discussion on a statistical table that indicated a European Jewish population of 11 million (including those in neutral or Allied countries, e.g., Britain, Sweden, Switzerland, etc.)—all would be included in the "final solution." Heydrich continued:

In the course of the final solution, the Jews should be brought under appropriate direction in a suitable manner to the east for labor utilization. Separated by sex, the Jews capable of work will be led into these areas in large labor columns to build roads, whereby doubtless a large part will fall away through natural reduction. The residual final remainder which doubtless constitutes the toughest element, will have to be dealt with appropriately, since it represents a natural selection which upon liberation is to be regarded as a germ cell of a new Jewish development (see the lesson of history).[14]

Although Heydrich does not mention those unsuited for road-building—the elderly, children, many women, the handicapped—the implication is clear: they were useless and would be annihilated immediately. The workers would be decimated by "natural selection," that is, by working them to death. However, the resilience of Jewish slave laborers from the Polish ghettoes prompted the proviso that "the residual final remainder" would "have to be dealt with appropriately," i.e. killed.

Historical research has shown that the annihilation of the Jewish people was not decided on at Wannsee, which was basically a meeting to discuss the best ways of implementing a decision that had already been reached, most probably in stages, towards the end of 1941. It followed, in a way logically, from the mass murder of all the Jews in the Soviet territories which had preceded it.

It was clear that methods used by the Einsatzgruppen to kill 1.4 million in the East were not adequate to deal with 10 million. The methods were not discussed at Wannsee; however, the first death camp using gas vans went into operation on December 8, 1941, at Chelmno in western Poland, five weeks before the Wannsee Conference.

To avoid protests from Germans who might object to the treatment of elderly people over 65 from Germany and Austria, especially those decorated for bravery in World War I, Heydrich reported that they would be sent to the Terezin ghetto in Bohemia (see Chapter 8).

The *Mischlinge* were the subject of much debate. The more extreme Nazis thought that all issue of Jewish-German marriages should be included in the "final solution." At Wannsee, however, it was suggested that *Mis-chlinge* who were neither married to Jews, nor members of the Jewish community, nor "behaved" like Jews, be given the option of deportation to death camps or "voluntary" sterilization. Although no clear policy was adopted, experiments in sterilization were made and undetermined numbers of *Mischlinge* were thus crippled. *Mischlinge* included in deportation transports suffered the fate of the Jews. A number of "Aryan" spouses of Jews, mostly women who refused to leave their spouses went with them to the East and shared their fate.

The Wannsee decision was to remove the Jews starting methodically from the West. Like some other operative decisions of the conference, it was not implemented. The mass murders actually started in Poland. Lublin ghetto was annihilated in March, 1942; other ghettoes in eastern and western Poland followed later in the spring and summer. The Warsaw ghetto was decimated in July-September; Slovakian Jews were deported between March and September 1942. The first Dutch, Belgian, and French Jews were shipped to death camps in July 1942 (a first transport from France was sent to Auschwitz in March). Few were put to work on road-building. Those who were not murdered immediately were put into concentration camps, usually Auschwitz; others provided slave labor for such German firms as I. G. Farben and Siemens. The importance of Wannsee lies in the fact that at that place and at that time the entire German bureaucracy became involved in the conscious effort to murder a nation.

Adolf Eichmann, formerly the SS officer in charge of forced Jewish emigration in 1938–41, was now in charge of a sub-department dealing with Jews, of the Reich Chief Security Office (RSHA), which was headed by Heydrich. RSHA controlled all SS police and terror actions, excluding concentration camps and death camps, which were run by a different SS bureaucracy. Eichmann's department, designated as IV B4 for most of the period, was in charge of arrests and the transportation of Jews to death and concentration camps. Special SS advisers on Jewish affairs attached to German embassies in satellite states throughout Europe were charged with facilitating deportations and were responsible to Eichmann. Eichmann was aided by Franz Novak, the transportation expert, Rolf Gunther, his deputy, Otto Hunsche, and others.

An intelligent and devoted bureaucrat, Eichmann was convinced of the importance of the task entrusted to him. He and his team were extreme, radical, ideological antisemites, quite contrary to the image he tried to create when in 1961 he was tried before a court in Jerusalem, and quite different from the way the philosopher Hanna Arendt, who considered him to be a very ordinary, banal personality, tried to portray him. He testified:

> I did not take on the job as a senseless exercise. It gave me uncommon joy, I found it fascinating to have to deal with these matters. . . . My job was to catch these enemies and transport them to their destination. . . . I lived in this stuff, otherwise I would have remained only an assistant, a cog, something soulless. . . .
>
> I thought it over, and I realized the necessity for it, I carried it through with all the fanaticism that an old Nazi would expect of himself and that my superiors undoubtedly expected from me. They found me, according to their experience, to be the right man in the right place. . . . This I say today, in 1957, to my own disadvantage. I could make it easy for myself. I could now claim it was an order I had to carry out because of my oath of allegiance. But that would be just a cheap excuse, which I am not prepared to give. . . .
>
> To be frank with you, had we killed all of them, the 10.3 million, I would be happy and say, Alright, we managed to destroy an enemy. . . .
>
> I suggested these words. [" Final Solution"] At that time I meant by this the elimination of the Jews, their marching out of the German Nation. Later. . these harmless words were used as a camouflage for the killing.[15]

CONCENTRATION AND DEATH CAMPS

Internment camps for civilians who for some reason were considered to be opponents of a regime were not invented by the Nazis. The Spaniards had set up camps for civilians in Cuba in 1898, and the British kept Boers in South Africa who were fighting them at the turn of the nineteenth century in such camps as well. The Soviets established camps for potential civilian opponents after they established their regime. Yet none of these were quite like the Nazi concentration camps. The first such camps were established in early 1933 by the SA. With the establishment of the first SS camp at

Dachau, near Munich, in March 1933, however, the SA was no longer involved in the camp system. The first inmates were opponents of the Nazi regime, such as communists, socialists, liberals, some clergy, and others considered disloyal by the SS. Until June 1938, Jews were interned, generally speaking, as members of such groups. After the so-called 'Kristallnacht' pogrom in November 1938, however, the percentage of Jews increased dramatically.

In 1939, these major concentration camps were in existence—Dachau, Oranienburg (later Sachsenhausen), Esterwegen, Buchenwald, Mauthausen, Ravensbrück (for women prisoners). Mauthausen in Austria was designated a punishment camp, which specialized in working people to death or killing them sadistically.

From early on, the camps were also designed to provide an economic base for the power of Heinrich Himmler's SS. Economically, however, the camps were a dismal failure. The slave labor provided by the concentration camp system was cost-inefficient. So-called out-camps *(Aussenlager)*, branches of the main camps, were largely slave labor camps. Generally, three types of camps existed: transition camps, labor camps, and concentration camps. There were also special camps for German youths, holding camps for candidates for possible exchange, and so on. In the wake of the "final solution" decision, death camps were established for the murder, almost exclusively, of Jews, either as separate institutions or as divisions of concentration camps.

To the Nazis, chronically ill people, habitual criminals, and mental patients had no right to live. In their anti-humane philosophy they followed the thinking of some western scientists who suggested that it was an economically and socially wasteful procedure to care for such people, and they rejected the prevalent notion that social institutions existed, among other things, also to do precisely that, namely take care of the most unfortunate and helpless members of society. Contrary to the Nazis, habitual criminality was, and largely still is, seen by democratic societies as a social problem to be dealt with by means other than those the Nazis employed, namely murdering them. On September 1, 1939, Hitler signed a decree "granting" the mentally and hereditarily sick people the "grace" of death. The Nazis defined euthanasia ("mercy" killing—in itself a very controversial term) so that it meant the murder of the helpless and the social misfits. In special institutions, German doctors killed, mostly by gas, at least 70,000 German citizens (including a few thousand Jews), by August, 1941; the total number throughout the war has been estimated at over 100,000. Officially, the euthanasia program was stopped after August 1941 because of the intervention of Protestant and Catholic clergy; actually, however, the killings continued until the end of the war (and even later).

Some people who lost their jobs after August 1941 were transferred to the mass murder of the Jews, employing identical or similar methods. Trucks were converted into hermetically sealed buses. Exhaust pipes of the bus were bent and inserted into the rear of the vehicle. As the van moved along, the one hundred or so people crammed inside were choked to death. When the vans arrived at the burial site, the corpses were unloaded into pits and covered with a layer of earth. Hundreds of thousands were killed in this manner at Chelmno, in the west Polish territory annexed by Nazi Germany, not far from Lódz, which began operating as the first death camp on December 8, 1941. Camps established later used more sophisticated methods of industrial mass murder.

Three more such camps were set up: Belzec, in eastern Poland, opened in March 1942 to kill Jews from the Lublin and Lwów areas. The second camp, at Sobibór, in the Lublin district, was ready in May 1942. Jews from various Polish districts as well as Dutch and French Jews were sent there. Treblinka, 50 miles northeast of Warsaw, originally a punitive labor camp for Poles, was converted in July to kill Warsaw Jews and, later, Jews from other areas in Poland and Western Europe. The estimated total number of Jews killed in those camps: Chelmno, 320,000; Belzec, 500,000; Sobibór, 250,000; Treblinka, 840,000.

Other death camps were organized differently and in a sense had special functions: Majdanek, near Lublin, was set up as a concentration camp in the summer of 1942 to produce military needs by Lublin SS commander Odilo Globocnik on Himmler's orders. Globocnik also was responsible for Belzec, Treblinka, Sobibór, and the so-called Aktion Reinhard of 1942, the code name for the mass murder action against Polish Jews (named after Reinhard

Heydrich who was killed by Czech freedom fighters in May 1942). Majdanek thus became a mass killing center as well as a concentration camp. It accommodated 50,000 inmates, and in the course of its history, 200,000 Poles and Jews died there.

Although no mass gassings took place at Mauthausen (the gas chamber was small) many Jews, as well as non-Jews, died there in a process the Nazis called "extermination through labor."

In Belzec, Treblinka, and Sobibór, the victims were gassed in specially constructed, hermetically sealed buildings. The person responsible for the first two, Christian Wirth, and some of his helpers were transferred from the euthanasia program. In August 1942 a German Christian named Kurt Gerstein managed to get himself sent to Belzec as a gas specialist to find out what was going on. He gave his eyewitness report to a Swedish diplomat, Göran von Otter, in August, who sent it to Stockholm where it went unheeded by the Swedish Foreign Office. His attempts to interest the Pope's representative in Berlin, papal nuncio Cesare Orsenigo, and a Swiss consul in his report fared no better. Gerstein described the destruction process at Belzec:

> A small special station with two platforms was set up against a yellow sand hill, immediately to the north of the Lublin-Lemberg [Lwów, today Lviv] railway. To the south, near the road, were some service buildings and a notice saying: "Waffen-S.S., Belzec Office". . . We saw no dead that day, but a pestilential odor blanketed the whole region. Alongside the station was a large hut marked "Cloak Room" with a wicket inside marked "Valuables." Further on, a hall, designated "Hairdresser", containing about a hundred chairs. Then came a passage about 150 yards long, open to the wind and flanked on both sides with barbed wire and notices saying: "To the Baths and Inhalation Rooms." In front of us was a building of the bathhouse type; left and right, large pots of geraniums and other flowers. On the roof, a copper Star of David. The building was labeled: "Heckenhold Foundation." That afternoon I saw nothing else. Next morning, shortly after seven, I was told: "The first train will be arriving in ten minutes." A few minutes later a train did in fact arrive from Lemberg, with 45 wagons holding more than 6,000 people. Of these 1,450 were already dead on arrival. Behind the small barbed-wire windows, children, young ones frightened to death,

women and men. As the train drew in, 200 Ukrainians detailed for the task tore open the doors and, laying about them with their leather whips, drove the Jews out of the cars. Instructions boomed from a loudspeaker, ordering them to remove all clothing, artificial limbs, and spectacles. Using small pieces of string handed out by a little Jewish boy, they were to tie their shoes together. All valuables and money were to be handed in at the valuables counter, but no voucher or receipt was given. Women and young girls were to have their hair cut off in the hairdresser's hut (an S.S.-Unterführer on duty told me: "That's to make something special for U-boat crews").

Then the march began. On either side of them, left and right, barbed wire; behind two dozen Ukrainians, guns in hand.

They drew nearer to where Wirth and I were standing in front of the death chambers. Men, women, young girls, children, babies, cripples, all stark naked, filed by. At the corner stood a burly S.S. man, with a loud priestlike voice. "Nothing terrible is going to happen to you!" he told the poor wretches. "All you have to do is to breathe in deeply. That strengthens the lungs. Inhaling is a means of preventing infectious diseases. It's a good method of disinfection." They asked what was going to happen to them. He told them: "The men will have to work building roads and houses. But the women won't be obliged to do so; they'll do housework or help in the kitchen." For some of these poor creatures, this was a last small ray of hope, enough to carry them, unresisting, as far as the chambers of death. Most of them knew the truth. The odor told them what their fate was to be. They walked up a small flight of steps and into the death chambers, most of them without a word, thrust forward by those behind them. One Jewess of about forty, her eyes flaming like torches, cursed her murderers. Urged on by some whiplashes from Captain Wirth in person, she disappeared into the gas chamber. Many were praying, while others asked: "Who will give us water to wash the dead?" (Jewish ritual).[16]

A Majdanek survivor described the camp's routine:

You get up at 3 a.m. You have to dress quickly, and make the "bed" so that it looks like a matchbox. For the slightest irregularity in bed-making the punishment was 25 lashes, after which it was impossible to lie or sit for a whole month.

Everyone had to leave the barracks immediately. Outside it is still dark—or else the moon is shining. People are trembling because of lack of sleep and the cold. In order to warm up a bit, groups of ten to twenty people stand together, back to back so as to rub against each other.

There was what was called a washroom, where everyone in the camp was supposed to wash—there were only a few faucets—and we were 4,500 people in that section (no. 3). Of course there was neither soap nor towel or even a handkerchief, so that washing was theoretical rather than practical. . . . In one day, a person there became a lowly person indeed.

At 5 a.m. we used to get half a litre of black, bitter coffee. That was all we got for what was called "breakfast." At 6 a.m.—a headcount *(Appell* in German). We all had to stand at attention, in fives, according to the barracks, of which there were 22 in each section. We stood there until the SS men had satisfied their game-playing instincts by "humorous" orders to take off and put on caps. Then they received their report, and counted us. After the headcount—work.

We went in groups—some to build railway tracks or a road, some to the quarries to carry stones or coal, some to take out manure, or for potato-digging, latrine-cleaning, barracks—or sewer repairs. All this took place inside the camp enclosure. During work the SS men beat up the prisoners mercilessly, inhumanly and for no reason.

They were like wild beasts and, having found their victim, ordered him to present his backside, and beat him with a stick or a whip, usually until the stick broke.

The victim screamed only after the first blows, afterwards he fell unconscious and the SS man then kicked at the ribs, the face, at the most sensitive parts of a man's body, and then, finally convinced that the victim was at the end of his strength, he ordered another Jew to pour one pail of water after the other over the beaten person until he woke and got up.

A favorite sport of the SS men was to make a "boxing sack" out of a Jew. This was done in the following way: Two Jews were stood up, one being forced to hold the other by the collar, and an SS man trained giving him a knock-out. Of course, after the first blow, the poor victim was likely to fall, and this was prevented by the other Jew holding him up. After the fat, Hitlerite murderer had "trained" in this way for 15 minutes, and only after the poor victim was completely shattered, covered in blood, his teeth knocked out, his nose broken, his eyes hit, they released him and ordered a doctor to treat his wounds. That was their way of taking care and being generous.

Another customary SS habit was to kick a Jew with a heavy boot. The Jew was forced to stand to attention, and all the while the SS man kicked him until he broke some bones. People who stood near enough to such a victim, often heard the breaking of the bones. The pain was so terrible that people, having undergone that treatment, died in agony.

Apart from the SS men there were other expert hangmen. These were the so-called Capos [Kapos]. The name was an abbreviation for "barracks police" [actually, in most camps these were the foremen, of different nationalities, especially Germans and Poles, but including some Jews, nominated by the Nazis from among the inmates—Y.B.] The Capos were German criminals who were also camp inmates. However, although they belonged to "us," they were privileged. They had a special, better barracks of their own, they had better food, better, almost normal clothes, they wore special red or green riding pants, high leather boots, and fulfilled the functions of camp guards. They were worse even than the SS men. One of them, older than the others and the worst murderer of them all, when he descended on a victim, would not revive him later with water but would choke him to death. Once, this murderer caught a boy of 13 (in the presence of his father) and hit his head so that the poor child died instantly. This "camp elder" later boasted in front of his peers, with a smile on his beast's face and with pride, that he managed to kill a Jew with one blow.

In each section stood a gallows. For being late for the head count, or similar crimes, the "camp elder" hanged the offenders.

Work was actually unproductive, and its purpose was exhaustion and torture.

At 12 noon there was a break for a meal. Standing in line, we received half a litre of soup each. Usually it was cabbage soup, or some other watery liquid, without fats, tasteless. That was lunch. It was eaten—in all weather—under the open sky, never in the barracks. No spoons were allowed, though wooden spoons lay on each bunk—probably for show, for Red Cross committees. One had to drink the soup out of the bowl and lick it like a dog.

From 1 p.m. till 6 p.m. there was work again. I must emphasize that if we were lucky we got a 12 o'clock meal There were "days of punishment"—when lunch was given together with the evening meal, and it was cold and sour, so that our stomach was empty for a whole day.

Afternoon work was the same: blows, and blows again. Until 6 p.m.

At 6 there was the evening headcount. Again we were forced to stand at attention. Counting, receiving the report. Usually we were left standing at attention for an hour or two, while some prisoners were called up for "punishment parade" —they were those who in the Germans' eyes had transgressed in some way during the day, or had not been punctilious in their performance. They were stripped naked publicly, laid out on specially constructed benches, and whipped with 25 or 50 lashes.

The brutal beating and the heart-rending cries—all this the prisoners had to watch and hear.[17]

Auschwitz

Auschwitz was established in 1940 as a concentration camp for Poles, and in 1941 it was to become a camp for Soviet POWs. It became a death camp for Jews in 1942; in October of that year Himmler ordered that Jews from all other camps should be concentrated at Auschwitz. Actually, it was not one camp but a system of camps, divided from 1942 on, into three main areas:

Auschwitz One—the central camp where, apart from prisoners, the camp commander's headquarters and the administration and the Gestapo offices were located. It also contained some workshops.

Auschwitz Two—Birkenau, the death camp, which included four gas chambers. Auschwitz Three—Monowitz, a slave labor camp where, among other industrial enterprises working for the German armament program, the I. G. Farben Buna-Werke factories, which produced synthetic rubber, were located.

In addition, the Auschwitz camp complex included outlying camps, where men and women worked as slaves under conditions that ensured a high mortality rate.

From May 1940 until the end of 1943, Rudolf Hoess was the commander of Auschwitz. After the war Hoess was tried in Poland and executed at Auschwitz in April 1947.[18]

In September, 1941, a first gassing experiment took place, the victims being Soviet POWs and a number of sick inmates.

In his autobiography, which he wrote while in prison, Hoess described the process:

> While I was away on duty, my deputy, Fritzsch, the commander of the protective custody camp, first tried gas for these killings. It was a preparation of prussic acid, called Zyklon B. which was used in the camp as an insecticide and of which there was always a stock on hand. On my return, Fritzsch reported this to me, and the gas was used again for the next transport. . . . Protected by a gas-mask, I watched the killing myself. In the crowded cells death came instantaneously the moment the Zyklon B was thrown in. A short, almost smothered cry, and it was all over. . . . I have a clearer recollection of the gassing of nine hundred Russians. . . . While the transport was detraining, holes were pierced in the earth and concrete ceiling of the mortuary. The Russians were ordered to undress in an anteroom; they then quietly entered the mortuary, for they had been told they were to be deloused. The whole transport exactly filled the mortuary to capacity. The doors were then sealed and the gas shaken down through the holes in the roof. I do not know how long this killing took. For a little while a humming sound could be heard. When the powder was thrown in, there were cries of "Gas!", then a great bellowing, and the trapped prisoners hurled themselves against both doors. . . . The mass extermination of the Jews was to start soon and at that time neither Eichmann nor I was certain how these mass killings were to be carried out. . . . Now we had the gas, and we had established a procedure.[19]

Eventually, five gas chambers were built in Auschwitz-Birkenau (four of them in Birkenau). Between April 1942 and November 1944, in addition to a number of Soviet POWs, the gas extinguished the lives of probably up to 6,000 Roma ('Gypsies') in 1944, around one million Jews (new estimates range between over 900,000 and 1.25 million).

"Zyklon B" (the German commercial name of the gas), or prussic acid derivative, supplied by two civilian companies, Degesch at Dessau and Testa

The Design of Auschwitz-Birkenau Concentration Camp

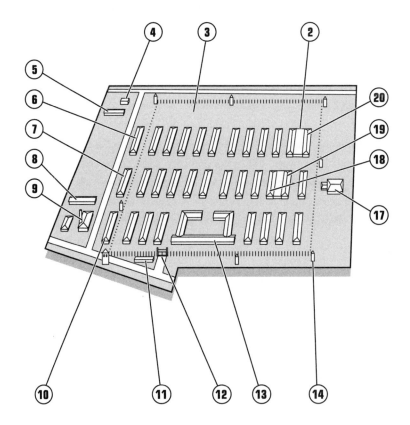

1. Gas Chambers and Crematoria
2. Black Wall
3. Living Barracks
4. Camp Commander's Quarters
5. Main Guard House
6. Command Post
7. Administration
8. Political Section
9. Crematorium
10. SS-Chief Medical Office
11. Block Commander's Room
12. Entry
13. Camp Kitchen
14. Watch Tower
15. Women's Camp
16. Watch Tower

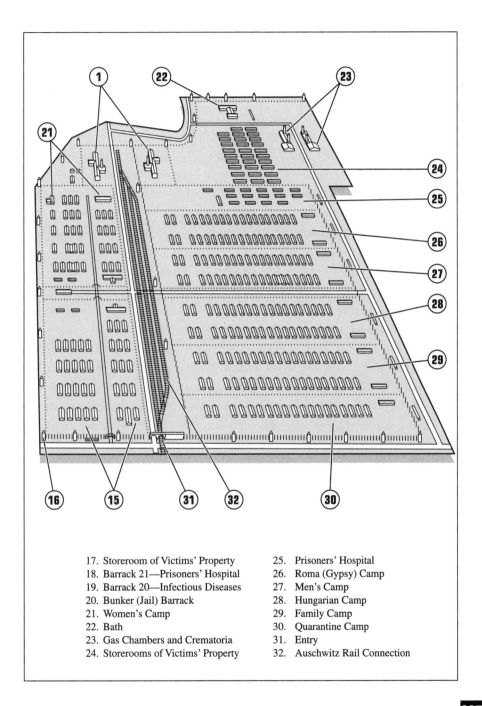

17. Storeroom of Victims' Property
18. Barrack 21—Prisoners' Hospital
19. Barrack 20—Infectious Diseases
20. Bunker (Jail) Barrack
21. Women's Camp
22. Bath
23. Gas Chambers and Crematoria
24. Storerooms of Victims' Property

25. Prisoners' Hospital
26. Roma (Gypsy) Camp
27. Men's Camp
28. Hungarian Camp
29. Family Camp
30. Quarantine Camp
31. Entry
32. Auschwitz Rail Connection

at Hamburg, was used. SS men dropped the gas, in crystal form, into the hermetically sealed room through a small opening in the ceiling. After a few minutes of intense suffering, the victims died. Sonderkommando (special unit) prisoners transported the bodies to a series of ovens where they were burned.

Later, to accommodate larger numbers, the victims were led, usually unsuspectingly, to the "disinfection baths," where they undressed and entered what looked like showers. Elaborate deception was practiced—people were told to mark the places where they had left their clothes so that they could find them after the "shower" and there were inscriptions "to the baths" on the wall. Hoess describes the process:

> The two large crematoria I and II [actually, II and III—Y.B.] . . . had five three-retort ovens and could cremate about 2,000 bodies in less than 24 hours. Technical difficulties made it impossible to increase their capacity. . . . They both had underground undressing rooms and gas chambers in which the air could be completely changed. The bodies were taken to the ovens on the floor above by means of a lift. . . . Owing to the wartime shortage of materials, the builders were compelled to economize during the construction of crematoria III and IV [actually, IV and V—Y.B.] and they were therefore built above the ground and the ovens were of a less solid construction. . . . The capacity of number V was practically unlimited, so long as cremations could be carried out both by day and night. . . . The highest total of people gassed and cremated within 24 hours was rather more than 9,000. This figure was attained in the summer of 1944, during the action in Hungary.[20]

Other sources estimate a higher maximum daily number of victims. In crematoria II and III, 2,500 people could be killed in thirty minutes. Because the ovens could not accommodate such numbers, the Nazis resumed the practice of burning bodies in large open pits, which had a capacity of 20,000. This occurred during the murder of Hungarian Jews in 1944.

The Sonderkommando, a special detachment of mostly Jewish prisoners, were forced to herd the victims into the gas chambers and helped them undress. The SS doctors and other SS men did the actual killing by introducing the gas into the chambers. Later the Sonderkommando had to extract gold teeth and remove rings from the bodies before burning the bodies in the ovens. They sorted the possessions of the dead in the so-called "Canada" area and sent them to Germany. Women's hair was used for mattresses for submarines. Children's clothes and toys and clothes of adults were distributed in Germany. Eventually, the Sonderkommando themselves were killed. Some committed suicide. The Sonderkommando could not be transferred to another detachment, for no witnesses were to be available to testify. Some managed to survive, however, among them Filip Müller, who was in the Sonderkommando from April 1942 to November 1944.[21]

Prisoners who became dazed and apathetic through starvation, thirst, maltreatment, and sheer exhaustion—little more than walking automatons—were called *Musulmans,* and were gassed. Ill persons in need of prolonged treatment were often killed by the injection of the poison phenol into their chests.

After May 1942, the need for labor increased. More war material was needed to combat increased Allied bombings. Himmler ordered a reduction in the death rate so that more workers would be available, but according to Hoess, Himmler's order was "mockery":

> Because of the increasing insistence of the Reichsführer SS [Himmler] on the employment of prisoners in the armaments industry, Obergruppenführer [General Oswald] Pohl found himself compelled to resort to Jews who had become unfit for work. The order was given that if the latter could be made fit and employable within six weeks, they were to be given care and feeding. . . . As far as Auschwitz-Birkenau was concerned, this order was sheer mockery. Everything was lacking. There were practically no medical supplies. . . . The food was completely insufficient . . . I do not believe that a single sick Jew was ever made fit again for work in the armaments industry.[22]

Thousands of concentration camp inmates were also used as human guinea pigs for medical experiments. Professor Carl Clauberg conducted sterilization experiments on women, in which a substance injected into the ovaries resulted in light temperatures, inflammation of the ovaries, and severe pain. Dr. Dora Klein, an inmate who was forced to serve as a nurse, reported:

> In accordance with what I could observe in block 10 [in Auschwitz, where the experiments took place], Clauberg obviously wanted to achieve temporary or permanent sterilization of women by a simple process, namely, the injection of a liquid of a certain composition into the ovaries. The treatment of women chosen for the experiments was harsh, even brutal, both at the hands of the doctors and the other medical staff. The women lived in a constant state of fear and uncertainty. They knew that they had to submit to some kind of experiments invented by the SS doctors, and that when their role ends—the role of guinea-pigs, they will be sent to Birkenau, where the gas chambers would be waiting for them. . . . I had the feeling that I was in a place which was half hell and half lunatic asylum.[23]

Dr. Horst Schumann of Hitler's Chancellery conducted sterilization experiments on 20- and 30-year-old inmates. Dr. Josef Mengele whistled operatic arias while "selecting" new arrivals for either the gas chambers, or the camp, including "medical" experiments. His experiments concerned twins and dwarfs. To test the effects of altitude on pilots, Jewish inmates were put into high pressure chambers; others were frozen to determine the best way to revive frozen German soldiers. Inmates were injected with viruses to test new drugs. "Medical experiments" were not limited to Jews; the bones of Polish women in Ravensbrück were removed from their bodies in transplantation experiments, and Roma ('Gypsies') suffered the same 'experiments' at Auschwitz as Jews did.. At public lectures on medical subjects, SS doctor Karl Gebhardt assumed "full human, surgical and political responsibility for these experiments."[24]

Many Jews and non-Jews tried to escape from Auschwitz, not only to save their lives but to inform the world of the Auschwitz horrors. A member of the Auschwitz underground managed to take three photographs of the crematoria compounds, including the burning of bodies in a pit. They were smuggled out of camp and sent to London. A Czech Jew, Siegfried Vítezslav Lederer, managed to escape on April 5, 1944. When he reached Bohemia, he told the underground in the Theresienstadt ghetto about Auschwitz. Rabbi Leo Baeck, formerly the leader of German Jewry and a member of the Terezin Judenrat, decided not to tell ghetto inhabitants that the transports to Poland meant death—he thought that such knowledge would only deprive them of a life- and morale-saving illusion.

Two Slovak Jews, Alfred Wetzler and Walter Rosenberg (Rudolf Vrba), escaped on April 7, 1944. Ernst Rosin and Czeszlaw Mordowicz followed on May 27. Both couples reached Slovakia. Wetzler and Vrba, both prisoner-clerks in the Auschwitz administration office, had taken with them a great deal of (necessarily inaccurate) statistical details of numbers of victims, but a most reliable account concerning the murder process and the camp generally. When they reported to the Slovak Jewish underground, a detailed thirty-page account of Auschwitz-Birkenau, including a map was prepared. The report, supplemented by the accounts of Rosin and Mordowicz and a report of a Polish officer who had escaped at about the same time, reached the Vatican and Switzerland in June 1944. The British and the Americans received the report, or shortened versions of it, via Switzerland and Sweden in the third week in June 1944. Similarly, Hungarian Jewry also received the gist of the report in April or May, and the full report in June.

In a letter written on May 18, 1944, the Slovak orthodox leader, Rabbi Michael Dov-Ber Weissmandel, demanded the bombing of the railroads leading to Auschwitz and the murder installations by the Western air forces. But nothing was done, although the Allies flew over Auschwitz many times in the late spring of 1944.

The population of concentration camps increased throughout the war. In Auschwitz there were 18,000 prisoners at the end of 1941; 74,000 in August 1943; and 66,000 in January 1945. According to German statistics, which may or may not be reliable, there were 95,000 inmates in concentration camps in mid-1942; 224,000 in August 1943; 524,286 (of whom 145,119 were women) on August 15, 1944; and 714,211 (of whom 202,674 were women) on January 15, 1945.

Of the Auschwitz inmates, approximately 70 to 80 percent were Jews. At least 30,000 non-Jewish Auschwitz inmates died during the war; in all the camps probably 500,000 non-Jewish victims died, including German opponents of the Hitler regime. Although they enjoyed a somewhat privileged status as compared to Jews and others, these German opponents of the regime were nevertheless subject to the death penalty whenever they clashed with authorities.[25]

The camp system was designed to kill Jews, either immediately upon arrival or after utilizing their labor. Their survival chances were somewhat higher if they arrived at the camp late in the war, because of the increased need for labor, or if they had special skills or were assigned relatively easy jobs. But for most—millions—that kingdom of death, the "Other Planet," as the novelist Yehiel Dinur ("Katzetnik") described it,[26] was an industrial machine designed to produce corpses.

The Nazi camp system developed slowly. Prior to the war, it was an instrument of terror used for intimidation ("reeducation" they called it) rather than for wholesale murder. During the war, however, releases from concentration camps became rare, and the purpose became twofold: murder, and exploitation of the victims' labor prior to death.

The commanders and sub-commanders in the camps were, in most cases, not sadists, nor were they uneducated. Many of them, such as the doctors and the engineers, were the products of the best Central European universities, which produced morally neutral, aseptic, "technically competent barbarians," to use a phrase coined by Franklin H. Littell.

The camp system was designed to deprive an individual of his/her humanity, of her/his capacity to behave in what in the West is commonly accepted as ethical conduct. And in many cases, the system succeeded. In an environment of extreme deprivation people fought to death over a better place to work, a better bunk, a piece of clothing, and a piece of bread. Mutual help, human behavior, the sacrifice of self ran counter to the all-pervasive camp system. The social habits of civilized society were nonexistent. The system was designed to have total control over the prisoners. But, because of the system's claim to totality, had only a few individuals kept their humanity, their ethical backbone, the whole system would have been a failure. What is amazing is that despite everything there were so many who were not broken.

Dutch Jews had a special treasure—tiny Torah [Bible] books. These Jews had arrived by the thousands and now there were scarcely a few hundred. But they kept to their fathers' traditions, even in Majdanek. I shall never forget a young, blond man from Holland who could not accept the order to be bare-headed. He got himself a tiny skullcap and wore it. During the most brutal exercises he used to fix the cap to his ears with thin pieces of string. The overseers sometimes saw this and beat him up severely.

Most of his Jewish countrymen acted in the same way. I find it difficult to report calmly on the two Dutch Jews who somehow got hold of Bibles and who pushed themselves into the middle of the columns marching out to work so as to be able to walk, read from the Bible, and avoid detection. I was told that they had found a few holy books in the crematorium and had hidden them in a place known to them alone. The barracks supervisors got tired of beating these stiff-necked people, and ignored them when they saw one of them at night, in the weak moonlight, burrow his eyes in the tiny pages and swallow each smudgy letter. I tried repeatedly to talk to them and call their attention to the dangers their actions were provoking. But they just listened silently, suspiciously, and then walked off without replying.

Their numbers grew smaller and smaller, but the few that remained, stead-fastly stood up to all kinds of suffering, as long as they could read a chapter in the Bible. I thought them to be happy, people who knew their days were num-bered and therefore did not permit the panic of hunger to uproot

in their hearts their last human feeling or divert them from the contempla-tion of the Day of Judgment. In those days of anguish and the fever of expecta-tion it so happened that I stood in the row next to two of them who were holding Bibles. They whispered to each other how to save the books when we would be taken away. And you were sorry you had no such worry, that you had no God in your heart to think about during your last hours. That you had no such holy con-cern for a book, while so many human beings were like dying candles.[27]

A young Jewish girl, Yoheved, managed to escape from the Bedzin ghetto to the "Aryan" part of town during the final liquidation of the ghetto. Passing as a Pole, she was sent by the Polish underground as a housemaid to a Gestapo family in Vienna. She spied on the Gestapo officer, was discovered, and was sent to Auschwitz as a Polish resister. Sent to the barracks (block) reserved for people awaiting execution the next day, she was recognized by a Jewish inmate, Yossel Rosensaft, who had been in the camp for some time and knew his way around. Rosensaft knew Yoheved's parents and tried to save her. He collected gold from the workers in "Canada," who sifted the clothes of the dead Jews and always found valuable rings, money, and so on, and offered it to an SS man who agreed to erase Yoheved's name from the execution list, give her a camp number, and transfer her to the women's camp. Today Yoheved is a member of an Israeli kibbutz.

Viktor Frankl, a famous psychologist and a prisoner in Auschwitz, wrote:

> I remember a personal experience. Almost in tears from pain (I had terrible sores on my feet from wearing torn shoes), I limped a few kilometers with my long column of men from the camp to our work site. Very cold, bitter winds struck us. I kept thinking of the endless little problems of our miserable life. What would there be to eat tonight? If a piece of sausage came as extra ration, should I exchange it for a piece of bread? Should I trade my last cigarette, which was left from a bonus I received a fortnight ago, for a bowl of soup? How could I get a piece of wire to replace the fragment which served as one of my shoe-laces? Would I get to our work site in time to join my usual working party or would I have to join another, which might have a brutal foreman? What could I do to get on good terms with the Kapo, who could help me to obtain work in camp instead of undertaking this horribly long daily march?
>
> I became disgusted with the state of affairs which compelled me, daily and hourly, to think of only such trivial things. I forced my thoughts to turn to another subject. Suddenly, I saw myself standing on the platform of a well-lit, warm and pleasant lecture room. In front of me sat an attentive audience on comfortable upholstered seats. I was giving a lecture on the psychology of the concentration camp! All that oppressed me at that moment became objective, seen and described from the remote viewpoint of science. By this method I succeeded somehow in rising above the situation, above the suffering of the moment, and I observed them as if they were already of the past. Both I and my troubles

became the object of an interesting psychoscientific study undertaken by myself. What does (Baruch) Spinoza (Dutch Jewish philosopher of the 17th century) say in his Ethics? "Emotion, which is suffering, ceases to be suffering as soon as we form a clear and precise picture of it."[28]

Not everyone became dehumanized. Finally, Filip Müller, who for two and a half years worked in the Auschwitz Sonderkommando, recounts in his testimony:

Now, when I watched my fellow countrymen walk into the gas chamber, brave, proud and determined, I asked myself what sort of life it would be for me in the unlikely event of my getting out of the camp alive. What would await me if I returned to my native town? It was not so much a matter of material possessions, they were replaceable. But who could replace my parents, my brother, or the rest of my family, of whom I was the sole survivor? And what of friends, teachers, and the many members of our Jewish community? For was it not they who reminded me of my childhood and youth? Without them would it not all be soulless and dead, that familiar outline of my home town with its pretty river, its much loved landscape and its honest and upright citizens? . . .I had never yet contemplated the possibility of taking my own life, but now I was determined to share the fate of my countrymen.

In the great confusion near the door I managed to mingle with the pushing and shoving crowd of people who were being driven into the gas chamber. Quickly I ran to the back and stood behind one of the concrete pillars. I thought that here I would remain undiscovered until the gas chamber was full, when it would be locked. Until then I must try to remain unnoticed. I was overcome by a feeling of indifference: everything had become meaningless. Even the thought of a painful death from Zyklon B gas, whose effect I of all people knew only too well, no longer filled me with fear and horror. I faced my fate with composure.

Inside the gas chamber the singing had stopped. Now there was only weeping and sobbing. People, their faces smashed and bleeding, were still streaming through the door, driven by blows and goaded by vicious dogs. Desperate children who had become separated from their parents in the scramble were rushing around calling for them. All at once, a small boy was standing before me. He looked at me curiously; perhaps he had noticed me there at the back standing all by myself. Then, his little face puckered with worry, he asked timidly: "Do you know where my mummy and my daddy are hiding?" I tried to comfort him, explaining that his parents were sure to be among all those people milling round in the front part of the room. "You run along there," I told him, "and they'll be waiting for you, you'll see."

. . . The atmosphere in the dimly lit gas chamber was tense and depressing. Death had come menacingly close. It was only minutes away. No memory, no trace of any of us would remain. Once more people embraced. Parents were hugging their children so violently that it almost broke my heart. Suddenly a few girls, naked and in the full bloom of youth, came up to me. They stood in front of me without a word, gazing at me deep in thought and shaking their heads uncomprehendingly. At last one of them plucked up courage and spoke to me: "We understand that you have chosen to die with us of your own free will, and we have come to tell you that we think your decision pointless: for it helps no one." She went on: "*We* must die, but you still have a chance to save your life. You have to return to the camp, and tell everybody about our last hours," she commanded. "You have to explain to them that they must free themselves from any illusions. They ought to fight, that's better than dying here helplessly. It'll be easier for them, since they have no children. As for you, perhaps you'll survive this terrible tragedy and then you must tell everybody what happened to you. One more thing," she went on, "you can do me one last favor: this gold chain around my neck: when I'm dead, take it off and give it to my boyfriend Sasha. He works in the bakery. Remember me to him. Say 'love from Yana.' When it's all over, you'll find me here." She pointed at a place next to the concrete pillar where I was standing. Those were her last words.

I was surprised and strangely moved by her cool and calm detachment in the face of death, and also by her sweetness. Before I could make an answer to her spirited speech, the girls took hold of me and dragged me protesting to the door of the gas chamber. There they gave me a last push which made me land bang in the middle of the group of SS men. Kurschuss was the first to recognize me and at once set about me with his truncheon. I fell to the floor, stood up and was knocked down by a blow from his fist. As I stood on my feet for the third time or fourth time, Kurschuss yelled at me: "You bloody shit, get it into your stupid head: *we* decide how long you stay alive and when you die, and not you. Now piss off to the ovens!" Then he socked me viciously in the face so that I reeled against the lift door.[29]

ten
WEST EUROPEAN JEWRY, 1940–1944

IN EASTERN EUROPE the Nazis felt free to engage in the most radical and murderous antisemitic policies. In Germany itself, fearing displeasure of the local population, they treaded very carefully. In Western Europe, however, the Nazis had to deal with a different kind of Jewish community. In Holland, Belgium, France, Denmark, Norway, and Italy, the Jews had acculturated to the political and economic life of the host countries. Jews spoke their languages, took part in their cultural life, and participated in their politics. As Jews observed their religious and ethnic traditions to various degrees, Jewish life in Western Europe was not dissimilar to Jewish life in Britain or America at the time.

FRANCE

Leon Blum, a French Jew and leader of the French Socialist party, was Prime Minister in 1936–38, and despite a strong French antisemitic tradition and the increasing influence of Nazi Germany, French Jewry enjoyed full equality prior to the outbreak of hostilities. The Jewish population was centered in Paris, Alsace-Lorraine, and broadly spread in other parts of the country.

Of the approximately 350,000 Jews in France at the time of its defeat in June 1940, 150,000 were French Jews proper, the self-styled "Israélites," whose ancestors had lived in France for centuries. The others they called the "Juifs." Of these, some 50,000 had fled from Central Europe between 1933 and 1939, 50,000 had fled from Belgium in May 1940, and 100,000 had immigrated from Eastern Europe from the early part of the century on. The old French Jewish element were largely middle-class businessmen and professional men. They were well integrated in French society and saw themselves solely as a religious community, represented by the Consistoire Central (central consistory), which had been set up by Napoleon in 1806. The "Juifs" were largely lower middle-class, left-wing, working people, who in part belonged to the anti-Zionist Bund, various Zionist-socialist parties, or the communists. Other "Juifs" were strictly orthodox, organized in small prayer communities according to their place of origin in Eastern Europe, and most of them continued to speak Yiddish.

Following the swift collapse of the French army and the French Republic in June 1940, thousands of Jews and non-Jews fled to the south, away from the invading armies. In the summer of 1940, 120,000 Jews remained in Paris; about 195,000 Jews were living in the south, including 30,000 Central European and 20,000 East European Jews. Many others were still in the army, or in refugee camps. The Jewish population was increased when Alsace-Lorraine was annexed by Germany and Alsatian Jews were expelled into France. Thousands managed to flee via Spain to Portugal, and in time escaped to North Africa and the Western Hemisphere. The Portuguese consul at Bordeaux, Aristides de Sousa Mendes, issued Portuguese transit visas to thousands of Jewish refugees in contravention of his government's instructions—perhaps the largest rescue action by a single individual during the Holocaust.

With the formulation of the "final solution," escapes were no longer tolerated. On May 20, 1941, Eichmann's department informed Gestapo branches in France and Belgium that "in the light of the final solution, which will undoubtedly be implemented, emigration of Jews from France and Belgium is to be prevented."[1]

The Southern (Vichy) Zone

The new collaborationist French government, under the aged Marshal Philippe Petain, established its center at Vichy in the south of France; its influence in the north was limited by the German military administration. The Vichy government embarked on antisemitic legislation as early as August 27, 1940, by abrogating a law forbidding antisemitic agitation. On October 3, Jews were defined as people who had at least two Jewish grandparents; Jews were forbidden to occupy public office; they were not permitted to serve in the legal profession, as teachers, in the armed forces, in banking, in real estate, and communications; their participation in other professions was limited. Ghettoes were not established, however, in France or anywhere else in Western Europe. But when an executive order was issued on October 4 providing for the arrest of all "foreign" Jews, 25,000 Central European refugees were sent to French concentration camps, along with Spaniards who had fled to France after fighting against the Franco regime. Large numbers of Jews, particularly elderly people, died from brutality in the concentration camp at Gurs. Even children were kept in camps, especially at Rivesaltes, but most of them were freed by 1942 through the intervention of French and American organizations.

On March 20, 1941, the Commissariat for Jewish Questions was established to oversee the execution of the French government's antisemitic policies. The first commissar was a veteran antisemitic politician, Xavier Vallat; he was replaced in June 1942 by an even more rabid antisemite, Darquier de Pellepoix.[2] On June 2, 1941, another order required the registration of Jews throughout France and the "Aryanization" of Jewish property, that is, its confiscation and transfer to non-Jewish ownership. Finally, on November 29, 1941, a French Judenrat was established. Called the UGIF (Union Générale des Israélites de France), it was charged, ostensibly, only with social aid programs. All Jewish organizations except for the rabbinate were absorbed into the UGIF, whose leadership was to be composed of eighteen members, nine each from the northern and southern zones, acting under the direction of Vallat's commissariat.

The traditional representation of French Jews, the Consistoire Central, opposed the establishment of the UGIF on the grounds that Jews who were French citizens should be treated as other Frenchmen, not separately as Jews. Their attitude implied that separate organizations for non-French Jews were acceptable. The representation of East European Jewry, the Federation of Jewish Societies (Fédération des Sociétés Juives), opposed the UGIF on the grounds that Jews should not be separated from Jews and that the antisemitic policy of the Vichy government had to be opposed. The other groups, the majority of old-established French Jewry, reluctantly accepted the UGIF despite their spiritual leaders' opposition. The UGIF also included organizations dealing with child care, especially Oeuvres de Secours d'Enfants (OSE). In both zones after July 1942, the security of children whose parents had been deported and, in time, that of all children, was a major problem. In time, the leaders of most of the organizations absorbed into the UGIF realized that the UGIF should be used as a "front" to allow rescue activities to continue, for the "front" provided not only legal status, but even limited financing from Vichy. This was especially so in the south where upper echelon Vichy antisemites who wanted to "productivize" the Jews by removing them from the middle classes and "returning them to the land" supported the agricultural settlements founded by the Jewish Scouts (Eclaireurs Israélites de France, EIF) who were members of the UGIF. In the northern, occupied zone, there was from the outset greater opposition to the UGIF, and the OSE and the EIF avoided handing over children to the UGIF whenever possible. Although much criticism has been leveled against UGIF, Vichy documents and testimonies of participants indicate that UGIF leaders used the UGIF as a legal cover and source of funds for rescue activities. The UGIF's president and his deputy—Raymond-Raoul Lambert and André Baur—were gassed in Auschwitz.

The Northern Zone

Jews in the occupied northern zone were subject to German military government and to such Vichy laws that did not contradict German military orders.

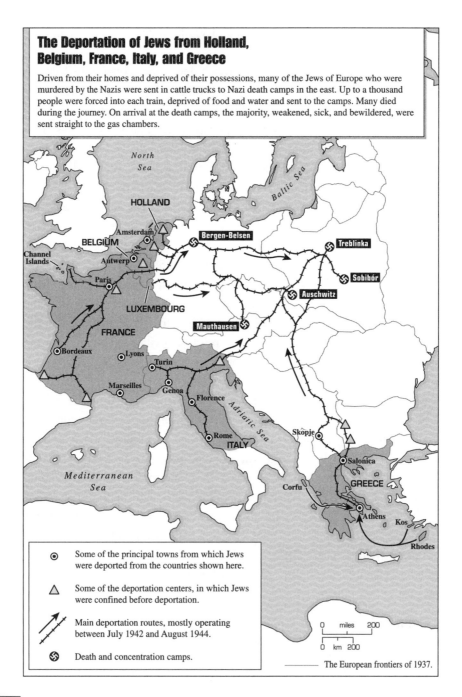

The Deportation of Jews from Holland, Belgium, France, Italy, and Greece

Driven from their homes and deprived of their possessions, many of the Jews of Europe who were murdered by the Nazis were sent in cattle trucks to Nazi death camps in the east. Up to a thousand people were forced into each train, deprived of food and water and sent to the camps. Many died during the journey. On arrival at the death camps, the majority, weakened, sick, and bewildered, were sent straight to the gas chambers.

North Sea

Baltic Sea

HOLLAND

Amsterdam

Bergen-Belsen

BELGIUM

Treblinka

Channel Islands

Antwerp

Sobibór

Paris

Auschwitz

LUXEMBOURG

Mauthausen

FRANCE

Bordeaux

Lyons

Turin

Marseilles

Genoa

Florence

Adriatic Sea

Skôpje

Rome

ITALY

Mediterranean Sea

Corfu

GREECE

Salonica

Athens

Kos

Rhodes

⊙ Some of the principal towns from which Jews were deported from the countries shown here.

△ Some of the deportation centers, in which Jews were confined before deportation.

Main deportation routes, mostly operating between July 1942 and August 1944.

卍 Death and concentration camps.

0 miles 200

0 km 200

—— The European frontiers of 1937.

252

In effect, Jewish matters were under the supervision of the German Foreign Office, through its ambassador in Paris, Otto Abetz, and the SS, who were acting in close cooperation with Abetz. The head of the SS in France, Obergruppenführer (Lieutenant-General) Karl A. Oberg, was in charge of the "experts" sent by RSHA, including Eichmann's aide, Theodor Dannecker.[3] However, SS control was weak, and it was the German Army that exercised political as well as military power and engaged in antisemitic activities.

An order on September 27, 1940, defined Jews in racist terms and forbade the return of those who had fled to the south. All Jews were to register and identify their businesses. "Aryanization" began, effected through the French bureaucracy. As of April 26, 1941, many occupations were closed to Jews, especially occupations in which Jews met with the public. A detailed index of Paris Jews, including their origin and their addresses and occupations, was prepared under Dannecker's supervision.

In May-August 1941, 3,100 Jews, mostly of Polish origin, were sent to camps at Pithiviers and Beaune-la-Rolande, and 4,300 Jews, including 1,300 French Jews ("Israélites") were sent to the camp at Drancy, which later became the transit camp to Auschwitz. In retaliation for an assassination attempt on a German air force officer, 1,000 French Jews, mostly lawyers and doctors, were arrested on December 12, 1941, sent to a camp at Compiégne, and later deported to the East. At the same time, 95 hostages, including 59 Jews were shot and a one billion-franc fine was imposed on the Jews. Young, healthy inmates who did not die of starvation at Compiégne, along with men from Drancy—a total of 1,112—were sent to Auschwitz on March 27, 1942—the first such transport from France.

Originally an internment camp, with a French commander and a certain amount of Jewish self-government, in which the sending and receipt of letters was permitted, Drancy's image about-faced when Alois Brunner, another one of Eichmann's men, took over in July 1942. Between July and the end of September, twenty-two trains, each carrying 1,000 people, left for Poland. The deportations began with a massive hunt for Jews in Paris on July 16. Although the Nazis had intended to apprehend between 22,000 and 28,000 Jews, rumors spread, apparently by French policemen, prompted many Jews to hide. The 12,884 men, women, and children who were caught were kept in a sports stadium (Velodrome d'Hiver), under the most terrible conditions, for some time; later they were transported to Drancy and eventually sent to Auschwitz. Small children were not immune.

> When the first tens of thousands of non-French Jews were rounded up in Paris in giant hunts, many thousands of small and very small children remained behind in apartments and on the streets. Before they could be tended by kind neighbors, 4,000 of them were collected and put into the sports stadium of the Velodrome d'Hiver. Children from the age of three up were torn away from their mothers, thrown on trucks. . . . Through the main thoroughfares of the city one could hear the screaming and the crying of the children and the long reverberating despairing cry "mummy, mummy". . . . Several days after the deportation of the adults, the four thousand children were loaded into cattle cars. Sixty children of all ages were thrown into each wagon. One pail with water was the whole furniture. No bench, no straw, no provisions were put at their disposal, and the children were sent away without any supervision. Then the doors and openings were hermetically sealed and after many more hours the trains slowly moved away. . . . A nurse, who alone among the many French officials present protested against this procedure and against the conditions in this transport, was given the following reply by the responsible doctor: "We normally expect about thirty percent loss during the journey."[4]

Between the first deportation transport in March 1942 and the last in July 1944, a total of 77,911 Jews were sent to Poland from Drancy. Fewer than 3,000 returned.

The agreement between the Nazis and the Vichy government, led by Prime Minister Pierre Laval, provided for the deportation of non-French Jews, although from the outset French Jews were also deported on occasion. In a cable to the head of the SS Security Police in Belgium on July 9, 1942, Dannecker reported:

> By arrangement with the French authorities we have been content to deport foreign and stateless Jews. French Jews have also been deported, but only as acts of reprisal. In due course efforts will be made to persuade Vichy to

deny French citizenship to masses of nationalized Jews, and that will permit their deportation.[5]

In August and September the Nazis were permitted by the French to deport more than 10,000 Jews from French concentration camps such as Gurs in the unoccupied southern zone as well. In the following two years, the SS deported Jews located by special anti-Jewish militia formed by the Vichy government, which, along with the French police force, tracked down Jews, including increasing numbers of French Jews. On the other hand, constant Nazi efforts to persuade Petain and Laval to deny French citizenship to naturalized Jews succeeded only in relation to those who became French citizens after 1933.

Beginning on May 29, 1942, in northern France, a yellow star inscribed Juif (Jew) had to be worn on the left breast of all Jews over age six. In the south the marking was not required even after the occupation of the southern zone by the Germans, nor were other anti-Jewish measures introduced, such as forbidding the employment of non-Jewish women in Jewish households or barring of Jews from public places.

Deportations of foreign and stateless Jews from Nazi-occupied France continued, as did the Franco-German controversy about denationalizing French Jews. As time went on, however, the attitude of the French population became more hostile toward the Germans, making the aims of the Nazis more difficult to achieve. The Nazis tried, unsuccessfully, through intimidation, to establish a kind of Jewish police force that would collaborate with them. They also released individuals from Drancy, promising them freedom if they identified friends and acquaintances. Unsuccessful in these pursuits, the Nazis began arresting inmates of the UGIF institutions, including children's homes. Klaus Barbie, the Gestapo commander at Lyon, cabled on April 6, 1944: "Early this morning the children's home at Aisier-Anne was emptied. A total number of 41 children aged 3–13 was seized. We also succeeded in catching all the Jewish working personnel comprising 10 persons, of whom 5 are women. No cash or valuables were found. I transferred them to Drancy on April 7, 1944 "[6]

On April 14, 1944, Helmut Knochen and his deputy, Brunner, signed an order to arrest Jews with French citizenship as well, except for persons in mixed marriages. On June 6, the Allies landed in Normandy, and in August France was liberated. Yet, as late as July, the Nazis and their French collaborators were still ferreting out Jews in hiding and sending them in special trains to Auschwitz. Others were murdered on the spot when transport to Drancy was no longer possible. The last Drancy inmates were scheduled to be shipped to Germany on August 13. But transportation difficulties intervened and when French and Allied forces liberated the area 700 Jewish inmates were found. However, as late as September, 100 Jews arrived in Auschwitz from Lyon by direct route four days before the town was liberated.

Algerian Jews Under Vichy Rule

In Algeria the Vichy government abolished the Cremieux decree of 1870, which gave local Jews equal status with Frenchmen, and introduced a number of antisemitic measures. On July 8, 1941, all Algerian Jews were required to register. On February 14, 1942, a General Union of the Jews of Algeria was set up to parallel the UGIF, and all Algerian Jews were forced to join. Dannecker in Paris had plans for shipping Algerian Jews to Auschwitz via Marseilles.

Similar measures were taken by the Vichy government in the French protectorates of Morocco and Tunisia. Thousands of Jewish refugees who had fled from France to North Africa in the wake of the French defeat in June 1940 were interned in slave labor camps by Vichy authorities, and a similar fate befell Jewish refugees who had volunteered for the French Foreign Legion in North Africa.

In 1940, one of the early underground groups supporting the Free French movement of General Charles de Gaulle was set up in Algiers by Joseph Aboulkar. Using a sports club as legal cover, the group met in the house of Joseph's father, Professor Henri Aboulkar, a respected member of the Jewish community. Contacts were established with the Gaullist underground in France and later with the American agent, Robert Murphy, with whom they worked in preparation for the American landings. Of the group's

800 members, only 400—including all the Jewish members—turned up on the night of November 7 and 8 when the time for action came. They nevertheless gained control of the city in a bloodless coup, taking prisoner the military commander, General Alphonse-Pierre Juin, and Petain's deputy, Admiral Jean Darlan, who was on a private visit to Algiers. The city's 11,000 Vichy soldiers and 2,000 militia were thus not a threat when the Americans landed on November 8. Had it not been for this successful coup, the occupation of the city by the Americans might well have been a protracted and bloody affair. Had the Vichy government managed to put up a real resistance to the Allies, hundreds of thousands of North African Jews might have been endangered.

The Italian-Occupied Zone of France

From 1940 on, eight provinces on the Riviera and in the mountains of southeastern France were under Italian influence. From November 1942 to September 1943, this area served as a refuge for Jews, because in November 1942, following the Allied invasion of North Africa, the whole southern zone was occupied by Axis forces; the eight provinces came under Italian rule, the rest under German occupation. In the Italian zone there were 20,000 Jews; after November 1942, however, Jews arrived in the Italian-occupied area in ever-increasing numbers. Not only from the southern zone but from the north, as far afield as Belgium and Holland.

The French police, especially the so-called Garde Mobile who searched intensively for Jews for deportation, were not allowed to function in the Italian zone because the Italians opposed such actions and all other anti-Jewish acts as well.

On January 13, 1943, the commander of the SS security police in France, Helmut Knochen, wrote to the Gestapo chief in Berlin, Heinrich Müller: "If the Italians are now taking all Jews of foreign citizenship under their protection it will make it impossible to continue to carry out anti-Jewish policy according to our conception."[7]

On February 12, 1943, Knochen again wrote to Müller: "The Italians live in the homes of the Jews. The Jews invite them out and pay for them.

The German and Italian conceptions seem here to be completely at variance ."[8] In yet another letter, on February 22, Knochen complained that when the Italian military authorities officially protested the arrest of 200 to 300 Jews in Lyon for deportation to Auschwitz the French police had to yield.[9]

Eichmann promised that the German Foreign Office would discuss the matter with Mussolini, and on February 25 and March 18 Ambassador Hans Georg Mackensen spoke with the "Duce" (Italian Leader). Proofs were submitted of Italian obstruction of French anti-Jewish actions. Even Gestapo chief Heinrich Müller was sent to Rome to persuade the Italians to conform to Nazi policies. As a result, the Italian government sent a police general, Guido Lospinoso, to south-east France as a special racial commissar for Jewish affairs. Müller reported that in the wake of "clear and definite instructions of the Duce, the Italian police sent Inspector-General Lospinoso and his adjutant, the Vice-Questor Luceri, with several other officers, to the Italian occupation zone, in order to regulate the Jewish problems there, in accordance with the German conception, and in the closest collaboration with the German police."[10]

But Müller was thoroughly mistaken. Lospinoso employed Angelo Donati, a Jewish bank manager who in World War I had been an Italian officer in charge of Franco-Italian military liaison. He was in close touch with Italian officers in the area and served as a contact between the Jews and the Italian military. Donati introduced Lospinoso, a devout Catholic, to Father Pierre Marie-Benoit, a Capucin monk, who persuaded Lospinoso to aid Jews out of religious motivations—Jews and Christians worshipped the same God.

In the friendly atmosphere of the Italian zone, Jewish organizations were able to aid refugees from the Nazi zone. A Jewish social aid committee issued identity cards to refugees and accommodated them in Alpine recreation hotels that had been assigned to the Jewish groups for use by refugees. Schools and vocational training courses were organized. A large proportion of the Jewish refugees concentrated in Nice until the September 1943 armistice agreement between Italy and the Allies.

Some historians argue that in refusing to denationalize the Jews, the Vichy government, particularly Pierre Laval, did not collaborate wholeheartedly with the Nazis. However, Laval fully collaborated in the deportation of foreign and stateless Jews and explicitly favored the deportation of children,[11] knowing full well what their fate would be. The French police and others fully collaborated in the antisemitic measures of the Vichy government as well. Most, though not all, Jews with French citizenship were saved. The number of Jewish victims in France would have been much greater if many Catholics and practically all Protestants had not aided the Jews.

BELGIUM

When the German army entered Brussels on May 16, 1940, the Belgian government fled to London. After signing a capitulation agreement on May 28, King Leopold III decided to stay in Belgium where he was treated as a privileged prisoner.

In Belgium, as in France, a military government was imposed, under General Alexander von Falkenhausen. In September 1940 a special department for Jewish affairs in the military administration contacted the parallel department in France to coordinate anti-Jewish activities. Before leaving for exile, the Belgian government had handed over the administration of the country to the general secretaries of the ministries, knowing that they would have to obey German orders insofar as they did not contradict the Belgian constitution or international law. Their bureaucratic traditions tied them to policies as expressed by the government-in-exile. Unlike the Vichy government, the local Belgian administration did not have an independent Jewish policy.

Prior to the outbreak of war, of the 90,000 Jews in Belgium—roughly 50,000 in Brussels, 30,000 in Antwerp and the others in smaller places— only 7,500 were Belgian citizens. The rest were foreign or stateless Jews, mainly East European immigrants and Central European refugees. When the Germans invaded Belgium on May 10, 1940, German citizens, including 8,000 Jews, were arrested by Belgian authorities and sent to France. During the fighting, tens of thousands of Belgians fled to France, including many Jews. Some Jews got as far as southern France, but many returned to Belgium in the summer of 1940 when no immediate anti-Jewish steps were taken. Toward the end of 1940, some 66,000 Jews were living in Belgium.

On October 28, 1940 the occupation authorities issued orders forbidding Jews to function as professionals and ordering them to register themselves, their businesses, and their property; all business transactions would henceforth require German approval. The Jews had to register, but only 42,000 to 43,000 Jews over the age of 15 complied.

With the exception of the diamond trade in Antwerp, which was largely Jewish-owned, Belgian Jews were not well-to-do. By the end of 1942, 20 percent of Jewish property had been transferred to non-Jewish ownership. On April 25, 1941, Jews were forbidden to enter public parks, and in the same month, Flemish supporters of the Nazis burned down two synagogues in Antwerp before a large crowd of onlookers.

In the autumn of 1941, anti-Jewish measures multiplied, again paralleling France and Holland. On October 29, 1941, Jews were forbidden to live outside Antwerp, Brussels, Liege, and Charleroi. On January 17, 1942, Jews were forbidden to change residence without official approval. On May 27, the yellow star was introduced (in France—two days later), and in October a curfew was imposed on Jews between 8 o'clock in the evening and 7 in the morning

On November 25, 1941, the Germans ordered the organization of a Judenrat, the Association des Juifs de Belgique (AJB), whose main tasks were to be social welfare, schooling (Jewish children were forbidden to attend general schools), old age and orphan homes, and so on. Before accepting the nomination to be AJB leader, Rabbi Solomon Ullmann, the chief rabbi of the Belgian army, received permission from the government-in-exile. Because Belgian municipalities refused to distribute the yellow star, the task was delegated to the AJB.

People were first deported to forced labor camps located in Belgium or in northern France (a section of northern France came under the jurisdiction of the German military administration in Belgium). A detention camp at Malines was converted subsequently into a transit camp for Auschwitz, paralleling Drancy in France. The AJB decided in July 1942 to send the following call for "labor duty in Germany" to Jews who had been designated by the Nazis, and who subsequently were sent to Auschwitz:

> The occupation authorities have transmitted to us today a call up order on your name for forced labor. The Association des Juifs de Belgique has been told to pass the order on to you as soon as possible. The authorities have assured us that this is really a matter of labor service and not of deportation. The harsh events of recent days force us to turn your attention to the fact that refusal to obey the order for labor service might bring with it serious consequences both to your family and to the Jewish population as a whole.[12]

Although it was not known that "forced labor" was a euphemism for ultimate death, the deportees might expect, at least, that conditions would be harsh, taxing, both physically and mentally, to even the strongest.

On August 29, 1942, a member of the AJB who was known to be a Gestapo collaborator was killed by a young Jew. The Nazis complained that the AJB was not collaborating sufficiently in preparing the "labor" call-up and threatened the wholesale deportation of Belgian Jewry. Ullmann and four other AJB members were arrested and interned at Breendonk, a camp for suspected communists, hostages, and other Nazi enemies. Later, two of the AJB members were sent to Auschwitz. Jews who survived the hard labor, starvation, cold, lack of medical attention, and torture at Breendonk were usually transferred to Malines, the transit point to Auschwitz.

The first transport from Malines to Auschwitz left on August 4, 1942. Although the ultimate destination of the transport was unknown, many Jews refused to obey the "invitation" to go to Malines and went into hiding because of the propaganda issued by the Jewish underground. Nevertheless, as of September 15, 1942, 10,000 Jews had been sent in ten trains, each carrying 1,000 men, women, and children, to the death camps. Trains became less frequent after September because of Jewish refusal to report. At first exempted, Jews who were Belgian citizens were included as well toward the end, despite a Nazi promise to the contrary given to Queen-Mother Elizabeth. As of July 1944 twenty-eight trains left Malines. Of the 25,437 deportees, 1,276 returned after the war.

More than half the Jewish population of Belgium survived the war, largely because of the help of the gentile population and the activities of various Jewish underground groups.

HOLLAND

On May 13, 1940, Queen Wilhelmina and the government fled to London; on May 14, the Netherlands fell to the Nazis. As in Belgium, secretaries-general of various ministries continued to carry on the day-to-day administration of the country. On May 21, Artur Seyss-Inquart, until then deputy governor under Hans Frank of the General Government in Poland, arrived in Holland as the Reichskomissar, the new Nazi ruler. The Nazi attitude toward Holland was different from their attitude toward Belgium and France. Seen as a Germanic country, Holland would sooner or later become part of Greater Germany—the elimination of the Jewish element was urgent, therefore, and had to be effected as it would be in Germany itself.

Of the 140,000 Jews in Holland at the time of the German occupation, more than 110,000 were Dutch; the others were refugees, mostly from Germany. About 80,000 Jews were living in Amsterdam. About half of them were engaged in industry and trade, and 5 percent were in the professions. Some 40,000 Jewish workers, mainly stevedores, sailors, and other harbor workers, lived in the slum sections near the harbor.

Although most Dutch Jews were of Ashkenazic (Central or East European) origin, 5,000 were Sephardic Jews, descendants of Spanish and Portuguese Jews who had come to the Netherlands after the expulsion of Jews from Spain in 1492. Dutch Jewry was organized in Ashkenazic and Sephardic synagogue associations, and a special committee, led by Professor David Cohen, a classical scholar, had looked after Jewish refugees since 1933. More than twenty Jewish newspapers (mostly in Dutch) were published, and a small Zionist movement was active. Assimilated into Dutch society, despite strong anti-Jewish sentiments among the more conservatively inclined parts of the population, Jews enjoyed complete equality, received financial support from the government for some institutions, and were active in the social and political life of the country. A decreasing birthrate and a high rate of out-marriage were threatening the future of a community that was both firmly Dutch and firmly Jewish.

On August 31, 1940, Jewish ritual slaughter was forbidden by the Nazis. On October 22, all Jewish businesses were required to register, and all Jewish financial holdings, privately and in banks, were to be declared. Jews were defined in racist terms. On January 10, 1941, Jews were required to register as "full" Jews or *Mischlinge*. Hans Rauter, the SS chief in Holland, and his boss, Seyss-Inquart, ordered the organization of a Judenrat (Dutch: Joodse Raad) to keep order in the Jewish Quarter, on February 12, after violent clashes between Jews and members of the Dutch Nazi party in the working-class slums of Amsterdam. A second clash, between an SS patrol and a Jew in another area of Amsterdam, provoked the arrest of 400 young Jewish men who were sent to Mauthausen concentration camp in Austria where they were killed.

As a result of these Nazi actions, Dutch workers called a general strike on February 25 in Amsterdam, which spread to other towns as well. Frightened by Nazi threats, the Judenrat asked the workers to stop the strike. Thus, the Judenrat aided the Nazis in suppressing the strike—the only massive non-Jewish action in Europe in support of Jews during the Nazi era.

An alternative Jewish group was led by Lodewijk Visser, the former president of the Dutch Supreme Court who was removed by the Nazis for being a Jew. With others, predominantly Zionists, he established a Jewish Coordination Committee, which declared that as Dutch citizens the Jews should have no direct contact with the Germans. To prevent the establishment of the Judenrat and to force Dutch officials to take a stand, Visser's committee wanted Nazi requests to be transmitted through the Dutch secretaries-general. However, Professor David Cohen, who was also a Zionist and originally a member of Visser's committee, broke with Visser and, along with a respected diamond merchant, Abraham Asscher, established the Judenrat. With the Jewish leadership split and with Nazi backing, Cohen soon gained control over the community. Visser died in the Hague on February 17, 1942, a disappointed and bitter opponent of the Judenrat and its works.[13] On May 12, 1941, the Nazis began the "Aryanization" of Jewish enterprises, and over the next two years, all Jewish property, with the exception of wedding rings and gold teeth, fell to the Nazis. Free travel was forbidden, as well as participation in almost all occupations. To isolate Jews from their non-Jewish environment, in August 1941 Jewish children were forbidden to learn in Dutch schools. In 1941, too, a Central Office for Jewish Emigration—later to organize the "emigration" of Jews to the death camps—was organized, headed by SS officer Ferdinand Aus der Fünten.

In January 1942 forced labor camps were set up in Holland, and Jews were crowded into the downtown area (ghetto) of Amsterdam. On April 29 the yellow star was introduced.

The deportations of Dutch Jews began in July 1942 and ended, in effect, in September 1943, though the remnants were deported in 1944. The main transit camp was at Westerbork, and a secondary camp was at Vught. In September 1943, the remaining 5,000 Jews, including Cohen and Asscher, were sent to the "privileged" Theresienstadt ghetto and survived the war. A few privileged Jews and most *Mischlinge* remained, but even many of these were deported early in 1944.

Most deportations commenced at Westerbork, usually on a Tuesday, when a train left for Auschwitz or Sobibór. Although the Judenrat cooperated with the Nazis, the Jewish population generally tried to evade the Nazi net. As early as August 13, 1942, SS officer Otto Bene reported that the Jews seem "to have become wise to the true meaning of labor conscription for the East and have ceased to report" for deportation.[14] With the help of their neighbors, 24,000 Jews went into hiding. Hiding was not easy in Holland—small houses without cellars (because of the prevalence of water under houses), land without hills or forests, and the orderly prewar police system made hiding extremely difficult. Of the 24,000 Jews underground, about two-thirds survived; the others, like Anne Frank, whose diary became famous after the war, were found, usually with the help of Dutch Nazis, who formed almost 10 percent of the Dutch population. Much of the Dutch bureaucracy, and the Dutch police, collaborated with the Germans.

Of the 103,000 Jews deported from Holland, 5,540 returned. In Holland, because of direct SS rule, a spineless Judenrat, Dutch Nazis, many collaborators, and difficult topographical conditions, 75 percent of the Dutch Jewish population perished, as compared with less than 30 percent of French Jews and 34 percent of Belgian Jews.

eleven
RESISTANCE

HENRI MICHEL, one of the most important historians of anti-Nazi resistance, wrote: "Self-respect dictated that one should not yield to the blandishments of collaboration."[1] But in the case of the Holocaust, no blandishments were offered. The smuggling of food necessary to survival was punishable by death, and the exercise of the right to life itself was considered a capital crime. The smuggling of food, therefore, became an act of resistance. In a dehumanizing environment, the maintenance of morale by cultural and educational activities was equally a form of resistance. During the Holocaust, resistance was any *group* action consciously taken in opposition to known or surmised laws, actions, or intentions directed against the Jews by the Nazis or their supporters.[2] There was, of course, a great deal of individual resistance as well; but that is difficult to define or analyze. One simply has to take it into account as well, without attempting to subsume it under some academic definition.

Open resistance was extremely difficult. Isolated from each other, especially in Eastern Europe, by both the Nazis and the largely indifferent or hostile local non-Jewish population, Jewish communities could accomplish little concerted activity. Annihilation, starvation, the rending apart of families, caused a weakening of the social fabric. No government-in-exile supported Jewish resistance, no arms were dropped from the sky, no recognition was given by the Western world to even the possibility of Jewish resistance. In the prewar Polish army, to all intents and purposes, no Jews were among the higher officer ranks; there was no access to arms caches; no cadres of noncommissioned Jewish officers existed. Even the belief in the possibility of resistance had to decline under the circumstances prevailing in Eastern Europe. In addition, the concept of annihilation was inconceivable to the Jews. Thousands of Jews died disbelieving what was going on before their very eyes. Elie Wiesel, author and survivor, wrote:

> We did not yet know which was the better side, right or left; which road led to prison and which to the crematory. But for a moment I was happy, I was near my father. Our procession continued to move slowly forward.
>
> Another prisoner came up to us:
>
> "Satisfied?"
>
> "Yes," someone replied.
>
> "Poor devils, you're going to the crematorium." He seemed to be telling the truth. Not far from us, flames were leaping from a ditch, gigantic flames. They were burning something. A lorry drew up at the pit and delivered its load—little children. Babies! Yes, I saw it—saw it with my own eyes . . . those children in the flames . . . I pinched my face. Was I still alive? Was I awake? I could not believe it. How could it be possible for them to burn people, children . . .and . . . my father's voice drew me from my thoughts: "It's a shame . . . a shame that you could not go with your mother. . . . I saw several boys of your age going with their mothers. . . ." My forehead was bathed in cold sweat. But I told him that I did not believe that they could burn people in our age, that humanity could never tolerate it. . . . "Humanity? Humanity is not concerned with us. Today, anything is allowed. Anything is possible, even these crematories."[3]

Jewish Revolts 1942–1945

Despite the overwhelming military strength of the German forces, many Jews, while weakened by hunger and terrorized by Nazi brutality, nevertheless rose in revolt against their fate, not only in many of the Ghettoes in which they were forcibly confined, but even in the concentration camps themselves, snatching from the very gates of death the slender possibility of survival.

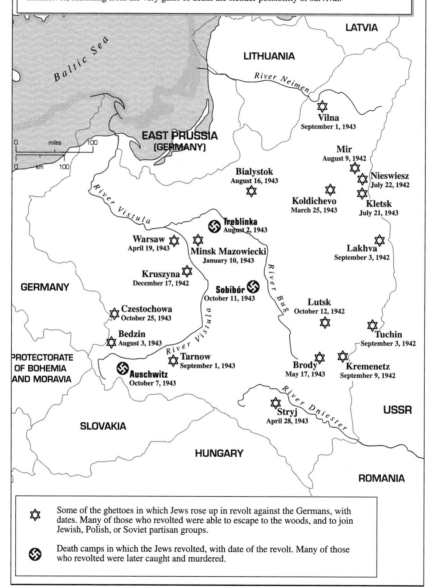

Baltic Sea

LATVIA

LITHUANIA

River Neimen

EAST PRUSSIA
(GERMANY)

Vilna
September 1, 1943

Mir
August 9, 1942

River Vistula

Bialystok
August 16, 1943

Nieswiesz
July 22, 1942

Koldichevo
March 25, 1943

Kletsk
July 21, 1943

Treblinka
August 2, 1943

Warsaw
April 19, 1943

Minsk Mazowiecki
January 10, 1943

Lakhva
September 3, 1942

Kruszyna
December 17, 1942

Sobibór
October 11, 1943

River Bug

Lutsk
October 12, 1942

GERMANY

Czestochowa
October 25, 1943

Bedzin
August 3, 1943

Tuchin
September 3, 1942

River Vistula

Tarnow
September 1, 1943

Brody
May 17, 1943

Kremenetz
September 9, 1942

PROTECTORATE
OF BOHEMIA
AND MORAVIA

Auschwitz
October 7, 1943

River Dniester

Stryj
April 28, 1943

USSR

SLOVAKIA

HUNGARY

ROMANIA

✡ Some of the ghettoes in which Jews rose up in revolt against the Germans, with dates. Many of those who revolted were able to escape to the woods, and to join Jewish, Polish, or Soviet partisan groups.

卐 Death camps in which the Jews revolted, with date of the revolt. Many of those who revolted were later caught and murdered.

The first and major problem, therefore, was to accept an impossible reality—a contradiction in terms. A small minority in Europe (about 10 percent in Poland, less than 1 percent in Germany, and even less in Western Europe), the Jews could not expect support from the general population. Without such support, open resistance was not feasible, until the sentence of death was accepted as fact. Only then did resistance become an option, for some at least, with the realization that death was inevitable in any case.

The cohesion of the Jewish family also militated against open resistance. Faced with the knowledge that going to the trains meant death, young persons refused to abandon parents, husbands to abandon wives, parents to abandon children, although one might argue that solidarity with one's family under those conditions was also an act of resistance.

Responsibility to the group was also a deterrent to resistance. Resistance would do but marginal harm to the Nazis; it would bring massive retribution on the Jews. Were individuals or groups entitled to endanger their communities or indeed their own families?

In Dolhynov, a small township in Belarus with 3,000 Jewish inhabitants, a resistance group was formed in late 1941 under the leadership of Yakov Segalchik and Leib Mintzel. Searching in the forest for Soviet partisans, they were caught by Byelorussian policemen and Germans, beaten up, and tortured. At night, with the help of an iron bar, they broke the barred windows of their cells and escaped into the ghetto. On the following day, March 15, 1942, the Dolhynov Judenrat leader, Nyumka Rayer, was told by the Nazis that all of Dolhynov's Jews would be killed if the two resisters did not come forward. The two escapees could not be found. On March 17, 1,640 Dolhynov Jews were murdered, with the help of the local non-Jewish population. Segalchik and Mintzel "sat in the ghetto, in hiding, with a heavy guilt-feeling: 'we were afraid of our neighbors, because many of them hated us with a murderous hatred, we were cursed in their eyes. They saw us as being responsible for the disaster that befell the town.'"[4]

And in Bialystok:

The incident occurred during the first day of the "action." Yitzhak Melamed belonged to a group that defended the house at Kopiecka street no. 29. As SS men and Jewish police entered the building, the Jews resisted. Melamed was among them. He held a bottle with acid in his hands and poured it straight into the face of the Nazi standing near him. The Nazi pulled his handgun but, blinded and confused because of the pain, he shot and killed one of the German policemen. At 2 P.M. Friedel [the chief hangman of the Bialystok ghetto] ordered the arrest of 100 persons. Without any ado, the Nazi murderers took hold of one hundred Jews whom they happened to see, most of them in the courtyard where Melamed was living; they were taken as hostages, so to speak, but were murdered immediately in a small garden near Nywelt street.

The Gestapo threatened reprisals more serious than the execution of a few hundred hostages. They declared that five thousand Jews would pay with their lives for the "crime" of an individual. At that point Melamed decided to hand himself over to the murderers. This happened on Sunday, February 7 [1943]. The "action" was temporarily stopped.

High Gestapo officials devoted that day to the interrogation of the imprisoned hero. "Why did you kill a German?" they asked. Melamed gave them a proud and forceful answer: "I hate you. I am sorry I killed only one German. I saw my parents killed in front of my eyes. In front of my eyes you murdered ten thousand Jews at Slonim [Melamed had fled to Bialystok from Slonim]. I am not sorry for what I did."

All during that day attempts were made to smuggle cyanide to him, but in vain. The military court sentenced him to death by hanging.

Next morning at 8, the gallows were ready at Kopiecka street. German gendarmes entered the ghetto. . . .All that time the Germans beat Melamed and tortured him. He did not weaken and did not beg for his life. Only once did he turn to his torturers and asked for some water, but even that request of the condemned man was refused. "You don't need any water anymore," the hangman joked. . . . He faced death quietly. Twice the rope was tied around his neck. The first time the rope tore. He managed to cry out: "You, the German murderers, will lose this war. Down with Hitler," and he spat into the face of the hangman. The second time the rope was tied around his neck, he cried out so that the whole street could hear it: "Murderers, you will pay for your deeds, your end is near."[5]

There were many like Melamed in the ghettoes and the camps. However, regarding this individual act of valor, what was the outcome? The death of one Nazi, Melamed's own death—and the deaths of a hundred other Jews. And in Dolhynov, the deaths of 1,640 people. Had the Germans not been provoked, would these people have survived? They were sentenced to death in any case. On another level, does anyone have the right to act when such acts might cause innocents to suffer reprisal? The moral question: to resist evil at whatever cost or to suffer evil to prevent, perhaps, extinction?

ARMED RESISTANCE

Who could be certain in late 1941 and early 1942 that the Nazis planned the murder of a people? Perhaps the acts of the Nazis were but a twentieth-century version of the persecution suffered by the Jews throughout the centuries. Perhaps this bizarre situation would soon end.

In the summer and autumn of 1941 at Ponary (Lithuanian: Paneriai), in a wood outside Vilna, thousands of Jews were murdered. In December 1941 the leaders of Hashomer Hatzair, the left-wing Zionist youth movement, who had returned to the ghetto after hiding with their friends, a group of nuns in a convent outside the city, considered the Nazi intentions:

Abba Kovner said: "We must not believe that those who were taken from us are alive. That their being led away was only deportation. Everything that has happened to us until now means Ponary—death. But even that fact is not the whole truth. The truth is larger and deeper than that by far. The murder of thousands is nothing but a prelude to the annihilation of millions. Their death is our total destruction.

I still have difficulties in explaining why Vilna is covered with blood and by contrast Bialystok is quiet. Why it happened this way and not otherwise. One thing is clear to me: Vilna is not just Vilna. Ponary is not just an episode. . . . There is a system. We are faced with a well thought-out system, whose inner workings are for the meantime hidden from us.

Is there any escape? No. If this is a system, then flight from one place to another is just an illusion, and like every illusion—bad. After all, who will flee from Vilna ghetto to Bialystok or Warsaw? Obviously, young, strong and agile

people. And in the burning city the weak, the elderly, the children will be left. . . .
Is there a possibility of rescue? Even if the answer is cruel, we must answer: no,
there is no rescue. And our answer must be even clearer: for individuals, for
tens and for hundreds—perhaps. For the people, for millions of Jews under German occupation, there is no rescue.

Is there a way out? Yes, there is a way out: rebellion and armed resistance."[6]

Kovner had absolutely no proof that there was indeed a "system" when
he spoke these words on December 31, 1941, in Vilna, but as a young poet
and youth leader, aged 23, he saw intuitively what the Nazis intended. Other
members of the group had other views:

Jacob Kaplan said: "We are members of the movement, and all our education to date, all our lives, were directed solely to Palestine. We have always
totally rejected the diaspora. A catastrophe is now overrunning European Jewry.
Possibly it will be broken in spirit as a result, but there is no certainty that it is
faced with total annihilation. And in the midst of this catastrophe we, a small
group of movement members, have been caught. In fact, it is just by chance
that we are here, because our place is in the Land of Israel, and there, in Palestine, is our way of-life and our aims. Now, too, aliyah [immigration to Palestine]
is the foundation of our lives. We must make every effort to save as many of our
members as possible. There are ways of rescue and of continuing our work.
The movement in Warsaw is active and we must go there, strengthen the movement cadre there and do everything to keep it alive. . . ."

Ruzhka Korczak: "The people will be annihilated and the movement cadre
will remain, will be saved. And those who will remain will carry on living and perhaps achieve aliyah to Palestine. And I am asking: Who of those who will remain
will have the courage to answer with his head held high when a child in Palestine
asks: and what did you do? What did all of you do when thousands and millions
died? Shall we answer the child: we saved our lives only, we looked for places to
hide and let ourselves be led to death powerless just like the others?

I think that just because we are so attached to the people, and the Jewish
center in Palestine is so dear to us, we must fight for the honor of the people, for
its values. . . ."

Adam spoke: "No one here spoke about a vitally important problem. I refer to the collective responsibility which all the Jews of the ghetto have to bear. How can we in our position think of resistance, of preparation for armed defence, when we all know that this may lead to wholesale, total disaster. After all, we have no certainty that we are immediately faced with a total annihilation of the ghetto and its total destruction. When we start our action—do we not endanger the whole ghetto? After all, this is not a question of our own readiness. We ourselves are ready—but do we have the right to take upon ourselves responsibility for all the Jews, endanger their lives, and thereby help in their murder in case of failure? None of the Jews of the ghetto will support us, will understand us, and many may possibly even curse us and become our enemy, because they will say that we are the cause of the catastrophe that overcame them."[7]

THE ATTITUDE TOWARD RESISTANCE IN THE GHETTO

Again, the Vilna ghetto can serve us as an example that will stand for many other places. There, as in many other ghettos, the Judenrat leaders taught that survival lay in submission, and the general population accepted that ideology. The resisters had no solution for the mass of the population. Nor did they have arms for those who might be able to bear them. A rebellion meant certain death for everyone. A slave labor economy seemed to provide at least the possibility of survival.

Itzik (Yitzhak) Wittenberg, the leader of the communist cell in the Vilna ghetto, was elected to lead the underground United Partisans' Organization (FPO), by all the ghetto groups and organizations, including the anti-Zionist Bund, the right-wing Zionist Revisionists, the main-line Zionist groups, and the leftist socialist-Zionists. The basic reason was the hope to receive help from the Soviets. Early in July 1943 a member of the Lithuanian communist underground caught by the Gestapo in Vilna town apparently identified Wittenberg for the Nazis. On July 8 the Gestapo demanded that the Judenrat surrender him. But he was warned and went into hiding. A week later the Nazis renewed their demand. The Judenrat leader, Jacob Gens, asked the FPO leaders to meet with him at midnight at his home. The FPO command group outside Gens's home became suspicious, and when Gestapo and Lithuanian policemen surprised Wittenberg in Gens's home and arrested him, they were momentarily overpowered by the FPO group and Wittenberg was freed.

Believing he had to betray Wittenberg to save the ghetto, Gens enlisted the aid of ghetto police and the "underworld," a group of criminals who supported him, to find Wittenberg. When they were unsuccessful, Gens spread the word throughout the ghetto that either Wittenberg would be surrendered or 20,000 men, women, and children of the Vilna ghetto would die. Everyone participated in the hunt—fathers, mothers, children, husbands, wives would not die because of one man. Alone and hated, the FPO members were attacked when their command post was located. A shot was fired. The attackers withdrew. A policeman loyal to Gens almost stumbled over the chief armory of the FPO. Another shot. The policeman was killed. Arguments began in the streets. FPO members tried to explain why the Nazis should not be trusted, that if Wittenberg was handed over, the ghetto would be doomed in any event, that in any case the ghetto's end was near, and that the only answer was resistance. Their arguments seemed to make sense. But then the commander of the ghetto police told the populace that the Nazis threatened to enter the ghetto immediately and destroy it if Wittenberg was not handed over. The FPO became, in the eyes of the ghetto, a threat to the life of every Jewish child.

The FPO members were not prepared to give up Wittenberg, but neither were they willing to turn their weapons against the ghetto. Wittenberg's communist cell decided that he should deliver himself to the Nazis, and the FPO command accepted the decision. Wittenberg went to the ghetto gate where Gestapo men were waiting. Although his comrades were unable to smuggle cyanide to him, he died before his interrogation, apparently supplied by Gens with cyanide before he left the ghetto for fear of compromising the Judenrat. The Nazis were so angry that they mutilated his body in revenge. The date: July 16, 1943. Thus, resistance was prevented by those in whose name it was to take place.

OTHER PROBLEMS OF ARMED RESISTANCE

The weapons supply was a major problem. Generally, Polish and other non-Jewish sources were unwilling to provide arms for the Jews. Consequently, arms were obtained either by purchase, for which a great deal of money was needed, or by theft from German stores. With Nazi guards at depots, and especially at the ghetto gates, smuggling bulky arms required ingenuity. In Vilna, arms were smuggled into the ghetto in potato carts with double bottoms; in Warsaw, carts transporting dead bodies to the cemeteries were also used. Occasionally, a guard at the gate could be bribed.

Without intelligence of Nazi activity, armed resistance could not commence. Nor could it commence without a plan. In the ghettoes of southeast Poland and Belarus, where forests were near, people could hide in the thickets at first. But where would they go from there? Would they find armed partisans? Would the partisans be antisemitic? Even anti-Nazi partisans (non-Jews) were just as happy to kill Jews as they were Germans. This also made resistance difficult. Should young men stay in the ghetto to fight a losing battle, or should they flee to the forests to fight against the Nazis, leaving the ghetto population helpless? In the ghettoes in Central and Western Poland, far away from forests, where the local population was likely to help the Nazis to round up the Jews, what should be done?

Despite such difficulties, armed resistance was employed in a considerable number of ghettoes. The most famous act of armed resistance occurred in the Warsaw ghetto.

THE WARSAW GHETTO REBELLION

Resistance in Warsaw, as in most other places, evolved slowly. Time was needed to accept the unbelievable. News of Nazi atrocities was believed more easily by young people than by adults who had difficulty grasping the fact that they had been sentenced to death for no reason at all. A small group of Zionist youth movement members left Vilna in December 1941 to travel across Nazi-controlled territories to bring the news of the murder of Vilna Jews at Ponary to Warsaw. When another Zionist youth emissary, Frumka Plotnicka, who left Warsaw in the autumn of 1941, and again in January 1942, for eastern Poland, returned, she reported on the murders that had been taking place there since June 1941. In March, 1942, Mordechai Tennenbaum, another Zionist youth leader, who later became the commander of the Bialystok ghetto uprising, arrived in Warsaw from Vilna; he reported on the organization of FPO in Vilna. Haika Grossmann,[8] also from Vilna, followed with more news. Escapees from east Poland also arrived in Warsaw, telling their stories of mass murder. Despite the news, the concept of mass annihilation was difficult to comprehend, although letters and underground newspaper articles indicate that an understanding of the situation was beginning to emerge.

Jacob Groyanovsky, a young man from the village of Izbica (Kujawska), near Lódz, managed to escape from the Sonderkommando (burial detail) at the Chelmno death camp in January 1942. Late in January or early in February 1942, he reached Warsaw. His detailed testimony, preserved in the Oneg Shabbat archives, was published in the underground press in February-March 1942. Although the adult community could not believe the "cobbler from Chelmno," as he was known, youth groups began to be convinced.

In April two Lublin refugees arrived with news of the deportation of the Lublin ghetto population. David Wdowinski, leader of the Zionist Betar[9] movement, and the two Lublin refugees went to the Judenrat leader, Adam Czerniakow, to inform him that the Jews were being mass-murdered everywhere. In his book, Wdowinski reported: "The two refugees from Lublin repeated to him what they had told me. He considered the news as exaggerated. Then he said he had the assurance of General Governor Frank, that three large ghettoes would remain—Warsaw, Radom and Krakow."[10] Whether Czerniakow actually considered the news exaggerated is not clear, for the next sentence seems to indicate otherwise, and in his diary on April 1, 1942, he wrote that 90 percent of the Lublin Jews were being deported.[11] The Judenrat, however, did not act—what could be done?

The first attempt to establish a Jewish fighting organization in March 1942, initiated by the leftist Zionist groups, Dror and Hashomer Hatzair, was torpedoed by the Bund, who claimed that the success of such an organization could be assured only with the aid of the Polish socialists.[12] In January 1942 the Polish Communist Party (PPR), which had been purged and dissolved by Stalin in 1938, was reconstituted. A ghetto PPR member, Josef Finkelstein-Lewartowski, attracted a number of young ghetto left wingers to the position of the PPR and its armed force, the Gwardia Ludowa (later, Armia Ludowa), which demanded immediate action against the Germans to aid the Soviet forces. The main Polish underground force, the Armia Krajowa (AK, Home Army), however, opposed such action until the last moment when German defeat was imminent.

The leftist Zionist groups acceded to Lewartowski's initiative when they found out that the AK would not help them, and in late March formed the 500-member Anti-Fascist Bloc, which also included the two main Zionist-socialist political parties, Left Poalei Zion and Poalei Zion Z.S. Rather than supply weapons to the ghetto, which is what the Zionists wanted, the PPR insisted on organizing groups to fight in the forests—a long distance from Warsaw. The Zionists, who thought the offensive should begin in the ghetto, reluctantly agreed. However, before the dispatch of the first groups to the forests, on May 30, the Gestapo arrested three communists, including the chief military expert in the ghetto, Andrzej Szmidt. The arrest resulted from the successful infiltration of the PPR in the city of Warsaw by the Gestapo and, in effect, brought about the dissolution of the Anti-Fascist Bloc. Additional arrests further weakened the PPR group in the ghetto.

These fruitless maneuvers generated despair and bitterness. Aside from the Anti-Fascist Bloc and the Bund, no other organizations were preparing resistance actions.[13] On April 18, apparently identified by Gestapo informers in the ghetto, 52 persons, including Bund and Zionist underground leaders, were murdered by the Nazis. Others on the list were forewarned and went underground.

On July 22, the eve of the ninth of Ab (in the Jewish calendar this is the day of mourning for the destruction of the Jewish temples in Jerusalem in B.C.E. 586 and A.D. 70) the great deportation from Warsaw began. On the second day of deportation, Czerniakow committed suicide, after he had been faced with the German demand to deport children. During the deportation, which lasted until September 12, 10,380 persons died or were murdered in the ghetto; 11,580 were sent to slave labor camps; about 8,000 managed to flee to the "Aryan" section of the city. Almost all of the estimated other 265,000 deportees died in the gas chambers of Treblinka.[14]

The Nazis forced some Treblinka victims to send postcards purporting to originate in various Polish towns back to the ghetto. As the cards began arriving in the ghetto, many refused to believe that their friends had been killed. In the first half of August a few young men managed to escape from Treblinka by hiding in the heap of clothes of those who had been gassed. When sufficient clothes had been assembled, the Nazis sent them out of the camp to sorting stations. The escapees hid in the wagons under the clothes.[15] The Bund sent Zygmunt Friedrich to Treblinka to find out if the rumors were true. When Friedrich got to Sokolow, a nearby town, he met an escapee, Azriel Wallach (a cousin of Maxim Litvinoff, the former Soviet foreign minister), who confirmed the rumors. The date: the first half of August.[16]

On July 23, the day of Czerniakow's suicide, the underground political groups met to consider alternatives. The representative of the religious groups, Rabbi Zishe Friedman, said that resistance would bring even greater disaster. The respected historian Isaac Schiper thought that the majority of the ghetto inmates would not be deported. Resistance, he thought, would provoke total annihilation, and one could not be responsible for such a tragedy. In any case, there were no arms and no time to train people. Unarmed protest was the only kind of resistance available. Diarist Hersh Berlinski rendered this account of Rabbi Friedman's statement:

> I believe in God and in miracles; God will not permit that His people of Israel should be destroyed, we must yearn for the miracle and it will occur. Resistance is hopeless. The Germans are capable of destroying us in a few days (as they did in Lublin). But if we act like this [i.e., in accordance with his advice], things can take a long time and a miracle will yet happen.[17]

Although a coordinating committee of the Bund and the former Anti-Fascist Bloc was set up, it could not act decisively in the panic that prevailed during the great deportation. Many activists of the various movements were shipped to Treblinka. The Bund waited in vain for arms or even a word of encouragement from Polish socialists. The PPR leaders told Lewartowski to save himself—they had no arms to give and no advice to offer. He was caught up in the deportation, however, and perished in Treblinka.

In this atmosphere of utter despair, representatives of three Zionist youth movements—Dror, Hashomer Hatzair, and Akiva[18]—met on July 28 to establish the Jewish Fighting Organization (JFO; ZOB according to its Polish initials). Four people were sent to the "Aryan" section of Warsaw to organize help and obtain arms. The Bund and the JFO printed wall placards calling on ghetto inhabitants to rebel and refuse to be deported. German-controlled warehouses were fired, and on August 20 Israel Kanal, a JFO member, shot and seriously wounded Josef Szerynski, the head of the collaborationist Jewish police, with the only weapon, a handgun, that the JFO had at that moment.

Five revolvers and eight light hand grenades were obtained and smuggled into the ghetto. Before they could be used, however, the Nazis caught a young man from a group sent by the JFO to fight in the forests, Israel Seltzer, who apparently broke down under torture and identified Josef Kaplan, the senior member of the five-man JFO leadership. Arrested on September 3, Kaplan was later killed. A second JFO member, the "military expert," Shmuel Breslav, was caught on the street. He was killed immediately when he tried to draw a knife on the Gestapo men. As the Nazis seemed about to track down the JFO, the five revolvers and eight light hand grenades were entrusted to a girl, who was to carry the "treasure" in a vegetable basket to a new hiding place. On her way, however, she was accidentally stopped by the Nazis, and the weapons were lost. On September 3, 1942, therefore, the Warsaw ghetto rebellion was stopped before it started: the two central members of the JFO command were dead, and the meager supply of JFO arms had been lost.[19]

When the great deportation ended on September 12, the remnants of the JFO met in a darkened room. Yitzhak Zuckerman, one of the three remaining JFO leaders, reported:

> I don't remember who was the first to talk—Aryeh [Vilner] or Zivia [Lubetkin]. The words were bitter, heavy, decision-laden words. There will not be any resistance by Jews. It is too late. The Jewish people are lost. If we failed to organize a Jewish force among hundreds of thousands in Warsaw, how can we succeed when there are only a few tens of thousands left?

The masses did not believe us. There are no arms, and it seems we will not get any. We have no strength to start anew. The people are being exterminated. Our honor—trampled. This small group can still save it. Let us go out tomorrow into the streets, let us put fire to the ghetto and attack the Germans with knives. We will die. It is our duty to die. And Israel's honor will have been saved. Days will come and it will be told: this poor nation had youth which saved its honor as best it could. Comrades added what each of them thought he had to say. One idea prevailed: despair controlled emotion, and emotion commanded action.

In this atmosphere of despair it was impossible to say anything else. Nevertheless, one of the comrades plucked up his courage and said: the emotions are true; the conclusions are mistaken. The disaster is great, and so is the shame. But the deed that is being discussed here is a deed of despair. It will leave no echo. There will be no revenge on the enemy. Our youth will disappear. We have suffered an untold number of setbacks, and will yet suffer more. It is necessary to start from scratch. . . .On that night we decided the fate of the January and April 1943 uprisings.[20]

The reaction of the Polish population of Warsaw was mixed—from sympathy to hostility. Thousands of Jews were hidden in the homes of Poles who were willing to endanger their own security. However, the majority reaction was hostility partly generated by fear, fear that the Poles would be next. The Polish underground army, the AK, refused all contact with the Jewish underground until September 1942. On November 10, the Polish commander, General Stefan "Grot"-Rowecki, issued order No. 71: "In connection with the extermination of the Jews by the occupant, there can be observed among the Polish public a fear that after the completion of this action the Germans will start liquidating the Poles in the same manner. I hereby order you to exercise self-control and calm the public." If the German aim was to "swallow our people," to "exterminate" the most nationalistically determined segment of the Polish people, the AK would fight. Until then, nothing would be done to provoke the Germans.[21]

Rowecki's order indicates that the AK did not intend to defend Poland's Jewish citizens from annihilation. Unless the Germans began mass murdering Poles in the same way, the AK would desist from any action against them.

In its resolution of November 27, 1942, which was one of the decisive public acts that persuaded the Western Allies that the annihilation of the Jewish people was indeed taking place, the Polish National Council in exile in London described in detail the destruction going on in Poland. An appeal was directed to the Western Powers to help. The number of victims, "over one million," was underestimated; more important, the appeal to the West was later balanced only slightly by a plea from the government in exile to the Polish population to aid their Jewish neighbors. The AK command in Warsaw never issued a parallel order to either its forces or the population generally.

The remnants of the ghetto—from 55,000 to 65,000 inhabitants—were clustered in a number of scattered areas. Although the official count of 35,000 was incorrect, the percentage of age groups seems to reflect reality. The highest proportion of deportees appears to have included the youngest and the oldest. Officially, no one over the age of 80 survived at all; only 45 people between the ages of 70 and 79 survived, and of the 31,458 children under 10 before the deportation, only 498 survived.

Guilt manifested itself among the distraught ghetto population, for every single person had lost relatives and friends to the Nazi *Moloch* (pagan god to whom children were sacrificed in Biblical times). "Had we resisted the Nazis earlier," they said, such resistance might have been more effective. And the desire for revenge became pervasive. The JFO killed Jacob Leikin, a senior Jewish police official, and because of such JFO activity, the Judenrat and the police were no longer respected or feared. In this atmosphere, it was easier for JFO to operate.

The remnants of the first JFO were strengthened and broadened. By the end of October the three original Zionist youth groups—Dror, Hashomer Hatzair, and Akiva—had been joined by other Zionist youth groups such as Gordonia and Noar Zioni. The decisive development, however, was that both the Bund and the communists joined, as well as some adult Zionist political groups. With the exception of the orthodox religious segment, which never joined the armed underground, and the Betar movement, which split off in the late autumn to create its own underground, a full unification had been achieved. The leaders included Mordechai Anielewicz of

Hashomer Hatzair, the JFO commander, who had been on a mission to southwest Poland when the great deportation started; Yitzhak Zuckermann of Dror[22] was his deputy; area commanders, such as Marek Edelmann of the Bund,[23] Zivia Lubetkin, Zuckermann's wife,[24] and Michael Klepfisz of the Bund,[25] a young engineer who was in charge of preparing hand grenades and explosives, Aryeh Vilner,[26] who was the chief negotiator for arms on the "Aryan" side, and others.

Parallel with the reestablishment of JFO, a Jewish National Committee was organized; it included representatives of all the groups participating in JFO with the exception of the Bund. Because the Bund did not want to belong to a political organization that included Zionists and communists, a Coordinating Commission, which included the Jewish National Committee and the Bund, was formed to function as the overall political body. However, these rather complicated political arrangements were less important than they seem: Although the youth movement leaders allowed their elders to set up a political framework that would enable the JFO to negotiate with Polish groups in the name of a united Jewish movement, the leadership remained firmly in the hands of Anielewicz, Zuckermann, Vilner, and the young leaders of the other groups.

Arms were bought or negotiated. With the help of the JDC, especially its treasurer, David Guzik, money was raised in the ghetto. People who had money were taxed; when they refused to pay the tax, force was used. The Judenrat and the Jewish police were pushed aside. By the end of 1942, the JFO was the decisive factor in the ghetto—this time with the growing mass support of the population.

In January 1943 in the wake of a visit to Warsaw by Himmler, the Nazis decided to deport 8,000 Jews to Treblinka. This time, however, they met with armed and unarmed resistance. On the morning of January 18, when German forces and their Lithuanian and Latvian helpers entered the ghetto, most people were out of sight in carefully prepared underground bunkers. The help given the Nazis by Jewish policemen was of little avail. The Germans shot about 1,000 people in the street, and soon began taking anyone they could find. Although between 6,000 and 6,500 people were deported, the JFO finally managed to go into action. One group of youngsters, under the command of Anielewicz, joined a column of Jews being marched toward the railway wagons, and on a prearranged sign attacked the guards. The short battle that ensued ended when German reinforcements arrived. A number of Germans and all the JFO members were killed with the exception of Anielewicz. In another incident two Germans were killed as they searched a house occupied by the group under Zuckermann where four revolvers, four hand grenades, acid, and iron bars were hidden. After similar incidents had occurred elsewhere in the ghetto, Anielewicz and his friends concluded that street fighting was pointless. They decided instead that by fighting from fortified positions in houses they could neutralize, at least somewhat, the German superiority in fire power.

Between January and April 1943 the JFO expanded and acquired more arms. In the late autumn of 1942 the Jewish Military Organization (JMO, or ZZW according to its Polish initials) was founded by Betar. Its membership included people of other persuasions as well, including communists. Pawel Frenkel headed its military force, David Wdowinsky, its political committee. By allying with two Polish underground groups, which, though part of the AK, maintained a semi-independent existence, the JMO was able to procure one or two light machine guns and some rifles. Major Henryk Iwanski and Captain Cesary Kettling were particularly helpful.

But relations between the JFO and the JMO were strained. The JFO wanted the JMO members to join the JFO, and the JMO wanted its commander to lead the united resistance. In the end, on the eve of the uprising, Anielewicz was accepted as the commander and the two organizations coordinated their activities, although they did not merge. The two groups together had 750 members at most, 500 from the JFO, 250 from the JMO. Almost every fighter had a revolver, and there were probably one to three light machine guns, a fairly large number of hand grenades, and fourteen rifles, whereas the SS and regular German army troops, probably more than 2,000 soldiers, had heavy equipment including artillery and tanks.

When the Nazis entered the ghetto on April 19, Passover Eve (which was also Hitler's birthday for which the Nazis hoped to make the liquidation of the ghetto a birthday present), they met with determined resistance. They retreated and a new commander, General Jürgen Stroop, took over. In the following days fighting extended throughout the ghetto. When the Germans set fire to the ghetto, heat forced many people out of their hideouts. The rebels fought German patrols at night. During the day the Germans, with the help of dogs or a few Jews who were promised their lives, tried to locate the bunkers in which people were hiding. The whole ghetto resisted—those who had arms fought, those without arms hid and refused to surrender.

Slowly, over weeks, many rebels and members of the ghetto population were caught or killed. On May 8 the bunker in which the JFO command was hiding during the day was located.

> At 8 A.M. the people in the bunker heard knocking from above. A state of readiness was declared immediately. After some time the knocking stopped. The Germans found the entrance, blew it open, and one of them entered. This was the result of a betrayal. The German who entered was killed. After some time the Germans brought a boring machine, placed it on the rubble on top, bore a hole into the bunker, and through it they introduced poison gas.[27] Some of the unarmed civilians went out and were caught by the Germans. When the fighters saw there was no way out, they decided to commit suicide. Lotek Rosenblatt gave his mother and her adopted daughter poison and they died. He shot himself. Rivka Pasmonek shot her girlfriend and then herself. This was what most people did. Mordechai Anielewicz was stunned by the poison gas. He put his head into a bucket of water standing on the floor in order to regain consciousness, and died.[28]

Some of the JMO fighters tried to escape through an underground passage from their central command post on Muranowska Square to the "Aryan" side, but they were caught and killed, including Pawel Frenkel. From early May, attempts were made to save the fighters by guiding them through the sewers to the "Aryan" side of the city. With the help of Polish sympathizers, including PPR members and Iwanski and his allies, a few dozen people survived in this way; others died in the sewers or were killed by Germans when they emerged on the "Aryan" side.

The rebels and the other Jews in the ghetto who managed to obtain arms (the so-called wild Jews) held out after May as well. At least one large armed group managed to cross to the "Aryan" side in late September. Polish sources indicate that armed Jews were found in the ruins and rubble in October 1943.[29] Total German casualties were small. Even if Stroop's figure of 16 is not accepted, the number of German dead cannot have been very great.

Polish sources indicate that AK provided 50 or 70 revolvers, some explosives, and instructions on how to make homemade explosive bottles. During the fighting the AK intervened twice: on April 19 or 20, 25 AK members tried unsuccessfully to explode a mine under the ghetto wall. In the short fight that ensued two AK members died. Reports on the second action, reported to have occurred April 23, are contradictory and it is not quite clear what transpired. The communist underground also staged two attacks on the Germans.

Officially, the Polish attitude favored the rebellion. On May 5, Wladyslaw Sikorski, the Polish prime minister in exile, broadcast a speech from London in which he termed the destruction of the Jews "the greatest crime in the history of mankind." He asked his people in the name of the government "to extend help to the martyred Jews." The next day, May 6, an announcement appeared in an underground newspaper in Warsaw expressing admiration and sympathy for the Jews who were "defending themselves valiantly."[30] AK help was minimal, however, and when Zuckermann asked for aid in leading fighters through the sewers, it was the communist underground, not the AK, that extended help.

The AK had considerable arms at the time. As early as 1941 the AK had 135 heavy machine guns, 190 light machine guns, and 6,045 rifles. The 60 revolvers they contributed to the JFO were hardly in line with the sentiments expressed by Sikorski. The communists had no large arms caches at the time, and their attitude toward the Jewish struggle was ambivalent in any event. However, both the AK and the communists made at least token attempts at armed action in which Polish fighters died. When Iwanski, his son, and some of his men joined his JMO friends in the battle for one day, his son lost his life. Polish sewage workers crept through the filth to rescue people from the ghetto. With an estimated 10,000 to 15,000 Jews on the "Aryan" side in the spring of 1943, a considerable number of Poles risked—and lost—their lives to hide them. Ringelblum and others, however, attest to the hostility of the majority of Warsaw's Polish inhabitants, a hostility that placed the lives of pro-Jewish Poles in jeopardy. Street hooligans called *szmalcowniki* (people looking for bribes) hunted Jews, extorted their money, and then handed them over to the Nazis.

No Jews were accepted into AK ranks outside of Warsaw. Ringelblum asks:

> What real meaning is there in passing a resolution to arm the Ghettoes when armed fighters are discouraged and not mobilized to fight against the common foe? This government attitude towards armed Jewish groups forces them to fight against everyone and leads to their being mercilessly liquidated by Polish partisan groups and by the rural population, who capture them and hand them over to the Germans. . . . The Polish population finishes off the remnant of the Jews left from the large Jewish communities. Jews are not admitted to Polish partisan groups, for no known reason. How mistaken this policy is, can be proved by the practice of the Polish Left, which has placed no restrictions on Jews.[31]

The AK political leadership in Warsaw, however, organized a group, Zegota, to aid Jews in October 1942. Headed by Colonel Henryk Wolinski, Adolf Berman, a member of the Jewish National Committee, and by Wladyslaw Bartoszewski, a Polish Catholic, Zegota saved an estimated 4,000 to 6,000 Jews.

Of those who hid, not many survived. They were found by the Nazis, often betrayed by their neighbors. When the Warsaw Polish rebellion broke out in the summer of 1944, and Zuckermann of the underground JFO issued a call to all Jews to join in fighting the enemy, about 1,000 Jews participated.

THE BIALYSTOK GHETTO REBELLION

In the Bialystok ghetto, which by early 1943 housed 40,000 people, two resistance groups developed. One group included a communist faction among others; the other group was led by Dror, under Mordechai Tennenbaum, who had reached Bialystok via Vilna and Warsaw, and included another communist faction, the other Zionist movements, and the Bund.

Hashomer Hatzair members belonged to both groups. As in Warsaw, obtaining arms was difficult. The Judenrat leader, Ephraim Barash, believed that an economically important ghetto would survive until liberated by the Soviet army. However, he did not fight against the underground; under certain conditions he said he would join it. By early 1943, no illusions regarding Nazi policies remained. But, Barash said, no actions should be undertaken until the annihilation of the ghetto was at hand—and he would be privileged to that information. Barash provided passes and hideouts for the underground. Although they disagreed on various points, the Judenrat leader and the resistance groups trusted one another.

Early in February 1943 the Nazis announced the deportation of 6,300 inhabitants. After a night of agonizing debate, Tennenbaum and his friends decided not to rebel—weapons were in short supply, a rebellion now would only be echoed by the deaths of the remaining ghetto population. But the resistance leaders did not judge the Nazis accurately—they took not 6,300 human beings but 12,000, and they killed 1,000 in the streets because of massive, though unarmed, resistance. Thus, Franci Horowitz, who taught literature in the local high school, fought the Nazis with her bare hands and then, to avoid deportation into the gas chambers, swallowed poison. Others remained barricaded indoors.

Believing that they should resist when the first Jew was taken, Hashomer Hatzair and one of the communist groups refused to accept Tennenbaum's decision. They planned to resist even though they had one revolver, one rifle, and some acid. Before they could attack, however, they were discovered by the Germans, apparently betrayed by a Jewish informer. They fought as best they could, pouring acid over the Germans, biting, and knifing. Some were killed immediately; others, including their commander, Adek Boraks, were put on the trains to Treblinka. Barash had refused to give them life-saving passes—they had rebelled against his position. On the train, they plotted to escape:

> In the death train an argument broke out. The boys decided that the girls should jump first, because the guards would notice that people were jumping, and further escape would be prevented. The first to jump would have the best

chances, but they would undoubtedly awaken the alertness of the Germans. The girls said: You jump first. You are more essential for the fighting which will no doubt continue after our deaths. In the end all of them jumped. Only Yentel and Shlomo came back. The train went quickly and there were distances of kilometres between those who jumped. Yentel saw Roshka, her friend, fall under the wagon and her two legs severed. She saw Zivia Kruglik hit by a hail of bullets nearby and die.[32]

Those who survived joined the group led by Tennenbaum, who succeeded in obtaining some rifles, revolvers, and hand grenades. As the Soviet army approached Bialystok, the Nazis decided to liquidate the ghetto on August 16, 1943—after Bialystok, only Lódz remained. Barash was taken by surprise. The JFO wanted to defend the strongpoints in the ghetto. Before they could act, however, the panic-stricken population was streaming toward the assembly points, and the JFO were likely to be left fighting in an empty ghetto. Their hope that the ghetto inhabitants would join them was not fulfilled. The frightful moral dilemmas that the young rebels had to face in relation to their families are exemplified in the memoirs of a girl fighter:

> I tried to make my way through the multitude, to Tepla street. What was I thinking about? I don't remember. I only remember that I was in a great hurry, because the last moments had come. Suddenly, in the throng, I saw my mother. I wanted to steal away and run, not to stop. I was afraid of this meeting, I was scared of seeing her in the transport. I was in a hurry. Where should she hurry to? Where should she turn? To a hideout? Where will she find one? I was afraid of seeing her wrinkled face, grown old before her time. Her gray hair. I was scared of seeing her in her loneliness. I backtracked, like a coward, like someone running from the battlefield. But she stopped me with her eyes.
> "Haika'le, whereto?"
> I was silent, I kissed her dry lips, her gray hair, and fled. I did not see her again.[33]

The resisters quickly changed plans and attacked the German forces through park areas, trying to break the German lines. During the day-long battle, most of the resisters fell in battle. Tennenbaum appears to have committed suicide two days later. Some who were taken alive when their ammunition gave out were killed or deported. Others fought back from hideouts in the empty ghetto for another few days. A group of girls survived, escaped into the city, and carried on their struggle. A Jewish partisan group fought in the forests near Bialystok.

THE RESISTANCE IN VILNA

On July 22, 1943, a week after the FPO was forced to surrender Wittenberg, thirty-four FPO members, under Joseph Glasmann, a leader of Betar and a member of the FPO command, left the ghetto for the Narocz forests, a considerable distance east of Vilna. Ambushed by a German patrol, some were killed; others managed to break through and reached their destination. The next day the families and the neighbors of some of those who had left (especially those who had been killed and identified) were murdered.

On June 21, 1943, Himmler had ordered that all ghetto laborers who were working outside the ghetto be replaced by non-Jews; the ghettoes were to be liquidated; Jewish workers who were essential were to be transferred to concentration camps. But beyond this general directive the liquidation of Vilna ghetto in September 1943 seems to have been due, in part, to the increase in partisan activities east of Vilna and the increased numbers of Jewish fighters in the groups. The two remaining ghettoes in Lithuania, Kaunas (Kovno) and Siauliai (Yid., Shavli), existed until the late spring of 1944.

On September 1 when German troops and Estonian pro-Nazi guards entered the Vilna ghetto and demanded 3,000 men and 2,000 women for work, FPO members began concentrating at two points in the tiny ghetto area. Before the arms could be distributed, however, German troops surrounded one FPO group, which had been betrayed by two supporters of Gens, the Judenrat leader. Some members escaped to the second assembly point. Armed, they occupied several houses on Straszun Street and waited for the German troops to enter; they posted a leaflet asking the population to join the rebels and refuse to obey Nazi orders. The Germans and Estonians ceased hunting when Gens suggested that the Jewish police would be more successful in rounding up Jewish workers. Gens, who knew of the FPO's mobilization on Straszun Street, feared the ghetto would be doomed if a clash occurred.

When only 600 men had been arrested by the Jewish police by evening, the Germans and Estonians again entered the ghetto and clashed briefly with an FPO outpost commanded by Yehiel Sheinbaum (who was the leader of a smaller resistance group that had joined the FPO shortly before the current action). With darkness approaching, the Germans withdrew. Again Gens intervened and promised to supply the workers. Between September 2 and 4 his policemen and an auxiliary troop of hardened criminals specifically recruited for the purpose caught several hundred men (the women volunteered in most cases to join their husbands) but not enough to fill the quota.

The FPO, now commanded by Abba Kovner, was in constant contact with Gens, who promised the people that they would be sent to work in Estonia. Although the FPO argued that they were going to Ponary to die, the people believed Gens rather than the FPO because others had been taken to Estonian camps prior to September.

The FPO did not take the offensive because of the same unanswerable moral question that plagued all ghettoes. As Abba Kovner wrote:

> As regards revolt, we agonized more than anything else over the moral aspect. Were we entitled to do this, and when? Were we entitled to offer people to go up in flames? Most of them were unarmed—what would happen to all of them? And if in the meantime it turned out that this was not liquidation? We were terribly perplexed as to what right we had to determine their fate.[34]

And Ruzhka Korczak wrote of the FPO:

> All its plans, all its expectations, all its prayers went up in smoke. . . . There is no longer any hope that the battle, which a handful of fighters, limited in number, would initiate, could turn into a mass defense. . . . The rebellion, should it break out, would be nothing but an act of individuals alone, of no wide-national value, and would not open the way to mass rescue.[35]

How Gens could have deluded himself into thinking that the Nazis would be satisfied with shipping a few thousand Jews to Estonia after they had encountered the FPO on September 1 is difficult to comprehend. In any case 11,000 to 12,000 Jews remained in the ghetto on September 5; 7,130 had been deported not to Ponary but to Estonia where they were murdered a few months later. During the month, small groups of FPO members left the ghetto for the forests. On September 23, the last group, 80 to 100 armed men and women, including the FPO leaders, crawled through the sewers for seven hours to escape to the forests. They refused to take non-combatants with them because to do so would have severely hampered their chances of a breakout. On the same day, the Germans and their auxiliaries sent the women with children to Majdanek and the old people to Ponary where they were killed. Able-bodied men and women were shipped to Estonia. The FPO fought in the forests of Narocz and Rudniki until the liberation of Lithuania in July 1944.

RESISTANCE IN OTHER GHETTOES

Armed groups existed in 24 ghettoes in western and central Poland: Warsaw, Krakow, Czestochowa, Wlodawa, Sosnowice, Tomaszow Lubelski, Kielce, Iwaniska, Chmielnik, Sandomierz, Józefow, Opatów, Kalwaria, Ozialoszica, Markuszew, Rzeszów, Miedzyrzec Podlaski, Opoczno, Tarnów, Pilica, Radom, Radzyn, Sokolów Podlaski, Zelechów. In northeastern Poland (western Belarus), in 110 ghettoes or other Jewish concentrations, there were 63 armed underground groups; in another 30 ghettoes, armed actions indicate the existence of some form of organization. About 25,000 people fled into the forests to fight, but most of them were killed before they could become members of armed groups. In Lithuania, underground organizations functioned in all four ghettoes—Vilna, Swiencionys (Swieciany, Swienczan), Kaunas (Kovno), and Siauliai (Shavli). Resisters from Kovno and Swieciany fled to the forests; in Kovno the Judenrat aided their escape.

In eastern Belarus there was a massive exodus into the forests. Some 7,500 persons are estimated to have left the Minsk ghetto (the fourth largest ghetto, with over 80,000 inhabitants), where the Judenrat was active in the resistance movement. In the Ukraine, most of which does not contain thick forests, over 4,000 Jewish partisans have been identified. Estimates for southeastern Poland are not available.

PARTISANS IN EASTERN EUROPE

During 1941 and 1942, the time of the annihilation of the Jewish population in Soviet areas occupied by the Germans, the partisan movement was in its infancy. Jews who fled to the forests often were unable to find partisan detachments. They were easily surrounded and murdered by the Germans, who were aided by local anti-Jewish peasants. In addition, some partisan detachments killed Jews. When the Soviet command gained control over these groups after May 1942, discipline was more or less enforced and partisan detachments grew in strength, but by that time most of the ghettoes no longer existed.

Partisans usually accepted new recruits only when they were armed. This made sense for the local population which could live in its towns and villages and did not have to join the partisans to save their lives. To the Jews, who had little access to arms, rejection by partisans meant death. Often, too, armed Jews were relieved of their arms and clothes and given token substitutes in return. No resistance to such iniquity was possible in the forest conditions. Nor was there any reprieve for Jewish women who were assaulted sexually by partisans.

Specifically Jewish units were frowned upon. The Soviet command, for its own reasons, mixed nationalities in so-called territorial (i.e., Belorussian, Ukrainian, etc.) units. A few Jewish units nevertheless survived, the most famous were those of the brothers Tuvia, Zusia, and Asael Belski in the Naliboki forests; the unit of "Uncle Misha" (Misha Gildenman) near Korzec in western Belarus; Dr. Yehezkel Atlas's unit in the same general area; and the large unit commanded by Abba Kovner in the Rudniki forests in Lithuania.

The overall figures for Jewish participation in Soviet partisan units are not known. The estimate of 15,000 Jewish partisans in western Belarus is an informed guess, and not even that is available for eastern Belarus, or for Russia itself. Although research is yet to be done, eyewitness accounts nevertheless indicate that there was mass participation of Jews in partisan activities in Eastern Europe.

In western and central Poland (the General Government), twenty-eight Jewish partisan units were active for more than a few months at least. Many of them were connected with, or acted in cooperation with, the Gwardia Ludowa or the Armia Ludowa (AL) of the communists. All but three groups were betrayed or discovered by the Germans and killed. The largest surviving group was that commanded by Yehiel Grynszpan in the Parczew forests of southeastern Poland. Thirteen additional detachments, also of the AL, were Polish-Jewish, with about one-third of Jewish fighters. Two thousand Jewish partisans were in those areas; in 1942 almost half those in the forests were Jewish, because the AK did not, as we know, want an armed struggle just then. (See above.) The total number of Jewish partisans in the Polish-Soviet area has been estimated at 30,000.

An estimated 2,500 Jewish fighters participated in a national uprising in Slovakia in August 1944. A Jewish unit of 161 men who had escaped from a forced labor camp fought SS troops at Batovany to cover the retreat of a Slovak unit. After the defeat of the uprising, some 1600 Jewish fighters joined 15,000 partisans in the Tatra mountains.

Several thousand Jews fought with the Tito partisans. Jews participated in underground activities in Bulgaria, an estimated 600 in the Greek partisan movement, and some 2,000 in northern Italy.

The rebellion in Warsaw was quite different from the fight in the forest: the forest presented both a hope of survival and of revenge. Jews were motivated to escape into the forest to survive and to avenge the deaths of parents, wives, husbands, other relatives and communities. The forest might—and in many cases did—offer the opportunity for both.

RESISTANCE IN CAMPS

Rebellion in the camps was rarely possible. The emaciated inmates from thousands of different localities, speaking different languages, lived in a state of terror in a kingdom of death. Nevertheless, rebellions occurred. There were non-Jewish underground organizations in some camps, and even arms were collected and stored. In Auschwitz and Buchenwald, especially, preparations were made for rebellion, although they never came to pass. The Buchenwald underground took over the camp when the SS guards fled as the American army approached. In the end only Jewish inmates rebelled in camps, which was only logical, perhaps, since they were doomed to death in any event, whereas the others might survive until Nazism's downfall. How such people—humiliated, degraded, dehumanized—were able to organize rebellions is difficult to comprehend. Fairly adequate descriptions of these Jewish acts of resistance are available.

Armed and unarmed rebellions occurred in Sachsenhausen, Auschwitz, Sobibór, Treblinka, Kruszyna, and Krychow. Organizations intending rebellion that in some cases brought about escapes existed at Plaszów, Ostrowiec Swietojarski, Budzyn, Poniatow, Trawniki, the Jewish POW camp at Lublin, and elsewhere. It should be noted that the only resistance at the camps came from the Jews. Even Russian prisoners of war, who were trained for combat, put up no resistance, except at Sobibór.

At Sobibór, where in 1942–43 some 250,000 Jews were murdered, Alexander Pechersky, a Jewish Soviet officer, organized a rebellion and a mass escape. To attack the camp's arsenal, Pechersky and his group had to kill the main Nazi officers first. On October 14, 1943, nearly a dozen of the camp's Nazi officers, lured separately into workshops on the pretext that an inspection was due or that something they had ordered was ready, were soundlessly killed with hatchets. Although the attack on the arsenal failed, the phone wires were cut and the arrival of Nazi reinforcements delayed. Of the 600 inmates, 400 rushed to the woods. Half of them died in the minefield surrounding the camp, and others were killed by Nazi search parties or the Polish fascist underground (the NSZ). Some 60 men and women, including Pechersky, survived, however, to join the Soviet partisans. Two days after the rebellion, Himmler ordered Sobibór dismantled.

A rebellion at Treblinka on August 2, 1943, allowed from 150 to 200 people to escape, but only 12 survived. At Sachsenhausen on October 22, 1942, young German Jews about to be transported to Auschwitz attacked their captors with bare hands; most of them perished.

The rebellion in Auschwitz was ignited by the murder of members of the Sonderkommando unit whom the Nazis employed to burn the bodies of the gassed victims. At the end of September 1944 Soviet forces were conquering Poland. Hungarian Jewry had been murdered, and large numbers of prospective victims were no longer available. Jews were no longer arriving at Auschwitz en masse. As the Sonderkommando were no longer needed, the SS forced the Sonderkommando leaders to "select" 300 men early in October. The 300 men—mostly Hungarian and Greek Jews—told the others they would rebel. Previously, the resistance movement in the camp, led by Josef Cyrankiewicz, who later became president of Poland, had promised the Sonderkommando that they would act if the Sonderkommando were endangered. Young Jewish women had smuggled explosives and small arms to the Sonderkommando. Now, however, the resistance organization told the Sonderkommando that they were not to rebel, that such an act might provoke the murder of the entire camp population—an argument that was echoed by the Judenräte in many ghettoes.

On October 7, as the SS began to separate the 300 men from the others, the men suddenly began throwing stones at the SS. Fire was set to crematorium no. IV. The Sonderkommando tried to break out of the camp. In another compound (crematoria II and III) several Soviet POW Sonderkommando killed a Kapo they hated; others pulled three hand grenades and a few revolvers that had been smuggled to them and escaped. As it was daylight, however, they were soon located and surrounded as they hid in a barn near the town of Rajsko. Most rebels were killed during the fighting; the others were caught and shot. Of the 650 men in the uprising, 450 died. A few SS guards were killed or wounded; one crematorium was burned. The few Soviet POW and Polish Sonderkommando also participated in the uprising.[36]

The act of escape itself can, in a sense, be considered an act of resistance. Of the 667 prisoners who escaped from Auschwitz, 270 were caught and, in most cases, killed. Because they were best able to survive in the Polish area around the camp and because they had the most privileged jobs in the camp—in hospitals, in artisan work details, and as secretaries—which made escape more possible, most escapees were Polish. The Soviet POWs were the second largest group; when Jews began to occupy some of the privileged jobs in 1943, 76 Jewish escapees followed. Barely a dozen managed to avoid capture once outside the camp, however.

RESISTANCE IN WESTERN EUROPE

In France, especially, Jews participated actively in the anti-Nazi underground movement. In Eastern Europe most Jews (with the exception of some communists and the few assimilated Jews) were motivated to resist because of their Jewish identity, although other considerations—victory against Nazism, victory of socialism, a free and independent socialist or liberal Poland—were also factors. In the West, specifically Jewish motivations were predominant with some but by no means all. However, that so many Jews participated in the resistance in the West was due, in large part, to their Jewish identity; that included many, if not most, Jewish communists.

In France, many Jews belonged to underground organizations or to Jewish groups that maintained links with such organizations. Until the German attack on Russia in June 1941, French communists did not oppose the Nazis. After the entry of the USSR into the war, French communists discovered their French anti-Nazi patriotism. However, a Jewish communist group organized against the Vichy government and the German occupation as early as July 1940, though no armed action took place. In the summer of 1941, the Main d'Oeuvre Immigré (MOI), a communist front organization of recent immigrants led by Jewish commanders, began armed actions against the German forces. Two young Jews executed the first overt armed act in Paris on August 2, 1941; one of them, Samuel Tyszelman, was shot on August 13. A special MOI Jewish unit executed approximately fifty acts of sabotage between May 1942 and May 1943, by which time most of the original members had been caught and executed by the Nazis. The remnants of the unit were transferred to the south where they organized four units to fight the Nazis as well as the Union des Juifs pour la Résistance et l'Entr'aide (Union of Jews for Resistance and Mutual Assistance, UJRE), which also included Zionist and Bundist groups.

In the south, in Toulouse, a small group of Jewish resisters was organized as early as August 1940 by the poet David Knout and the engineer

A Nazi soldier guards these people in the Warsaw Ghetto as they huddle against a wall. Notice the bullet holes in the wall.

As Jewish resistance ends in the Warsaw Ghetto, armed soldiers round up men and women.

These Jews are being marched through the streets of Warsaw. Their destination will be trains that take them to the Nazi death camps.

As a Swedish diplomat in Hungary, Raoul Wallenberg issued Swedish passports to Jews and helped Jews receive food and medical care. When the war ended, Wallenberg was imprisoned in the Soviet Union on charges that he was a spy. He was never heard from again.

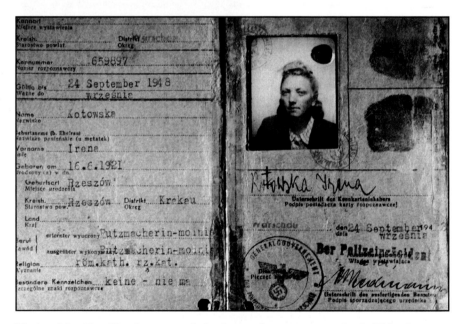

Having false identification papers helped some Jews to escape death. This photo shows the false identification card of Rose Stein-Braseliten. Using the name Irena Kotonska, she was able to hide outside the Warsaw Ghetto in an area where Aryan Germans lived.

This photo shows the entrance to the German concentration camp at Auschwitz-Birkenau.

These Hungarian families have just arrived at Auschwitz.

As Hungarian Jews got off the trains, they were separated from their families. Nazi guards selected those who would be forced to work or take part in horrible experiments and those who would be taken immediately to the gas chambers.

These Jews have just arrived at Auschwitz and have been selected as "unfit" and "useless." They are being led off to the gas chamber to die within an hour of this photo being taken.

These women and children at Auschwitz await "the bath." Doors marked "the bath" actually led into the gas chamber.

At this concentration camp in the Ukraine, men serve as forced laborers to move piles of dirt in small wheelbarrows.

Here, prisoners at the Mauthausen camp are forced to carry heavy loads of earth to help build the camp. Jews and others worked at these camps in horrible conditions. The Nazi goal was to work prisoners to death.

This photo of Anne Frank is taken from her diary. The diary records, "This is a photo as I would wish myself to look all the time. Then I would maybe have a chance to come to Hollywood." She died in a concentration camp at age 16.

Dit is een foto, zoals ik me zou wensen, altijd zo te zijn. Dan had ik nog wel een kans om naar Holywood te komen.

Anne Frank.
10 Oct. 1942

(translation)
"This is a photo as I would wish myself to look all the time. Then I would maybe have a chance to come to Hollywood."
Anne Frank, 10 Oct. 1942

As U.S. troops march through a concentration camp at the end of World War II, they pass rows of bodies. These victims provide a clear indictment of the gruesome reality of Nazi plans for extermination.

These Jewish survivors look defiant as U.S. soldiers liberate the death camp at Auschwitz. The men were starved and exhausted. As one survivor later said, "We were like a bit of sandpaper, which, rubbed a few times, becomes useless and is thrown away to be burned with the garbage."

These female prisoners cover their heads with scarves as they leave the Terezin camp in Czechoslovakia at the end of World War II.

After World War II, twenty-two Nazi leaders were tried at the International War Crimes Tribunal for War Crimes and Crimes Against Humanity in Nuremberg, Germany.

Israeli soldiers proudly display the flag of the new State of Israel in July 1948. The photo was taken just months after Israel declared its independence.

Abraham Polonsky, a Palestinian Jew. They assumed the rather grandiloquent name Jewish Army (Armée Juive, AJ). After the extensive deportations of the summer of 1942, the AJ was joined by the scouting movement, Eclaireurs Israélites de France (EIF), and the united Zionist youth movement, Mouvement de la Jeunesse Sioniste (MJS), and became, as in Warsaw, the Organisation Juive de Combat (Jewish Fighting Organization, OJC).

Most of OJC's membership was provided by the EIF, originally a traditional, non-Zionist, typical French-Jewish youth group. Active only in the south, the EIF's agricultural enterprise was at first supported by the Vichy government; the head of the movement, Robert Gamzon, was a member of the French Judenrat, the UGIF (see Chapter 10). During the summer deportations of 1942, the EIF's ideology changed—they became pro-Zionist and religious, as well as radical, in an anti-Nazi sense. The maximum number of AJ-OJC members can be estimated at 2,000, including some small *maquis* groups (forest partisans) in the Black Mountain area of southwestern France and city guerilla units in Paris, Grenoble, Marseilles, and Toulouse. The OJC smuggled hundreds of youngsters intent on joining the Allied forces over the Pyrennees into Spain. In all, the OJC claimed credit for 1,925 armed actions, mainly immediately prior to and after the June 1944 Normandy landings: 750 sabotage attacks on railways, the demolition of 32 Nazi factories and the sabotage of 25 others, and so on. The casualties were heavy—1,000 OJC members died.

Organized Jewish groups, especially OJC and the health organization OSE (see Chapter 10), saved thousands of lives by falsifying documents. With the help of French institutions and individuals, various Jewish groups were able to hide up to 7,000 children. Many French Catholic prelates and all Protestant pastors actively opposed the Vichyite and Nazi Jewish policies, and hid Jews or supported rescue actions, along with a large and growing part of the French population. As a result, about two-thirds of French Jewry was saved. Apart from organized Jewish groups, many individual Jews participated in general French resistance groups.

Although many Jews participated in Belgian resistance groups, their number and role still await research. A small, specifically Jewish group led by Jacques Gutfreund was active in armed action and sabotage. A number of people escaped when a special unit of Belgians and Jews derailed the only deportation train to Auschwitz to be stopped anywhere in Europe on April 19, 1943, the same day the Warsaw ghetto rebellion erupted and the Anglo-American Bermuda conference began (see Chapter 12).

Because of political and topographical factors, relatively few armed actions occurred in Holland, although underground resistance groups were active. Jews in the Dutch resistance were few. A group of young Jews from the Netherlands—mostly German refugees—were smuggled into France with the help of Joop Westerweel, a member of the Plymouth Brethren and a teacher, who was killed in the process. Most of them became active in the OJC.

The first act of resistance to the Nazis in Germany was engineered by a Jewish unit of the communist underground (separate, on the insistence of the parent group) led by Herbert Baum. When they set fire to a Nazi exhibition in Berlin on May 12, 1942, all were caught, and all but two or three were killed.

The main expression of Jewish resistance could not be armed, could not be violent. There were no arms; the nearby population was largely indifferent or hostile. Without arms, those condemned to death resisted by maintaining morale, by refusing to starve to death, by observing religious and national traditions. Armed resistance may be a marginal comment on the Holocaust, but it is written in very large letters indeed.

twelve
RESCUE?

WAS IT POSSIBLE to save the Jews? Who was in a position to help? Some Jews survived the Holocaust—could more have survived? Was anything done to save the nearly 6 million Jews who died?

A "rescue" is effected when a danger to life is perceived. When a danger to life is not perceived, "rescue" is less urgent or justifies less sacrifice. When was the threat to life perceived by the Jews? When did this perception become general among non-Jews? Did the early known facts, that is, facts prior to the knowledge of mass murder, justify rescue?

SUMMARY, 1935–1939

As discussed earlier, German Jews reacted to the Nazi rise to power with both flight and a determination to stick it out in the fatherland. Until 1935, the majority of Germany's Jews wanted to stay, in the hope that the Nazis would not survive; at the same time, however, thoughts of emigration persisted, a calm, gradual, organized emigration that might extend over something like a twenty-five year period. However, as it turned out, there was nothing like that span of time available to the potential victims.

From 1935, emigration was seen as the only solution, and in 1938, especially after Kristallnacht, almost all Jews wanted to escape to anywhere at any price. Why? How did they perceive the threat they were facing?

Some say that the threat to physical existence should have been obvious by 1933 or 1935. However, Nazi propaganda did not utter explicit threats of murder until the end of 1938, when they were thought of as merely ravings of some extremists. Until mid-1938, Jews were rarely put into concentration camps as Jews. The Nuremberg Laws seemed to guarantee at least life and limb if not spirit. The 1936 Olympics brought another reprieve. Nobody imagined mass murder. The Jews' own traditions of humanism and liberalism contributed to their delusions.

The term *rescue* as used in the thirties, meant the rescue of a community, its property, and its future. When the Zionist movement in April 1933 discussed the establishment of a Rescue Fund, a Palestinian Jewish labor party leader said: "Zionism must provide an answer for the rescue of the Jews in Hitlerite Germany—that is, a planned, gradual emigration of German Jewish youth, preferably to Palestine." Rescue in the thirties also meant the maintenance of Jewish life in Germany for those who could not yet emigrate, and for those who would never emigrate for reasons of age or professional status. Jewish organizations abroad supplied the funds to the best of their ability during the world economic crisis of the thirties. In 1935–36, for example, approximately 100,000 German Jews were supported by the JDC; in the thirties, 37,000 persons underwent vocational retraining, largely to prepare themselves for emigration. When Jewish children were no longer allowed to attend German schools, 167 Jewish schools were opened. All this was rescue, in a way, too.

Many Jewish organizations tried to effect entry of German Jews into various countries. The Zionist efforts were directed toward the creation of a Jewish Palestine capable of absorbing a maximum number of Jews. Other local Jewish organizations tried to regulate, limit, or even prevent the immigration of Jewish refugees for fear of the reaction of their national authorities. In the Netherlands, for example, the Committee for Special Jewish Affairs, led by Professor David Cohen, who later became the leader of the Dutch Judenrat, limited immigration and assisted in the expulsion of "undesirable" newcomers. French Jews tried to halt the immigration of Jews into France several times, especially in 1938. When war broke out in 1939, some French Jewish groups refused to help German and Austrian Jewish refugees who had been interned by the French as "enemy aliens." However, Polish, Italian, Yugoslav, and British Jews organized to welcome and absorb their unfortunate brethren from Germany.

A persecuted minority was emigrating. Was there not a moral obligation of the liberal countries to open their doors? In August 1939 the Nazi paper *Der Weltkampf* stated: "We are saying openly that we do not want the Jews, while the democracies keep on claiming that they are willing to receive them—and then leave the guests out in the cold! Aren't we savages better men after all?"[2]

In 1933–35 James G. McDonald, the League of Nations "High Commissioner for Refugees" (Jewish and others), tried to aid the hapless Jews. In the face of strong restrictionist, isolationist, and antisemitic currents, the Roosevelt administration did not attempt to liberalize the quota system, fearing that even the limited quotas in force might be abolished.[3] The most that could be achieved—in 1938–1939—was the maximum use of the German-Austrian quota. When 908 refugees from Hamburg on board the *St. Louis* were denied entry to Cuba in 1939, the United States did not make an exception (see Chapter 6).[4]

In Britain the restrictionist policy was changed in 1938–39 (see Chapter 6). Soviet Russia was certainly not interested. Other countries took in relatively small numbers of refugees. Overall, the Jewish problem was seen as a relatively minor side issue.

That the fate of the Jews had universal moral and political implications was not grasped. Antisemitic undercurrents in even the most liberal circles vitiated against aid to Jews. The Jews, in effect, were doomed before the first shot was fired.

POLAND AND LITHUANIA, 1939–1941

When the Nazis conquered Poland, no threat of annihilation was perceived by the Western world. However, the threat of extinction by starvation and disease was perceived, and by early 1942 Polish Jewry, partly through the Warsaw JDC, was not entirely unsuccessful in fighting it, despite terrible losses of life in 1941.

The Poles, frightened and threatened themselves, were largely indifferent to the Jewish situation. According to Ringelblum and others, the Polish population wanted to isolate the Jews. Although acts of friendship occurred, the overwhelming impression indicates Nazi success in isolating the Jews from the Poles. Such contact that did occur was usually with the negative elements, such as the Polish police force, the "blue" police, which was organized by the Nazis specifically to harass the Jews, and Polish smugglers who brought food into the ghetto at high prices, though without them starvation would have been even worse. Few Jews attempted to hide among the Poles until the murder actions began in 1942. The only organized Polish help available was that extended by the Polish Social Aid Committee, led by Prince Adam Ronikier, which provided aid to all groups in Poland, including the Jews. However, there were the many instances of help—among old friends, colleagues, neighbors. Sometimes help was motivated by hatred of the Nazis. The Catholic Scout movement, a tiny but heroic minority, saw it as a moral imperative to help their Jewish comrades, the left-wing Zionist Socialist Hashomer Hatzair movement. Serving as couriers between the ghettoes, Irena Adamowicz and her fellow scouts entered the ghettoes disguised as Jews to give material and moral aid and to help prepare for the ghetto rebellion.

According to the Molotov-Ribbentrop treaty of August 23, 1939, Lithuania was to have come under German influence. However, on September 28 additional arrangements between the USSR and Germany provided for ethnic Polish regions to come under German domination and Lithuania to come under Soviet influence. On October 10, the Lithuanians were forced to agree to the presence of Soviet armed forces within their country, but Vilna, the ancient capital of Lithuania, would revert to that country.

During September and October 1939, hundreds of thousands of Jews escaped from German-held Poland to Soviet-occupied Polish territory, including the leaders of the Zionist youth movements, some of the most famous yeshivot and their teacher-rabbis, and Polish Jewish political leaders. When rumors spread that Vilna was to be handed over to Lithuania, members of organized Jewish groups began moving toward the city, which was going to become the capital of a neutral country.

Lithuanian troops occupied Vilna on October 28. Because of the instability prevailing in the whole region, the Soviets did not prevent the entry of Jews into Vilna until mid-November. After that time, border crossings became increasingly difficult. Young Jews and local villagers led people across the new Soviet-Lithuanian borders. When caught by the Soviets, the refugees were interned or shipped to Siberian forced labor camps. The crossings stopped in January-February 1940 when they became too risky. Some 14,000 Polish-Jewish refugees had entered Lithuania, including 2,611 yeshivot students and rabbis and 2,065 members of Zionist youth movements.

The old, liberal element of the Lithuanian government was friendly and understanding. Contrary to Western countries, they did not intern the refugees, although they themselves were in a most precarious situation vis-a-vis the Soviet threat. Sooner or later Lithuania would be swallowed by Germany or the USSR. There was no practical way out for Lithuanian citizens. The Polish-Jewish refugees, as aliens, had a better chance of leaving the country for a haven abroad.

The American Jewish emigration society HIAS (Hebrew Sheltering and Immigrant Aid Society) obtained 137 entry visas for Western countries. In addition, the Jewish Agency for Palestine persuaded the British government to honor 406 immigration certificates for Palestine granted to Poles prior to the outbreak of war. The emigrants flew from Riga, Latvia to Palestine via Stockholm.[5] The central figure in this rescue effort was a young Jewish Agency official, Zvi Brick (Barak). When the Soviets annexed Lithuania in June 1940, Brick's work ended, for it seemed that no escape would be possible from the Soviet empire.

Under Soviet occupation, antisemitism, which had become increasingly prevalent in the late thirties, went underground. Whereas only seventy-four Jews had served in the Lithuanian administration previously, Jews now entered the administration, especially those branches of the economy in which they had been prominent, such as trade and industry. Jewish youths entered universities without hindrance. However, the communization of private property deprived Jewish traders, industrialists, and even many artisans of their livelihood, and all Jewish national institutions, including newspapers, political parties, and the Jewish school system, were abolished or denied all autonomous Jewish content. Both Lithuanians and Jews faced exile to Soviet camps if they were identified as enemies of the regime, and proportionately more Jews than Lithuanians suffered deportation in this way. The refugees from Poland were in imminent danger.

After the Soviet annexation of the country, the refugees, with the help of an American Jew—Moses W. Beckelman, who represented the JDC—tried to get out of the Soviet Union. A number variously estimated between 1,500 and over 2,000 escaped to Japan due to the efforts of the Japanese vice-consul in Kovno (see below). An additional 1,200 escaped to Palestine, after the British consul's reluctant agreement to honor some 800 legal certificates of entry to Palestine. As the date of the latter's departure from Kovno (September 4, 1940) approached, Brick and his staff helped to speed up the technical preparations. Inventive minds forged another 400 visas, but what about the official seal, normally displaying two very British lions? In Kovno, the lions miraculously became pussycats. After all, who in Kovno had ever seen a real lion? Although this was but a small percentage of the 14,000 refugees and 250,000 indigenous Lithuanian Jews, more than 3,000 persons had been saved.

JEWISH-GENTILE RELATIONS IN EASTERN EUROPE

Obviously, the relationships affecting that major concentration of the Jews in Europe, namely, Polish Jewry, are of central importance in a brief examination of the rescue problem. The attitude of the surrounding Polish population was an important determining factor in the fate of the Jews.[6]

The accusation of Jewish-Soviet cooperation in Eastern Polish areas occupied by the Soviets in 1939 was leveled by many Poles throughout the war, and persists to this day. There was some truth to this. Soviet occupation was better than Nazi rule, and the Soviets abolished the restrictions that had prevented Jews in Poland from entering universities, the administration, and some trades. However, the fact that Jewish attitudes changed as the Soviets restricted religious life, abolished all Jewish institutions, and confiscated property, was ignored by Polish public opinion. According to Polish figures, 264,000 Jews were deported into Soviet exile or Soviet camps, or between 17 and 20 percent of the Jews in Soviet-occupied Eastern Poland. This percentage is similar or even higher than that of Polish deportees at Soviet hands. During the war itself, in the absence of any substantial help extended by Poles or Ukrainians, the Soviet army and the return of the Soviet regime were seen by the Jews as the only hope for rescue. Jewish forest and ghetto fighters sought aid from the Soviets. The Poles, who feared Soviet rule no less than they hated the Nazi conquerors, could not identify with the Jewish attitude.

By involving Poles in the looting of Jewish apartments and property, such as furniture and clothing, the Germans created a situation in which these persons hoped the Jews would not return. In some cases, Jewish property was handed over to Polish families for safe-keeping. Although some property was protected, other items were appropriated by Poles who had no wish to see the Jews return to claim them. In his detailed account of this situation, Ringelblum recorded the remarks of people who said that Hitler at least, as disastrous as he was, had dealt with the Jewish question and solved it.[7]

Intensive Nazi antisemitic propaganda also left its mark. The Catholic clergy, by and large, and with a few honorable exceptions, echoed antisemitic sentiments. By isolating the Jews behind barbed wire, the Nazis facilitated the identification, and eventually destruction, of the Jews as a foreign minority. From mid-1943 on, an extreme right-wing organization, the National Armed Forces (NSZ), openly advocated the murder of all Jews; after the unification of the NSZ with AK, the AK's anti-Jewish bias became even more marked. Only in Warsaw were some Jews allowed to join the AK. Accusing Jewish fighters in the forests of banditry, AK General Tadeusz

Bor-Komorowski ordered their liquidation on September 15, 1943.[8] When the Jews began trying to escape from the ghettos to hide among Poles in 1942, groups of *szmalcowniki* (blackmailers) waited for them, robbed them, and handed them over to the Germans.

The Polish attitude toward the Jews can be understood within the context of the Nazi attitude toward Poland. Possibly up to three million Poles lost their lives under the German occupation, a process that can be defined as selective genocide. The Polish intelligentsia, the Catholic priesthood—especially in Western Poland—and a large peasant population fell victim to the Nazi desire to eliminate the proud Polish nation. In contrast to other European nations, practically no political figures in Poland cooperated politically with the Germans.

Although antisemitism was widespread and help to Jews was not common, the populations of various areas reacted differently. In Volhynia, in what was then eastern Poland, for example, where the Poles themselves were a persecuted minority among Ukrainians, there was a willingness to help the Jews. In the Lublin area and in Krakow, Poles were more willing to hide Jews than elsewhere. Among the Catholic clergy, the Archbishop of Lwow, Count Andreas Szeptycki, ordered his clergy to save Jews, as did the Ursuline sisters and some village priests. In Warsaw in 1942–43 thousands found hiding places among Polish neighbors—both working-class people and professionals—who risked their lives. A total of possibly 1 percent of the Jewish population successfully hid in the Polish ethnic area. There were heavy penalties for hiding Jews: in many cases entire families were killed and their property burned when it was discovered that they had hidden Jews.

In October 1942, Henryk Wolinski, a Polish liberal, organized a group called Zegota, under the auspices of the Polish underground, which was loyal to the London government-in-exile. Using about 1 percent of the funds transmitted from London to Poland for the use of the underground, Zegota was able to save some 4,000 children and adults in Warsaw and, to a degree, in Krakow. Zegota included in its ranks such Catholic liberals as Wladyslaw Bartoszewski[9] as well as Jewish underground leaders; its secretary was Adolf Berman, a member of the Jewish National Committee.

The Avenue of the Righteous

Hiding a Jew in one's house or on one's property carried grave risk. Other forms of help included supplying forged identity and ration cards, finding employment, accepting Jews into underground movements, smuggling people from one place to another, supplying temporary shelter and food, and so on. Apart from the desire for profit, which operated with many people who gave shelter or aid to Jews, a strong humanitarian motive also prevailed. Other motivations included religious conviction, political ideologies, and personal friendships. The Jews have come to call those who helped "the Righteous," and trees have been planted as living memorials to them in the Avenue of the Righteous at the Holocaust Memorial of Yad Vashem in Jerusalem.

Otto Busse. The director of a German factory in Bialystok, Otto Busse accompanied his Jewish workers into the ghetto, smuggling milk, butter, and potatoes past the ghetto guards. During and after the August 1943 ghetto rebellion, Busse hid Jewish fighters in his factory and, despite his pacifist views, supplied them with arms. He also gave his Jewish friends money and medicine, which enabled them to survive on the "Aryan side." When a resistance fighter asked for money to live, he burst into tears, opened his safe, and said: take as much as you want. Somehow Busse obtained the plans of Germany military camps and the plan for the German anti-aircraft defense in Bialystok, which he gave to the resistance fighters. He found rooms for the Jewish fighters to live in and places to hide equipment, including arms, and Jewish escapees. He put his car—a rare commodity in those days—at the disposal of the Jewish refugees. Above all, he tried to find Jews who had escaped from the ghetto in order to hide them. He even wanted to rescue Jews from Majdanek. When the Russians approached, the Jewish fighters offered to let him stay with them and be saved. But Busse said that as a German he had to pay for what his nation had done. He joined the German army, was captured by the Russians, and spent five years in Russia doing heavy labor.

Paul Grüninger. After the annexation of Austria, many Jewish refugees were denied entry into Switzerland by the Swiss authorities. Paul Grüninger, a police officer in charge of the Swiss border police near St. Gallen, knew that Nazi concentration camps awaited those who tried to leave and failed. He disobeyed orders and allowed a large number of Jews to cross illegally into Switzerland. Discovered, he was put on trial by the authorities and discharged, losing his pension rights. He lived for many years earning a modest living as a teacher's helper. Those he saved never knew his name. When his name and actions became known in 1969, he, too, was honored by the planting of a tree in his name in Jerusalem.

Ona (Anna) Simaite (Shimaite). A Lithuanian, Ona Simaite was described by one of those she helped:

> She came to us as one of the first non-Jews to enter the ghetto, and then came to the ghetto gate almost every day. She served as a contact and a messenger for hundreds of Jews whom she did not know, carrying letters that for those Jews were of vital importance. She went to Gentile neighbors to ask for clothes and other valuable articles that the Jews had left, and brought these things to their owners. Often she was cursed by these "good people" who had patiently waited for the liquidation of the owners of these things. Often these pieces of property saved their owner from death by starvation. Her own ration cards Shimaite used only for potatoes and cabbage. All the rest: bread, marmalade, some margarine, cheese—she sent to the ghetto children, especially the orphans.
>
> She wanted to save the cultural treasures of the Jews. She hid in her apartment all the books and writings that she managed to obtain. A few days before the liquidation of the ghetto, Shimaite took a ten-year-old girl, arranged Aryan papers for her through a lawyer, showing that the girl was her sister's daughter.
>
> The forgery was discovered, and she was sentenced to death. Her friends paid a high ransom for her and she was released. She was tortured by the Gestapo in order to betray the hiding places of Jews. She told her story: "I prayed that I should not open my mouth at that time. I mixed up names and

addresses, so that I should not remember them. I do not believe in God—but prayed with all my heart." Her prayer was heard: She did not reveal a thing.[10]

Raoul Wallenberg. The efforts of Raoul Wallenberg to aid the Jews are described in Chapter 13. He, too, has a place among the "Righteous."

Anna Masczewska. Mordechai Seifert, known by the Polish diminutive Maczek, lives on a kibbutz in Israel. All he knows about himself is his name. Probably born near or in Krakow he was three years old when the war broke out. When a Polish woman, Anna Masczewska, found him in an orphanage, she took the circumcised toddler into her home where she and a Catholic parish priest cared for him during the Nazi occupation. When the Nazis searched her home for hidden Jews, Anna handed Maczek to the priest. Maczek still remembers how, at the age of five and six, he assisted the priest at mass, swinging the incense around, walking behind him through the church. When the war ended, Anna took Maczek to a Jewish children's home and said: "This is a Jewish child; I have kept him throughout the war, he belongs to your people, take him and look after him." Anna Masczewska died, the priest's name is unknown.[11]

Sempo (Chiune) Sugihara. A *yeshiva* student in Lithuania heard from the Dutch consul that no visas were required for Curacao, a Dutch possession in the West Indies, and that the Soviets would issue transit visas to Japan for non-Soviet citizens (such as Polish refugees), provided Japanese transit visas for Curacao had been obtained. Although refugees would not be admitted to Curacao, no visa was required. The Japanese consul at Kovno, Sempo (Chiune) Sugihara, who had been ordered by the Soviets to leave Lithuania by August 31, 1940, and his German aide, Wolfgang Gudke, decided to issue Japanese transit visas to Jewish refugees. Working day and night, he issued thousands of visas by August 31.

Not all the visa holders escaped, but probably between 1,500 and 2,000 managed to get to Japan, and from there to the Western Hemisphere or Shanghai. The efforts of Sempo Sugihara are remembered. In the Avenue of the Righteous at the Holocaust Memorial of Yad Vashem in Jerusalem, a tree has been planted in his name.

Do these people not deserve a forest?

THE RESCUE OF BULGARIAN JEWS

Bulgaria during the war was a Nazi satellite nation, ruled by a fascist government under King Boris. Some 50,000 Jews lived there, an ancient, largely Sephardic community some of whose antecedents dated from Roman times. They were mostly lower-middle-class people or artisans, with a very small group of wealthy merchants at the top.

Eichmann had no great difficulty in obtaining Bulgarian agreement to deport Jews from "New" Bulgaria, that is, Yugoslav and Greek territories occupied by Bulgaria, and in March 1943, 11,343 Jews were deported to their deaths from Macedonia and Thrace. This was brutally executed by Bulgarian police and troops, with the express agreement of the king, Boris.

In "Old" Bulgaria, the situation was different. Although Bulgarian fascists were not averse to taking over the meager possessions of the Jews, and there was no real opposition to these acts of robbery, an agreement of February 22, 1943, between the Nazis and Alexander Belev, the commissar for Jewish affairs, to deport 8,000 Jews from "Old" Bulgaria, along with the Jews from the newly annexed territories, was not fulfilled because of a combination of factors. The Jews of one of the towns, Kyustendil, persuaded their fascist parliamentarian, Dimiter Peshev, a vice-president of the Sobranje (Parliament), to oppose deportation. Some high dignitaries in the Orthodox church intervened, and the underground Communist party, and other groups came out and demanded that no deportations should take place. The king yielded, and the deportation was averted.

In May and June 1943 Sofia Jews were expelled to the countryside and economic expropriation and slave labor followed, but no deportations occurred. Apparently, the news of the fate of Polish Jews had reached Bulgarian politicians. By March–April 1943 the Germans had been defeated in

Stalingrad and North Africa. There was, it seems, no great wish to make the Bulgarian situation worse than it threatened to be. Yet, at the same time, other satellites—Croatia, Slovakia, Vichy France—continued their anti-Jewish policies. The stand taken by Bulgaria was, therefore, in that sense, extraordinary.

RESCUE OPERATIONS IN WESTERN EUROPE

With the conquest of Western Europe by the Nazis in May-June 1940, the hope prevailed that the Nazis would be satisfied with discrimination, expropriation, and occasional reprisals. The war had severed all communications with Eastern Europe, so that the situation there was not known to the Jews in Western Europe. The Nazis did not show their intentions in these countries immediately. Consequently, more than half of the Belgian Jews who had fled to southern France during the fighting returned. Even after the discriminatory laws began to operate in late 1940 and 1941 and conditions seemed precarious, no danger to life was perceived. The Nazis helped to create such illusions by opening in May 1941, for example, a Central Office for Jewish Emigration in Amsterdam. And Gertrude Van Tijn, the JDC's representative in Holland, was sent to Lisbon to discuss Jewish emigration to the United States.

France

In France, it seemed at first that those most endangered might flee to the southern unoccupied zone under the direct rule of the Vichy regime. Jewish organizations of East European origin and those representing East European Jews in France—such as the Fédération des Sociétés Juives and the child-care society OSE—directed their activities from their southern headquarters. The Israelite Jews, that is, the old-established French Jews, thought that the Nazis would concentrate on non-French Jews; they were certain that the Vichy government would protect "their" Jews.

Even when the deportations started in 1942 the fate of the deported was uncertain. Reports on the deportees by French Jewish organizations occasionally depicted places in Poland where Jewish Councils govern, "the old people do not work. The children go to Jewish schools. Men and women capable of working are put to hard labor in factories and mines. Nourishment and lodging are reasonable." [12]

At the same time it was clear that the children deported from France in the summer of 1942 were dead: "The extirpation of Jewry is finally to be accomplished by the methodical extermination of the children." [13] Inconclusive information nevertheless bred fear, and there were BBC broadcasts from London, which from the early summer of 1942 and especially from December 1942, gave reasonably accurate information regarding the fate of the Jews in Nazi Europe. Rescue in the West took place in this contradictory atmosphere. In France, for example, local and international organizations, Catholic and Protestant church leaders, peasants, underground groups, and others, at Jewish initiative, participated in large-scale rescues, especially of children. The Jewish groups included the OSE, the EIF (the French Scouts), the AJ-OJC (the Jewish resistance group), and the JDC.

Until July 1942, the various groups helped people to escape to the unoccupied zone in the south and established an interfaith and international committee at Nimes, which helped many thousands of Jews and others—chiefly Spanish Republicans—in French concentration camps such as Gurs and Rivesaltes. By obtaining permission of the local police prefect, thousands of children were removed from Rivesaltes and placed in children's homes or with families. The OSE especially expanded its children's home to accept these children, whose parents stayed behind barbed wire.

With the July 1942 deportation, the OSE realized that drastic, illegal action was necessary to save the children. George Garel, the young Jewish owner of an electrical appliance shop in Lyon, organized an underground group to save the children. On August 26, 1942, backed by a Catholic group led by a Jesuit, Father Pierre Chaillet, a Jewish convert to Christianity, Abbe Abraham Glasberg, and a Protestant group led by Pastor Marc Boegner, Garel penetrated the camp at Venissieux, where Jewish families were held in transit to Drancy and Auschwitz. He obtained the permission of parents to take 108 children to trucks waiting at some distance and placed them among Christian homes and institutions. On September 2, when the Gestapo demanded that Cardinal Gerlier of Lyon return the children, the Cardinal did not know where they were.

Most members of the Circuit Garel, as Garel's underground organization came to be known, were non-Jewish volunteers. They hid the children with peasants, in town homes and Christian institutions. In most cases, the people who hid these children knew immediately or shortly thereafter that their charges were Jewish. Most of them received the minimal sum of 600 francs a month, smuggled in by the JDC, for the upkeep of the child. No Jewish child was betrayed to the Nazis, even if on occasion the monthly payment was late. Many foster families refused to give up their charges after the liberation.

Garel's workers succeeded in providing the children with a basic Jewish education or at least a Jewish awareness, thus fulfilling the wishes of the parents. Monthly visits to each child took place to ensure both its physical and spiritual well-being. The same applied to children hidden with Christian institutions. In relatively few cases did Christian institutions or individuals misuse their position to influence children to abandon their faith. A group of Jewish girls who were hidden in a nunnery converted, out of despair, after the war. They joined the order of the Sisters of Zion and consecrated themselves to action in support of Jews.

In the action to save Jews, Archbishop Jules-Gerard Saliége of Toulouse and Bishop Pierre-Marie Theas of Montauban were especially active. Saliége in particular demanded that his parish priests help Jews. Although the situation in France cannot be compared with that of Poland, French collaborators and fascists were diligent in their pursuit of Jews. Those caught hiding Jews in France and other West European countries were sent to concentration camps.

During 1942–44 children were smuggled also into neutral Switzerland and Spain. The Swiss accepted children up to the age of 16, and children brought to the frontier had to prove their true identity and age, because children over that age, and adults without children were refused entry and were usually delivered to the Vichy French or the Germans. In addition, passeurs (border smugglers) were used, although they were often far from reliable. Some children fell into German hands, and they and their guides, for example, Marianne Cohen and Mila Racine, were killed. Older children were smuggled across the wild terrain of the Pyrennees, largely by OSE and EIF members of the AJ-OJC underground. Help by the French people was essential. The mayor of the border town of Annemasse aided many children's groups; a tree has been planted in his honor in the Avenue of the Righteous at Yad Vashem in Jerusalem.

Some 7,000 Jewish children were saved. About 1,300 children were smuggled into Switzerland, and about 100 were taken to Spain, financed largely by JDC in Switzerland. Although close to 76,000 died, two-thirds of the Jews in France survived, including 8,500 children.

Denmark

Denmark was conquered by the Nazis on April 9, 1940. Because the Nazis saw the Danes as an "Aryan," "Nordic" people equal, in principle, to the Germans, Denmark was treated with some consideration, though the main reason for a relatively easy occupation regime was economic: Denmark supplied close to 10 percent of Germany's food needs. The monarchy, the Parliament, and the democratic government continued to function. Danish meat, eggs, and butter continued to flow into Germany. The Danes resisted all attempts at Nazification; they showed, the Nazis were later to complain, no understanding of racist principles. The 8,000 Jews in Denmark were in effect protected by the Danish people.

However, as Danish resistance acts multiplied, German-Danish relations deteriorated, and on August 29, 1943, the Nazis instituted military rule, took the king prisoner, and disarmed the tiny Danish army. Although Nazi representatives in Copenhagen warned Berlin against anti-Jewish actions, in the end they agreed to the deportation of Danish Jews, for which preparations began in the late summer of 1943. On September 17 the Nazis confiscated the card index of the Jewish community in Copenhagen, despite strong Danish protests. Dr. Werner Best, the German ambassador to Denmark, thought that a successful deportation of the Jews would arouse a bitter Danish reaction and thus be against the best interests of Nazi Germany; after the war he claimed that the raid of September 17 was intended to warn the Jews, and this may or may not have been the case: Best was playing a double-faced game, and he pushed the deportation plans. Other German officials in Copenhagen, influenced by the humanistic atmosphere in Denmark, warned the Danes. Rabbi Marcus Melchior spread the deportation rumors on September 29 in the synagogue, but no further action by the Jewish community took place.

The Nazi ships in Copenhagen harbor awaiting the arrival of Jews waited in vain. On the night of October 1–2, the Nazis caught only 284 persons. The Danish underground transported 7,229 Jews and 686 non-Jews married to Jews to Sweden. In the end, a total of 477 Jews were caught and shipped to the ghetto of Terezin (Theresienstadt) in Bohemia. In the process, the Danish resistance united and organized. Aage Bertelsen, a teacher, ran a rescue operation for three weeks that saved some 700 people. Also very active were Protestant pastors, trade-union activists, and doctors and nurses. Danes protected Jewish apartments and their contents and saved Torah scrolls from synagogues. Food parcels sent to deportees in Terezin were received there from February 1944.

The Danish rescue action was largely spontaneous, a reaction to the Nazi disregard of Danish national pride and Danish traditions and religious and political convictions. The Jews were Danish citizens or lived under Danish protection and their persecution was understood by the Danes as an attack on their national integrity. Although some antisemitism existed in Denmark prior to 1940 (and still does), a whole people understood that the deportation of the Jews endangered them as socialists, Protestants, liberals, or, simply, as Danes.

It should perhaps be noted that in the atmosphere of true humanism in Denmark even the Nazis acted differently, though the fact that all this took place in late 1943, when many Nazis realized that the war was lost, also helped; however, had other populations decided to protect "their" Jews, the perpetrators might possibly have been similarly influenced. It should also be noted that the Jews of Denmark were saved not by themselves, but by the Danes.

THE ATTITUDES OF THE MAJOR POWERS
The USSR, 1939–1942

Soviet ideology saw the war first as a struggle between German and Western imperialisms, between which there was little to choose. After the Nazis attacked the USSR on June 22, 1941, the war became a world struggle of "progressive humanity" against fascism, and in Russia it became the Great Patriotic War against the German fascist invaders. A Soviet attitude toward the murder of Jews simply did not exist. Soviet ideology was incapable of differentiating or of understanding the particular, the individual. On the other hand, the success of the heroic Soviet struggle against the invaders saved those Jews that managed to survive.

Early in the war, as Jews tried to escape into the Soviet interior, Soviet guards stationed along the pre-1939 borders prevented Jews in the Baltic countries and eastern Poland from crossing. Later the guards were removed and thousands escaped into the Soviet heartland. Nobody cared for these multitudes in the chaos of the Soviet defeats in the early stages of the war. Masses of Jews—and others—died of starvation or typhoid, especially in central Asia, where most of them fled.

Of the estimated 400,000 Polish and Baltic Jews who fled into the USSR, some 250,000 survived. Appeals to Soviet Russia to intervene to save Jews were not answered, nor were appeals to bomb Auschwitz in 1944. All contacts with the Nazis aimed at rescuing people were disallowed by the Soviets, an attitude that was not, most probably, the result of an official anti-Jewish position, but simply of a disregard for human life, exacerbated by the severe suffering of the Soviet population.

The extent of the German mass murder of Soviet citizens is unknown. Many millions perished—from starvation, random shootings, the effects of the war on whole areas, reprisals against areas supporting anti-German partisans, and in concentration camps. About 3.3 million Soviet POWs died of hunger and diseases in German POW camps. Yet the Soviets always had difficulty in acknowledging that whereas the majority of the Russian, Ukrainian, Belorussian, and Lithuanian populations survived, the Jews did not. The struggle against evil is always particular, never general—a concept that Soviet ideology never recognized.

The United States, 1939–1942

Throughout most of the war, the American government, as well as most non-Zionist Jewish groups, clung to the delusion that the Nazis were persecuting the Jews because of their political or religious beliefs. This basic misinterpretation was, of course, rooted in the fear of identifying the struggle against Nazism with a "Jewish" cause. Widespread antisemitism in the United States and strong remnants of isolationist sentiment may help to explain this position, which resulted in American policies lagging several steps behind the Nazi onslaught. Whereas the Nazis talked openly of their anti-Jewishness, the Anglo-Americans were hiding shamefacedly behind such euphemisms as "persecutees," "political and racial refugees," and the like. The Nazis persecuted and killed Jews. The Allies protested against Nazi persecution of "persecutees."

> There was no need to know of the mass murder (up to 1942) in order to save as many European Jews as possible by bringing them into the New World. What was published in the American press was quite sufficient: the persecutions and deportations of German Jews until 1938; the pogroms of November 1938; the mass arrests of Jews and their murderous treatment in the Nazi concentration camps in 1938 and 1939; the establishment of the ghettoes, and the attendant waves of hunger, epidemics, and death, all this was presented in the press, photographed by newsmen who until 1941 could still visit Eastern Europe. The suffering of hundreds of thousands, soon of millions, was evident for consciences to be aroused, for steps to be taken. Nothing was done.[14]

The United States in effect closed its gates to emigration from Europe in 1940–41, when German and West European Jews were still allowed to emigrate. Although the country was neutral, antisemitic tendencies were strong. In five polls between March 1938 and April 1940 some 60 percent of those responding thought that Jews had objectionable qualities. In 1940-41, 17 to 20 percent of the population saw the Jews as a menace to the United States. They were believed to be more of a threat than the Germans and far more dangerous than Catholics or Blacks. In ten surveys between 1938 and 1941, 12 to 15 percent were ready to support a general antisemitic campaign. An additional 20 percent were sympathetic to such a policy and 30 percent opposed it. The remainder did not much care either way. Antisemitism in America actually increased during the war and started to decline only at the end of it.[15] The accusation generally leveled against the Roosevelt administration for its lack of action to save the Jews must be seen in the context of American public opinion: Could a democratic government go far beyond an intolerant, prejudice-ridden, antisemitic public? Could the American government run the "danger" of being accused of fighting a war for the Jews, as the Germans said in their propaganda? Could a liberal President intent on mobilizing his people for a tremendous war effort risk unpopularity because of a minority against whom such prejudices were held?

Britain, 1939–1942

In fighting a desperate battle for its own survival, much of the time alone (June 1940-June 1941), Britain undoubtedly saved civilization. Britain's defense saved the Jews of Palestine, North Africa, and much of the British empire from the fate of European Jewry. Had Britain been defeated, the fate of American Jewry, given American antisemitism, might well have hung in the balance. The British, of course, fought only for themselves, but the defense of their own interests coincided with the defense of civilized humanity, including the Jews.

The May 1939 White Paper on immigration to Palestine stated that immigration would end after 75,000 had been admitted between 1939 and 1944. In view of bitter Jewish opposition to this policy and the expected pressure for more immigration after the 75,000 had been admitted, the British were in no hurry to grant the promised 75,000 entry permits. When war broke out, the British decreed that no enemy nationals could enter Palestine, which, in effect, closed the doors to those who needed rescue most.

In reacting to British policies, Jewish organizations tried desperately to continue the illegal immigration stratagems that had been practiced prior to 1939. Such ventures were supported by Eichmann's Gestapo until the end of 1940. The Nazis wanted to be rid of the Jews and the emissaries from Palestine wanted to save Jews—even enemies can agree when the goal is the same, despite opposite intentions. Between September 1939 and March 1941, twenty-three ships carrying 10,628 refugees from Nazi-held areas left for Palestine. They came in much the same way as they had come before the war: overcrowded, unseaworthy boats brought desperate people who knew, even prior to the era of mass murder, that they were fleeing for their lives.

The British made every effort to stop the ships. The British navy hunted them on the seas; British diplomats in Balkan countries tried to persuade local governments to stop the "traffic." In their miscomprehension of Nazism, the British thought that German agents would infiltrate the ships and thus arrive in Allied-held areas. The thought of introducing agents among the "Jewish parasites" never occurred to any Nazi. In addition, the British feared that Jewish immigrants in Palestine would provoke the Arab world to rise in rebellion. Although hypothetical arguments are just that, the fact remains that when Britain was strong, no country rebelled, whereas when Britain was weak, disturbances and rebellions, or underground preparations for anti-British moves took place (Iraq, April-June 1941; Egypt, 1942). Jewish refugees fleeing for their lives had nothing to do with this.

In November 1940, three ships, the *Milos,* the *Pacific,* and the *Atlantic,* carrying 3,551 passengers, arrived at Haifa. The transport was organized by Berthold Storfer, a Jewish operator, under Gestapo supervision, with the help of Zionist groups in the Reich. The British decided to deport the refugees to Mauritius in the Indian Ocean, but on November 25 the Haganah, the Jewish underground organization in Palestine, blew up the French ship *Patria,* on which the *Milos* and *Pacific* passengers had been concentrated for deportation, in order to prevent it. Two hundred and fifty people lost their lives. The *Atlantic* passengers were transferred by force to a British ship and exiled to Mauritius for the duration of the war.

The last large ship, the *Darien,* reached Palestine in March 1941. The British were unable to deport the passengers because no shipping space was available. After a year in an internment camp, the passengers were released. Most of the men volunteered for the British army.

In December 1941, an old tugboat, the *Struma,* reached Istanbul from Rumania with 769 people on board. The motor failed and could not be repaired. The Bulgarian captain refused to permit the passengers to land or to keep them in an internment camp. The British refused to allow them entry to Palestine, although the Jewish Agency offered the use of 769 permits out of the 75,000 allocated to them. After two months in Istanbul, the British finally agreed to allow the children entry to Palestine, but the Turks refused to disembark either adults or children. On February 24, the helpless ship was towed into the Black Sea by the Turks and sunk as an enemy ship by a Soviet submarine. One person survived.

Public Information About the Holocaust, 1942–1944

The Western press published information regarding the Nazi treatment of the Jews. On January 7, 1942, Soviet Foreign Minister Vyacheslav Molotov published an announcement in *Pravda* that detailed some mass executions and—for the first and last time during the war—specifically mentioned Jews. The *Pravda* report was reproduced in the West. However, all such information—and there was much more in 1941–42—was classified as exaggerated wartime propaganda in the West. Such "stories" could not be true—the concept of the annihilation of a whole people was simply incomprehensible. The Western countries were dealing with more pressing matters—a war that was not going too well and the sorrows and sufferings of millions. A British official wrote about the "wailing Jews."

The first detailed account of mass murder reached the West in May-June 1942.[16] The report, prepared by the Bund leadership in Poland, said that the Germans had "embarked on the physical extermination of the Jewish population on Polish soil." The number of victims was estimated at 700,000. In

June and July, the gist of the report was broadcast over the BBC and published in the press, first in Britain and then in the United States. But it was not really absorbed or believed. It could not be true; it was exaggerated; things like that did not happen in the twentieth century.

On August 8, 1942, Dr. Gerhart Riegner, the World Jewish Congress representative in Geneva, cabled his office in New York and London that the Nazis planned to kill all the Jews in Europe in the coming autumn. The information had been provided by a German industrialist via a Swiss business friend. The cable continued: "Methods under discussion including prussic acid. We transmit information with all necessary reservation as exactitude cannot be confirmed."[17] Considered to have been the first official source of information regarding the mass murder of the Jews, the cable set in motion a process that ultimately made the West at least partly aware of what was happening. However, the information in the cable was hedged with qualifications, and the Americans decided to double-check. The investigation by the Americans led them to the International Red Cross, whose executive officer, Professor Carl J. Burckhardt, was interviewed by the American consul in Geneva, Paul C. Squire, on November 7. Burckhardt verified the Riegner cable.

The Polish government-in-exile had been the first official body to lend unhesitating credence to the reports on planned mass murder. Since June, they had been bombarding the Americans and the British with demands to recognize the facts and to do something about them. Polish statesmen, such as Stanislaw Mikolajczyk, the minister of home affairs in the London government, had tried to arouse the Western Allies.

To see for himself what was happening, Jan Karski (a pseudonym), a Polish patriot and Catholic humanitarian, visited the Warsaw ghetto after the summer 1942 deportation. Disguised as a guard, he then managed to enter what he thought was the Belzec death camp (it was probably a slave labor camp next to it) for one day where he witnessed mass murder. Late in 1942 the Polish underground sent him to report on the situation in Poland in general to the Polish government-in-exile in London. He spoke to both the Polish premier, General Sikorski, and Anthony Eden, the British foreign secretary, and included a detailed statement on what he had seen in Warsaw and Belzec. He then traveled to the United States and reported to President Roosevelt. His report was a major factor in informing the West, but no action followed.[18]

Information regarding the facts of the Holocaust became available in late 1942. Perhaps naturally, though, people refused to internalize it. To protect themselves against the impact of the information, Jews themselves refused to believe it, and many of them refused to internalize the information until after the war. The same difficulty, in different degrees, was experienced by non-Jews. Until information is internalized and becomes knowledge, action is not possible. It took time until the information was believed. By December 17, 1942, when the Americans and the British finally announced that the Nazis were indeed murdering the Jews of Europe, most European Jews were dead. The politicians who drafted the statement privately expressed their doubts about its truth even after its publication.

But the situation in America and Britain was not the same. In America, a hostile State Department, in which an alleged pathological antisemite was responsible for refugee affairs, found itself faced with a deep cleavage in public opinion regarding Jews.

In Britain, a mostly indifferent if not anti-Jewish coalition government, though headed by the pro-Jewish Churchill, faced an enraged public that demanded, in late 1942 and early 1943, action to save the Jews. In the lead were the Anglican Archbishop of Canterbury and the Catholic Archbishop of Westminster, the independent MP for Oxford, Eleanor Rathbone, lords, members of the House of Commons, local trade unionists, village pastors— letters from all areas of Britain reached Parliament and the press in support of action to save the Jews. Although antisemitism was not absent in Britain, the wind did seem to be blowing in the opposite direction.

In this atmosphere, the American State Department and the British Foreign Office met at the Bermuda Conference on Refugees on April 19, 1943 (it so happened that that was the day on which the Warsaw ghetto rebellion began). Little was accomplished. Negotiations with the Nazis to rescue Jews and others were not allowed. No food would be sent to camps or ghettoes.

No ships would be made available for those refugees who might manage to escape on their own. Two small refugee camps were opened in North Africa, and the IGCR (Intergovernmental Committee on Refugees), of Evian vintage, was resuscitated. The public in both countries was told that momentous decisions had been reached, but could not be divulged for security reasons. It was a blatant lie.

The record of the great democracies in 1939–43 does not generate a sense of pride, to put it mildly.

thirteen
THE LAST YEARS OF THE HOLOCAUST, 1943–1945

BY THE SPRING OF 1943, 2.7 million of the 3.3 million Jews of Poland were dead (hundreds of thousands had fled to the USSR on the outbreak of German-Soviet hostilities in June 1941 or had been deported to the USSR by Soviet authorities prior to the outbreak of war). The Jews remaining in Poland were in concentration or slave labor camps or hiding among the non-Jewish population. Two ghettoes remained, Bialystok in the east and Lódz in the west. In August 1943 the Bialystok ghetto was destroyed and its inhabitants murdered. Lódz remained, with 69,000 inmates in early 1944.

In Lithuania, the Vilna ghetto was abolished in September 1943; its working population was sent to concentration camps in Estonia; women, children, and the elderly were killed in Ponary or Treblinka and Majdanek. The Kovno and Shavli ghettoes existed until July 1944 in reduced form.

Elsewhere in Europe, Jews no longer lived freely by the end of 1943.

The Jews of Poland 1939–1945

Amounting in all to 3,351,000 people by 1939, the Jewish community in Poland provided one of the most flourishing cultural, political, and social manifestations of Jewish life in the whole history of Jewish dispersal. Less than 369,000 survived the war, making a total death toll of at least 2,982,000 of whom nearly one million were teenagers, children under the age of 12, and babies.

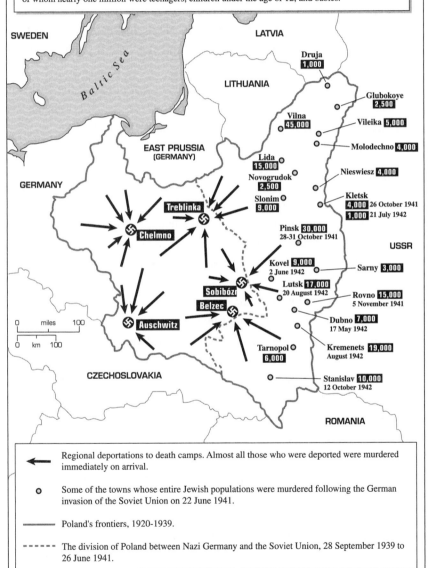

SWEDEN

LATVIA

Baltic Sea

Druja
1,000

LITHUANIA

Glubokoye
2,500

Vileika **5,000**

Vilna
45,000

Molodechno **4,000**

EAST PRUSSIA
(GERMANY)

Lida
15,000

Nieswiesz **4,000**

GERMANY

Novogrudok
2,500

Slonim
9,000

Kletsk
4,000 26 October 1941
1,000 21 July 1942

Treblinka

Chelmno

Pinsk **30,000**
28-31 October 1941

USSR

Kovel **9,000**
2 June 1942

Sarny **3,000**

Lutsk **17,000**
20 August 1942

Sobibór

Rovno **15,000**
5 November 1941

Belzec

Dubno **7,000**
17 May 1942

miles 100

Auschwitz

Kremenets **19,000**
August 1942

km 100

Tarnopol
6,000

CZECHOSLOVAKIA

Stanislav **10,000**
12 October 1942

ROMANIA

← Regional deportations to death camps. Almost all those who were deported were murdered immediately on arrival.

○ Some of the towns whose entire Jewish populations were murdered following the German invasion of the Soviet Union on 22 June 1941.

—— Poland's frontiers, 1920-1939.

- - - - - The division of Poland between Nazi Germany and the Soviet Union, 28 September 1939 to 26 June 1941.

Italian Jews were caught up in the Holocaust by the German invasion of Italy in September 1943; of some 45,000 Italian Jews, 8,000 died—a high proportion survived because of aid received from the Italian population and the local Catholic priesthood. In Holland and Belgium, with few exceptions, only Jews in hiding survived; in France, too, Jews with French citizenship were endangered. In 1943 the Nazis murdered 65,000 Greek Jews, mainly in the Saloniki community and the Greek islands (Rhodes, Corfu, and others).

Most of the approximately 5.8 million Jews who died in the Holocaust were dead by the time the Soviet army recrossed the Polish border in 1944. By the time of D-Day, June 6, 1944, not too many were still alive.

ROMANIA

Of the 765,000 Jews in Romania, 300,000 lived in Bessarabia and Bukovina, the areas that Romania was forced to surrender to the Russians in June 1940. In the wake of this debacle, and the forced surrender of northern Transylvania to Hungary and southern Dobrudja to Bulgaria that followed, King Carol's dictatorship came to an end. From September 1940, Marshal Ion Antonescu shared power with the fascist-terrorist Iron Guard under Horia Sima, thus placing the country under indirect German domination.

Romanian antisemitism was particularly virulent. In a country of great class contradictions, in which the peasants were poor and bitter and the middle classes saw the Jews as hostile competitors, antisemitism was a safety valve used to divert discontent from the real problems. During the fascist government of Octavian Goga and Alexander Cuza (late 1937–early 1938), and King Carol's dictatorship (1938–1940), a series of antisemitic laws were enacted that deprived most Jews of their livelihoods and civil rights and threatened them with denaturalization. Fortunately, antisemitism was tempered by corruption; even more fortunately, Romanian Jewry enjoyed the leadership of a remarkable individual, Dr. Wilhelm Filderman, head of the Union of Rumanian Jews. Although the strong Zionist movement opposed Filderman's liberal, assimilationist approach, it accepted his leadership in relationships with Romanian society. Strict orthodoxy was observed by a small minority; most Jews observed a liberal or tolerant orthodoxy under Rabbi Alexander Shafran, an ally of Filderman's.

The Iron Guard—or the Legionnaires, as they were called—gained great influence in the truncated country. Their program centered around the Jewish "problem": If the Jews were removed and their property confiscated, Romania would flourish. Their participation in government intensified the anti-Jewish line in the streets and in propaganda. A few "legal" measures were taken. An office of "Romanization" was established to transfer Jewish, Greek, and Armenian property to Romanian hands; Jewish agricultural property was confiscated; and Jews in private commerce and industry were dismissed on October 5 and November 16, 1940.

In January 1941 the Iron Guard rose in rebellion against the government of the military leader, Ion Antonescu. In the course of the fighting on January 19–20, 1941, some 120 Jews were literally butchered and their bodies were hung like cattle carcasses in a Bucharest slaughterhouse. In the end, Antonescu defeated the Iron Guard, whose leaders fled to Germany.

Romania became Germany's close ally in March 1941 when German troops were stationed on Romanian soil. The Romanian military were eager to reconquer the lost provinces of Bessarabia and northern Bukovina and to see Russian power removed as far as possible from their borders. They accused the Jews of having welcomed the Soviets into these areas and of having attacked the withdrawing Romanians in June 1940. Although the latter accusation was founded on only one or two isolated incidents, the former statement had some truth to it: many Jews preferred the Soviet regime, despite its destruction of organized Jewish life, to the lethal antisemitism of the Romanian administration. At any rate, when the Germans invaded Russia with the aid of the Romanian army, a series of brutal mass murders took place. On June 29 a pogrom took the lives of 11,000—some were killed in the town of Iasi and some died in closed cattle cars that were shunted from place to place.

In the reconquered provinces of Bessarabia and Bukovina, Romanian troops and police murdered Jews, with some help from Einsatzgruppe D. In July and August 1941 about 100,000 Jews were killed in mass shootings, during aimless and endless marches of men, women, and children, and by drowning in the Dniester River. Romanian attempts to send the remaining Jews, including Jews from Central Romania, across the Dniester to the Ukraine met with German resistance—they were already fully occupied in murdering Ukrainian Jews. However, on August 30, 1941, a German-Romanian agreement was reached at the town of Tighina that allowed the Romanians to deport Jews into the Ukrainian area between the Dniester and the Bug, now called Transnistria.

From September on, about 185,000 Jews were deported from the reconquered provinces and from the region of Dorohoi in "Old" (Central) Romania. In the late autumn and winter they were driven into the townships and villages of Transnistria. The "lucky" ones lived in the ghettoes of Moghilev, Shargorod, and Copaigorod, where they suffered from starvation and typhoid. Most people were "housed" in pigsties and village stables or slave labor camps on the shores of the Bug. In the Auschwitz gas chambers and the shooting pits of Russia, death came quickly. In the pigsties of Transnistria, under Romanian guards, death was slow. Children often kept themselves alive longer by stealing, working for local peasants for a little food, and, in the case of adolescent girls, selling themselves for prostitution. Most victims were starved to death in a small number of horrible camps near the river Bug.

In Bucharest, in the meantime, Filderman tried to intervene with the government to alleviate conditions. He was well aware of the Antonescu regime's intention to murder the Jews. A German memorandum of October 17, 1941, stated that the Jews were being "evacuated from the Bukovina and Bessarabia into two forests in the Bug river area." So far as the writer of the memorandum could learn, "this *Aktion* is based upon an order issued by Marshal Antonescu. Purpose of the *Aktion* is the liquidation of these Jews."[1] But Romania was not Germany, and Antonescu was not Hitler. Although the regime was corrupt, liberal remnants survived, and Filderman, who knew the dictator personally (they had gone to school together), was an impressive personality with connections to the court of the child king, Michael, and to political and religious leaders. He bombarded Antonescu with memoranda that pointed out the damage his antisemitic policy would cause to the Romanian economy, and drawing on his experience as a lawyer, he tried to use Romanian laws to limit anti-Jewish measures. He played on Romanian national pride in an effort to separate Romanian and German Jewish policy. Some support was given by the Apostolic nuncio, Andreas Cassulo. Even some antisemitic orthodox prelates were persuaded to intervene. Liberal Romanian intellectuals were also approached. Filderman secretly supported the small anti-Nazi underground movement, led by socialists and communists. Although he was unable to prevent deportations, his interventions may have contributed to stopping the executions. Money was transferred to Transnistria, though in insufficient amounts. Goods, such as salt, were sent in late 1942 and 1943, to some places at least. Filderman himself was deported to Transnistria for a short time; with an iron hand, he put some semblance of order into the Moghilev ghetto and acted to protect the orphans. He was helped by a Red Cross delegation under Charles Kolb; the main actual work was done by Romanian Jews, particularly a young community leader named Fred Sharaga.

Filderman fought the Nazi design to deport all Romanian Jews to their deaths. Gustav Richter, Eichmann's adviser on Jewish affairs in Bucharest, demanded that the Romanians surrender their Jews. A Jewish Central Committee, led by a Jewish convert to Christianity, Dr. Nandor Ghingold, had been organized as a Judenrat under the direction of a corrupt Jew-hater, Radu Lecca, the 'Commissar for Jewish Affairs'. "It is planned," Eichmann reported on July 26, 1942, "to remove the Jews of Romania in a series of transports beginning approximately September 10, 1942, to the district of Lublin, where the employable segment will be allocated for labor utilization, while the remainder will be subjected to *Sonderbehandlung*" (special treatment—the Nazi cover word for murder).[2] But the deportations did not take place. Why?

The reasons seem to be complicated. The German army had not supplied promised materiel to the Romanian army in the USSR, and the Romanians had suffered severe losses in the course of the German summer offensive of 1942. In addition, Italy and Hungary had not deported their Jews, whereas the German satellites Croatia and Slovakia, upon whom the Romanians looked with disdain, had done so. Antonescu hardly wanted to be counted among the lesser fry. A slight inflicted upon Rada Lecca during his visit to Berlin in August 1942 added fuel. The Romanians decided to postpone the deportations—they were no longer that sure of German victory and were in no hurry. In addition, the Judenrat was helpless; its authority was not recognized by the Jews who continued to see Filderman as their leader. Interventions of religious and political figures, initiated by Filderman, appear to have at least contributed to Romanian wavering and their withdrawal from full support of the Eichmann program.

Of the 380,000 Romanian Jews who died, 260,000 were killed in Bessarabia, Bukovina, and Transnistria by the Romanians, and 120,000 in northern Transylvania, which had come under Hungarian rule in 1940. Most Jews of 'Old' Romania survived, a paradox in a country of such widespread antisemitism. The result in Romania was different because of a combination of Romanian self-interest, national pride, realpolitik, and the fearless stand of the Jewish leaders.

THE RESCUE NEGOTIATIONS

Prior to the outbreak of war, the Rublee-Schacht negotiations pointed to a possibility of, in effect, buying the Jews from the Nazis (see Chapter 6). The Nazis were then pursuing two parallel policies: forced emigration, which became shortly thereafter planned expulsion, and emigration by ransom, which is what the Rublee-Schacht agreement, in effect, amounted to. In 1939–41 emigration was still permitted in most of the Nazi domain. Between the beginning of planned mass murder in June 1941, in the conquered Soviet areas, and the cessation of legal Jewish emigration in October 1941, the two policies were pursued simultaneously: murder in the East, emigration (though partial) elsewhere.

Slovakia

In 1940, some 90,000 Jews lived in Slovakia, where a puppet fascist government, led by a Catholic priest, Father Jozef Tiso, fulfilled all Nazi wishes. Deportations to Poland began in March 1942 with the arrest and transport of 16-year-old girls to Auschwitz. The Tiso government actually initiated the deportations, and of course the Germans agreed; their contribution was expert advice, organization and efficiency, which were supplied by Dieter Wisliceny, the Gestapo expert on Jewish affairs attached to the German embassy at Bratislava. For each Jew deported to Poland, the Tiso government paid the Nazis 500 RM.

A Judenrat imposed on the Jewish community was led, in early 1942, by Arpad Sebestyen, who was loathed for his sheer inefficiency and abject slavishness toward authority. However, an illegal leadership group, called the "working group," was formed; it was led by a Zionist-secularist woman, Gisi Fleischmann, who had been active in philanthropic causes and was the local JDC representative. The outstanding personality in the group led by her was a young, orthodox, anti-Zionist, religious fanatic, Rabbi Michael Dov-Ber Weissmandel, who was her relative.

Although they did not initially know that deportations meant death, Weissmandel and Fleischmann desperately tried to stop them. They approached Wisliceny with an offer of money through the intermediary of a Jewish traitor who collaborated with the Nazis, Karel Hochberg. Weissmandel told Hochberg in June 1942 that he represented a world association of rabbis and could therefore pay in foreign currency. According to Weissmandel's memoirs, Wisliceny rose to the bait: If half the bribe of $50,000 was paid within two weeks, the deportations would cease for seven weeks; if the other half was then paid, deportations would cease completely. The Slovaks would have to be bribed separately. Again, according to Weissmandel, the "working group" collected $25,000 locally from Jewish businessmen who had held on to prewar dollars. The deportations stopped. But the second half of the bribe could not be collected—the JDC was not able to transfer cash from Switzerland, and Hungary's Jews refused to help. In September three Slovakian transports were sent to Poland. Finally, orthodox circles in Hungary collected the remaining sum. Two more transports were sent to Poland after the second $25,000, again according to Weissmandel, was paid but after that no more deportations took place for two years.

Although Weissmandel and Fleischmann assumed that the deportations ceased because the bribe had been paid, it is today quite clear that that was not the case. On June 26, Wisliceny and the German ambassador, Hanns

Ludin, met with the Slovak prime minister. In a report on that meeting and in a separate report to his Foreign Office, Ludin said that the deportations were stopped because of church pressure and the corruption of Slovak officials who had exempted 35,000 Jews for economic reasons.[3]

Ludin's statements, however, were only partly true. Nothing like 35,000 Jews had been exempted. By June, nearly 50,000 Jews had been deported, and another 8,000 went in the September transports; between 7,000 and 9,000 had fled to Hungary, 24,000 remained. Some were lucky enough to receive Slovak exemptions for economic reasons, others were held in three labor camps, still others hid among the population. The Vatican indeed intervened in March and June, and it appears that this had some effect. The chief reason for the stoppage of the deportations appears to have been the bribing of the totally corrupt Slovak officials.

The request by Slovak officials in May 1942 to see the paradise the Germans were building for the exiled Jews in Poland, caused perhaps by some stirrings of conscience, was denied in the usual Nazi style.

After the war Wisliceny said that he gave the money (he said it was $20.000) to Eichmann, who must have reported to Himmler. The bait was obviously not the paltry sum of money but the prospect of contacts with Weissmandel's "world association of rabbis" and their vast influence on America. After the war, Weissmandel put it this way: "Apart from the money, they wanted in this way to get in touch with Jews in the U.S., for some political reason that was more important to them than the extermination of Jews."[4] What was that political reason?

In the course of negotiating the bribe, Weissmandel wrote a letter on prewar Swiss paper using an old Underwood typewriter. He signed the letter "Ferdinand Roth," representative of World Jewry. Even after the war, during his trial in Bratislava, at the end of which he was sentenced to death and executed, Wisliceny still stuck to his belief that he had been in touch with the leadership of World Jewry through Ferdinand Roth. Wisliceny apparently took the letter to Berlin, though we do not know what the Nazi reaction to it was.

In November, the working group again approached Wisliceny and asked what the price would be for stopping the deportations throughout Europe.

After protracted negotiations, Wisliceny offered, supposedly in the name of his SS chiefs, to stop deportations from Western Europe and the Balkans for $2–3 million. Further negotiations on Poland and the actual Reich area might follow. By getting the money from abroad, Wisliceny apparently hoped to establish contact with "World Jewry" for his bosses. However, as he never received their approval to offer what he offered, or to ask for a specific sum of money—it was basically his own initiative, after he had received an initial permission from Himmler to speak to the Jews—his "offer" was a sham.

The working group thought that Wisliceny was speaking for Himmler, and therefore asked for the initial 10 percent of the bribe demanded by the Nazi, i.e., $200,000, from the Jewish organizations with which it was in contact. However, most Jewish aid organizations in the free world—the JDC, the World Jewish Congress, and others—rejected the Europa Plan, as it came to be called, as a blatant Nazi attempt to extort money; they did not believe deportations would cease. The Allies, of course, would not permit ransom monies to be transferred legally, and no such sums could be smuggled out of Switzerland—the only possible venue—illegally. Only the Jewish Agency and the Histadruth, the workers' trade-union organization in Palestine, and their representatives in Istanbul managed, somewhat belatedly, to send $184,000 illegally to Bratislava. There is no way of knowing whether the money actually got there. In the meantime, in August 1943, Wisliceny told Fleischmann that the negotiations were in abeyance, but that the Nazis might well renew them (he had received an order from Himmler to stop them).

Hungary

The Jewish population in Hungary in 1941, after the annexation of Czechoslovak, Romanian, and Yugoslav territories, totaled 725,000. Along with some 62,000 converts to Christianity—a result largely of anti-Jewish discrimination which drove many people to change their religion for economic and social reasons—there were some 800,000 Jews by Nazi definition.[5] A majority was "neologue," or liberal, in the religious sphere, and a strong minority were strictly orthodox. Both groups were acculturated and thought of themselves in terms not dissimilar from those current among German Jews earlier on: they were Hungarians of the Jewish religion, wanted to have as little as possible to do with Jews elsewhere, and rejected Zionism. The Zionists, a small minority among Hungarian Jews, were led by a gifted engineer, Otto Komoly.

Since 1919, Hungary had been ruled by Admiral Miklos (Nicholas) Horthy, whose authoritarian, aristocratic regime had shown its sympathy for Italian fascism and German Nazism early on. Antisemitism was built into the regime; Jews were defined as a race; and a *numerus clauses* operated in universities (only 6 percent of the student body could be Jewish) until 1928. In 1938 and 1939 antisemitic laws limited the percentage of Jews in most branches of the economy. Within the next few years, marriages between Jews and Christians were forbidden, the official status of the Jewish religion was abolished, and Jews were removed from the army—they had to serve in labor battalions instead. Prior to Hungary's entry into the war on Germany's side in June 1941, the slave labor battalions numbered 52,000. More were recruited later, and some 40,000 were sent to the Russian front, where at least 30,000 died from maltreatment and execution. Any thought of Jewish resistance, consequently, was impossible—the young men were simply not there.

Throughout this period, the official Jewish community was largely led by Jewish notables who desperately tried to be counted as Hungarians. Their efforts to alleviate some of the worst effects of official policy by private interventions and pleadings were only very partly successful.

In July–August 1941, 18,000 Jews from the Hungarian-occupied Carpatho-Ukraine (formerly part of Czechoslovakia, today part of the Ukraine) and of Northern Transylvania were deported to Poland, as "aliens," although most had been born in what was Hungarian territory in 1941. At Kamenets Podolskiy in the Ukraine on August 27–28, 16,000 were murdered by SS General Franz Jäckeln's Einsatzgruppe troops and Hungarian auxiliaries. A similar outrage was perpetrated at Novi Sad in the Hungarian-occupied area of Yugoslavia by Hungarian troops against Jews and Serbs.

In the face of these developments, Komoly's small Zionist group initiated flight and evasion tactics. The Zionist leaders included Dr. Reszoe Kasztner, a newcomer from recently annexed Transylvania, and Joel Brand, a refugee from Germany, who established an essential link to the Hungarian secret service. In order to save some of the Kamenets Podolskiy deportees and later to bring Polish Jews to Hungary, Brand also organized an underground railway. Zionist youth movements, especially Hashomer Hatzair and Maccabi Hatzair, as well as orthodox groups, helped some 7,000–9,000 Jews from Slovakia to enter Hungary during the spring 1942 deportations from that country to Poland. In early 1943, Komoly and Kasztner set up a Zionist Aid and Rescue Committee, known by its Hebrew title Va'adah (Committee), to direct these and other activities. The youth movements worked independently, although they acknowledged the Va'adah as the leader of underground Zionist activities and coordinated their activities with them, at least partly.

Until early 1944 Hungary seemed a haven of relative security. Although the young men were in labor battalions, where losses were high, the general Jewish population lived among the host peoples with but marginal discomfort, compared with the situation of Jews elsewhere. Because of their sense of security, Hungarian Jewry, like other Jewish populations, were able to delude themselves into thinking that "it could not happen here." The "it" in the phrase indicates that they knew what was happening in Poland and elsewhere, contrary to the postwar claims of many Hungarian Jews. Information was provided by Hungarian soldiers on leave from Russia, discharged members of Jewish labor brigades, Polish Jews who had escaped to Hungary, and by the BBC. But knowing the facts is not always the same as accepting the facts. To survive, many had to deny what they knew. The later claim that had someone—their leadership, Kasztner, or anyone else—only told them, they would have behaved differently, cannot be taken at face value.

Fearing that the Hungarian government was seeking a separate peace with the Allies, the Germans occupied Hungary on March 19, 1944. Adolf Eichmann directed a Sondereinsatzkommando (Special Task Group) of trusted Gestapo and SS men. A Judenrat was established under Court Councilor Samu Stern, an acquaintance of Horthy's. To avoid a repetition of the Warsaw ghetto rebellion, Eichmann promised the Jews that nothing would happen to them if they cooperated. Judenräte were established in every Jewish community throughout the country. Laws and regulations identifying Jews, expropriating their property, and progressively isolating them from their surroundings followed. Two Hungarian Nazis, Laszlo Baky and Laszlo Endre, who became secretaries in the new pro-Nazi Ministry of the Interior, worked with Eichmann to plan the ghettoization and deportation of Hungarian Jewry. On April 7 instructions were sent to the provinces to move the Jews into ghettoes; implementation began on April 15. The local population neither resisted the new regime nor objected to the ghettoization of the Jews. As in Poland, their cooperation was purchased with permission to loot Jewish property that was not stolen by the Hungarian gendarmes. The ghettoization and subsequent deportation, with all their attendant brutalities, was executed by the Hungarian gendarmes.

On April 27 and 28 two trains carrying 4,000 persons left for Auschwitz. Then, by province, between May 14 and July 9, a total of 437,000 followed. Approximately 100,000 who were capable of work were sent to the labor camp in Auschwitz or to other camps in Germany. Some 75 percent were gassed immediately on arrival. Because the crematoria could not handle such volume, open pits were again resorted to.

The floor of the backyard of crematorium V was littered with amorphous heaps of corpses. One after the other the bodies were dragged out by the bearers who placed them side by side on their backs in a long row where their teeth were removed, their body orifices searched for hidden valuables, and the hair of the women cut off. Only then were the corpses released for cremation.

As it began to grow light, the fire was lit in two of the pits in which about 2,500 dead bodies lay in piles one on top of the other. Two hours later all that could be discerned in the white-hot flames were countless charred and scorched shapes, their blackish-phosphorescent hue a sign that they were in an advanced stage of cremation. At this point the fire had to be kept going from outside because the pyre which at first protruded about half a meter above the edge of the pit had, in the meantime, gone below this level. While in the Crematorium ovens, once the corpses were thoroughly alight, it was possible to maintain a lasting red heat with the help of fans, in the pits the fire would burn only as the air could circulate freely in between the bodies. As the heap of bodies settled, no air was able to get in from outside. This meant that we stokers had constantly to pour oil or wood alcohol on the burning corpses, in addition to human fat, large quantities of which had collected and was boiling in the two collecting pans on either side of the pit. The sizzling fat was scooped out with buckets on a long curved rod and poured all over the pit causing flames to leap up amid much crackling and hissing. Dense smoke and fumes rose incessantly. The air reeked of oil, fat, benzole and burnt flesh.[6]

Komoly and the Va'adah members could not stop the disaster. The arms they had managed to collect—150 pistols, 40 grenades, 3 rifles, and 2 machine guns, only one of which was serviceable—were insignificant. Neither the Hungarian establishment nor the general population was inclined to help. The small anti-Nazi underground was inefficient and depended, at one point, on documents forged by the Zionist youth movements. Nor was the church a source of aid. Catholic Cardinal Jusztianian Seredi declared on June 29:

> We do not deny that a number of Jews have executed a wickedly destructive influence on the Hungarian economic, social and moral life. . . .We do not doubt that the Jewish question ought to be settled in a lawful and just way. Consequently we raise no objections to steps being taken so far as the financial system of the state is concerned. Neither do we protest against the objectionable influence being eliminated; on the contrary, we would like to see it vanish. However we would be neglecting our moral and episcopal duties were we not to guard against justice suffering damage and against our Hungarian fellow-citizens and our Catholic faithful being wronged merely on account of their origin.[7]

Seredi then refused "all responsibility for the consequences" of the deportations, thus washing his hands, like Pilate of old, of the whole affair. The Vatican, on the other hand, on May 15 declared in a note to the Hungarian government that "the whole world knows what deportation means in practice." It then continued that the apostolic Nuntiature protested against these measures "not from a false sense of compassion, but on behalf of thousands of Christian converts; it once again appeals to the Hungarian government not to continue this war against the Jews beyond the limits prescribed by the laws of nature and the commandments of God."[8]

The deportations could be stopped, perhaps, by other means. Energetic attempts were made to inform the free world of the events in Hungary. The World Jewish Congress, through its Geneva representative, Dr. Gerhart Riegner, the Zionist representatives in Geneva, and various diplomats focused the attention of both the press and governments on the Hungarian tragedy. The WJC and other Jewish organizations tried to persuade the International Red Cross and some neutral countries to intercede with Horthy to stop the deportations.

The War Refugee Board

On January 21, 1943, Riegner had transmitted a particularly harrowing account of what was happening in Europe. On February 10 Minister Leland Harrison in Berne received the State Department's order not to transmit messages from "private individuals," that is, Riegner, unless they were of great importance. Throughout 1943, the U.S. State Department—that is, Breckinridge Long, the antisemitic official responsible for the Visa Section—procrastinated, sabotaged proposals, and distorted messages relating to Jews emanating from Switzerland. A group of young non-Jewish Treasury officials—John W. Pehle, Raymond Paul, and Josiah E. DuBois, Jr.—obtained documentary proof of the State Department's policy and submitted a "Report to the Secretary on the Acquiescence of this Government in the Murder of the Jews," to Secretary of Treasury Henry Morgenthau, Jr. Morgenthau toned down the report and with Pehle and DuBois submitted it to Roosevelt on January 17, 1944, as a "Personal Report to the President." In addition, a group of young right-wing Palestinian Zionist activists who at that time lived in the United States, organized public events and conducted a very successful public campaign intended to move the Administration to engage in rescue. The group, around Hillel Kook (a.k.a Peter Bergson), impacted on Congress where a move against Roosevelt on the Jewish refugee question became a real threat.

On January 22, 1944, as a result, President Roosevelt signed an order establishing the War Refugee Board, whose task was to "take all measures. . . consistent with the successful prosecution of the war" to "rescue the victims of enemy oppression." The WRB was to deal with rescue, transportation, maintenance, and relief; it was to deal with civilians whose lives were endangered within Nazi-controlled territory as well as without. Not only relief, but rescue. The WRB was to engage in negotiations with foreign governments; it could employ personnel without regard to Civil Service laws and the Classification Act; it was to appoint special attaches to U.S. representatives abroad. It could "communicate with enemy territory to carry out the purpose of the order." Government agencies had the duty to extend to the WRB shipping, supplies, and other assistance. In effect, the WRB, by implication, was empowered to negotiate with the enemy to save lives. The presidential press release accompanying the order mentioned "the plan to exterminate all the Jews and other persecuted minorities," although the Jews were the only minority who were threatened with complete annihilation. The WRB, in effect, was officially permitted to break practically every important law of a nation at war in the name of an outraged humanity.

Roosevelt's establishment of the WRB appears to have been motivated by a combination of political and humanitarian considerations. The climate of public opinion was changing in America. Attacks in the press and in Congress on government inaction in matters of rescue, especially of Jews, were multiplying. In Congress, the impact of the effective publicity campaign organized by the Peter Bergson group had, as we have seen, become a threat to the Administration. Non-Jewish America was beginning to realize what was happening. Antisemitic sentiment was at its peak, but began to decline. Action to fit the new mood was both politically expedient and, perhaps, in accordance with the president's own personal feelings. The establishment of the WRB may illustrate a political situation in which realpolitik was influenced by moral considerations. The establishment of the WRB, whatever its actual effectiveness, then acquires an importance as a major event in the history of the war: Was the war not fought to preserve the ethical values embodied in practical politics?

On March 24 a presidential declaration warned the Hungarians that collaboration with the Germans in the persecution of Jews and others would not be tolerated. In the following weeks the WRB, and especially its energetic representative in Berne, Roswell D. McClelland, persuaded other countries to intervene in Hungary. Whether because of that, or because of their own perspective on what was happening, Switzerland, the International Red Cross, the Vatican, and the Swedish government contacted Horthy in an attempt to stop the deportations. The Vatican intervened on June 25 (influenced, perhaps, by the liberation of Rome by the Allies on June 6). On June 30 the Swedish king interceded on behalf of the Jews in a personal letter to Horthy. On July 2 the American Air Force bombed Budapest heavily. Convinced, erroneously, that the raid was in retaliation for deportation of the Jews, Horthy stopped the deportations on July 9, temporarily, as he told the German ambassador. Eichmann nevertheless managed to deport one more trainload of Jews.

The awakening of the American conscience was important, though it came much too late. With the exception of some 12,000 to 15,000 who were sent to the environs of Vienna, all the Jews from the provinces had been deported to Auschwitz. Only the Jews of Budapest, some 180,000, remained.

Trucks for Lives

The Zionist Va'adah in Budapest was aware of the Europa Plan negotiations in Slovakia. Komoly and Kasztner, the heads of the Va'adah, also decided to negotiate—Komoly would try to reach the Hungarian government and the underground; Kasztner would try to continue where the Europa Plan had left off; Brand would establish escape routes to Slovakia and Romania. An orthodox group and the Zionist youth movements, led by Rafi Benshalom (Friedl), engineered the flight of a few thousand people to both countries. Komoly's negotiations were fruitless. Kasztner met with Wisliceny and offered the equivalent of $2 million (as in the Europa Plan negotiations) for the ransom of Hungarian Jewry. Although the Nazis accepted the offer and promised that deportations would not occur, they actually viewed the $2 million as an "installment" on the road to "real" negotiations. It is not clear whether Himmler was informed of these early negotiations, and if so, what his reaction was.

However, preliminary contacts ended abruptly on April 25, 1944, when Eichmann himself ordered Brand to appear before him. He offered to release one million Jews (i.e., not only the Jews of Hungary) in return for war materiel and other goods. In subsequent meetings the ransom became more specific: 10,000 trucks and quantities of tea, coffee, sugar, and soap. The trucks would not be used against the West but against the Soviets—a clumsy Nazi attempt to split the Allies. To negotiate via the Jewish Agency for Palestine with the Western Allies to get the goods, Brand would be sent to wherever he chose—he chose Istanbul. He would have a limited, though undefined, amount of time to get results. If the goods did not arrive, the Jews would be killed. When the Allies agreed to the plan, the first group of Jews would be released. On May 19 Brand arrived in Istanbul.

The Va'adah was unhappy with the choice of Brand for the mission. Why was Brand chosen, and not Kasztner? Joel Brand had been educated in Germany, had been a communist opponent of the Nazis, was arrested by them in 1933 and released in 1934, when he went to Budapest and joined the Zionist movement. Resourceful, brave, and intelligent, Brand was also a heavy drinker and an adventurer with contacts in the Hungarian secret service.

However, a second figure was involved in the mission: Andor (Bandi) Grosz. Grosz, a convert, was a smuggler and a cheat. He had joined the German military secret service (the Abwehr), which was directed by the conservative anti-Hitlerite Admiral Wilhelm Canaris, to escape punishment in Hungarian courts of law. In 1943 Grosz managed to be sent to Istanbul, where he worked for the Hungarian counterespionage unit as well as the American OSS and the British Intelligence Service. The Va'adah also contacted Grosz, and he became a courier of the Palestine Jewish emissaries in Turkey, transmitting letters to and from Istanbul and Hungary. Today we know that most, if not all of these letters and messages were caught and read by the German espionage agency. In February 1944 when Himmler's SD finally managed to dissolve the Abwehr, the SD itself became Germany's espionage and counterespionage agency. But the fight between the Abwehr and the SS (the parent body of the SD) had so disorganized the German services that by 1944 the only effective German contact with Western intelligence agencies was the quadruple, low-level agent, Bandi Grosz.

The leader of the SD, Walter Schellenberg, and his boss, Heinrich Himmler, were in early 1944 looking for a way to contact the Western Allies. The war was lost, unless Germany could be saved by a separate peace with the Anglo-Americans. Himmler also knew that a strong, conservative opposition was bent on trying to eliminate Hitler. If they succeeded, Hirnmler's SS, rather than the disunited and inefficient rightists, would gain control of Germany. In the meantime, Abwehr contacts could be used to establish a dialogue with the West. But Brand was not the best choice for establishing contacts. It was Grosz who was entrusted with the offer to the Americans of a meeting with German military intelligence officers in a neutral country to discuss the possibility of a separate peace. As a petty criminal, he could always be disavowed if necessary—in the meantime, he would be useful in establishing first contacts. On May 19 Grosz accompanied Brand to Istanbul—or, perhaps, Brand accompanied him.

Grosz contacted Allied intelligence. Brand, who had a general notion of Grosz's assignment, impressed on the Jewish Agency that the lives of a million people hung in the balance. He knew that the Hungarian deportations had started on May 14. The director of the Jewish Agency's political department, Moshe Sharett (who later became Israel's foreign minister and second prime minister), was refused permission by the Turks to come to Istanbul to meet with Brand. The Turks wanted Brand to leave Turkey, but Brand desperately tried to avoid returning to Hungary where he would be killed unless he had something to show for his efforts. After at first refusing to accept him, the British finally agreed to receive him, and he left Istanbul for British-held territory on June 6. Grosz had already done so on June 1. Brand was promised that he would be permitted to return to Hungary after meeting with Sharett, but after a long discussion between the two in Haleb in Syria, he was spirited away by the British to be detained in Egypt.

In Cairo, Brand and Grosz were interrogated, and the purpose of their missions became clear. The Allies of course rejected any idea of separate peace negotiations with the SS. The British refused to negotiate via Brand, although they saw him as an honorable representative of the Jews and released him after a few months. The Americans, mainly the WRB, at first viewed the offer of the emissaries as a tool to be used to gain time for rescue. The Russians refused to permit any effort to be made to save the lives of people under Nazi rule.

It appears that the SS offer was serious, though this has been disputed by some historians. Because the Nazis believed the Jews controlled the West, they could be used as hostages. Their ransom might bring not only valuable war materials to a besieged Germany (this probably was the story Himmler "sold" to Hitler; Himmler's Nazi competitors knew nothing about Grosz) but might well move the Allies toward negotiating with the SS.

On June 2, 1944, a demand to bomb Auschwitz and the railways leading to it, which originated with Rabbi Weissmandel, was transmitted to the United States government by the Jewish Agency and the Agudat Israel orthodox group in America. A parallel demand was made of the British. American planes were actually bombing eastern Germany, and targets near Auschwitz were severely hit. The British procrastinated. Churchill's demands that the bombings be executed were sabotaged by the Foreign Office and the Air Ministry. In any case, the British were using only night bombers at the time, and these could not be used for precision bombing far away from the home base. Since January 1944, the policy of the Combined Chiefs of Staff in Washington had been to concentrate on military targets only. Auschwitz was "civilian." America rejected the proposal to bomb Auschwitz on July 4, 1944, over the signature of John McCloy. They could have bombed it, though it is not clear what the effectiveness would have been (post-war interviews with Nazi leaders seemed to indicate that the Germans could quite easily have continued murdering Jews even without the gas chambers). Yet the Jewish inmates of Auschwitz were fervently hoping for such a bombardment, even if many of them would have been killed by imprecise Allied bombing. In the end, it was not a question of how many Jews would have been saved, but of a demonstration of Allied concern for a people that was being annihilated that was important. The Allies, through the bombing of the gassing installations, could have demonstrated such a concern, but chose not to do so.

Four Jewish men who escaped from Auschwitz in April and May 1944

(Rudolf Vrba, Alfred Wetzler, Arnolt Rosin and Czeslaw Mordowicz) delivered the full story, and drew detailed maps of the death installations and the concentration camp at Auschwitz, to the Jewish leadership in Slovakia in April 1944. By mid-June, the Auschwitz report was in the hands of the Vatican, the International Red Cross, and representatives of the Allies and Jewish organizations in Switzerland and Sweden. Diplomatic cables summarized the report for the British and American governments. Partly believed, partly rejected, the report did not reverse the decision regarding the bombing proposal. The full report did not reach the WRB until early November, when a shaken and distraught Pehle tried unsuccessfully to revive the bombing proposal. In any case, the gas chambers at Auschwitz— the site of an estimated million murders at least—were closed in early November. Auschwitz was liberated by the Soviets in January 1945. Was there no alternative to the policy adopted by the Allies?

The Mayer Negotiations

The failure of the Brand mission did not dissuade the Nazis from using the Jews as a pawn to entice the Allies into negotiations. The Nazis contacted Jewish individuals and groups in Istanbul and Lisbon with offers to negotiate. Although the British refused, the WRB agreed to negotiate, intending to drag on discussions in the hope of saving lives until victory came. The person chosen to handle the negotiations was a Swiss citizen, Saly Mayer, the JDC representative in Switzerland. The instructions from Washington, which were transmitted by Roswell D. McClelland at Berne on August 21, 1944, stated that the United States "cannot enter into or authorize ransom transactions of the nature indicated by German authorities. If it was felt that a meeting between Saly Mayer and the German authorities would result in gaining time, the War Refugee Board has no objections to such a meeting."[9] Mayer could not offer goods or money, nor could he speak in the name of the JDC.

Colonel Kurt Becher, a confidant of Himmler's in Hungary, was assigned to negotiate by the SS. The Jews of Budapest, whose deportation had been "postponed," were the first subjects of negotiation. In addition, a transport of 1,684 Jews organized by Kastner in June 1944, which included not only his family and friends but representatives of all levels of Hungarian Jewry, was part of the bargaining package. After agreeing to send these people to a neutral country in exchange for a high ransom, the Nazis sent them instead to Bergen-Belsen, where people who might be exchanged for Germans abroad were imprisoned. The release of some members of that group was a precondition of the first Mayer-Becher meeting, which took place on the border bridge at St. Margarethen, between Switzerland and Germany, on August 21. On that day 318 Hungarian Jews arrived in Switzerland from Bergen-Belsen.

The Mayer-Becher negotiations continued until February 1945. Mayer managed to shift the discussion from goods and trucks to ransom money. He far exceeded the terms of his brief. A conservative, deeply religious, eccentric Jewish industrialist and philanthropist with a rather misanthropic bend, Mayer talked money to the Nazis, though he was expressly forbidden to do so. He ignored the Swiss government's warning on August 8 that Jews who escaped as a result of a ransom deal would be refused entry into Switzerland. And he actually bought Swiss tractors and shipped them to Germany to give the Nazis a reason to continue the negotiations.

On August 25 Himmler ordered that the deportations from Budapest be stopped—arguably, this was due, in part at least, to the negotiations and the German desire to continue them. In December the other members of the Kastner transport from Bergen-Belsen arrived. In the meantime, Mayer was trying to persuade the Nazis to permit the Red Cross to take over all "civilian" internment camps, Jewish and non-Jewish (i.e., slave labor, and concentration camps; at that time, the only death camp still operating was Auschwitz). The Red Cross would be using Allied monies and this would, in effect, constitute payment to the Nazis. But the Nazis wanted to contact the American government, an intention of which Mayer was well aware. On November 5 Mayer pulled off a major coup: He arranged a meeting between the Nazi Becher and the American diplomat McClelland in Zurich, at which he demanded that the Nazis stop all killings, release the orphans, and agree to the intervention of the Red Cross. Though the SS accepted Mayer's Red Cross idea only in part, and kept harping on the subject of ransom, Mayer did succeed in saving some lives. To have the clout that would allow the talks to continue, Mayer persuaded the Americans to transfer $5 million of JDC money to Switzerland to show the Nazis that he could deliver the goods (the money was so tied up, however, that he could not have used it).

In an effort to reach the Americans, the Nazis tried other approaches. In 1943, Himmler had sent Schellenberg to Sweden to try and negotiate with the Americans. In 1944, he met with a formerly pro-Nazi Swiss politician, Jean-Marie Musy, and sent emissaries who then contacted the WRB representative in Sweden, Iver Olsen. To Musy, Himmler released 1,200 Jewish inmates from Theresienstadt on February 5, 1945.

On January 15, 1945, a desperate Himmler asked his aide: 'Who is it that the American government is really in contact with. Is it a Rabbi-Jew or is it the Jioint [sic]?'[10] (The JDC was known in Europe as the Joint.)

In Budapest, in the meantime, the Jewish population was moving between the poles of hope and despair. On August 25 General Geza Lakatos formed a new Hungarian government that was bent on taking Hungary out of the war. But on October 15, when Horthy made a radio announcement that Hungary was surrendering to the Allies, the Germans took over Budapest and nominated Ferenc Szalasi, the leader of Hungary's Nazi party, the Arrow Cross, to be the new head of government. The indiscriminate murder of Jews commenced—many were brought to the banks of the Danube, shot, and dumped into the river. In the chaotic conditions of a Budapest beleaguered by Russian forces, Jews were killed by Hungarian Nazis without pretext. Earlier on, the Jews had been forced into special houses in the ghetto, identified with a Star of David. To build fortifications on the Austro-Hungarian border, the Germans took, on the order of Eichmann, approximately 30,000 Jewish women and men from these houses—mostly women, because Jewish men had been in labor battalions since early in the war. Thousands died on the march, without proper food or shelter, from Budapest to the border between November 8 and November 27.

Neutrals became more helpful as the realization dawned of the atrocities committed against the Jews. Among the rescues of this period, that originated by Raoul Wallenberg is perhaps the best known. A scion of a well-known Swedish family of bankers, Wallenberg offered to go to Hungary on a rescue mission, with the blessing of the WRB and the OSS, and with $100,000 provided by the JDC. In July 1944, he became third secretary to the Swedish ambassador in Budapest, Carl I. Danielsson, who had already given Swedish protection papers to some 400 Jews with Swedish connections. Wallenberg provided 4,500 such papers in the course of the following months, especially after the Arrow Cross takeover on October 15. He established his protegees in a number of "Swedish houses" procured for that purpose, and closed his eyes to the forgery of more Swedish protection papers by the Zionist underground.

Wallenberg was later to be arrested by the Soviets, to whom the moral imperatives moving a rich banker to endanger his life in order to save some Jews must have seemed incomprehensible and suspicious. He disappeared in a Soviet dungeon, and was probably murdered by his captors in 1947.

More important practically was the work of Charles Lutz, the Swiss consul, who gave shelter to a member of the Va'adah, Moshe Krausz. Krausz persuaded Lutz to issue Swiss protection papers to more than 8,000 persons who had been promised emigration to Palestine. The examples of Lutz and Wallenberg had a snowballing effect. Representatives of the International Red Cross, the Vatican, Spain, Portugal, and Turkey also issued protection papers to a limited number of Jews. The Arrow Cross Hungarian Nazis did not always respect these papers, however, and many victims died with the papers in their pockets. But as the pressure on the Hungarian Nazis mounted, the Szalasi regime at least formally declared its willingness to recognize the papers on October 29. Another force in restraining the Arrow Cross appears to have been Kurt Becher, the SS man in charge of the Mayer negotiations. Afraid both for his own skin—he was a devoted Nazi[11]—and for the success of the Swiss negotiations, he tried to put brakes on both the Hungarians and Eichmann, who represented the fanatic faction in the SS.

The majority of the Jews of Budapest, however, were rescued by the Zionist youth movements. Unknown at the time, because they operated illegally, they included Rafi Benshalom (Friedl), Moshe Alpan, Peretz Revesz, Zvi Goldfarb, and Efra Teichmann. Having decided that armed resistance would be hopeless, whereas a rescue operation might succeed, their workshop for forging protection papers produced tens of thousands of sophisticated documents—they supplied the anti-Nazi Hungarian underground as well. They operated the Swiss and Swedish houses and organized children's houses, where with Red Cross protection, they cared for the children until liberation. Disguised as Nazis, they "arrested" Jews in transit to the Danube for execution and liberated them; they rescued people from Nazi prisons in a similar manner. Some 50,000 Jews were thus "protected," and thousands of children were saved. Remnants of the Budapest Judenrat also became effective in rescue work in the confines of the ghetto that the Hungarian Nazis established in Budapest in the last few months of their terror regime.

In February 1945 when Budapest was liberated, 119,000 Jews had survived in the city; 11,000 returned from laboring on border fortifications. By August 1945, 72,000 others returned, including those who had been deported to Austria rather than Auschwitz in June 1944 (some 15,000) and those who had survived slave labor in Auschwitz and other camps. The returnees included Jews from areas that had been annexed by Hungary from 1938 on.

THE WAR ENDS

The war against the Jews continued as the Allies closed in on the crumbling Nazi empire. In early November 1944 the Auschwitz gas chambers were dismantled. As the Allied armies approached, some 300,000 to 400,000 Jews were evacuated from other camps to be used to build fortifications in the mountains of southern Germany and Austria. The mass murder of the Jews was to remain a secret—the bodies had been burned, nothing but ashes and mountains of eyeglasses, women's hair, children's toys, and clothes remained. To eliminate the testimony remaining in the mass graves throughout Eastern Europe, Himmler ordered SS commander Paul Blobel to organize Commando 1005, a contingent of Jewish slaves, which was to open the mass graves and burn whatever remained. Although many such graves were opened and the evidence destroyed, many remained untouched and were uncovered after the war. The quick Soviet advance in Estonia prevented the complete destruction of the bodies of Vilna Jews, which had been placed on pyres and burned. When Majdanek was liberated in July

1944, the Russian reports on what they found there were viewed with disbelief in the West.

From November–December 1944 inmates of a number of camps, especially in the East, were marched off into the rapidly contracting inner area of Hitler's "Thousand Year Reich." Most of the inmates at Auschwitz had been marched off on January 18, 1945; when the Russians arrived on January 26, only a few thousand ill persons remained. The pattern repeated itself: last minute mass murder, and marches of those who were able to walk into the German-held interior. Sometimes they were transported in open railroad cars in mid-winter, with next to no clothing or food. Hundreds of thousands of walking skeletons, dirty, hungry, thirsty, were marched under heavy guard from camp to camp, sometimes backtracking on their path because of changes in the war situation or conflicting orders. Those who lagged behind were shot. One survivor recalled:

> A few days later the camp was evacuated. Before we left, everyone was given a bread ration. And then we set out on our march, in a cloud of dust and escorted by large numbers of SS guards. We had not been told where we were making for, but judging from the position of the sun we were marching in a southwesterly direction.
>
> After only a few kilometres the first few collapsed. Anybody unable to get up was immediately shot. Even now, when their time was so obviously almost up, the SS took care to remove every last trace of their crimes. After the first few corpses had been flung onto the side of the road, an SS-Unterführer ordered ten men, including me, to step aside. We were told to wait by the roadside.
>
> Meanwhile the last stragglers in the column had dragged themselves past the spot where we were still waiting in the company of the Unterführer who did not deign to speak to us. After an hour a horse-drawn vehicle appeared from the direction in which the column had disappeared. The driver, an elderly member of the Volkssturm (elderly or very young German civilians called up at the last moment and given arms), reversed and stopped. We were ordered to load the corpses on his vehicle. With his cart piled high with bodies he drove to the cemetery in the next town. There a largish grave had been dug in the meantime into which we threw the nameless corpses. Then we continued on our way in

the wake of the marching column. I mused wryly on the strange fate which had once more put me in a team whose job was the removal of corpses.

As we passed through a village or hamlet with our giant hearse the inhabitants, as soon as they set eyes on its grisly load, turned away in horror and disappeared into their houses. One could see that many felt sorry for us and would have liked to help. Outside a few of the houses small heaps of apples, carrots, and bread had been placed which we picked up and devoured ravenously. When I had eaten my fill I decided to lay in a small store. From a barn I took a piece of cord which I tied round my waist. Then I stuffed anything edible I could find inside my shirt so that nothing could fall out. The next few days were to prove that I had done the right thing.

Our march ended in a wood not far from Gunskirchen near Wels [Austria], inside a few wooden barracks surrounded by watch-towers. There was not an SS man in sight. We had no roll-call, did not work. Now and then a few cauldrons of soup appeared. Of discipline there was not a trace. Lying on the barracks' floors were hundreds of emaciated forms, apathetically drowsing and looking as if the last spark of life had departed from them.

I had taken up residence in one of the barracks, perched on a narrow rafter, strapping myself in with a belt so as not to have to keep holding my balance, and covering myself with a blanket. There was, needless to say, never any question of proper sleep. Below me the moaning and groaning continued day and night. Dead bodies lay strewn all over the place, no one concerning themselves with their removal: the stench took one's breath away. Besides, I had to take care not to make a wrong movement, or else I might have fallen 3 metres. It was here that the wisdom of hoarding food inside my shirt became apparent. Of course, if the others had discovered my secret supplies I should have been lost. Thus I only dared to eat in the dark, chewing my precious food slowly and, most importantly, noiselessly. With alarm I watched my little hoard getting smaller every day. . . .

My physical and spiritual state of health was deteriorating rapidly. Still lying precariously perched on my rafter, I watched rather impassively as scores of lice were walking all over my blanket. I scarcely any longer noticed the moaning and groaning in the barracks below me. I felt somnolent, as though I was just about to drop off to sleep. Then all of a sudden from all around us there came the noise of fighting. The chattering of machine guns and the bursting of shells made me feel wide awake. Before long people burst into the barrack, their arms raised, and shouting exuberantly: "We are free! Comrades, we are free!"

It was, incredibly, a complete anti-climax. This moment, on which all my thought and secret wishes had been concentrated for three years, evoked neither gladness nor, for that matter, any other feelings inside me. I let myself drop down from my rafter and crawled on all fours to the door. Outside I struggled along a little further, but then I simply stretched out on a woodland ground and fell fast asleep.

I awoke to the monotonous noise of vehicles rumbling past. Walking across to the nearby road I saw a long column of American tanks clanking along in the direction of Wels. As I stared after the convoy of steel giants I realized that the hideous Nazi terror had ended at last.[12]

How many marched, how many died in the last months? In April and May 1945 the camps in Germany itself and the wandering columns of women and men were finally liberated: Buchenwald was freed on April 11 by the Americans, Bergen-Belsen by the British on April 15, Dachau and Mauthausen on April 29 and May 3, respectively, by the Americans, Terezin (Theresienstadt) on May 9 by the Soviets.

The last, and perhaps ultimate, horror was uncovered by the British in Bergen-Belsen. Neither a death camp nor even a concentration or labor camp, Bergen-Belsen was a "convalescent" camp. Prisoners too weak to work were transported there in large numbers in February and March 1945. In early March, of 41,520 persons, 26,723 were women. By that time the camp administration was breaking down, although the guards were at their posts. The water supply was no longer sufficient and the food was a watery soup with rotten vegetables. In March, 18,168 people died of starvation. On March 31 new arrivals had increased the population to 44,060, and early in April 30,000 more arrived. On April 15 there was no food at all to feed 60,000 people who were dying of starvation and typhoid. *Prior* to liberation 37,000 people died. *After* liberation another 14,000 succumbed, despite the heroic efforts of a British medical team. Most of the inmates were Jewish. When films of Bergen-Belsen were released, the world looked on in horror.

During the last weeks of the Reich, Himmler continued to negotiate with Count Folke Bernadotte of Sweden, Musy of Switzerland, and others—he even met a representative of the World Jewish Congress, Norbert Masur, on April 21. Contrary to the wishes of the extreme SS faction—Ernst Kaltenbrunner, head of the security services, Eichmann, and others—Himmler wanted to keep some Jews alive to serve as hostages. Occasionally, his associates intervened to prevent the mass murders that the extreme faction demanded. In that sense, the negotiations pursued since 1942 served some purpose until the end—Ravensbrück, Bergen-Belsen, Buchenwald, and other camps were abandoned to the Allies without fighting.

WAS RESCUE BY NEGOTIATION POSSIBLE?

Throughout their rule, the Nazis advocated two alternative solutions, sometimes one to the exclusion of the other, sometimes both simultaneously: expulsion or sale of Jews, and mass murder. However, expulsion or sale were but a step towards a final goal of annihilation, as the Nazi leadership aimed at catching up with those who had escaped its clutches temporarily, in the long run. In the end, therefore, murder was the intention.

Because the Nazis saw the Jews as non-human, they could be sold—in exchange for peace with the West, for instance, to save the tottering Nazi empire. That seems to be the thread running through the story starting with Weissmandel's supposed deal with Wisliceny in Slovakia in June, 1942, and ending with the Mayer-Becher talks in early 1945. In other words, murder was inherent in Nazi ideology, but there were, apparently, temporary alternatives. To realize these alternatives, the West needed different priorities: the preservation of human lives required a higher priority than military considerations. By negotiation, by bombing, and other means, some Jews—and others—could have been saved.

Hitler himself was perfectly consistent. He began his political career with an expression of his view that the central problem facing the world was the removal of the Jews. In his political testament on April 29, 1945, the day he committed suicide, he wrote:

Centuries will pass away, but out of the ruins of our towns and monuments the hatred against those finally responsible, whom we have to thank for everything, international Jewry and its helpers, will grow. . . . I left no one in doubt that this time . . . the real criminal would have to atone for his guilt, even if by more humane means [gassing?—Y.B.]. . . . Above all I command the leadership of the nation and the followers to observe punctiliously the racial laws and to show unrelenting resistance to the poisoner of all the nations of the world, international Jewry.[13]

Nazism ended the way it began—by attacking Jews. To the Nazis, the Jews symbolized humanism, morality, monotheistic religion, democracy, and the rule of law, all those pillars of civilization that they tried to destroy.

THE HOLOCAUST—SUMMING UP

What "Caused" the Holocaust?

Historians agree that the Holocaust resulted from a confluence of various factors in a complex historical situation. The interpretation favored here is that antisemitism fostered throughout the centuries in European culture is centrally important, the basic fact being that the Jews were (and are) a minority civilization in a majority environment. In periods of crisis, instead of searching for the solution of such crises within the majority culture, the majority *may* tend to project blame for the crisis on a minority which in some ways stands out in the public mind, is familiar and weak. As the originators and bearers of an important part of civilization, the Jews are a "father civilization" against which pent-up aggressions are easily unleashed. Christianity's long quarrel with a religion that, according to the church fathers, should not really exist exacerbated the dangers. The view of the Jews as a satanic force out to control the world, developed in the Middle Ages, was reinforced in the crises accompanying the emergence of liberalism, democracy, and the industrial world by the modern secularist biological theories of "blood" and "race." In this connection it is important to state that none of these racialist theories are grounded in scientific fact. All so-called "races" are in fact mixed. All modern humans originate from Africa, and their color has changed (or has not) over hundreds of thousands of years because of climatic and environmental conditions. Blood does not define any group, because the same blood groups are found in different human societies. The Old Testament (the Jewish Bible) preempted modern science when it developed a monotheistic approach which implied that as there is only one God, the father of mankind, all humans are essentially equal.

Violence against Jews was perpetrated not only in Germany. Antisemitism is a Euro-American phenomenon, the oldest prejudice of humanity. With the globalization of human civilization, antisemitism has spread beyond Euro-America to other continents. Without denying the universality of antisemitism, and the fact that antisemitism in pre-Hitler Germany was no more prevalent than in some other countries, the development of the Holocaust by German National Socialism (Nazism) can be explained by specific factors operating in Germany:

1. The destruction of a German national identity and the retardation of the development of a national unity resulting from the Thirty Years' War (1618–1648), and the consequent division of Germany into a large number of separate political entities. This in its turn retarded the economic and social developments in Germany and especially the rise of a strong middle class that would have a vital interest in the establishment of a strong democracy. There were important efforts made in Germany in the nineteenth century towards such a development, but they succeeded only in part.

2. The identification of an integral German (völkisch) nationalism with both Germanic Christianity and German pagan anti-Christian traditions, all of which excluded Jews. The struggle for a German national identity always explicitly excluded Jews from the definitions of German nationhood.

3. German romanticism, which by and large rejected liberal and democratic traditions, though it originally rebelled against autocratic regimes.

4. The German defeat in World War I and the resulting desire to reassert German collective strength.

5. The economic crises of the early, and then the late, twenties, and the resulting destruction of objective and subjective security for the group, the social class, and the individual.

6. The central and crucial element of the long-standing tradition of anti-semitism in "explaining" crises and social problems

Holocaust and Genocide—Is There a Difference?

Every Jew—man, woman, and child—was to be killed. The Roma ("Gypsies"), Poles, Russians, Czechs, and Serbs were not to be totally annihilated. Their leaders and their national, economic, political, cultural, and religious life were to be destroyed, and widespread massacres of innocents from among all these peoples were committed—hence the term *Genocide*—but the majority was not to be killed; they were to be used as slaves. The Genocide of the Roma, for instance, was to engulf most wandering, and some settled people of that nation. In Poland, some would be voluntarily or forcibly Germanized; the intelligentsia was mass murdered, large numbers of the Catholic priesthood underwent martyrdom, whole Polish areas were depopulated, cultural institutions were closed, millions of Polish people became slaves in Nazi industries. But although possibly up to three million Poles died, and the German policy towards them must be defined as genocide, the masses of the Polish people survived.

In the original definitions of the term Genocide by lawyer Rafael Lemkin (1943) there is an interesting contradiction: on the one hand, Lemkin defines Genocide as the "extermination" of a people; but on the other hand, he goes into great detail describing the selective mass murder of leadership by the perpetrators, the destruction of religious life, the appropriation by the perpetrators of economic advantage, and the moral corruption of the victims. Obviously, if people are murdered, they cannot be victimized by moral corruption. Lemkin's definitions were in essence, and with some amendations, taken over by the United Nations in its Genocide Convention of 1948, which has been signed by most countries of the world. What is suggested here is that of the two definitions offered by Lemkin, the second is what is here called *Genocide,* and the other, the first, the total "extermination," is *Holocaust.* Obviously, they are closely interrelated.

It is unfortunately essential to differentiate between different types of evil, just as we differentiate between types of good. If we do that, we can see a continuum from mass brutalization, mass murder for political or religious or other reasons, through Genocide to Holocaust. Mass brutalization began, in our century, with World War I and the massive murder of soldiers (by gas, for instance) that took place then. This appears to have prepared the world for the shedding of all restraints imposed by the relatively thin veneers of civilization. The next step is Genocide, and Holocaust is then defined as the extreme case, the farthest point of the continuum. It then becomes not only the name by which the planned murder of the Jewish people is known, but a generic name for an ideologically motivated planned total murder of a whole people. There have been a number of genocides in the twentieth century from the genocide of the Herrero people in what today is Namibia, at the hands of the then German Imperial Army (in the first decade of the twentieth century), through the Armenian genocide in World War I, the genocide of the Assyrian people in Iraq in the twenties and thirties, the genocide of the Roma ('Gypsies') and the Poles in World War II, the auto-genocide in Cambodia in the seventies, the genocide of the Tutsi in Rwanda in the nineties, and several genocidal acts that do not fit into the UN definition, but are clearly of the same basic quality as genocides, such as those in the Balkans in recent times. There are no gradations as between all these attacks on people—one cannot (and should not) say that one is "better" or "worse" than the other. Nor is there a gradation of suffering. None of the people described here as victims of genocide or Holocaust suffered more or less than the other. The differences lie in the motivations of the murdering groups, in other words in the ideologies that led to the mass murder, and in the regimes that perpetrated them. The victims here are the crucial factor, because there will always be more victims than perpetrators, and it is vitally important to examine why the victims were victimized, what social life they had developed prior to their victimization, and what their reactions were to their being targeted. It is also important to state that efforts were and are made to overcome the tendency of victim societies to perpetuate their subjective feelings of remaining victims—a potentially dangerous tendency.

Theodicy—Where Was God? Where Was Man?

Obviously, the Holocaust poses serious questions as to the credibility of both religion and humanism. Ultraorthodox Jewish theology justifies the Holocaust as an act of God, a punishment for sins committed by the Jewish people against their God. That children were punished for the sins of their parents, a contradiction of the teachings of Judaism, and that millions of devout Jews suffered for the transgressions of others are not explained. This approach, popular enough among the extreme orthodox, is rejected by most scholars. Others argue (Rabbi Joseph D. Soloveichik) that as God's intervention in history cannot be understood or explained in human terms at all, the question is not what, or why, God did or did not do but whether man follows God's commands. In this view, Auschwitz is the result of man's betrayal of God. Another Jewish view (Rabbi Eliezer Berkowitz) sees the contradiction between free will and a constant presence of God as a possible explanation of the withdrawal of God from His creation (the "Hiding of the Face"). Elie Wiesel is torn between the impossibility of both God's presence and His absence in Auschwitz. Emil Fackenheim, in a series of penetrating analyses, accepts God's presence in history but limits it in accordance with Divine will. The rise of Israel in the post-Holocaust world is a hopeful sign of a return of the Divine presence, and the command of Auschwitz is to preserve the Jewish people. Richard Rubenstein sees the Holocaust as a tool used by the dark forces in human society to eliminate superfluous populations in a cold world devoid of Divine presence. Alexander Donat draws atheistic conclusions: A God that permits the murder of millions of innocent children, either by His presence or His absence, is a Satan and cannot therefore exist. Morality is man-made and must be defended by human effort.

The credibility of Christianity in the wake of the Holocaust has been questioned by Franklin H. Littell and A. Roy Eckardt, among others: How can the murder of the Messiah's people in the midst of Christendom by baptized apostates be justified? The martyrs of the Church Struggle against

Nazism and the Righteous among the Nations are but a footnote to the Holocaust, which to some Christian theologians is a main theological crisis of the present generation. On the Catholic side, John Pawlikowski, Rosemary Ruether, and others grapple with the responsibility of Christianity for the Holocaust.

Littell, Eckardt, Pawlikowski, and I have suggested that an "early warning system" be instituted to detect in Western democracy the signs of anti-democratic tendencies, racism, intolerance, and prejudice that breed genocide (see Bibliography). The Holocaust would then become a tremendous warning signal to be addressed when trying to avoid becoming either perpetrator or victim. In the meantime, however, it has become painfully obvious that in fact no early warning is needed, because in all recent genocidal or similar events the warning had been given by observers, mass media, military people, and politicians well in advance of the tragedies happening. What seems to be needed is not early warning, which is there, but early preventive action by an international community aware of its responsibilities. Non-action is actually not cost-effective: in the end, it costs more to repair the results of these man-made tragedies than it would have been to prevent them.

Consequences of the Holocaust

During the Holocaust, probably 5.8 million Jewish people died, that is, more than one-third (about 34 percent) of the Jewish population.[14] From the liberated Nazi camps, weeping skeletons of men and women emerged. Among them were 200,000 Jews. These have to be added to the 210,000 that survived in France, about 37,000 in Belgium, 20,000 in the Netherlands, probably close to two million in the Polish-Soviet area (including the internal parts of the former Soviet Union), 350,000 in Romania, 130,000 in Hungary, and smaller numbers elsewhere. Including Soviet Jewry, part of whom were never under Nazi rule, Great Britain and the neutral countries, about three million Jews were left in Europe out of the original nine million Jews before the war.

Prior to 1939, the Jewish populations in Eastern Europe were growing,

TABLE 13.1

JEWISH LOSSES IN THE POLISH-SOVIET AREA

Jews in Poland 1939[a]	3,351,000	
Jews in USSR 1941 [b]	3,100,000	
Jews in non-Polish territory annexed by USSR 1939–41	554,000	
Total Jews in Polish-Soviet area 1941		7,005,000
Jews in Polish-Soviet area 1945[c]	1,910,000	
Polish survivors and repatriates from USSR	300,000	
Total survivors		2,210,000
Jewish military casualties, Polish and Soviet		230,000
Total casualties, excluding military casualties		4,565,000
Total survivors and casualties		7,005,000

a Polish government figures.

b population of 3,020,000 in 1939 plus natural increase by June 1941.

c Natural increase from 1945 to 1959 deducted from 1959 population of 2,268,000.

whereas in Western Europe the tendency was toward less, or zero population growth. Jews in the Western Hemisphere followed the West European pattern after the Holocaust, which must be seen as having accelerated a downward tendency in Jewish population. In 2000, only the Jewish population in Israel is growing. The populations of almost all other Jewish communities are either stagnant or declining, thus creating a threat to the existence of the Jewish people.

The loss of Jewish cultural centers during the Holocaust has created the need for an immense rebuilding program. Some orthodox institutions and scholars were rescued, and their heirs survive in the United States and Israel. These have succeeded in rebuilding a whole minority world of religious institutions and talmudic academies. About 20 percent of Jews in

TABLE 13.2.
TOTAL JEWISH LOSSES IN THE HOLOCAUST

Polish-Soviet area (approx.)	4,565,000
Germany	125,000
Austria	65,000
Czechoslovakia	277,000
Hungary	402,000*
France	83,000
Belgium and Luxemburg	24,700
Holland	106,000
Italy	7,500*
Norway	760*
Romania (excluding Bessarabia, northern Bukovina, and northern Transylvania)	271,000–287,000
Yugoslavia	60,000–67,000*
Greece	60,000–67,000
Total	5,700,000–5,860,000

*May be underestimated.

Israel and less than 10 percent in the United States belong to orthodox or ultra-orthodox groups. Only small remnants of the Zionist youth movements survived and contributed to the new centers of Jewish life in Israel. However, the survivors, most of whom were not orthodox, rebuilt their lives, and at the beginning of the third millenium still have a very important and constructive influence on Jewish societies. Their influence is also felt through their children and grandchildren, keepers of their family traditions.

The Holocaust trauma of mass murders of a large part of the Jewish civilization left indelible marks on individuals, families, and on the attitudes of the Jewish people as a whole—probably for many generations to come. By no means all of these influences are positive; Jewish society may be described as a traumatized group, and it will take a very long time before the effects of the Holocaust are properly internalized and absorbed.

It is essential to realize that we live in an era in which Holocausts are possible, though not inevitable. The Holocaust was produced by factors that still exist in the world, factors such as deep hatreds, bureaucracies capable and willing to do the bidding of their superiors, modern technology devoid of moral directions, brutal dictatorships, and wars. If this is so, who can say which peoples could be the future victims, who the perpetrators? Who might the Jews be the next time?

fourteen
AFTERMATH
AND REVIVAL

MORE THAN 11 MILLION prisoners of war and "displaced persons" of many nations were liberated from Nazi slavery at the end of the war. The roads of Europe were filled with people going home. The liberating armies were intent on returning these multitudes to their homes both to ease the pressure on scarce military resources and to aid the liberated countries to reactivate their economies. Some groups faced special problems: The Roma who had survived the war continued to be hunted and discriminated against in postwar Germany and elsewhere in Europe (to this day); the Nazi collaborators—especially those in the Ukraine and the Baltic countries—who feared reprisal on returning to their countries; and many from the Soviet sphere who refused to return to countries where personal and political freedoms were denied. The formerly occupied countries of Europe, especially Poland and the Soviet Union, were destroyed and had to be rebuilt. In some of them that process has not been completed, six decades after the war.

Of the 200,000 Jews liberated from the camps, roughly three-quarters returned to their own countries: Most Hungarian Jews, the largest contingent, returned to Hungary, Czechoslovak Jews to Czechoslovakia, and so on. But some 55,000 Polish and Lithuanian Jews remaining in Germany in the summer of 1945, had nowhere to go. Those who tried to go back were greeted with hostility by their neighbors, many of whom had profited from looted Jewish property. Immediately after the war the Jewish Brigade, which was established by the British in September 1944 from among Palestinian Jewish recruits in the British army, began searching for survivors. The soldiers were, in their majority, also members of the Palestine Jewish armed underground, the *Haganah*. In army trucks identified by the Star of David and the blue-white Jewish national colors, the brigade visited liberated camps to help Jewish inmates, who were the targets of antisemitic outbursts by their brutalized fellow inmates even *after* liberation. Through contact with the brigade, many inmates decided to try to reach Palestine. By August 1945, 15,000 former inmates had been smuggled across the border into Italy by the brigade where they were under the jurisdiction of the United Nations Relief and Rehabilitation Administration (UNRRA), with additional aid supplied by the JDC. Most of those remaining in the liberated camps had a single goal: emigration to Palestine, to help found an independent Jewish community.

A major factor in the formation of an autonomous Jewish DP (displaced persons) leadership in postwar Germany were the Jewish military chaplains in the U.S. Army. Among these, a decisive influence was exercised by Rabbi Abraham J. Klausner, who was instrumental in helping set up the initial organization of the Munich-based Central Committee of Liberated Jews in Bavaria. In the British zone of occupation in North Germany, a similar role was played by a survivor, Joseph (Yossel) Rosensaft.

The Allied armies were irritated by the Jews: The Jews did not want to return to their former homes; they tried to set up independent organizations; and they demanded separate Jewish camps. The Allies did not recognize the Jews as a separate entity, and the struggle was quite bitter. American public opinion was aroused by both a feeling of guilt derived from the Holocaust, and the letters received from soldiers in occupied Germany that described the treatment of the Jews. In June 1945 President Truman asked a law professor at Princeton, Earl G. Harrison, to look at the situation of the DP camps and to report specifically on the Jewish situation. In his initial report to the president, in early August, Harrison accused the U.S. Army of negligence, of continuing Nazi practices of discrimination (which was a vast and unjust exaggeration), and of not supplying proper food and clothing. He proposed to set up Jewish camps, on the model of those set up by the Jews themselves under Rabbi Klausner's guidance. He also suggested that 100,000 Jews be permitted to go to Palestine, thus solving the DP problem in Germany and allowing some leeway to gather in more survivors from the rest of Europe.

When President Truman released the Harrison report to the public at the end of September 1945, he also submitted a request to British Prime Minister Clement Attlee to admit 100,000 Jews to Palestine. The British, however, had concluded that, in view of their shaky hold over the Middle East and its natural resources, they could not permit such a move. On September 21 the Labor cabinet in Britain, which had come into power after the July 1945 general election, decided to devise a way to hand over the rule of Palestine to the Arabs without causing too great a disturbance among the Jews and their supporters. In the meantime, a monthly quota of 1,500 Jewish immigrants would be permitted. Truman's proposal for the admission of 100,000 was impossible. However, to avoid a clash with the United States, Foreign Minister Ernest Bevin proposed an Anglo-American Committee of Inquiry to consider what to do with the Jewish survivors in Europe, whom Bevin wanted to return to their countries of origin. After some wrangling, the committee in November 1945 was also given the task of proposing a solution to the Palestine problem.

In the meantime, however, many Holocaust survivors in Poland and the other eastern countries began organizing to move toward Palestine, without waiting for representatives of Palestine Jewry or the Zionist movement. When the ghetto fighters, the forest partisans, and those who had been hiding returned to their former homes, they were greeted by death, and streets empty of friends and relatives. The reality could not be faced. As one of them said:

Who will release us from the pain in our hearts, from the lonesomeness and destruction that call out at us from every street corner and every clod of earth? Around us victory trumpets are blown every day. There is a tremendous desire to live and we—we try to run away from ourselves. Can one demand that we eat flesh off the altar of death? When we heard of the liberation of Kovno, we rushed there like mad. Each one went to his home with a pounding heart. We went to our house in Milados 7 [an address in Kovno—Y.B.]. Heaps of rubble and burnt bricks— that is all that remained. . . . And a mail-covered plaque, with the number 7 inscribed on it in shining white, remained, as though to protest the destruction of the house and its occupants.[1]

In addition, the rabid antisemitism of the local population persisted. "In the village of Eisiskes in the Vilna area five of the few Jews who had survived were murdered. Their bodies were brought to Vilna for burial. In some of the pockets of their clothes the following inscription, in Polish, was found: 'This will be the fate of all surviving Jews.'"[2]

There was no point in staying. The only hope for survival, they were convinced, lay in the Jewish homeland—in Palestine. At first, small groups organized, independent of each other, in localities liberated by the Soviet army as early as the spring of 1944. By December 1944, they were in touch with each other and converged on Lublin, the location of the Soviet-controlled Provisional Government of Poland. In January 1945 ghetto fighters from Warsaw joined them. Led by Abba Kovner of Vilna, they set up a clandestine organization called Brichah (Flight) to lead the refugees out of Poland to the coasts, the jumping off place to Palestine. Kovner himself had moved to Romania in March 1945, while the war was still on, to search for a way to Palestine. The Brichah organization in Poland included a director, local branches, "points" at the borders for illegal crossings, and workshops to supply forged papers to allow escape from Soviet-controlled areas.

In July 1945 Kovner and his group met with Palestinian Jewish soldiers in Italy. In a speech before the Jewish Brigade on July 17, 1945, Kovner said:

> But what are we to do if in our sick souls—or are they healed already?—we bear not only the vision of the past, but also that of the future. And we feel with all our senses the breath of the approaching slaughtering knife. The knife which lies in ambush in every corner, on every path and highway of Europe. The new knife was born on the fields of Majdanek, Ponar, and Treblinka where millions of the masses of tens of nations saw how it was done—so easily, so simply, and so quietly.[3]

The deep pessimism about the future expressed by Kovner was shared by many survivors—another Holocaust was more than a possibility. To guard against that possibility, they would build and fortify a Jewish homeland in Palestine.

During 1946, some 175,000 Jews returned to Poland from the Soviet Union, as a result of a special arrangement made between the Polish and Soviet governments in the summer of 1945. The communist-dominated Polish government tried to persuade the returning Jews to stay in Poland to help build a new Polish society. In the newly annexed ex-German area of western Poland, lands and parts of towns were set aside specifically for the Jews. However, the same causes that made the original Brichah groups leave Poland operated now as well. Nothing remained of the original communities from which the returnees had fled to the Soviet Union. Friends and relatives were no more. It was impossible, psychologically, to reestablish a thriving Jewish life in a graveyard. To compound such misery, antisemitism was rampant in Poland. Between the end of the war and the summer of 1946, hundreds of Jews were murdered throughout Poland—some were thrown off moving trains by antisemites who had been well taught by the Nazis. On July 4, 1946, in an action reminiscent of the Middle Ages, the Jewish survivors in the town of Kielce were accused of blood libel, of killing Christian children for ritual purposes. In the pogrom that followed, in which government forces participated and the local bishop refused to intervene, forty-two Jews were brutally killed. The Kielce pogrom provoked a mass flight. Within three months, some 100,000 Polish Jews and others from neighboring countries fled to the American and British zones of Germany. The Brichah organization, flooded with requests to leave the country, managed with difficulty to organize the illegal mass exodus. In the midst of the flight movement, in August, the Polish government agreed unofficially to aid the exodus by permitting exit from Poland into Czechoslovakia. The main Brichah route led through Czechoslovakia to Bratislava and from there to Vienna. From Vienna, the refugees were moved by Brichah organizers via Salzburg into either the American zone of Germany or southward into Italy. Another route went via the Polish-dominated harbor of Sczeczin to Berlin and the West. Brichah continued its operations—from Poland, Rumania, Hungary, Czechoslovakia, and Yugoslavia—until well into 1948. A total of 250,000 Holocaust survivors were moved by Brichah into Germany, Austria, and Italy with the aim of ultimately arriving at the coasts—the largest organized, illegal, mass movement in the twentieth century.

However, because the British had closed Palestine to Jewish immigration, the Jews could not continue their journey. To locate a temporary home, the chairman of the Jewish Agency executive board, David Ben-Gurion, went to Frankfurt in October 1945 to persuade General Eisenhower and his chief of staff, General Walter Beddel Smith, to permit free Jewish entry into the American occupation zone. Although the American military, which was friendly toward Jewish aspirations at that time and also wary of any repetition of the Harrison Report scandal, did not explicitly promise to accept Jewish refugees arriving from Eastern Europe, neither did it voice any serious opposition.

In the American zones of Germany and Austria, Jews lived in DP camps where no employment was available and the barely sufficient food and clothing allotments were supplemented to some extent by the JDC. However, although far from ideal, the camps provided a necessary temporary refuge.

The political and social organizations in the camps were overwhelmingly directed toward immigration to Palestine, but not all Jewish DPs in Germany, Austria, and Italy wanted to reach Palestine. Palestine at that point was rent by difficulties, armed conflict, and an uncertain future—the war-weary Jewish refugees had every incentive to seek alternative refuge. But in the end only about one-third of the 300,000 East European Jewish refugees in Central and Western Europe chose to go to countries other than Palestine.

In the political sphere, British opposition to Jewish immigration to Palestine presented a number of difficulties. At the end of April 1946, the Anglo-American Committee of Inquiry reported that the immigration of 100,000 Jews into Palestine was a logical and positive step. It also recommended that the British mandate in Palestine be ended and that a bi-national Arab-Jewish state be established there.

Contrary to Bevin's promise to the members of the Anglo-American Committee of Inquiry, the British government did not implement its unanimous recommendations. Instead, a new Anglo-American committee of "experts" was appointed to find a compromise between the anti-Zionist British policy and the American demand for immigration. This group of "experts" proposed to freeze the development of the Jewish National Home in Palestine, to end immigration after accepting 100,000 Jews, and to retain British rule in Palestine. A loud outcry erupted in the United States against this development, and under the pressure of public opinion, Truman repudiated the "experts" proposals and announced in early August 1946 that he did not support the compromise.

The American position derived from both political and humanitarian motives. The Jewish DPs in the American zone were a restless element and an obstacle to any rapprochement with the emerging West German state, which was becoming a major priority of American global policy with the developing confrontation with the Soviet Union. Both Truman's political inclinations and American public opinion favored the immigration of the Jewish DPs to Palestine. But no American statesman in his right mind wanted any part of the Palestine embroglio—let the British, the Jews, and the Arabs sort it out.

In 1945–46, the illegal Jewish underground in Palestine, the Haganah, took matters into its own hands. The Mossad, the illegal immigration department of the Haganah, formed a clandestine high command in Paris, led by a founding father of Israel's Labor party, Sha'ul Avigur, who had also founded the Mossad. With tremendous difficulties, ships were bought and fitted out, foreign crews and Palmach (Haganah elite troops) volunteers were enlisted, and a complicated radio communications system was set up. Jews in Europe and elsewhere were offered the risk of an illegal journey to Palestine.

Despite the danger of being discovered and arrested by the British, and despite the overcrowded and hazardous conditions on the small, unsuitable boats, thousands thronged to take the trip: families, small children, pregnant women, older people, DPs from Germany, Austria, and Italy, North African Jews in Arab countries, Romanian and Bulgarian Jews in Soviet-controlled areas—not even a reasonable proportion of those who wanted to risk such a journey had the opportunity to do so. Between August 1945 and May 1948, sixty-five ships brought 69,878 people to the shores of Palestine. In 1946 alone, twenty-two ships brought 21,711 people: 7,451 on eleven ships from Italy, 3,777 on four ships from France, and the rest from Yugoslavia, Rumania, Greece, and other places. To accomplish this exodus, a whole network of disguised emissaries, camps, and transports was devised with the support of French people, Italians, Yugoslavs, and others, who disliked the British policy of preventing Holocaust survivors and other Jews from achieving what they considered to be self-determination.

In Palestine itself, a guerrilla war of increasing venom was waged against the British by right-wing split-offs from the Haganah, the National Military Organization (NMO, or IZL; Heb., ETZEL), led by Menachem Begin, and the Fighters for the Freedom of Israel (FFI; Heb., LEHI), founded by Abraham Stern (known also as the Stern Group and by the British as the Stern Gang), who was murdered by a British policeman in February 1942. The NMO, which numbered some 1,500 members in 1945, had started its armed campaign as early as January 1944 in direct response to the news about the Holocaust. Begin, who had fled to Vilna early in the war, and had spent time in a Soviet concentration camp, reached Palestine with Polish troops who were moving from the USSR to fight alongside the British in the Mideast in 1942. The IZL viewed British rule in Palestine as an accessory to the murder of the Jews of Europe. They intended to force the British from Palestine and to establish an independent polity. The Haganah itself, which was subject to control by the Jewish Agency, was also motivated by the situation in Europe. When it became clear in the summer of 1945 that the newly elected British Labor government would permit neither sizeable Jewish immigration nor Jewish political autonomy in Palestine, Haganah joined the two smaller groups in what was termed the Jewish

Resistance Movement to attack British objectives. From October 1945 to July 1946, the guerrillas attacked railways, bridges, military airfields, oil refineries, and other targets. The Haganah and the IZL did not attack civilians and in most cases warned the British prior to the attack to avoid human casualties. Whereas the aim of the IZL was to rid Palestine of the British, the Haganah, including its elite corps, the Palmach, commanded by Yigal Allon, was more concerned with changing British policy toward Jewish Palestine. The leaders of the Jewish Agency, by and large, still hoped for an accommodation with Britain that would restore the old alliance of the Zionist movement with the British.

In the face of these difficulties, the British government, prodded by Ernest Bevin, decided to act forcefully. On June 29, 1946 ("The Black Sabbath" as it was later to be called), the British army, 90,000 men strong and equipped with modern weaponry, descended on the Haganah. Open resistance was out of the question: The Haganah had, on paper, 36,000 members, but only 2,000 were trained Palmach troops; another 3,000 to 5,000 could be considered half-trained; they were equipped with about 10,000 rifles and 132 machine guns. In any case, the Haganah command was taken by surprise. One of the three main Haganah arms caches—which contained the "heavy" armaments, 94 two-inch mortars and 2 three-inch mortars—was uncovered at Kibbutz Yagur near Haifa. Jewish Agency leaders who were in Palestine were arrested. Ben-Gurion was in Paris at the time and the Haganah commander, Moshe Sneh, managed to evade the British and fled abroad. A legendary Haganah field commander, Yitzhak Sadeh, who later became the father of the Israeli armored forces, took over.

Haganah was hard hit by the British action. It ceased participating in the armed struggle against Britain not only because of the blow it had received but because the Haganah command considered an armed struggle with a superior force to be a waste of Jewish strength. The Haganah would attack the British through illegal immigration and public opinion; armed Jewish strength would be reserved for possible war against the surrounding Arab states, which certainly would oppose the establishment of a Jewish polity. In 1946–47, therefore, Haganah desisted from most armed attacks on the British, whereas the two other groups carried on.

On July 22, the IZL blew up the wing of the King David Hotel in Jerusalem that housed the British civil administration in Palestine, with the sanction of the Haganah. Despite strong British denials, the evidence indicates that the IZL warned the British prior to the attack. The message was not broadcast to the people, however, and more than 90 Britons, Arabs, and Jews died. Because of the loss of life, the Haganah ended its association with the IZL. The King David explosion marked a turning point in the escalation of the armed struggle in Palestine.

The second British blow fell on illegal immigration. In August 1946 the British government declared that illegal immigrants would be stopped and shipped to detention camps in Cyprus. Of the 69,000 immigrants mentioned earlier some 51,000 (and 2,000 who were born there) spent up to two years in the Cyprus detention camps. Despite the deterrent of the camps, large numbers of DPs continued to volunteer for the journey organized by the Mossad. In July 1947, the *President Garfield,* which was bought in America by the Mossad and renamed *Exodus 1947,* brought 4,200 would-be immigrants from France. The British returned the immigrants on three British ships to Port-de-Bouc on the Riviera. However, contrary to their expectations, the French authorities refused to disembark the passengers against their will; the ships finally docked at Hamburg, where the passengers were forced to disembark in the British zone of Germany. In returning the immigrants to the country responsible for their suffering, the British only succeeded in making them more determined than ever to reach their ancient homeland. Nor did the action enhance the British image in the worldview; the sight of the British navy chasing rickety ships crowded with refugees across the seas was not a pleasant one.

In August 1946 an impasse developed. Weakened by the war, the British could not impose a pro-Arab solution in Palestine without American backing. The United States, torn between a desire to solve the European DP problem and pro-Arab interests, thought a compromise was possible. On October 4, 1946, President Truman issued a declaration that stated that a compromise between the partition as proposed by the Jewish Agency and the British pro-Arab solution "would command the support of public opinion in the United States." The press, and the British, interpreted this—

wrongly—as support for partition, i.e., for the establishment of a Jewish State in Palestine. To Bevin, the Palestine situation was insoluble: The Jews wanted a state, the Arabs would go to war to fight it, and he would not use force against American wishes and, in fact, against public opinion in a war-weary Britain. Consequently, Britain relinquished the Palestine problem to the United Nations in February 1947, hoping that pro-British and pro-Arab views would prevail. The UN set up yet another commission to examine the related problems of the Jewish DPs in Europe and Palestine.

After touring Europe and Palestine in the summer of 1947, the United Nations Special Commission on Palestine proposed a complicated partition plan. Surprisingly, a Russo-American alliance supported the establishment of a Jewish state. The Soviets wanted the British out and the Americans, in effect President Truman, despite his opposition to a Jewish State, and after zigzags and tactical turnabouts, decided ultimately—against the wishes of his State Department—to support Jewish independence. Among other bene-fits, it would finally resolve the DP issue. American policy was also deter-mined to a large extent by the pressure of Holocaust survivors and American public opinion, which, by and large, supported the Jews: Americans were convinced that the world was in debt to the Jews; religious Americans recog-nized the validity of the Jewish desire to return to their ancient home; and American soldiers returning from Europe had seen what the Nazis had done to Jews and others. Public opinion in a democracy is a powerful force, and in this case it operated in favor of the Jews. American Jewry also contributed to the outcome: Under the charismatic leadership of Rabbi Abba Hillel Sil-ver of Cleveland, it created a grass-roots political organization in the Zionist movement that successfully influenced non-Jewish America to support the Jewish stand. Truman, a weak president who desperately needed the Jewish vote in the congressional elections of 1946 and the presidential elections of 1948, could not do without the support of pro-Jewish public opinion. In a dramatic autumn UN session in New York, the General Assembly voted by a two-thirds majority to sanction the partition of Palestine, on November 29, 1947.

Palestinian Arabs and the Arab states surrounding Palestine opposed the decision by force. Because Palestine's Arabs were not organized and because their prewar leader, Haj Amin el-Husseini, had supported Nazism and was consequently no longer viable, the main struggle actually involved the Jews and the Arab states.

Although the martial skills of the Jews were viewed with disdain by their enemies and friends alike, and military equipment was scarce, the Jews, that is, the Haganah, fought a bitter war successfully. After establishing the State of Israel on May 14, 1948, the Jewish forces, aided by Czechoslovak armaments delivered with Soviet connivance, pushed back Arab invaders from Egypt, Syria, Jordan, and Lebanon. Many Holocaust survivors from Europe and Cyprus lost their lives on the battlefields of an emergent Israel. When the war ended in early 1949, with an armistice that was to be broken by more bitter wars in the decades to come, 6,500, about 1 percent of the Jewish population in Palestine, had died, most of them Palestinian Jews who had grown up there; but Holocaust survivors had played their part, had fought and suffered additional, grievous losses on the battlefield, and by the end of the war close to a half of Israel's soldiers were recent immigrants. Political independence, the return of the Jewish people to world history, had exacted a heavy price. A mass exodus to the new State of Israel commenced. By 1950–51, two-thirds of the DPs had come to Israel, one-third went elsewhere.

The State of Israel did not result from the Holocaust; in fact, had the Holocaust not occurred, it is more than likely that Israel may have arisen quicker and better and more securely. Had the war continued for another year or more, it is doubtful whether any Jews would have survived to demand immigration to Palestine. Therefore the equation is: more Holocaust, less Israel. Hence the argument that Israel was created by the Holocaust is as erroneous as it is popular. But there is no doubt that the pressure exercised by the Holocaust survivors in the DP camps decisively influenced the establishment of Israel; it is therefore true to say that the *results,* or the after-effects, of the Holocaust had an important influence on the processes that led to the rise of Israel.

Some religious Jewish leaders have claimed that Israel was in some sense a recompense by God for the murder of the Jews during the Holocaust. However, on both historical and theological grounds, most Jews reject this theory today as utterly repugnant. Other theologians, Jewish and Christian, argue that the rise of Israel is a sign of God's presence in history; to some Christians, especially, Israel's return to political history is a matter of profound theological import in the light of God's promise. For others, this is a purely political development, and for Palestinian Arabs it is a disaster—hundreds of thousands were displaced as a result of the fighting: they fled, or were uprooted by the Jewish forces.

From a historian's point of view, the problem is no less complicated. The rise of an independent Israel is indeed difficult to understand, especially by those who subscribe to the theory of Jewish submissiveness.

The frightful trauma of the Holocaust is now, decades after the event, beginning to emerge as a constituent factor in Jewish psychological make-up. It could happen again, and not necessarily to Jews, but to anyone by anyone. Increasing numbers of non-Jews are equally concerned with the event, its causes and aftereffects, and for not dissimilar reasons. The Holocaust is a meeting place between Jewish and non-Jewish history. As a major event of the twentieth century, it is a watershed. As a warning, it may be most crucial; as a precedent, it could be disastrous. It has become a symbol for genocide, for mass murder, for 'ethnic cleansing' for hatred of foreigners, for racism and antisemitism. The reasons for that seem to be that it was an extreme, unprecedented form of genocide, and it happened to a people whose traditions and contributions to civilization have an important place in humanity's consciousness.

On its margins, the acts of the rescuers show us that human beings can choose between evil and good. Most people at that time chose evil, or turned away so as not to see it. But some chose good, and thus provide us with a hope for the future: we are capable of being rescuers, just as we are capable of being evil-doers.

People very seldom learn from history; sometimes, however, they do. Can our generation be such an exception? Which shall we choose?

APPENDIX

HIMMLER'S "REFLECTIONS ON THE TREATMENT OF PEOPLES OF ALIEN RACES IN THE EAST"

FILE NOTE OF HIMMLER'S, May 28, 1940, concerning the handling and distribution of his memorandum on the treatment of alien races in the East (Translation of Document NO–1881, Prosecution Exhibit 1313, Nuremberg Trial Documents).

The Reich Leader SS
Special Train, 28 May 1940
Top Secret

On Saturday, 25 May, I handed my memorandum on the treatment of peoples of alien race in the East to the Führer. The Führer read the six pages and considered them very good and correct. He directed, however, that only very few copies should be issued; that there should be no large edition, and that the report is to be treated with utmost secrecy. Minister [Hans Heinrich] Lammers [Chief of the Reich Chancellery] was likewise present. The Führer wanted me to ask Governor General [Hans] Frank [General Governor of occupied Poland] to come to Berlin in order to show him this report and to tell him that the Führer considered it to be correct . . . .

A secret memorandum handed to Hitler by Himmler on May 25, 1940 (Translation of Document NO–1880, Prosecution Exhibit 1314, Nuremberg Trial Documents).

For the files

(stamp) Top Secret

Reflections on the Treatment of Peoples of Alien Races in the East

Concerning the treatment of peoples of alien races in the East we have to see to it that we acknowledge and cultivate as many individual ethnic groups as possible, that is, outside of the Poles and the Jews, also the Ukrainians, the White Russians, the Gorals, the Lemkes and the Kashubes [small ethnic groups linguistically and culturally related to the Poles]. If other small and isolated national groups can be found in other places, they should be treated the same way.

What I want to say is that we are not only most interested in not unifying the population of the East, but, on the contrary, in splitting them up into as many parts and fragments as possible.

But even within the ethnic groups themselves we have no interest in leading these to unity and greatness, or perhaps arouse in them gradually a national consciousness and national culture, but we want to dissolve them into innumerable small fragments and particles. . . .

There must be no centralization toward the top, because only by dissolving this whole conglomeration of peoples of the Government General, amounting to 15 million, and of the 8 million of the eastern provinces [the parts of Western Poland annexed by Germany after Poland's defeat in 1939], will it be possible for us to carry out the racial sifting which must be the basis for our considerations: namely, selecting out of this conglomeration the racially valuable and bringing them to Germany and assimilating them there.

Within a very few years—I should think about 4 to 5 years—the name of the Kashubes, for instance, must be unknown, because at that time there won't be a Kashubian people any more (this also goes especially for the West Prussians). I hope that the concept of Jews will be completely extinguished through the possibility of a large emigration of all Jews to Africa or some other colony. Within a somewhat longer period, it should also be possible to make the ethnic concepts of Ukrainians, Gorals and Lemkes disappear in our area. What has been said for those fragments of peoples is also meant on a correspondingly larger scale for the Poles.

A basic issue in the solution of all these problems is the question of schooling and thus the question of sifting and selecting the young. For the non-German population of the East there must be no higher school than the four-grade elementary school. The sole goal of this school is to be—

Simple arithmetic up to 500 at the most; writing of one's name; the doctrine that it is a divine law to obey the Germans and to be honest, industrious, and good. I don't think that reading is necessary.

Apart from this school there are to be no schools at all in the East. Parents, who from the beginning want to give their children better schooling in the elementary school as well as later on in a higher school, must make an application to the Higher SS and Police Leaders. The first consideration in dealing with this application will be whether the child is racially perfect and conforming to our conditions. If we acknowledge such a child to be of our blood, the parents will be notified that the child will be sent to a school in Germany and that it will permanently remain in Germany.

Cruel and tragic as every individual case may be, this method is still the mildest and best one if, out of inner conviction, one rejects as un-German and impossible the Bolshevist method of physical extermination of a people.

The parents of such children of good blood will be given the choice to give away their child; they will then probably produce no more children so that the danger of this subhuman people of the East *(Untermenschenvolk des Ostens)* obtaining a class of leaders which, since it would be equal to us, would also be dangerous for us, will disappear—or else the parents pledge themselves to go to Germany and to become loyal citizens there. The love toward their child, whose future and education depends on the loyalty of the parents, will be a strong weapon in dealing with them. . . .

NOTES

Chapter 1
Who Are the Jews?

1 B.C.E. (before the common era) and C.E. (common era) are used in this book. They are the Jewish equivalents of B.C. (before Christ) and A.D. (anno Domini, the year of the Lord).

2 Vatican 11, October 1965.

3 Quoted in Franklin H. Littell, *The Crucifixion of the Jews* (New York, 1975), pp. 27–28.

4 Quoted in Fred Gladstone Bratton, *The Crime of Christendom* (Boston, 1969), pp. 84–85.

5 *Patrologia,* Series Latina XLII, vii. 9.

6 See Bernhard Blumenkranz, *Die Judenpredigt Augustins* (Basel, 1946), pp. 99–100. On the general context, see William Nicholls, *Christian Anti-semitism*, (Northvale, NJ, 1993), pp. 153–188.

7 St. Augustine, *The City of God (De Civitas Dei)*, trans. Marcus Dods, New York, 1950, pp. 656–657.

8 From a letter to the Duchess of Brabant, quoted in Edward H. Flannery, *The Anguish of the Jews* (New York, 1965), p. 95.

9 Quoted in Martin Gilbert, *Exile and Return* (London, 1978), pp. 20–21.

Chapter 2
Liberalism, Emancipation and Antisemitism

1 Shmuel Ettinger, Roots of Modern Antisemitism, in: *Catastrophe of European Jewry* (Jerusalem, 1976), pp. 3–40.

2 Quoted in Lucy S. Dawidowicz, *The War Against the Jews, 1933–1945* (London, 1975), p. 32.

3 Le Contemporain, Revue Catholique 16 (1878):58–61, quoted in Johannes R. von Biberstein, *Die These von der Verschwörung, 1776–1945* (Bern, 1976), pp. 161–62.

4 Biberstein, *Die These*, p. 163.

5 George L. Mosse, *Germans and Jews* (New York, 1970), p. 60.

6 Mosse, *Germans and Jews*, p. 76. On the general context, see Shmuel Almog, ed., *Antisemitism Through the Ages* (Oxford, 1988).

7 Mosse, *Germans and Jews*, p. 63.

8 Based on the accounts in Nicholls, *Christian Antisemitism*, pp. 323–345; and John Weiss, *Ideology of Death,* (Chicago, 1996), pp. 80–190.

Chapter 3
World War I and Its Aftermath

1 E.g., Oswald Spengler, *The Decline of the West* (New York, 1947).

2 E.g., Arnold Zweig, *The Case of the Sergeant Grisha* (New York, 1928).

3 Cf. Richard G. Hovanissian, ed., *The Armenian Genocide* (New York, 1992), esp. pp. 21–79, 280–310; Vahakn N. Dadrian, *The History of the*

Armenian Genocide, (Providence, R.I., 1995); on Turkish denial, see Akcam Taner, *The Genocide of the Armenians and the Silence of the Turks,* in: Levon Chorbajian, and George Shirinian, eds., *Studies in Comparative Genocide,* (New York, 1999).

4 Quoted in: Yehuda Bauer, *My Brother's Keeper* (Philadelphia, 1974), p. 31.

5 *Sprawy Katolicke*, October 11, 1936, and *Gazetta Swiateczna*, no. 2915 (1936), quoted in the Catholic Press Agency statement of January 25, 1936.

6 Shimshon Kirschenbaum, *Toldot Yisrael Ba'Dorot Ha'aharonim* (Jewish History in Recent Times), (Tel Aviv, 1975), p. 149.

7 Bauer, *My Brother's Keeper,* pp. 61–62.

8 Henry L. Feingold, *Zion in America,* (New York, 1974), p. 265.

9 Feingold, *Zion in America*, p. 120.

10 Not to be confused with the Allgemener Yiddisher Arbeter-Bund, the Jewish socialist anti-Zionist movement in Eastern Europe.

11 David S. Wyman, *Paper Walls: America and the Refugee Crisis, 1938–1941* (Amherst, Mass., 1968), pp. 15–21.

12 Wyman, *Paper Walls*, p. 17.

13 Charles H. Stember, et al., *Jews in the Mind of America* (New York, 1966), pp. 84–85, 130–33, 208, 210; quoted in Wyman, *Paper Walls*, pp. 22–23.

14 Feingold, *Zion in America*, p. 281.

Chapter 4
The Weimar Republic

1 "The Outlaws," in: Ernst von Salomon, *The Answer of Ernst von Salomon,* trans. Constantine Fitzgibbon, (London, 1954), p. x.

2 Quoted in Heinz Höhne, *The Order of the Death's Head* (London, 1969), p. 17.

3 Joachim C. Fest, *Hitle,* (New York), 1975, p. 116.

4 See Ian Kershaw, *Hitler, vol. I, 1889–1936, Hubris* (London, 1998), pp. 3–69.

5 Ibid., pp. 81–87.

6 Robert Payne, *The Life and Death of Adolf Hitler* (New York, 1973), pp. 197–198.

7 *Hitler's Secret Book,* (New York, 1961), pp. 146–159,215; Joachim C. Fest, *Hitler*, pp. 594–603.

8 Himmler's Memorandum, "Reflections on the Treatment of Alien Races in the East", handed to Hitler 5/25/1940, IMT, Nuremberg Trial Document NO–1880. German original in: Vierteljahreshefte für Zeitgeschichte, 1957, Vol. 2, pp. 196–198.

9 Ibid.

10 Conference at Hermann Göring's Headquarters, 11/12/1938, IMT, Nuremberg Trial Document, PS–1816.

11 Ackermann, Josef, *Heinrich Himmler als Ideologe,* (Göttingen, 1970), pp. 178–194 (esp. p. 194).

12 Documents on German Foreign Policy, 1918–1965, Series E (1933–1937), Vol. 5, 2 (Göttingen, 1972), pp. 793–795 (in German). Also quoted in: Yehuda Bauer, *"Genocide: Was it the Nazis' Original Plan,"* in: The Annals of the American Academy of Political and Social Science, July 1980, vol. 450, p. 38.

Chapter 5
Evolution of Nazi Jewish Policy, 1933–1938

1 William L. Shirer, *The Rise and Fall of the Third Reich* (London, 1962), p. 194.

2 Lucy S. Dawidowicz, *The War Against the Jews*, pp. 57–58; Kershaw,

Hitler, pp. 80, 100–101. On the general context, see Saul Friedländer, *Nazi Germany and the Jews, vol. I* (New York, 1997), pp. 9–173.

3 Lucy S. Dawidowicz, *A Holocaust Reader* (New York, 1976), p. 45.

4 Dawidowicz, ibid., pp. 47–48.

5 Dawidowicz, ibid., p. 46.

6 Bernhard Lösener, *"Als Rassereferent im Reichsministerium des Innern,"* (As Race Expert in the Reich Ministry of the Interior), VJHfZ (Vierteljahreshefe für Zeitgeschichte), 9 (1961): 264–266.

7 Uwe D. Adam, *Judenpolitik im Dritten Reich* (Jewish Policy in the Third Reich) (Düsseldorf, 1972), pp. 159–166.

8 Official population figures: 185,246 Jews. The inclusion of converts to Christianity, or people not declaring for any religion, would add 15,000 and possibly more persons of Jewish origin.

9 Yehuda Bauer, *My Brother's Keeper* (Philadelphia, 1974), pp. 222–223.

10 Bauer, ibid., pp. 97–98.

11 Herbert Rosenkranz, *Reichskristallnacht* (Vienna, 1968).

12 Published in: *Jüdische Rundschau* (Journal of the Zionist organization in Germany), No. 79–80, 10/4/1933.

13 Yad Vashem Archive, Jerusalem, JM/2245.

14 Max Domarus, *Adolf Hitler, Reden und Proklamationen,* ed. Max Domarus, (Neustadt, 1962), Vol. I, p. 537.

15 Ibid., Vol. 1, pp. 538–539.

16 Martin Bormann, who later became chief of Hitler's Party Chancellery and Heinrich Himmler's rival.

17 Rudolf Hess. He went to England in 1940 to try and reach a peace settlement between Britain and Germany.

18 Nuremberg Trial Document PS–1816.

19 Josef Bürckel.

20 Germany prior to Anschluss.

21 Nuremberg Trial Document PS–1816.

22 *Das Schwarze Korps* (weekly paper of the SS, ed. by Günther D'Alquen), Berlin, November 24, 1938.

Chapter 6
German Jewry in the Prewar Era, 1933–1938

1 Bundesarchiv Koblenz, Neue Reichskanzlei, File L-1431.

2 Nora Levin, *The Holocaust* (New York, 1973), p. 60.

3 *Jüdische Rundschau,* No. 77, 9/24/1935.

4 Arthur D. Morse, *While Six Million Died: A Chronicle of American Apathy* (New York, 1967), p. 191.

5 David S. Wyman, *Paper Walls,* (University of Massachusetts Press, 1968), p. 4.

6 Bauer, *My Brother´s Keeper,* p. 148.

7 Bauer, *Ibid.*

8 Ibid., pp. 278–80, 288–89.

9 Frederick O. Bonkovsky, *"The German State and Protestant Elites,"* in Franklin H. Littell and Hubert G. Locke, eds., *The German Church Struggle and the Holocaust* (Detroit, 1974), p. 137.

10 Bonkovsky, ibid., p. 134.

11 Ibid. p. 138.

12 Jacob Robinson, *And the Crooked Shall Be Made Straight,* (Philadelphia, 1965), p. 125.

13 Bonkovsky, *The German State and Protestant Elites,* p. 143.

14 Franklin H. Littell, *The Crucifixion of the Jews,* (New York, 1975), pp. 50–51.

15 Gordon C. Zahn, *German Catholics and Hitler's Wars,* New York, 1962, and Guenther Lewy, *The Catholic Church and Nazi Germany* (New York, 1965).

16 Lewy, *The Catholic Church*, p. 284.

17 See Benedicta Maria Kempner, *Priester vor Hitler's Tribunalen* (Munich, 1966), and Reimund Schnabel, *Die Frommen in der Hölle* (Berlin, 1967).

18 Littell, *Crucifixion of the Jews*, pp. 44–45, 57.

Chapter 7
Poland—the Siege Begins

1 Yehuda Bauer, *My Brother's Keeper,* (Philadelphia, 1974), pp. 182–209.

2 Ibid., p. 189.

3 *Sefer Hazvaot* (The Book of Atrocities), ed. Benjamin Mintz and Joseph Klausner, (Jerusalem, 1945), p. 86.

4 Danzig, Western Prussia, Posen, and eastern Upper Silesia were to be incorporated into Germany; most of the remaining occupied Polish territory would comprise the General Government.

5 The earliest reference to the German plan to establish ghettoes.

6 Lucy S. Dawidowicz, *A Holocaust Reader* (New York, 1976), pp. 59–64.

7 Sara Selwer-Urbach, *Mib'ad Halon Beiti* (Outside My Window) (Jerusalem, 1964), p. 54.

8 *Documents on the Holocaust*, ed. Yitzhak Arad, Yisrael Gutman, Abraham Margaliot (Jerusalem, 1981), p. 227.

9 Emmanuel Ringelblum, *Notes From the Warsaw Ghetto,* ed. and trans. Jacob Sloan (New York, 1958), p. 86.

10 Martin Bormann to Party Leaders, July 13, 1943, *Documents on the Holocaust,* pp. 342–343.

11 Dawidowicz, *A Holocaust Reader, p. 60.*

12 It is possible that Moshe (Muniek) Merin, Judenrat leader in the Zaglebie (Sosnowice-Bedzin) area, based his policy on the assumption that Germany would win the war, but there is no clear evidence to substantiate such a suspicion.

13 Aharon Weiss, *Jewish Leadership in Occupied Poland—Postures and Attitudes,* Yad Vashem Studies 12 (1977):335–65.

14 Natan Eck, *Sho'at Ha'am Hayehudi Be'eropa (*The Catastrophe of the Jewish People in Europe), (Jerusalem, 1978), p. 36; Isaiah Trunk, *Judenrat,* (New York, 1972), p. 8.

15 Mark Dworzetzki, *Yerushalayim De'litta Bameri Uvasho'ah* (Jeruslaem of Lithuania [i.e. Vilna—Y.B.] in Resistance and Holocaust) (Tel Aviv, 1951), p. 114.

16 Moreshet Archive, Givat Haviva, Israel, D.1.1.920.

17 Moreshet Archive, Givat Haviva, Israel, D.1.1.920.

18 Ruzhka Korczak, *Lehavot Ba'efer* (Flames in the Ash), (Tel Aviv, 1965), p. 125.

19 Moreshet Archive, Givat Haviva, Israel, D.1.1.920.

20 Czerniakow was referring to the leaders of the Jewish political parties who fled after the German occupation.

21 Raul Hilberg, Stanislaw Staron, and Josef Kermisz, eds., *The Warsaw Diary of Adam Czerniakow* (New York, 1979), pp. 285, 295, 350, 376, 381, and 384.

22 Jonah Turkow, *Hayo Haita Warsha Yehudit (*There Once Was a Jewish Warsaw), (Tel Aviv, 1969), pp. 116–17.

Chapter 8
Life in the Ghettoes

1 Dawidowicz, *The War Against the Jews, 1933–1945,* p. 242.

2 Shimon Huberband, *"Kiddush Hashem"* [The sanctification of the Lord's name], MS, Ringelblum Archives (Tel Aviv, 1969), pp. 32–33.

3 According to Jewish tradition, meat and milk products and the dishes in which they are cooked and served must be kept separate— "Thou shalt not boil a kid in his mother's milk" (Exod. 22:19). Some scholars argue that the dietary laws are actually a compromise solution and that Judaism basically is inclined toward vegetarianism.

4 *The Warsaw Diary of Chaim A. Kaplan*, trans. and ed. Abraham I. Katsh (New York, 1973), pp. 202–03.

5 Literally, "number"; the reference is to the number ten, the requisite number of men for congregational worship.

6 Josef Bor, *The Terezin Requiem,* (New York, 1978).

7 Yitzhak Rudashevsky, *A Diary of the Vilna Ghetto, June 1941–April 1943*, ed. P. Mateuko , (Tel-Aviv, 1973), p. 67.

8 Altmann's letter arrived in Palestine via the Red Cross; it is reprinted in Bracha Habbas, *Michtavim Min Hageta'ot* (Letters from the Ghettoes) (Tel Aviv, 1943), pp. 401–43. Altmann died after the Warsaw ghetto rebellion.

9 Ringelblum, *Notes,* see above, ch. 7, note 9 (New York, 1958).

10 IMT (International Military Tribunal) Trial of Major War Criminals, Nuremberg, 1947–49, L-180, vol. 37, p. 672.

11 Ephraim Oshri, *The Book of Ephraim's Sayings* (Hebrew), (New York, 1949), p. 96; quoted in: Jacob Robinson, *And the Crooked Shall be Made Straight,* (Philadelphia, 1965), pp. 185–186.

12 The Festival of Lights (Hanukka—about the time of Christmas) celebrates the victory in the second century BCE of the priest Mattathias and his five sons (the Hasmoneans) over the Greco–Syrian king Antiochus, who tried to banish the Jewish religion.

13 Ephraim E.g., Oshri, *Sheeloth Utshuvot Mima'amakim (*Questions and Answers from the Depths), (New York, 1949).

14 "Singer" (Hebrew, hazzan). The cantor leads a congregation in prayer, especially the singing. The rabbi usually presides but does not lead the singing.

15 Sara Nishmit, *Ma'avako shel Hagetto* (The Struggle of the Ghetto), (Tel Aviv, 1968), p. 50.

Chapter 9
The "Final Solution"

1 Heinz Höhne, *The Order of the Death's Head,* (London, 1969), pp. 353–54; Dawidowicz, *The War Against the Jews*, pp. 123–24.

2 Several German documents are explicit. Thus, Himmler's Circular Memorandum of October 9, 1942, says that after executing the less useful Jews, the remaining Jews, who were to become laborers, were to be sent to concentration camps "in the eastern part of the General Gouvernement, if possible. Even from there, however, the Jews are someday to disappear, in accordance with the Führer's wishes" (Dawidowicz, *A Holocaust Reader,* [New York, 1976], p. 104).

Himmler's letter of October 2, 1943, to Oswald Pohl and others stated his wish to concentrate the Jewish remnants in camps in eastern Poland: "However, there too, the Jews should disappear one day, in accordance with the Fuhrer's wish" (Heiber, Helmut, ed., *Reichsführer, Briefe an und von Himmler,* (Reichsführer, Letters to and from Himmler), Stuttgart, 1968, doc. 150, p. 151).

Heydrich explained at the Wannsee Conference on January 20, 1942: "In lieu of emigration, the evacuation [i.e. mass murder—Y.B.] of the Jews to the east has emerged, after an appropriate prior authorization by the Führer, as a further solution possibility" (Raul Hilberg, *Documents of Destruction,* [Chicago, 1971], p. 92).

On July 28, 1942, Himmler wrote to the minister in charge of the conquered eastern territories: "The occupied eastern territories will become free of Jews [Judenfrei]. The execution of this very difficult order was placed on my shoulders by the Führer. No one can relieve me of this responsibility in any case" (Heiber, doc. 130, p. 134).

3 "In the Name of the Führer," July 13, 1943, IMT (Nuremberg trial documents) NO 2710, and *Documents on the Holocaust,* pp. 342–43.

4 Dawidowicz, *A Holocaust Reader*, p. 132.

5 Uwe D. Adam, *Judenpolitik im Dritten Reich* (Düsseldorf, 1972), pp. 303–316; Hans Mommsen, *The Realization of the Unthinkable,* in: idem, *From Weimar to Auschwitz* (Princeton, NJ, 1991); Martin Broszat, *Hitler and the Beginning of the Final Solution,* Yad Vashem Studies, vol. 13, 1980, pp. 73–125; Eberhard Jäckel, *The Holocaust, Where We Are, Where We Need to Go,* in: Abraham J. Peck, ed., *The Holocaust in History,* Bloomington, Ind., 1998.

6 Ulrich Herbert, *Nationalsozialistische Vernichtungspolitik* (Frankfurt, 1998). This slender volume contains the summaries of findings of a number of youngish German historians that point to the conclusions mentioned in the text.

7 *Pravda,* 1/7/42, quoted in: Walter Z. Laqueur, *The Terrible Secret,* (London, 1980), p. 69.

8 According to German sources, 33,771 were killed on September 29 and 30, 1941.

9 Benjamin West, *Bekhavlei Klaia* (In the Throes of Destruction), (Tel Aviv), 1963, p. 47.

10 West, *Bekhavlei,* p. 47; see also Bingel, Erwin, *"The Extermination of Two Ukrainian Jewish Communities,"* Yad Vashem Studies, vol. 3, 1959, pp. 283–99.

11 Richard Breitman, *Official Secrets,* Allen Lane, Penguin, London, 1999.

12 Dawidowicz, *A Holocaust Reader*, p. 72.

13 Hilberg, *Documents*, p. 92.

14 Hilberg, *Documents*, p. 94; corrected slightly in accordance with German original.

15 Gideon Hausner, *Justice in Jerusalem* (New York, 1966), pp. 10–11, 40.

16 Saul Friedländer, *Kurt Gerstein: The Ambiguity of Good*, trans. Charles Fullman, (New York, 1969), pp. 106–108.

17 Y. Pfeffer, in: Golan, Shamai, *Ha-Shoah* (The Holocaust), (Jerusalem, 1976), pp. 186–189; the testimony is translated from the Hebrew and appeared originally in *Miparashat Ha-Shoah,* (From the Story of the Holocaust), ed. Yisrael Kloisner (Jerusalem, 1946), pp. 241–43.

18 Rudolf Hoess, *Commandant of Auschwitz: The Autobiography of Rudolf Hoess,* (London, 1959), pp. 163–65.

19 Hoess, *Commandant*, pp. 163–65.

20 Ibid., pp. 215, 216.

21 Filip Müller, *Auschwitz Inferno,* (London, 1979).

22 Hoess, *Commandant*, p. 217.

23 Ota Kraus, and Erich Kulka, *Noc a Mlha,* (Night and Fog), (Praha, 1966), pp. 287–288.

24 Hilberg, *Documents*, p. 603.

25 Martin Broszat, *Konzentrationslager*, in: Hans Buchheim, Martin Broszat; Hans–Adolf Jacobsen; and Herbert Krausnick, *Anatomie des SS-Staates*, Olten und Freiburg, Vol. 2, 1965, pp. 149–160.

26 See Dinur, Yehiel, (Katzetnik) in: *Eduyot* (Testimonies [of Adolf Eichmann's trial]), Jerusalem, 1963, Vol. 2, pp. 1122–1124.

27 Mordechai Striegler, *Tanakh Be'Majdanek* (The Bible in Majdanek), in: *Ha-Shoah* (The Holocaust), ed. Shamai Golan, (Tel Aviv, 1976), pp. 189– 190.

28 Viktor E. Frankel, *Man's Search for Meaning: An Introduction to Logotherapy,* (Boston, 1967), pp. 116–117.

29 Filip Müller, *Auschwitz Inferno,* pp. 111–14.

Chapter 10.
West European Jewry, 1940–1944

1 Nuremberg Document NG: 3104, quoted in: Helmut Krausnick, *Judenverfolgung*, in: Hans Buchheim, *Anatomie des SS-Staates*, Vol. 2, p. 371.

2 Darquier lived in exile in Spain; he continued his anti-Jewish campaigns in the French press until his death.

3 A chief executioner of the Jewish people, Dannecker committed suicide after the war.

4 Yehuda Bauer, *American Jewry and the Holocaust,* (Detroit, 1981), p. 235.

5 Archive of the Centre de Documentation Juive Contemporaire, Paris, File XXVb; also in: *Recueil de Documents des Dossiers des Autorités Allemandes,* ed. Beate and Serge Klarsfeld, Paris, 1980, p. 1051.

6 Archive of the CDJC, File VII-10.

7 Leon Poliakov, and Jacques Sabille, *Jews Under the Italian Occupation,* (Paris, 1955), p. 50.

8 Ibid., p.62.

9 Ibid., pp. 64–66.

10 Ibid., p.73.

11 Michael R. Marrus, and Robert O. Paxton, *Vichy France and the Jews* (New York, 1985), p. 263.

12 Lucien Steinberg, *La Revolte des Justes,* (Paris, 1970), p.252.

13 Joseph Michman, *The Joodse Raad in the Netherlands,* Yad Vashem Studies 10 (1974): 48.

14 Jacob Presser, *Ashes in the Wind* (New York,1969), p. 150.

Chapter 11
Resistance

1 Henri Michel, *The Shadow of War* (London, 1965), p. 247.

2 Yehuda Bauer, *The Jewish Emergence from Powerlessness* (Toronto,1979), p.27.

3 Elie Wiesel, *Night* (New York, 1970), pp. 41–42.

4 Shalom Cholawski, *Al Naharot HaNiemen veha Dniepr* (On the Shores of the Rivers Niemen and Dniepr), (Tel-Aviv, 1982), pp. 145–146.

5 Ber Mark, *Der Oifstand in Bialystoker Getto* (The Rebellion in the

Ghetto of Bialystok), Warszawa Z.I.H., 1960; Sara Bender, *Mul Mavet Orev* (In the Face of Death), (Tel-Aviv, 1997), pp. 211–213.

6 Ruzhka Korczak, *Lehavot B'efer* (Flames in the Ash), (Tel Aviv, 1965), pp. 49–50

7 Korczak, *Lehavot* pp. 50–51.

8 She later became the main figure in the Jewish resistance group in Bialystok after the rebellion, and later still a member of the Israeli Knesset (Parliament).

9 A right-wing Zionist youth movement founded in 1925 by Ze'ev Jabotinsky.

10 David Wdowinski, *And We Are Not Saved* (London, 1964), p. 55.

11 Adam Czerniakow, *The Warsaw Diary of Adam Czerniakow*, eds. Raul Hilberg, Staron Stanislaw, and Josef Kermisz (New York, 1979), p. 339.

12 Yisrael Gutman, *The Jews of Warsaw, 1939–1943*, Bloomington, 1982, pp. 168–169.

13 The postwar claims of the right-wing Zionist Betar movement to have had a resistance organization in Warsaw in early 1942 appear groundless. The leader of the movement, David Wdowinski, after relating his attempt to persuade Czerniakow to do something, stated: "I came away empty-handed, without accomplishing anythlng. On my own responsibility, as head of apolitical party, I could do nothing. . . . In order to save our youth, the Betarim, we sent them through devious ways and means to the peasants and farmers of Hrubieszow County. . . . A part of this youth went into the forest as partisans, and another part came back to Warsaw where they created the nucleus of the later uprising in the Ghetto. In April-May of 1942, therefore, the greatest part of the Revisionist youth movement was out of the Warsaw Ghetto. But even if they had been there, we, Revisionists, could not take upon ourselves as a single party the organization of an eventual resistance. Such a

resistance had to have behind it the backing of the great majority of the population. We did not have it" (Wdowinski, pp. 55–56).

14 Gutman, p. 213.

15 David Nowodworsky in his testimony to Abraham Levin on August 28, 1942, in: Levin, Abraham, *Pinkaso shel Hamoreh Miyehudiya* (The Notebook of the Teacher from Yehudiya) Lohamei Hagetaot (Israel), 1969, p. 115.

16 Gutman, *Jews of Warsaw*, p. 222.

17 Berlinski, Hersh, *Zikhronot*, in: Yalkut Moreshet, no. 1(1963): 9–10.

18 A liberal, middle-of-the-road Zionist secular youth movement.

19 Gutman, pp. 243–245.

20 Yitzhak Zuckerman, *Yemei September, 1942,* in: Yalkut Moreshet no. 16 (1973), pp. 32–33.

21 Szwarcbart Material, M-2/5, Yad Vashem Archive, Jerusalem.

22 Died in Israel, in 1981.

23 A doctor in Lódz in 2000.

24 Died in Israel in 1979.

25 Died in the uprising.

26 Died in the uprising.

27 The only use of poison gas in World War II except, of course, in the gas chambers.

28 Haim Primer, *Min Hadlekah Hahi* (From That Conflagration), Lohamei Hagetaot, (Israel, 1961), pp. 236–37.

29 Aryeh Neyberg, *Ahronim* (The Last Ones), (Tel Aviv, 1958), pp. 189–91; Helena Balicka-Kozlowska, *Mur Mial Dwie Strony*, (Warsaw, 1958), p. 53.

30 Nahman Blumenthal, and Jozef Kermisz, *Meri VeMered Begetto Warsha* (Resistance and Rebellion in the Warsaw Ghetto), (Jerusalem, 1965), p. 295.

31 Emmanuel Ringelblum, *Polish-Jewish Relations During the Second World War,* eds. Joseph Kermisz and Shmuel Krakowski (New York, 1976), pp. 220–21.

32 Haika Grossman, *Anshei Hamachteret* (The Underground People), (Tel Aviv, 1965), pp. 209–210.

33 Grossman, p. 284.

34 Yitzhak Arad, *Ghetto in Flames: The Struggle and Destruction of the Jews of Vilna* (Jerusalem, 1980), p. 418.

35 Ibid., p. 417.

36 Filip Müller, *Auschwitz Inferno,* (London, 1979), pp . 153–60.

Chapter 12
Rescue?

1 Berl Katznelson, *Ktavim* (Writings), (Tel Aviv, 1947),Vol. 6:159–60.

2 Arthur D. Morse, *While Six Million Died,* (New York, 1968), p. 288.

3 See David S. Wyman, *Paper Walls,* 1938–1941 (Amherst, Mass., 1968).

4 Bauer, *My Brother's* Keeper, pp. 277–80. The *St. Louis* was one of a number of ships bringing illegal Jewish immigrants to Latin American countries. Efforts of the JDC and HIAS ultimately brought about acceptance by the local governments in most, though not in all, cases. The Cuban government, especially, was out to get large sums of money for its different, mutually hostile factions (one of which was led by the future dictator, Fulgencio Batista). When the JDC did not come up with a $450,000 bribe for each of two factions quickly enough, the ship was

turned out of Havana harbor (June 2, 1939). Gustav Schröder, its humanitarian German captain, managed to bring the ship to Europe slowly enough to allow time for the JDC to find refuge for the passengers in Western Europe. While the *St. Louis* was sailing along the U.S. coast, a U.S. coast guard cutter made sure the refugees, threatened with concentration camps if they returned to Germany, would not land on American soil.

5 The airline had employed Hermann Göring many years before.

6 Ringelblum, *Polish-Jewish Relations During the Second World War;* for a sociological discussion of this factor, see Helen Fein, *Accounting for Genocide,* (New York, 1979).

7 Ringelblum, op.cit., pp. 182–85.

8 Shmuel Krakowski, *The War of the Doomed* (New York, 1984), p. 14.

9 Wladysla Bartoszewski, and Zofia Lewin, *The Righteous Among the Nations* London, 1969.

10 Shamai Golan, *Hashoah* (The Holocaust), (Tel Aviv, 1976), pp. 268–70.

11 Yehuda Bauer, *The Holocaust in Historical Perspective* (Seattle, Wash.), 1978, pp. 92–93.

12 Bauer, *American Jewry and the Holocaust*, p. 246.

13 Ibid.

14 Bauer, ibid., pp. 80–81.

15 Charles H. Stember, et al., *Jews in the Mind of America* (New York, 1966), pp. 53–55, 84–85, 123–24, 127–33, 208–10.

16 Yehuda Bauer, *When Did They Know?*, in: *Midstream*, Vol. 14, No. 4, (April 1968): pp. 51–58.

17 Morse, *While Six Million Died*, p. 8.

18 Jan Karski [pseudonym], *The Story of a Secret State* (Boston, 1944).

Chapter 13
The Last Years of the Holocaust, 1943-1945

1 Raul Hilberg, *The Destruction of the European Jews* (New York, 1985), p. 493.

2 Ibid., p. 501

3 Ibid., pp. 467–68.

4 Michael D. B.Weissmandel, *Min Hametzar (*From the Depth), (New York, 1960), p. 45.

5 Bauer, *The Holocaust in Historical Perspective,* pp. 94–155; and idem, *The Jewish Emergence From Powerlessness,* Toronto, 1979, pp. 7–25.

6 Müller, *Auschwitz Inferno*, p. 136.

7 Hilberg, *Destruction of the European Jews*, pp. 539–40.

8 Ibid.

9 War Refugee Board cable 2867, War Refugee Board Archive, Roosevelt Library, Hyde Park, N.Y.

10 Bauer, *Jewish Emergence From Powerlessness*, p. 23.

11 A multimillionaire, Becher lived out his life in Bremen.

12 Müller, pp. 169–71.

13 *Documents on the Holocaust*, ed. Yitzhak Arad, Yisrael Gutman, Abraham Margaliot (Jerusalem, 1981), pp. 162–63.

14 *Encyclopedia of the Holocaust,* ed. Yisrael Gutman (New York), 1990, Appendix.

Chapter 14
Aftermath and Revival

1 Dov Levin, *Mineged Laport Hatshi'I,* (Facing the Ninth Fort), in: Sefer Hapartizanim (The Partisans' Book), ed. Shalom Cholawski, (Tel Aviv, 1958), p. 257.

2 Ruzhka Korczak, *Lehavot Ba'efer* (Flames in the Ash), (Tel Aviv, 1965), p. 305.

3 Bauer, *The Jewish Emergence From Powerlessness*, p. 63.

BIBLIOGRAPHY

one
WHO ARE THE JEWS?

History of the Jewish People

Baron, Salo W., *A Social and Religious History of the Jews*. New York, 1952.

Ben-Sasson, H. H., and Ettinger, S., eds., *Jewish Society Through the Ages*. London, 1971.

Roth, Cecil. *A Short History of the Jewish People*, rev. ed. London, 1959.

Christian-Jewish relations

Almog, Shmuel, ed., *Antisemitism Through the Ages*. Jerusalem, 1988

Brown, Michael, *Approaches to Antisemitism*. New York, 1994.

Flannery, Edward H. *The Anguish of the Jews: Twenty-three Centuries of Anti-Semitism*. New York, 1965.

Gade, Richard E., *A Historical Survey of Anti-Semitism*. Grand Rapids, 1981.

Littell, Franklin H., *The Crucifixion of the Jews: The Failure of the Christians to Understand the Jewish Experience.* New York, 1975.

Nicholls William, *Christian Antisemitism.* London, 1993.

Parkes, James, *The Conflict of the Church and the Synagogue: A Study in the Origins of Anti-Semitism.* New York, 1969.

Prager, Dennis, *Why the Jews?* New York, 1983

Ruether, Rosmary, *Faith & Fratricide.* New York, 1974.

Tal, Uriel, *Christians and Jews in Germany: Religion, Politics and Ideology in the Second Reich,* 1870–1914. Ithaca, N.Y., 1975.

Trachtenberg, Joshua, *The Devil and the Jews.* Philadelphia, 1993

two
LIBERALISM, EMANCIPATION, AND ANTISEMITISM

Baron, Salo W., "The Modern Age," in L. Swartz, ed., *Great Ages and Ideas of the Jewish People.* New York, 1965.

Ben-Sasson, H. H., and Ettinger, S., eds. *Jewish Society Through the Ages.* London, 1971.

"Emancipation," *Encyclopedia Judaica,* Vol. 6, cols. 696–718. Jerusalem, 1971.

three
WORLD WAR I AND ITS AFTERMATH

The situation of Jews in various countries

Encyclopedia Judaica: "Germany," Vol. 7, cols. 482–88; "Poland," vol. 13, cols. 738–52; "Russia," Vol. 14, cols. 444–72; "United States of America," Vol. 15, cols. 1622–35.

Flohr, Raul, Mendes, R., and Reinhartz, Joshua, eds., *The Jew in the Modern World: A Documentary History.* New York, 1980.

American Jewry

Feingold, Henry L., *Zion in America.* New York, 1974.

Stember, Charles H., et al. *Jews in the Mind of America.* New York, 1966.

Wyman, David S., *Paper Walls: America and the Refugee Crisis, 1938–1941.* Amherst, Mass., 1968.

Wyman David S., *The Abandonment of the Jews.* New York, 1984.

The Armenian people
Dadrian, Vahakn N., *The History of the Armenian Genocide.* Providence, R.I., 1995.
Hovanissian, Richard G., *The Armenian Genocide.* New York, 1992

The Zionist movement
Laqueur, Walter Z., *A History of Zionism.* New York, 1976.

 four

THE WEIMAR REPUBLIC

The Weimar Republic and the growth of national socialism
Bracher Karl D., *The German Dictatorship.* London, 1970
Laqueur, Walter Z., Weimar, *A Cultural History.* London, 1974.
Mosse, George L., *The Crisis of German Ideology: Intellectual Origins of the Third Reich.* New York, 1964.
Mosse, George L., *The Nationalization of the Masses.* New York, 1975
Sheridan, Allen W., *The Nazi Seizure of Power—The Experience of a Single German Town,* New York, 1984
Weiss, John., *The Ideology of Death.* Chicago, 1996.

Adolf Hitler and his aides
Fest, Joachim C., *Hitler.* New York, 1975.
Fleming, Gerald, *Hitler and the Final Solution.* Berkely, 1984.
Hitler's Secret Book. Trans. by Salvator Attanasio. New York, 1961.
Jäckel, Eberhard, *Hitler in History.* Hanover, 1984.
Kershaw, Ian., Hitler. London, 1999.
Spielvogel, Jackson J., *Hitler and Nazi Germany.* Prentice Hall, 1996.

Nazi antisemitism
Cohn, Norman, *Warrant for Genocide, the Myth of the Jewish World Conspiracy and the Protocols of the Elders of Zion.* New York, 1967.
Friedländer, Saul, *Nazi Germany and the Jews.* New York. 1997
Gordon, Sarah., *Hitler, Germans, and the "Jewish Question".* Princeton, 1984.

Kater, Michael H., *Everyday Anti-Semitism in Prewar Nazi Germany,* in: Yad Vashem Studies, vol. 16, Jerusalem, 1984.

five
THE EVOLUTION OF NAZI JEWISH POLICY, 1933–1938

The Nazi seizure of power
Bracher, Karl D., *The German Dictatorship.* London, 1970.

Dawidowicz, Lucy S., *The War Against the Jews: 1933–1945.* New York, 1976.

Friedländer, Saul, *Nazi Germany and the Jews.* New York, 1997.

Hilberg, Raul, *The Destruction of the European Jews.* Chicago, 1961.

Krausnick, Helmut, and Broszat, Martin, *Anatomy of the SS State.* London, 1973.

Viereck, Peter, *Metapolitics—the Roots of the Nazi Mind.* New York, 1961.

The Relations of German Churches to the Nazi regime and Christian Attitudes toward the Jews
Conway, John S., *The Nazi Persecution of the Churches, 1933–1945,* New York, 1968.

Eckardt, Roy A., *Elder and Younger Brothers.* New York, 1967.

Lewy, Guenther, *The Catholic Church and Nazi Germany.* New York, 1965.

Littell, Franklin H., *The Crucifixion of the Jews: The Failure of the Christians to Understand the Jewish Experience.* New York, 1975.

Littell, Franklin H., and Locke, Hubert G., eds., *The German Church Struggle and the Holocaust.* Detroit, 1974.

Michael, Robert, *Theological Myth, German Antisemitism and the Holocaust: The Case of Martin Niemöller,* in: Holocaust and Genocide Studies, vol. 2., no. 1, Oxford, 1987.

six
GERMAN JEWRY IN THE PREWAR ERA, 1933–1938

Reactions of German Jewry to the rise of Nazism
Ball-Kaduri, K. J., *The National Representation of Jews in Germany,* in: Yad Vashem Studies, vol. 2, Jerusalem, 1958.

Friedländer, Saul, *Nazi Germany and the Jews.* New York, 1997.

Margaliot, Abraham, *The Dispute Over the Leadership of German Jewry (1933–1938),* in: Yad Vashem Studies, vol. 10, Jerusalem 1974.

Simon, Ernst, "Jewish Adult Education in Nazi Germany as Spiritual Resistance," in *Leo Baeck Institute Yearbook,* vol. 1. London, 1956: pp. 68–104.

Western attitudes toward the Jewish situation in Nazi Germany

Bauer, Yehuda, *My Brother's Keeper.* Philadelphia, 1974.

Feingold, Henry., *The Politics of Rescue.* New Brunswick, N.J., 1970.

Morse, Arthur D., *While Six Million Died: A Chronicle of American Apathy.* New York, 1967.

Wyman, David S., *Paper Walls: America and the Refugee Crisis, 1938–1941.* Amherst, Mass., 1968.

seven
POLAND—THE SIEGE BEGINS

Hilberg, Raul, *The Destruction of the European Jews.* Chicago, 1961.

eight
LIFE IN THE GHETTOES

Polish and Soviet ghettoes

Arad, Yitzhak, *Ghetto in Flames: The Struggle and Destruction of the Jews of Vilna.* Jerusalem, 1980.

Bauer, Yehuda, *The Holocaust in Historical Perspective.* Seattle, 1978.

Dawidowicz, Lucy S., *The War Against the Jews, 1933–1945.* New York, 1976.

Dobroszycki, Lucjan, *The Chronicle of the Lodz Ghetto.* New Haven, 1984.

Friedlander, Albert, *Out of the Whirlwind.* New York, 1976.

Gutman, Yisrael, *The Jews of Warsaw.* Bloomington, Ind., 1982.

Kaplan, Chaim, *The Warsaw Diary of Chaim A. Kaplan*; ed., Abraham I. Katsh, New York, 1973.

Klein, Gerda, *All But My Life.* New York, 1971.

Korczak, Janusz, *Ghetto Diary*. New York, 1978.

Porat Dina, ed., *The Kovno Ghetto Diar.* Cambridge, MA, 1990.

Ringelblum, Emmanuel, *Notes from the Warsaw Ghetto: The Journal of Emmanuel Ringelblum,* ed. and trans. Jacob Sloan. New York, 1958.

—*Polish-Jewish Relations During the Second World War,* ed. J. Kermisz and S. Krakowski. Jerusalem, 1974.

Rudashevski, Yitzhak, *The Diary of the Vilna Ghetto: June 1941–April 1943*. New York, 1972.

Trunk, Isaiah, *Judenrat: The Jewish Councils in Eastern Europe Under Nazi Occupation*. New York, 1972.

Wiesel, Elie, *Night*. New York, 1970.

Leadership in the ghettoes

Bauer Yehuda, and Rotenstreich, Nathan, ed., *The Holocaust as Historical Experience,* New York, 1981.

Czerniakow, Adam, *The Diary of Adam Czerniaków,* ed. Raul Hilberg, Staron Stanislaw, and Josef Kermisz. New York, 1979.

Elkes, Joel, *Values, Belief and Survival*. London, 1997.

Margaliot, Abraham, *The Dispute over the Leadership of German Jewry,* in: Yad Vashem Studies, vol. 10, 1974.

Patterns of Jewish Leadership in Nazi Europe, 1933–1945. Proceedings of the Third Yad Vashem International Historical Conference, April 1977. Jerusalem, 1979.

Weiss, Aharon, *Jewish Leadership in Occupied Poland,* in: Yad Vashem Studies, vol. 12, Jerusalem, 1977.

nine
THE "FINAL SOLUTION"

Concentration camps, death camps, and mass murder

Hilberg, Raul, *The Destruction of the European Jews*. Chicago, 1961.

Hoess, Rudolf, *Commandant of Auschwitz: The Autobiography of Rudolf Hoess*. Cleveland and New York, 1960.

Höhne, Heinz, *The Order of the Death's Head: The Story of Hitler's SS.* New York, 1970.

Krausnick, Helmut, and Broszat, Martin, *Anatomy of the SS State.* London, 1973.

Müller, Filip, *Auschwitz Inferno.* London, 1979.

The Concentration Camps, Gutman, Yisrael and Saf, Avital, ed., Jerusalem, 1984.

Wiesel, Elie, *Night,* New York, 1970

The "Final Solution" and life in the camps

Becker, Jureck, *Jacob the Liar.* New York, 1974.

Bor, Joseph, *Terezin Requiem.* New York, 1963.

Borkin, Joseph, *The Crime and Punishment of 1. G. Farben.* New York, 1978.

Borowski, Tadeusz, *This Way to the Gas, Ladies and Gentlemen.* New York, 1976.

Cohen, Elie A., *The Abyss: A Confession.* New York, 1973.

De Pres, Terrence, *The Survivor: An Anatomy of Life in Death Camps.* New York, 1977.

Donat, Alexander, *The Holocaust Kingdom: A Memoir.* New York, 1965.

Fenelon, Fania, *Playing for Time.* New York, 1977.

Ferencz, Benjamin, *Less Than Slaves.* Cambridge, Mass., 1979.

Frankel, Viktor E., *Man's Search for Meaning: An Introduction to Logotherapy.* Boston, 1967.

Friedländer, Saul, *Kurt Gerstein: The Ambiguity of Good.* New York, 1969.

Katzetnick 135633 [pseudonym], *Atrocity.* New York, 1963.

Kraus, Ota, and Kulka, Erich, *The Death Factory: Documents on Auschwitz.* Oxford and London, 1966.

Levi, Primo, *Survival in Auschwitz.* New York, 1961.

Nyszli, Miklos, *Auschwitz: A Doctor's Eyewitness Account.* New York, 1960.

Semprun, Jorge, *The Long Voyage.* New York, 1964.

The Concentration Camps, Gutman, Yisrael and Saf, Avital, ed., Jerusalem, 1984.

Wiesel, Elie, *Night.* New York, 1970.

ten
WEST EUROPEAN JEWRY, 1940–1944

The fate of French Jews

Marrus Michael R. and Paxton, Robert O., *Vichy France and the Jews,* New York, 1981.

Poliakov, Leon, and Sabille, Jacque, *The Jews Under the Italian Occupation.* Paris, 1955.

The fate of Dutch Jews

Frank, Anne, *The Diary of a Young Girl.* New York, 1958.

Michman, Joseph, *The Controversial Stand of the Joodse Raad in the Netherlands: Lodewijk Visser's Struggle,* in: Yad Vashem Studies, Vol. 10, Jerusalem, 1974.

Presser, Jacob, *The Destruction of the Dutch Jews.* New York, 1959.

Ten Boom, Corrie, *The Hiding Place.* New York, 1974.

The fate of Belgian Jews

Belgium and the Holocaust, Michman, Dan ed., Jerusalem, 1998.

Flinker, Moshe, *Young Moshe's Diary: The Spiritual Torment of a Jewish Boy in Nazi Europe.* Jerusalem, 1965.

eleven
RESISTANCE

Jewish Resistance During the Holocaust, Gutman, Yisrael, ed., Jerusalem, 1970.

Arad, Yitzhak, *Ghetto in Flames: The Struggle and Destruction of the Jews of Vilna.* Jerusalem, 1980.

Bauer, Yehuda, *The Jewish Emergence from Powerlessness.* Toronto, 1979.

Cholawski, Shalom, *Soldiers From the Ghetto.* New York, 1980.

Donat, Alexander, *The Holocaust Kingdom: A Memoir.* New York, 1965.

Garlinski, Joseph, *Fighting Auschwitz.* New York, 1975.

Gutman, Yisrae, *The Jews of Warsaw.* Bloomington, Ind., 1982.

Krakowski, Shmuel, *The War of the Doomed.* New York, 1984

Levin, Dov, *Fighting Back.* New York, 1997.

Meed, Vladka, *On Both Sides of the Wall: Memoirs from the Warsaw Ghetto.* New York, 1972.

Rose, Leesha, *The Tulips Are Red.* New York, 1978.

Zuckerman, Yitzhak, ed., *The Fighting Ghettos.* New York, 1971.

twelve
RESCUE?

Bauer, Yehuda, *American Jewry and the Holocaust.* Detroit, 1981.

Bauer, Yehuda, *The Holocaust in Historical Perspective.* Seattle, Wash., 1978.

Bauer Yehuda, *Jews For Sale?* New Haven, 1994.

Bartoszewski, Wladyslaw, and Lewin, Zofia, *The Righteous Among the Nations.* London, 1969.

Friedländer, Saul, *Pius Xll and the Third Reich: A Documentation.* New York, 1966.

Hochhuth, Rolf, *The Deputy.* New York, 1964.

Karski, Jan., *Story of a Secret State.* Boston, 1944.

Lowrie, Donald A., *The Hunted Children.* New York, 1963.

Rescue Attempts During the Holocaust, Gutman, Yisrael, ed., Jerusalem, 1976.

Ringelblum, Emmanuel, *Polish-Jewish Relations During the Second World War,* ed. J. Kermisz and S. Krakowski. Jerusalem, 1974.

Wasserstein, Bernard, *Britain and the Jews of Europe.* New York, 1979.

Wyman, David S., *Paper Walls: America and the Refugee Crisis, 1938–1941.* Amherst, Mass., 1968.

Wyman, David S., *The Abandonment of the Jews.* New York, 1984

Yahil, Leni, *The Rescue of Danish Jewry.* Philadelphia, 1969.

thirteen
THE LAST YEARS OF THE HOLOCAUST, 1943–1945

The fate of Hungarian and Romanian Jews

Bauer, Yehuda, *Jews For Sale?* New Haven, 1994.

Braham, Randolph L., *The Destruction of Hungarian Jewry: A Documentary Account.* New York, 1963.

—*The Politics of Genocide in Hungary.* New York, 1980.

Breitman, Richard, and Kraut, Alan M., *American Refugee Policy and European Jewry, 1933–1945.* Bloomington, 1987.

Fisher, Julius S., *Transnistria.* New York, 1959.

Rescue Attempts During the Holocaust, Gutman, Yisrael, ed. Jerusalem, 1976.

fourteen

AFTERMATH AND REVIVAL

Bauer, Yehuda, *Flight and Rescue: Brichah.* New York, 1970.

Bauer, Yehuda, *Out of the Ashes.* Oxford, 1989.

Crossman, Richard, *Palestine Mission.* London, 1947.

Crum, Bertrand, *Behind the Silken Curtain.* New York, 1947.

Dinnerstein, Leonard, *America and the Survivors of the Holocaust.* New York, 1982.

INDEX